AID AND DEVELOPMENT

THE JOHNS HOPKINS STUDIES IN DEVELOPMENT

Vernon W. Ruttan and T. Paul Schultz, Consulting Editors

Aid and Development

**ANNE O. KRUEGER,
CONSTANTINE MICHALOPOULOS,
AND VERNON W. RUTTAN**

with Keith Jay, Gayl Ness, J. Dirck Stryker,
Vasant Sukhatme, and Hasan A. Tuluy

THE JOHNS HOPKINS UNIVERSITY PRESS
BALTIMORE AND LONDON

The Johns Hopkins University Press, 701 West 40th Street, Baltimore, Maryland 21211
The Johns Hopkins Press Ltd., London

The paper used in this publication meets the minimum requirements of American National Standard for Information Sciences—Permanence of Paper for Printed Library Materials, ANSI Z39.48-1984.

Library of Congress Cataloging-in-Publication Data

Krueger, Anne O.
  Aid and development / Anne O. Krueger, Constantine Michalopoulos, and Vernon W. Ruttan with Keith Jay . . . [et al.].
    p. cm. — (The Johns Hopkins studies in development)
  Bibliography: p.
  Includes index.
  ISBN 0-8018-3798-7 (alk. paper)
  1. Economic assistance—Developing countries. 2. World Bank.
3. Developing countries—Economic conditions. I. Michalopoulos, Constantine.
II. Ruttan, Vernon W. III. Title. IV. Series.
HC60.K78   1989
338.91′09172′4—dc19   88-35920
                                               CIP

Contents

List of Tables and Figures

Tables

Figures

Preface

The collaboration that led to the writing of this book extends back to 1982. Early in that year Anne O. Krueger and Vernon W. Ruttan were awarded a contract by the Department of State and the United States Agency for International Development (US/AID) to conduct a study of the impact of assistance on economic development. A draft report was submitted to the State Department and US/AID at the end of the year. Constantine Michalopoulos, chief economist at US/AID at the time, helped to design the scope and terms of reference for the project, and Keith Jay, the US/AID contract monitor, helped to coordinate reviews of the initial draft report (Krueger and Ruttan, 1983).

The objective of the study was to evaluate, from existing literature, the effectiveness or impact of development assistance. Because of the limited study period, we had to restrict both our historical perspective and the geographic coverage. Fortunately, we were able to draw on the work of a number of colleagues: Vasant Sukhatme wrote "Development Assistance, Savings, Investment and Economic Growth," Gayl Ness wrote "The Impact of International Population Assistance," Vasant Sukhatme wrote "Assistance to India," and Dirck Stryker and Hasan Tuluy wrote "Assistance to Ghana and the Ivory Coast." Several graduate students devoted the summer of 1982 to identifying and summarizing relevant literature for us. They included Charles Adelberg, Marsha Blumenthal, Susanna Fishel, Mary Forsberg, John Klock, Kent Miller, and Arnold Sheetz.

When the report was completed, we initiated a series of discussions on the possibility of writing a more definitive book on the practice and impact of development assistance. By that time Krueger had taken leave from her position as professor in the Department of Economics at the University of Minnesota to assume the post of vice president for economics and research at the World Bank. Constantine Michalopoulos left US/AID to join the World Bank in October 1982. During 1985 and 1986 Ruttan redrafted a number of the report's chapters and worked with the authors of the sector and country case studies to update their chapters. In early 1987, after Krueger had left the World Bank, the draft was again reviewed and revised.

During part of the period when the volume was being prepared a number of the other authors were affiliated with US/AID or the World Bank; some still are. The views presented here are solely those of the authors and should not be interpreted as reflecting those of US/AID, the World Bank, or any other institution with which the authors are affiliated.

We are indebted to Mary Strait and Sylvia Rosen for editorial assistance in translating our drafts into a manuscript that could be transmitted to the Johns Hopkins University Press. The final drafts were typed and retyped by Judy Berdahl, Susan Bifulk, and Marilyn Clement.

AID AND DEVELOPMENT

1

Introduction

ANNE O. KRUEGER, CONSTANTINE MICHALOPOULOS, AND VERNON W. RUTTAN

Foreign aid is an instrument used by a government to strengthen the economy of another country. The first major foreign economic assistance program was the Marshall Plan, officially the European Recovery Program. It was put together hastily in 1948 to revive the war-torn economies of Western Europe. The plan provided $13 billion ($60 billion in 1985 dollars) through the Organization for European Economic Cooperation (now the Organization for Economic Cooperation and Development) over a period of four years. It succeeded beyond the greatest hopes of its initiators. By the early 1950s the Western European economies had achieved such large gains that they were able to maintain rapid rates of growth through their own efforts.

The Marshall Plan was hardly under way when the developed countries turned their attention to problems of economic growth and stability in the developing world. The breakup of the colonial regimes, the polarization of World War II alliances, the aspirations of people and governments in newly independent countries, and the threat of both political and economic instability, particularly in East and South Asia, focused Western attention on the economic and security problems of the developing countries of Latin America, Asia, and Africa.

Official commitment by the United States to assist in the development of poor countries dates to the fourth point in President Harry S. Truman's inaugural address on 20 January 1949 and to the subsequent passage of the Act for International Development in June of 1950. Truman proposed that the United States commit itself to "a bold new program for making the benefits of our scientific advances and industrial progress available for the improvement and growth of underdeveloped areas" (Truman, 1949, p. 125; Kennedy and Ruttan, 1986).[1]

Commitment by the United Kingdom and developed countries of the British Commonwealth (Australia, Canada, and New Zealand) began with the signing of the Colombo Plan in Ceylon (now Sri Lanka) in January 1950. Initially, aid was extended to the successor states of British India. Additional

South and East Asian recipient nations were included when the United States and Japan later joined the Plan as donor nations.

The Historical Setting

The commitment by the United States and other developed countries to development assistance was much more tentative than the rhetoric of Truman's 1949 inaugural address or the initial communiqué of the Commonwealth ministers who formulated the Colombo Plan. Substantial resource transfers to the developing countries at a level approximating the Marshall Plan levels were not achieved until the early 1960s (Little and Clifford, 1965, p. 24). As late as 1960 the United States was the source of well over half of all development assistance, with most of the rest supplied by four European countries to their current or former colonies (OECD, 1985, pp. 92–99).

By the early 1960s the International Bank for Reconstruction and Development (IBRD, the World Bank) and its associated institutions, the International Finance Corporation (IFC) and the International Development Association (IDA), were emerging as an important source of development lending (Mason and Asher, 1973, pp. 1–35). The articles of agreement for both the International Monetary Fund (IMF) and the World Bank had been drawn up at the Bretton Woods conference on postwar economic policy in July 1944. The founders visualized the IMF as supporting the liberalization of trade and payment regimes. The Bank's primary role, at least initially, was to support reconstruction rather than development. However, when other institutions devoted to reconstruction came into being, particularly the Marshall Plan and the United Nations Relief and Rehabilitation Administration (UNRRA), and Bank membership was expanded to include the new postcolonial states, the Bank was pushed into taking a more active role in development.

A variety of motives led to the expansion of bilateral assistance programs in the late 1950s and early 1960s. In the United States, the late 1950s became a period of rising concern about security because of the perceived threat of Chinese expansionism in Asia and concern with the potential impact of the Cuban revolution on political developments in other Latin American countries. The Kennedy administration argued that the security concerns arising from internal turmoil in developing countries, especially in Latin America, could best be addressed through faster development and the strengthening of economic and political institutions. Based on this premise, the United States launched the Alliance for Progress in Latin America and increased economic aid worldwide. Expanded commitment by the United Kingdom, France, and Belgium followed the emergence and admission into the United Nations of a large number of former colonies as independent nations. When the German, Italian, and Japanese economies recovered from World War II and began to compete for new markets, they also initiated programs of financial and technical assistance (Little and Clifford, 1965, pp. 1–50; White, 1974, pp. 195–238; OECD, 1985, pp. 39–45).

Emerging as a major issue on the international agenda in 1960, development assistance was able to draw on the substantial institutional infrastructure that had grown up during the 1940s and 1950s. The 1945 commitment in the United Nations charter to "employ international machinery for the promotion of economic and social advancement of all peoples" was followed by the creation of a series of U.N. specialized agencies, such as the U.N. Food and Agriculture Organization; the U.N. International Children's Emergency Fund; the U.N. Educational, Scientific and Cultural Organization; and the U.N. Expanded Program of Technical Assistance, a forerunner of the U.N. Development Program (Little and Clifford, 1965, pp. 45–49; Mason and Asher, 1973, pp. 11–35).

The major source of experience with large-scale resource transfers among governments in the 1940s and 1950s was the transfer of resources from the United States to Western Europe under the Marshall Plan. An important institutional innovation of the Plan was joint donor-recipient coordination of economic aid within a framework of national and regional planning. The Plan's success exerted great effect on subsequent development thought and practice. The experience seemed to confirm the feasibility of accelerating economic growth through large-scale augmentation of international financial flows.

A second major body of experience derived from large-scale financial transfers involved support for economic stability and political security in countries on the periphery of the Communist bloc. This support was initially extended to Greece and Turkey, and subsequently to South Korea, Taiwan, South Vietnam, and Laos. The experience in these countries provides some of the important lessons regarding tradeoffs between short-term and long-term security and development objectives (chapter 5).

Bilateral technical assistance has a longer history of institutional evolution than bilateral financial transfers. It draws on two major bodies of experience: (1) the effort by colonial governments to develop their dependencies, that is, to make the colonies "pay" or at least avoid the drain on metropolitan resources (Mukerjee, 1972; Davis and Huttenback, 1986); and (2) the agricultural research and technology transfer capacity established by the major colonial powers in many of their colonies to support growth of commodity exports (Masefield, 1972). During the 1950s several colonial powers, particularly the British, were providing assistance to develop institutions of governance and to manage economic affairs. After independence these institutions evolved into programs of development assistance and cooperation (OECD, 1985, p. 40).

Official commitment by the United States to a major technical assistance effort for the development of poor countries dates, as noted earlier, to the fourth point in President Harry S. Truman's January 1949 inaugural address. At the time of Truman's address the United States had already engaged in a modest technical assistance effort under the Marshall Plan. It also had acquired some experience with technical assistance during the interwar and war years primarily in Latin America (Glick, 1957, pp. 3–43). By 1950 other official and unofficial agencies had accumulated substantial experience with technical assistance. A strong tradition of technical assistance had been established by religious and some private voluntary agencies in the fields of health, education, and agriculture (Maddox, 1956). The Rockefeller Foundation had initiated important programs in health, education, and agriculture in Latin America during the 1940s (Mosher, 1957). By the early 1960s these several traditions of bilateral and multilateral assistance were beginning to merge into a common body of experience and doctrine.

During the early and mid-1960s development assistance became much more highly institutionalized. In 1960 a Development Assistance Group, later renamed the Development Assistance Committee (DAC), was formed within the Organization for European Economic Cooperation (OEEC), which was later reconstituted as the Organization for Economic Cooperation and Development (OECD). The World Bank strengthened its capacity for development assistance by organizing two affiliated institutions: the IFC, established in 1956 to strengthen the Bank's capacity to make capital available to the private sectors in developing countries, and the IDA, established in 1960 to provide the Bank with a "soft loan" fund. The latter was supported by donor member "contributions," rather than "capital subscriptions," to countries whose economies were not strong enough to justify loans at market or near-market interest rates. By the mid-1960s the World Bank was joined by three regional development banks—the Inter-American Development Bank (IDB) in 1959; the African Development Bank (AfDB) in 1964; and the Asian Development Bank (ADB) in 1966 (Mason and Asher, 1973, pp. 578–90). The impetus for the regional banks was the perceived need for institutions with special sensitivity to regional needs. The World Bank also began to sponsor consortia of "donors" for some major aid recipients to improve coordination between bilateral and multilateral assistance program activities (White, 1967).

The 1960s was a period of great optimism about the possibilities of development. Academic communities and development assistance agencies agreed that large increments of concessionary aid directed to supporting comprehensive development plans would, over a period of several decades, result in self-sustaining growth throughout the developing world (Mikesell, Kilmarx, and Kramish, 1983, pp. 5, 6).

The U.S. commitment to these goals faltered during the war in Vietnam. By the mid-1970s U.S. aid commitments had declined, and they have never regained, in real terms, the levels achieved in the mid-1960s. The declines were more than offset, however, by the commitments of other DAC members, by multilateral assistance, and by the Organization of Petroleum Exporting Countries (OPEC).

The 1960s was a decade of unusually rapid growth in the developing world. Growth was somewhat slower during the 1970s but still exceptional by historical standards. The 1970s was also a period of severe questioning of what had appeared to be promising approaches to development assistance in the early 1960s. The development community itself challenged what came to be viewed as excessive reliance on large-scale capital transfers. One group of scholars, led by Ian M. D. Little, Anne O. Krueger, Jagdish Bhagwati, and Bela Balassa, stressed the critical importance of liberal trade and exchange rate policies to facilitate economic growth (Mikesell, Kilmarx, and Kramish, 1983, pp. 17–19).

Another criticism, from within the aid community itself, was that the capital-intensive industrialization policies of the 1960s had contributed to the worsening of income distribution in developing countries. To meet the basic material and nonmaterial needs of the poorest people in the poorest countries, the International Labour Organization, the World Bank, and the U.S. Agency for International Development initiated programs to impact directly on employment and income distribution. In retrospect, some of the distributional concerns appear to have reflected the spillover from domestic political stress within the developed countries rather than from analyses of the objective changes in the developing countries.

During the 1970s development assistance was also under almost continuous criticism from outside the traditional community—from both the radical left and the radical right (Ayres, 1983, pp. 11–16, 230–32; Riddell, 1987, pp. 129–75). The right emphasized the role of foreign aid in politicizing economic activity in less developed countries (Bauer, 1972, pp. 20–22, 84–88; Bauer, 1981, pp. 131–34; Krauss, 1983; Lal, 1983; Bauer, 1984, pp. 38–72; Toye, 1985) and in contributing to the expansion of public sector enterprise and employment. Critics alleged that aid strengthens the control of the central planning and financial institutions over private sector economic activity. Access to external resources, it was argued, tends to obscure the burden of economic inefficiency resulting from the poor performance of public enterprise and the distortions resulting from planning and control.

The critics from the right also pointed to the failure of development assistance to affect "the prime determinants of material progress [which] are people's economic aptitudes, their social institutions, and political arrangements" (Bauer, 1972, p. 100). While not denying that foreign aid augments the resources available to recipient countries, the critics on the right insisted that "if a country . . . cannot readily develop without external gifts, it is unlikely to develop with them" (Bauer, 1972, p. 100). Some critics on the right argued that while economic assistance is ineffective for stimulating economic development, it does effectively promote political stability in the recipient country. Other conservatives argued that the short-term perspective of donors and the political backlash effects in recipient countries cause development assistance to be as ineffective in achieving the political objectives of the donors as it is in achieving the development of the recipient countries (Bauer, 1972, p. 126).

The criticisms of the left were of the opposite nature. Based upon the implicit premise that assistance is effective, they emphasized the external, rather than the internal, constraints on development. At its extreme, the left criticism tended to view development assistance as an imperialist conspiracy—as an instrument designed to reward the political, economic, and bureaucratic elites of the developing countries for acquiescing in the exploitation of their resources and people (Hayter, 1971).

From a populist perspective, critics focused on the technocratic biases in the organization and management of aid resources, on the perverse effects of development assistance on the growth of entrepreneurship and institutional development, and on income distribution and welfare in the developing countries (Griffin and Enos, 1970; Franke and Chasin, 1980). The costs of modernization were said to be borne by the poor, and the gains realized by the wealthy. In contrast to the critics from the right, the critics from the left saw these results as deriving, not from the growing power of the state, but from the weakness of the public sector in dealing with both external and internal organized interests.

By the mid-1980s much of the fire and rhetoric of the arguments of the 1970s had been muted. During the 1980s both development thought and development policy were strongly influenced by the effects of a global recession that interrupted a quarter-century of remarkably rapid economic growth in both developed and developing countries.

A convenient marker for the emergence of the new set of concerns was Mexico's move to reschedule its debt in August 1982. In 1982 and 1983 almost as many developing countries entered into debt rescheduling negotiations as in the previous twenty-five years (World Bank, 1984a).

These debt problems emerged at a time of transition for the international economy. For most heavily indebted developing countries, difficulties associated with the reduction in capital inflows, the worldwide recession, and their internal economic policies resulted in abrupt slowdowns in growth, if not outright declines, in per capita income. Problems of resuming growth and debt have continued to occupy the attention of the IMF, the World Bank, and other multilateral and bilateral donors. Aid disbursements have grown at a slower rate during the 1980s than during the 1970s, although official flows have become much more important as private flows to developing countries have declined sharply (OECD, 1985, pp. 59–62).

Aid flows have been substantially redirected both among regions and among countries during the 1980s. In general, financial flows to developing countries as a group have fallen sharply. This change reflects primarily the drastic reduction in net commercial bank lending, which fell from $36.5 billion in 1982 to almost zero in 1987. In Africa the deteriorating economic environment has resulted in a shift in aid resources from long-term development projects to either short-term recovery programs or structural reforms designed to facilitate sustainable growth in the medium term. A substantial increase has occurred in external aid flows to the least developed countries, when measured as a share of external receipts, of national savings, or of national income. This increased aid flow has been a response more to efforts to support policy reform than to specific project opportunities.

The global economic crisis has contributed to an emerging climate of "aid fatigue" on the part of some developed country governments and development assistance constituencies. Development assistance by the United Kingdom has declined since the late 1970s. In the United States failure to pass aid legislation has frequently led to funding by continuing resolution. By contrast, aid levels have continued to increase in Japan and Italy.

Surveys of public opinion in both the United States and other donor countries suggest that public attitudes toward foreign aid programs are increasingly critical (Rielly, 1983; Mosley, 1985), although respondents consistently show a deep concern with the plight of needy people in other countries. The polls also reveal a deep division between "opinion leaders" and the general public. Opinion leaders indicate less concern than the general public with poverty in the developing world, but at the same time they are less skeptical about the economic and security benefits to donors and recipients of foreign assistance.

The typical response by the foreign assistance community to public skepticism about foreign aid is to intensify efforts to persuade reluctant governments and the general public that foreign economic assistance is beneficial. The most recent official effort is the study by Robert Cassen and Associates, *Does Aid Work?* (1986),[2] which was commissioned by the Task Force on Concessional Flows (established by the Development Committee, a joint ministerial committee of the boards of governors of the World Bank and the IMF). Task force members represented the leading donor nations and some recipient countries.

The official reports typically have been supplemented by studies conducted by interest groups or public affairs institutes associated with the aid effort. These studies are often cast in a reform mode that attempts both to blunt the arguments of the more extreme critics of assistance policy and to contribute to the debate about assistance policy reform. The recent study by Roger C. Riddell, of the United Kingdom's Overseas Development Institute, *Foreign Aid Reconsidered* (1987), is one of the more serious scholarly attempts to recapture a middle ground. In the United States the Overseas De-velopment Council has issued a number of studies of development assistance policy that also are directed to a middle ground (Feinberg, 1986; Lewis and Kallab, 1986).

The Book Plan

We have grouped the chapters in this study of the effects of development assistance into three major sections. Part I focuses on the evolution of devel-opment thought and policy. In chapter 2 we provide a guided tour through the literature on development thought. The purpose of this excursion is to draw the implications of the advances in our understanding of the process of eco-nomic development for economic policy. Thus a major theme is to increase understanding of the policy environment in which individual economic deci-sions are made, although policies are not substitutes for natural resources, physical capital, or the quality of a nation's labor force. In chapter 3 we trace the evolution of thought on development assistance. Not surprisingly, it has taken considerable intellectual energy to clarify the role that the transfer of resources and knowledge plays in the development of poor countries.

The focus of part II is on how the policies of aid donors and recipients influence the effectiveness of assistance. In chapter 4 we examine how the macroeconomic and sector policy regimes that prevail in developing countries contribute to the erosion or enhancement of development assistance effects. Donor policies, the context of development assistance, are an important de-terminant of the impact of development assistance. Often, assistance is pro-vided to further donor economic or strategic interests. In chapter 5 we discuss the donor policies that enhance or reduce the effectiveness of assistance. In chapter 6 we trace the evolving system of interaction or dialogue between donors and recipients of aid on the policies that accompany the transfer and use of assistance resources. Many of the issues discussed in chapters 4–6 have been the subject of popular critiques of assistance regimes but have re-ceived less attention in the professional literature. To write these chapters, we drew on our own experience as well as on the available literature. Evidence on the macroeconomic significance of development assistance (on savings, investment, and growth) is presented in chapter 7. A large body of evidence indicates relatively high rates of return to individual projects, but evidence from cross-country studies of the differential impact of development assis-tance has been less conclusive.

In part III we turn to the sectoral impacts of development assistance. Chapter 8 is a review of the evidence on the impact of assistance for the development of physical infrastructure: transportation, power, irrigation, and telecommunications. In the 1950s and 1960s a very large share of both bilateral and multilateral assistance was devoted to large infrastructure projects. Initially, the evaluations tended to be quite critical, although the evidence now available permits a more thorough assessment. By the mid-1960s a major shift toward assistance to sustain growth in agricultural production had occurred. It was followed in the 1970s by an effort to strengthen rural community physical and institutional infrastructure. In chapters 9 and 10 we review the evidence on the impact of assistance to expand agricultural production and to improve the quality of life in rural areas.

One of the newest and most controversial areas of development assistance has been population policy and fertility control. In chapter 11 Gayl Ness assesses the impact of international assistance on national population programs.

Several areas of sector development assistance have not been treated explicitly. Among the most important are assistance for the development of financial institutions, assistance for the development of the manufacturing industry, and assistance to the education sector. We examine these issues in the context of studies of several countries in part IV.

Part IV comprises four chapters that present five country studies. The countries were chosen for different reasons. Chapter 12 discusses assistance to India. India is important not only because of its size and the amount of aid it has received but also because a great deal of development thought has originated in, and has been stimulated by, the country's development experience and policy discussions.

Chapters 13 and 14 discuss assistance to Korea and Turkey respectively. Both Korea and Turkey were early recipients of aid. Their responses to external assistance, however, have been quite different. Turkey's per capita income was higher than Korea's when they started receiving aid, but by 1985 Korea's per capita income was double that of Turkey. By the early 1980s Korea no longer needed concessional finance, while Turkey has again found it necessary to draw on external assistance.

Chapter 15 discusses assistance to Ghana and the Ivory Coast. These two countries are interesting because of the differences in their development. At independence in 1957 Ghana was relatively well developed and had one of the highest per capita incomes in black Africa. In contrast, the Ivory Coast was far behind Ghana at the time of its independence in 1960, yet twenty years later it was far ahead of Ghana. The reasons for the different performances of the two countries are reviewed.

In part V, consisting of a single, final chapter, we attempt to draw some lessons from the development assistance experience examined. We also attempt to address how useful the lessons of the past may be in the economic and political environment that will confront aid donors and recipients in the future.

Perspective

In developing this book our shared judgment was that if assistance to support economic development in poor countries is to be successful in enhancing the quality of life and the even less tangible dimensions of economic and political development, it must be capable of generating the new income streams needed to enhance personal and social consumption. This view focused our attention on the contribution of aid to enhancing the capacity of poor countries to achieve and sustain rapid rates of economic growth. Therefore, we tried to extract from the literature what could be learned about the economic impact of development assistance and to assess the factors that have contributed to the success or failure of development efforts that are measured primarily in economic terms.

In our review of the literature we were impressed by how much of the seminal work in the field of development thought and development policy had its origins in the 1950s and 1960s. This was the period when development thought became the center of interest for scholars, who were attracted by the challenge of development policy in terms of both the development assistance agencies and the new national governments.

The body of literature on development assistance and development impact continued to grow during the 1970s and 1980s. The research units of the bilateral and multilateral assistance agencies became important sources of literature on development processes, policy, and impact. But there has been no new synthesis comparable to the advances of the 1950s and 1960s. Indeed, development thought and practice continue to be bound by the theoretical insights and policy perspectives that emerged during the 1950s and 1960s.

In this book we have drawn some of the implications from the wider body of research and experience that is now available. We hope that this assessment of the current state of knowledge may provide a basis for a continuing dialogue in development thought and practice.

Part One

THEORY

2

Development Thought and Development Assistance

ANNE O. KRUEGER
AND VERNON W. RUTTAN

Donor agencies have extended foreign assistance from one country to another for a variety of motives. Recipients also have had different motives for seeking assistance. In both cases, the motives sometimes have not been consistent with developmental purposes. The analysis in this volume is directed at assessing how effectively aid has supported development and examines donors' motives only insofar as they impinge on effectiveness.

The evaluation of aid effectiveness is possible only if the underlying development process is understood. There are two reasons for this. First, without such an understanding, assessment of the contribution of aid would be impossible. Furthermore, aid constitutes but a small portion even of most poor countries' resources and is highly fungible, hence, aid effectiveness must be considered within a country's overall growth framework. Our starting point in this chapter is the evolution of development thought in relation to development policy.

Until World War II, growth was not a conscious policy objective even in most industrial countries.[1] Insofar as some governments attempted consciously to stimulate economic growth, little or no systematic knowledge was available to guide their efforts. Furthermore, many now-developing countries were colonies until after 1945. As they attained independence and set economic development as a prime objective, economists turned their attention to what at the time seemed to be relevant issues and policies. The early development theories were relatively simplistic.[2] As experience mounted, theory and policy were altered, and they interacted with experience to build a knowledge base for understanding the development process.

The purpose of tracing the evolution of thought about the development process is to lay the analytical basis for later chapters. It is also intended to assess how far thinking about development has progressed. It would be unfair to assess the effectiveness of aid in earlier years without some understanding of the thinking about the development process that was prevalent then.

Economic development, or even economic growth, was not a major theme in modern economic thought until well into the 1950s. Development thought, however, has been strongly influenced by the "magnificent dynamics" of the classical economists, particularly Malthus and Ricardo. Other precursors were the members of the German historical school, from List to Sombart, who outlined a series of stages of economic development. These stages were little more than simple expository devices and had only a minor impact on economic policy. When Marx invested his growth-stage sequence with a sense of historical inevitability, he provided the ideology for the forced-draft industrialization policies pursued by the Soviet Union. Schumpeter's brilliant speculations on the roles of technical change and the entrepreneur in economic growth, of course, were formulated to apply primarily to the already advanced capitalist economies (Schumpeter, [1911] 1934). Three particularly important landmarks in the problems of developing economies were Colin Clark's massive statistical study, *The Conditions of Economic Progress* (1940), and the studies by Paul Rosenstein-Rodan (1943) and Kurt Mandelbaum (1947) on problems of industrial development in eastern and southeastern Europe.

In the five sections of this chapter, the history of development thought is necessarily presented in brief. The first section sketches the state of thought as of the early 1950s, when attention was turning to the economic objectives of developing countries and how foreign assistance might facilitate their achievement. The second section identifies some of the early lessons and insights. The next section indicates how the simple early paradigms led to a more complex appreciation of the development process. Because foreign assistance is essentially government-to-government and development policy is inherently government policy, the fourth section addresses the role of government in development as it is presently understood. The final section provides a broad picture of where development economics stands now and some of the important questions that stem from our current understandings.

Early Postwar Development Thought: The Simple Solutions

The most striking aspects of "underdevelopment," as it was then known, were the extremely low income accruing to workers and the remarkable similarity of economic structures across the developing countries. Substantial proportions of their populations depended upon subsistence agriculture, and only relatively small fractions of their labor forces were engaged in industrial activities. Exports were limited to a few primary commodities, and imports met the demand for most manufactured goods. Although many observers commented on, for example, the needs for public health, education, and technical assistance in those countries, emphasis was placed on two factors as primarily responsible for low incomes: (1) the very low capital stock per person and (2) what were widely believed to be significant "market failures."

Undoubtedly, the capital stock of developing countries was low relative to that of the developed countries. Even casual observation confirmed the lack of roads, irrigation, electrical power–generating capacity, communications facilities, buildings, and machinery and equipment. It was believed that because incomes were low, only relatively low savings rates could be expected. Low savings rates, in turn, seemed to imply low rates of investment. The explanation of underdevelopment as the result of a vicious circle in which low incomes led to low savings, which led to low rates of capital formation and small amounts of capital for each person to work with and hence low productivity, which in turn kept incomes low, generated a policy prescription: find the means to raise the rate of capital accumulation.

A closely related observation that later was largely discredited tended to reinforce the idea that a significant segment of the labor force in developing countries was idle. This phenomenon was referred to as "disguised" unemployment, meaning that farm workers were less than fully employed and would willingly work more hours and days were opportunities available. By implication, the marginal product of labor was zero, either because some workers could leave agriculture and others would work more hours to maintain total output or because idle household members would willingly undertake tasks with positive marginal products (Eckaus, 1955). Thus, it was thought that not only was capital scarce but the resources complementary to capital were, in effect, free goods. Capital accumulation, therefore, should have a very high return.

When the observation that developing countries were predominantly rural and agricultural was combined with the perceived lack of capital, the development process was viewed as one of "structural transformation"; that is, its purpose was to find means to increase the rate of capital accumulation so that the structure of economic activity would shift from rural-agricultural to urban-industrial activities. In 1940 Colin Clark had provocatively and painstakingly classified economic activities as primary, secondary, and tertiary, including: (1) farming and mining, (2) industrial (manufacturing, construction, and electric power generation), and (3) tertiary or service (e.g., health care, education, wholesale and retail trade, finance). Growth was envisioned as taking place as capital stock increased and capital was allocated largely to secondary activities and labor (according to this line of reasoning, labor was essentially costless) migrating from primary to secondary employment.

Given such a view of the development process, the question was, how could it be achieved? This brought into focus the second factor thought to be responsible for low incomes, namely, that many more significant market failures occur in developing than in developed countries. It was based in part on the belief in the existence of disguised unemployment and in part on the belief that in most developing countries the majority of the poor follow traditional patterns of behavior and are unresponsive to incentives. The economic behavior of peasants was assumed to be essentially irrational. Some commentators even asserted that peasants' utility of income was limited and that should returns to labor increase, the number of hours per day worked would diminish at least proportionately. The belief in pervasive market failure gained support from the apparent power of a number of economic agents: rural landlords who held monopsony power over their tenants and were also moneylenders, which made the credit market seem highly imperfect; monopsonistic traders; and industrialists who were the sole producers of goods. Entrepreneurship appeared to be lacking. Distrust of the market and of market mechanisms was buttressed by the view that the demand for exports of primary commodities was income- and price-inelastic and therefore, the prospects of developing countries' export earnings growing rapidly were dim. This "elasticity pessimism" was widespread, especially when commodity prices fell sharply at the end of the Korean War.

If accelerated capital accumulation is thought to lead to the structural transformation that is the essence of development, and markets cannot be relied on to function well enough to do the job, then the policy prescription seems to be straightforward: government must become a major actor in the economy. In this role, it has the responsibility not only to intervene to raise the savings rate but also to allocate the resulting investable resources among different economic activities. Thus, private economic activity must be regulated by government because monopolists cannot be relied upon to behave in socially valuable ways. The attention of development economists, consequently, focused on (a) devising analytical techniques to determine investment allocations across economic activities and (b) developing planning methods and models that could be used as analytical instruments to support the policymakers charged with the mobilization and allocation of resources.[3]

India's prominence among developing countries made it the focus of much development thought. Several plans—one by the colonial government and one by leaders of the movement for independence—were drawn up before independence.[4] Subsequently, a planning commission was put in place by the new government. At the core of the commission's work were the policy measures that in the 1950s were widely believed to be conducive to development. They included an outline of planned government expenditures on infrastructural activities, macroeconomic objectives and projections, and somewhat detailed specific industry and commodity output targets for the entire economy. "Investment" licenses regulated the expansion of productive capacity to ensure that overexpansion in some industries did not occur at the expense of others.

Several points should be noted here, however, because they relate to the beliefs about development policy current at the time. First, had the Indian planners trusted the international market, they need not have been so concerned with detailed output levels; they could have exported those goods for which "overcapacity" had been built. Second, the planners envisaged savings as within the government's power to raise. And third, the underlying belief was that the government would have to carry out or enforce its plans; incentives to induce the types of economic activity desired received minor attention. In fact, import prohibitions provided powerful incentives for domestic production, but the planners did not envisage the successful encouragement of exports through exchange rate policy or the liberalization of the financial system as a major means of inducing savings increases. Incentives were given major attention only in those areas in which the government thought it could correct market failure; for example, to implement a "small savers" scheme, the government established outlets that paid low nominal rates to attract rural savings.

In sum, Indian planning, reflecting the views of the time, relied on government to raise and allocate resources and to control private economic activity. The economists or policymakers concerned with development never considered the fact that these activities might overtax the administrative capabilities of the government and/or divert its attention from essential tasks and from tasks for which government had a clear comparative advantage.

During the 1950s a number of attempts were made to extract the lessons from the initial implementation of development programs by the developing countries and from the financial and technical assistance endeavors of the developed countries. Two of these programs, one centered at the Massachusetts Institute of Technology Center for International Studies (MIT-CENIS), the other at the National Planning Association and the University of Chicago (NPA-Chicago), substantially influenced development thought and development policy in the late 1950s and the 1960s.

The perspective that characterized the MIT-CENIS study was that the economic development of underdeveloped areas requires a deliberate, guided, and intense effort over one or two decades to move an economy from stagnation to development. This view was encapsulated in metaphors such as "big push," "take-off," and "minimum critical effort" (Hirschman, 1982; Rostow, 1985, pp. 36–56).

The implications of the MIT perspectives were embodied in a series of proposals for a dramatic increase in the level of capital transfers to the countries of South Asia and Latin America (Millikan and Rostow, 1957).[5] If the amount of aid to all countries was to be sufficiently large to remove lack of capital as a bottleneck to growth, then a commitment of $10–12 billion ($42–50 billion in 1985 dollars), in the form of loans or grants, would be required over a five-year period. The MIT proposals were influential in shaping the thinking of the Eisenhower and Kennedy administrations on the role of economic assistance in foreign policy (Rosen, 1985, pp. 101–7; Rostow, 1985, pp. 3–12, 84–196).

During the mid-1950s, Theodore W. Schultz, of the University of Chicago, directed an ambitious study for the National Planning Association on the organization and impact of technical assistance in Latin America.[6] The authors of the individual studies took the value of technical assistance as self-evident and focused on the policy and administrative reforms needed by recipients and donors to make technical assistance more effective. A more coherent view did emerge, however, in Schultz's own writing, in which he argued that "for poor countries, and for rich countries as well, much and probably most economic growth does not come from additional inputs of the conventional types" (Schultz, 1956a, p. 17). He saw it as coming instead from two neglected variables: (a) the quality of people as productive agents, and (b) the level of the productive arts—of technology (p. 19). Investment in these nonconventional inputs, rather than additional conventional inputs, he argued, has permitted some countries to grow rapidly (Schultz, 1956a). By the early 1960s Schultz's insights were beginning to be articulated by others at Chicago, particularly Harry G. Johnson (1963) and Gary S. Becker (1964), in what Johnson termed a "generalized human capital" approach.[7] These ideas were formulated more precisely with respect to agricultural development by Schultz in his 1964 book, *Transforming Traditional Agriculture* (see esp. p. 145).

By the mid-1960s the Chicago and MIT perspectives were beginning to converge, largely because of the crises associated with the lagging growth of agricultural production in South Asia. A landmark in the convergent perspective was the 1964 conference on Productivity and Innovation in Agriculture in Underdeveloped Countries, sponsored by CENIS (Millikan and Hapgood, 1967). After the conference knowledgeable development theorists or practitioners could no longer assume that a combination of massive capital transfers and simple technical assistance was sufficient to generate growth, particularly in the agricultural sector, without investment in human capital, development of technology consistent with resource endowments, and appropriate economic incentives.

It was not until two decades later, however, that the insights into the role of human capital began to be effectively incorporated into growth theory. In his 1985 Marshall Lectures, Robert E. Lucas (1988) incorporated human capital into a Solow-like growth model that lent itself to the quantification of both formal education and learning-by-doing, as well as technical change.[8] He went on to show that human capital formation occurs most rapidly in an environment in which new goods are continuously being introduced and then argued that an export-oriented economy provides the most favorable environment for the continuous introduction of new goods and, hence, for the formation of human capital.

Complications to the Simple Model

Throughout the 1950s the simple capital-accumulation-cum-market-failure view of development was the predominant intellectual basis for development policy and foreign assistance (chapter 3). Many countries experienced accelerated rates of growth, especially in contrast with the 1930s and 1940s. In most, savings rates rose surprisingly rapidly, thereby permitting a fairly sharp increase in the rate of capital accumulation. Nonetheless, a number of problems arose. In trying to understand what was happening, development economists articulated new insights, although they were not directly integrated into the simple model until well into the 1960s.

Four lines of the new thinking deserve mention here:

First, one cannot simply "transfer resources out of agriculture and into industry." Evidence had mounted that the neglect of agricultural production could severely constrain development. Lewis (1954), Jorgenson (1961), and Ranis and Fei (1961) developed "dual economy" theories in which a "marketed surplus" from agriculture had to increase if development was not to falter (Krishna, 1967). Increased agricultural output was necessary to support the outmigration of labor from agriculture. Early studies of supply response demonstrated that production was not so inelastic with respect to price as had earlier been thought. Careful analysis of peasant households in developing countries had revealed little "disguised unemployment" in case after case; productivity was painfully low, and peaks and troughs occurred, but to "transfer labor out of agriculture" without a loss in output was simply not possible (Krishna, 1967; Behrman, 1968; Askari and Cummings, 1976). In other words, agricultural production had to increase in the course of development. Therefore, resolving problems associated with agricultural development was a prerequisite for satisfactory and sustained industrial growth.

Second, employment issues are at once different from those previously considered and somewhat less readily amenable to quick resolution by government policy. Most developing countries achieved fairly rapid rates of increase in industrial output in the first years of a conscious development strategy. Although the starting base was very low, the annual rates of growth (at domestic prices) exceeded 5 percent and often 10 percent in a number of countries for sustained periods. Surprisingly, however, industrial employment failed to grow at anywhere near the rate of industrial growth, and urban employment growth often lagged behind even the natural rate of increase of urban population, which did not permit significant outmigration from rural areas. Thus it was recognized that capital accumulation alone could not increase employment or living standards for most of the population.

Third, the belief in structural rigidities was questioned. The views of the Latin American "structuralist" school, led by Raul Prebisch (1959), that "structural transformation" was a prerequisite for economic development were especially important in contributing to skepticism about the functioning of markets in developing countries; however, empirical examination failed to support the structuralist interpretation of inflation. Evidence mounted that by and large, inflation in Latin America can be explained by the same monetary phenomena and budgetary deficits as in other parts of the world.

Fourth, when country after country encountered balance of payments difficulties, a model of growth was formulated in which foreign exchange, alongside capital, was seen as a scarce factor in development. The balance of payments difficulties experienced in country after country were generated, in large measure, by planners' underestimation of the future growth of imports and the overestimation of the rate of growth of exports. Carlos Diaz aptly noted that import substitution turned out to be import intensive (Diaz-Alejandro, 1965).

The pervasive "foreign exchange shortage" that became a stylized fact of development by the early 1960s led to the development of the influential "two-gap" model of development (Chenery and Bruno, 1962; Chenery and Strout, 1966). In this formulation, labor remained essentially a free good, and capital was still needed for growth; but instead of focusing only on capital accumulation, the two-gap model posited a second constraint on output growth: imports were needed in fixed proportion to both investment and output of import substitution industries because newly established factories could not operate without the intermediate goods and raw materials that were not produced at home. In the two-gap model, export growth was exogenous at a predetermined rate, and the domestic savings rate was taken as given. Output expansion could occur only with new capital and imports. Depending on the parameters for a particular country, either the savings or foreign exchange constraint was the limiting factor to growth. Hence, the term "two-gap model": a gap existed between domestic savings and investment or between foreign exchange demand and supply. At early stages of development, foreign exchange, rather than savings, was conjectured to be the binding constraint. (The use of the two-gap model in the programming of economic assistance is discussed in chapter 3.)

Each of the preceding lines of thought pointed toward a sector or an issue that had been overlooked in the simple models of the early postwar years and focused attention on factors in addition to capital accumulation that were important in development. Subsequently, the implications for aid policy in the two-gap and the Ranis-Fei and Jorgenson models were recognized (see chapter 3).

Toward a More Complex Perspective: Private Behavior

If early development thought implicitly or explicitly assumed market failure and irrational behavior by individual economic agents, the thrust of

development economics ever since has been the recognition that private behavior is much more rational and responsive to the incentives in the economic
environment than was earlier thought. When confronted with an apparent failure of markets to function as forecast in the 1950s, almost all development
economists instinctively ascribed the failure to irrational behavior, nonrespon-
siveness to price, or monopoly behavior of one sort or another (including
inequality of asset holdings). In contrast, the development economist of the
1980s is far more likely to inquire why people are behaving as they are, on
the assumption that their behavior is most likely a rational response to current
incentives.

This change in perspective draws on seven interrelated advances in the
understanding of development processes: (1) the development of the theory
of human capital provides an economic rationale for various phenomena previously regarded as "cultural"; (2) the mounting evidence that peasant responses to market incentives and technical opportunities are more significant
than had been anticipated; (3) the response of entrepreneurs to incentives for
industrialization in country after country has eroded the belief in a lack of
entrepreneurship; (4) if technical change is to become an efficient source of
new income streams, the new technology must be consistent with the factor
endowments in the country or region in which it will be used; (5) institutional
innovation also represents an important source of new income streams; (6) the
development of the economics of information reveals that the apparent
anomalies of interconnected factor markets can in fact be efficient market
responses to the costs of acquiring information; thus even tenancy and sharecropping, which earlier had appeared to be inefficient and hence probably
irrational traditional arrangements, may be rational responses to the difficulties associated with the high costs of obtaining information or the lack of it;
and (7) experience with alternative trade regimes indicates that "elasticity
pessimism" is unfounded, and slow export growth is attributable more to
supply difficulties than to foreign demand. Let us briefly consider each of
these seven advances in turn.

1. In early development economics, low levels of literacy, short life ex-
pectancies, poor health, and rapid population growth rates, which made the
challenge of development and raising living standards difficult, were basically
regarded as noneconomic phenomena. This view began to change in the early
1960s with the new understanding of the role of human capital in economic
development (Schultz, 1961; Becker, 1964). The initial simple assertion was
that acquiring education is an investment, as is the allocation of time and
effort in job search, migration, or improvement in health. Investment in education covers both the amount of income forgone and the direct costs of
schooling. Under economically rational behavior, a choice to make this investment depends on the higher future income a person might expect to receive by virtue of the additional education.

The human capital approach is not inconsistent with the view that many people will choose more education regardless of the return. But the founders of the human capital school insisted that for most people, a positive real rate of return is needed to induce more investment in oneself. Thus, the higher the return, the greater the number or fraction of an eligible population that will make such investments and the higher the investment per person.

The early work on human capital and its focus largely on individual decisions was highly influential in affecting thinking about development. Subsequent work has extended the analysis to family decision making (e.g., choice of family size) (see Binswanger and Rosenzweig, 1984). Such choices are recognized now as far more rational economic responses to circumstances than was assumed earlier. Quite aside from their welfare implications, policies that ignore the existing incentive framework are likely to be ineffective.

The other insight that emerges from the human capital literature is that people are as important a resource as physical capital. Even people in developed countries who are regarded as unskilled have sizable amounts of human capital. Literacy is a virtual prerequisite for most "unskilled labor," and the rate of return to primary schooling is especially high (Psacharopoulos and Woodhall, 1985, pp. 29–71). An efficient means of resource accumulation, then, is to invest in both humans and machines to the point where the rates of return are approximately equal.

2. The rationality of peasant behavior began to be recognized during the 1950s. Peasants' responses to changes in the prices of individual agricultural commodities and to prices confronting producers could not be ignored. T. W. Schultz's work on traditional agriculture (1964) eventually persuaded many development economists that small peasants usually respond rapidly to incentives. Peasants who refuse to adopt new techniques often have good reasons: risks are unacceptably high; soil erosion would quickly result; or a technique is not as productive in a local region as officials assume. On the other hand, when a potential for change has a demonstrated payoff and acceptable levels of risk, peasants adapt very quickly. Thus, in a case where agricultural extension agents fail to persuade peasants to undertake the new techniques they are recommending, Schultz's presumption is that the agents are ignorant of the conditions confronting the peasants, the exact opposite of the earlier presumption of peasant irrationality. Thus a very different role for government in fostering economic development is implied (see below).

3. Although no systematic body of theory was formulated with respect to entrepreneurship,[9] the experience in country after country was that whatever the incentive structure erected by the government, private entrepreneurs respond to it. When governmental controls are designed to prohibit profitable private undertakings, smuggling, gray markets, and other mechanisms for avoiding the controls quickly spring up. When import substitution activities are made highly profitable, investment in the protected industries increases.

And when incentive structures are dramatically altered (e.g., in Korea after 1960), the rapidity and magnitude of the response surprises all observers.

4. Technical change also has come to be seen as largely an endogenous economic phenomenon. During the initial period, when capital accumulation was the focus, emphasis was placed on the direct transfer of technology (capital-intensive "turn-key plants" and large-scale farming systems) from developed to developing countries. In environments with widely different factor endowments the borrowed technology often was commercially viable only when it was protected by high tariffs or other barriers, which made it a burden rather than a source of economic growth. In the case of agriculture, it became apparent that peasant farmers in the tropics had access to more productive crop and animal technologies only when the new technologies were developed in the same agroclimatic and socioeconomic environments as that in which the technology would be used.[10]

Hayami and Ruttan (1985), for example, demonstrated that major differences exist between the types of technical change developed for land-abundant American agriculture (basically mechanical to augment scarce labor on abundant land) and those adopted in land-poor Japan (mostly new chemical technologies enhancing the productivity of land). Teece (1977) investigated the costs of adopting existing patents in foreign locations and demonstrated that the costs are a very significant barrier, often almost equal to those in the initial location. The clear implication of this entire line of work is that most technical change to increase future earnings streams requires the investment of resources and is seldom possible as a "free" or almost-free good.

5. Greater recognition has been given the role of institutions. Both the American institutional school and Marxian ideology had emphasized the constraints on development associated with traditional property, market, and government institutions (Zingler, 1974). This perspective was pervasive in development economics during the 1950s and 1960s. Beginning in the mid-1960s a new view began to emerge: institutional innovations, along with changing resource or factor endowments, are a productive source of new income streams (Schultz, 1968; North and Thomas, 1970), and modern technical change is dependent on the invention of new institutions—the industrial research laboratory and the agricultural experiment station. In both the Schultz and North-Thomas works, differences and changes in resource endowments play a role in the efficient evolution or design of institutional innovations in a manner analogous to the design of efficient technical change.

Access to the knowledge and technology in the developed world requires investment in scientific and technical education and in the institutionalization of agricultural and industrial research capacity. This institutionalization usually must be calculated in terms of decades rather than the traditional three- or five-year project cycles of bilateral and multilateral assistance agencies. But the developed countries and the assistance agencies must be prepared to make the required investments so that developing countries can have access to the very large income streams that become available as the technological disequilibria with the developed world are narrowed.

6. From the perspective of economics of information, the apparently irrational market structures observed in many developing countries, as well as tenancy and sharecropping arrangements, can be interpreted as rational responses to uncertainty and the high costs of information.[11] For example, providing a sharecropper fertilizer may not improve the landlord's return, because the cost of monitoring its use may be excessive. If, however, the landlord can make a tie-in arrangement with the sharecropper, as a moneylender or as a marketer, the result may be advantageous to both parties.

Not all decisions are entirely rational from an economic perspective, nor are all individuals equally responsive to changes in economic incentives; however, enough evidence has emerged that people act in their own self-interest to cast doubt on the extent of market failure in developing countries and to indicate that failure is certainly less pervasive than was earlier thought. Much remains to be learned about economic behavior in both developed and developing countries, of course, but there is far less basis in the 1980s than in the 1950s and 1960s to presume that policies for growth should differ significantly between developed and developing countries because of differences in the degree of market imperfection.

7. Experience with alternative trade regimes led to another advance in development economics. When commodity prices fell sharply in the mid-1950s, the typical policy response was to intensify protection for balance-of-payments reasons, often with little regard for the original "industrialization" or infant industry aims. The alternative—adjusting incentives to encourage exports—was not adopted, partly because of "elasticity pessimism." Domestic inflation rates exceeding the world rate with fixed nominal exchange rates, rising costs of inputs (as imports were prohibited once domestic production started), and sharp increases in demand for imports because of the "import intensity" of import substitution resulted in the slow growth of export earnings, thus making elasticity pessimism a self-fulfilling prophecy (Diaz-Alejandro, 1965).

Meanwhile, articulation of the concept of the effective rate of protection and empirical estimates of high and variable rates of protection in a large number of developing countries demonstrated that highly protected industries are usually high-cost and inefficient and that growth based upon them can not long be sustained (Krueger, 1978). Moreover, the rates of growth measured at domestic (protected) prices greatly overstated actual industrial growth because of the heavy weight given to protected industries. Conceptual developments may by themselves have challenged the dominance of the two-gap model later, but in fact the challenge came from evidence derived from the analysis of both cross-country and individual country experience on the effectiveness of incentives and a move to "outer-oriented" trade strategies. The latter actually consisted in providing incentives to sell on the international market at least as great as the incentives for selling on the domestic market.

The Korean experience was perhaps the most dramatic (chapter 13). Exports indeed were responsive to incentives; their failure to grow in the 1950s was due more to normal supply responses (emanating from overvalued exchange rates and strong inducements to pull resources into import substituting industries) than to any failure of world demand or structural rigidity (Mason et al., 1980). The subsequent institution of a series of macroeconomic and trade policy reforms, combined with implicit export promotion policies, was followed by rapid growth in industrial output, total factor productivity, and exports.

By the 1970s the developing countries as a group were markedly increasing their share of world exports of manufactures—the most rapidly growing segment of the market—and the elasticity pessimism hypothesis was discredited by experience. The success of the countries that switched strategies also provided evidence of the importance of incentives and the responsiveness of individuals to them (see Krueger, 1984a).

Toward a More Complex Perspective: Government Behavior

In early development thinking, "the government" was assumed to be an instrument that could be readily used to promote social welfare without imposing large costs on economic growth. It was seen as a selfless, monolithic entity whose objective function was simply to promote the cause of development (on the assumption that it was what people wanted) consistent with the social good.[12]

Experience and analysis demonstrated that this view is far too simple. "Government" consists of various decision makers, many of whom have particular interests (rather than some vaguely defined common good) at heart; laws and regulations are not automatically and costlessly implemented and enforced; pressure groups emerge and divert resources to their own favorable ends; and resource constraints narrow the choices available to governments.

When the understanding of individual behavior improved, the question arose whether market failure is as pervasive as was initially believed. As long as it was assumed that governments could effortlessly implement a correction for market failure, the presumption of government responsibility for economic activity in all its dimensions remained. No one was about to assert that any market functions perfectly (in the textbook competitive sense).

Experience demonstrated, however, that governments are not the perfect and costless economic agents that had been implicitly assumed; government intervention is often perverse and often has a negative impact on economic growth. The considerable analysis of how trade policy actually works in contrast with the textbook theory of how it might be implemented led some trade theorists to enunciate the theory of economic policy in the presence of distortions, noting in particular that when contrasted with the distorted situation, not all policy interventions improve welfare, and to recognize that other manifestations of government failure (e.g., high-cost parastatals, inconsistent and contradictory policies, and rent seeking as a major economic activity) cast doubt on earlier assumptions about government behavior.

The combination of these insights with growing appreciation of individuals' responsiveness to incentives began a reexamination of the role of government in the development process.[13] The first line of research (e.g., Krueger, 1978) focused on how policy, as opposed to intentions, actually worked. Trade interventions were so visible and costly that estimates of effective rates of protection, domestic resource costs, and other analyses of trade regimes convinced most observers that existing policies were irrational: nothing in the infant industry argument (or in optimal tariff theory) could justify the prevalence over several decades of rates of effective protection ranging up to over 1,000 percent.

Experience with costly trade regimes led a number of trade theorists to develop the second important line of research: the theory of first- and second-best policy (see Bhagwati, 1971). In essence, the types of policy instruments that had been employed in trade regimes were found to be frequently second- or third-best, or even ineffective, in terms of achieving desired results. Among the externalities that might justify encouragement to infant industries, protection in most cases was likely to be inferior to the direct encouragement of an activity such as workers' training or to fail completely (Baldwin, 1969).

Bhagwati demonstrated the same sorts of principles for other perceived distortions: if a factor-market distortion was believed to exist, the first-best policy would be to intervene in the factor market; the second-best would be a production subsidy; and the third-best, a tariff. Not only were these instruments unequivocally ranked but it could be demonstrated also that the highest attainable level of welfare with a tariff (even at the optimal rate) is below the attainable level with a production tax, which in turn is below that achievable with the first-best intervention (see Krueger, 1986). Production externalities and other rationales for intervention could be similarly analyzed; only in the case of trade monopoly power was trade intervention a first-best instrument.

When the theory of optimal policy is contrasted with the highly protectionist trade policies adopted by many developing countries, it is hard not to conclude that motives other than the improvement of welfare, as assumed in the theory, guided policy formulation and that at best, the theory of optimal policy conveniently legitimizes the measures adopted for other reasons.

Experience with technological transfer led to recognition of the importance of institutional changes. But other factors also contributed. Motivated by the spread of smuggling, tax evasion, and economic activity designed to profit by controls, the economics of rent seeking, or "directly unproductive activities," was developed. Resources allocated to increasing a claim against fixed government licenses were costly and yielded no social (but possibly a high private) return. The positive and welfare economics of the economics of policymaking, in which public agents are considered to be self-serving, is less advanced than the theory of optimal policy design. To date, most development economists are convinced that reassessment of many propositions earlier taken as givens is in order. One no longer can assume that any textbook policy (e.g., tariff, quantitative restriction, food subsidy, credit rationing, or tax) works as intended. Nor can it be assumed that they will not in themselves set in motion political forces to amend such policies. This view of developing countries in which the government is an independent actor, bureaucrats pursue personal interests, and private interests exchange economic for political resources led to the rise of a more sophisticated perspective on government behavior.

Economists working primarily on problems of the developed economies in the 1960s and 1970s generated a new "political economy" literature, which explored the effectiveness with which legislative bodies and bureaucracies translated individual preferences into public policy.[14] Hence, it became clear that public sector enterprises (e.g., government bureaus, regional and local development authorities, and nationalized industries) could not be expected to follow the maximization rules implied by enabling or funding legislation or by planning agencies. The behavior of managers of such institutions is influenced by their individual objective functions and by the economic and political structure and product markets in which they generate and allocate resources.

Beginning in the early 1970s economists and political scientists in the field of international development began to explore the implications of rent seeking (Krueger, 1974b; Tollison, 1982), corruption (Bhagwati and Hansen, 1973; Pitt, 1981), and institutional organization (Bates, 1981) for the implementation of public policy and the behavior of public institutions. Economic historians (North and Thomas, 1970) and development economists (Ruttan, 1978; Ruttan and Hayami, 1984) explored the implications of differences or changes in resource endowments and in levels and rates of growth in demand for institutional innovation and development.

The effect of this new body of theoretical and empirical research was to interpret institutional change as largely endogenous, rather than exogenous, to national economic and political systems. Institutional innovation and reform influence resource acquisition and at the same time are resource-using activities. It is no longer possible to treat institutional change or technical change as disembodied manna from heaven, or as a costless transfer arising out of technical assistance or policy dialogue. In both developed and developing economies property rights are costly to design and enforce, market development and exchange consume resources, information is scarce and expensive to acquire, and policy decisions and implementation draw heavily on both political and economic resources. The view that "getting policies right" involves little more than an exercise of careful analytical skill by planning commissions combined with the enlightened application of "political will" by legislative and executive bodies has given way to a more sophisticated understanding of the forces that bear on the formulation and implementation of economic policy.[15]

The Role of Policy in Development

The preceding lines of thought leave many questions unresolved and lead to a general rethinking of the role of government in development. The conclusions that stand out clearly, however, center on the importance of policy and especially on the avoidance of policies that may have major negative consequences for development.

In this section, the implications of current understandings of individual and governmental behavior on economic policy in support of development are reviewed, and then some of the unanswered questions—we hope future research will shed light on them—are briefly sketched.

First, the role of policy. Both the insights into behavior and the distinctly different experiences of countries with entirely different policy stances have convinced all observers of the overriding importance of policy framework in determining the success of development efforts. To be sure, any policy framework will appear more successful in an environment of the world economy's rapid growth, and when more concessional flows and other resources are available for augmenting domestic resources. Nonetheless, the differences in performance between, for example, Far Eastern exporters and heavily inward-oriented Latin American countries both during times of rapid growth in the international economy and the worldwide recession of the 1980s are testimony to this difference.

The process of development can be viewed as one of accumulating productive resources (both quantitatively and qualitatively, including human capital) per person and of increasing the efficiency of resource use. Initially, development thought focused on the problem of resource accumulation, on the implicit assumption that the resources would be efficiently used. Theory and practice demonstrated, however, that the efficiency with which resources are employed depends heavily on the economic environment in which private and public decisions are made.

That environment has three major, albeit interrelated, components: (a) the physical, institutional, and human infrastructure; (b) the macroeconomic framework; and (c) the microeconomic incentive structure. Clearly, growth cannot proceed without the simultaneous development of the physical, institutional, and human infrastructure necessary to support it. Early insights into the necessity for better transport facilities, a more effective communications system, a reliable power supply, widespread access to education, public health, enforcement of contract with respect to financial agreements, and so on, were valid, but their importance relative to the seemingly more directly productive investments in industrial development was often underestimated. The infrastructure available at any moment sets an upper limit on economic activity; below that limit a weak infrastructure may impose sharply rising costs of additional output. No development program can proceed for long if it does not provide for expansion of infrastructural capacity. And for some purposes (e.g., development of new export industries), neglecting the development of reasonably efficient communications, transport, and financial facilities can effectively foredoom whatever efforts may be made. (See, for example, Morawetz's [1981] revealing description and analysis of the competitive advantages of the Far Eastern textile and clothing exporters over their Colombian counterparts.)

If the importance of infrastructure was recognized but unappreciated, the role of macroeconomic policy was almost entirely neglected. High and fluctuating rates of inflation (especially when nominal exchange rates are held constant and only reluctantly altered), low nominal and negative real interest rates, and large fiscal deficits that either drain resources from the private sector or result in buildups of foreign debt are all deceptive insofar as growth apparently can continue for periods of several years even with such policies in place. Yet they are inherently unsustainable and their costs mount. When the time comes, a balance of payments crisis, a debt crisis, or a rate of inflation that is regarded by all segments of society as intolerable can wipe out the apparent gains of past growth over several years of stagnation or even declines in output.

Finally, microeconomic incentives clearly matter, and matter greatly. If the macroeconomic environment is neglected and the infrastructure underappreciated, analysts may be positively wrong about the responsiveness of individuals to incentives. Price controls (often imposed to contain inflation) lead to gray markets, resource misallocation, and worse. When the controls are sustained, savings rates fall and capital takes flight. Where producer prices of agricultural commodities have been suppressed, negative output responses are much greater than expected (Ghana's loss of share in cocoa and Sudan's loss in cotton are but two cases in point of a much more general phenomenon). Appreciating real exchange rates result not only in the failure of new export activities to grow but also in the decline in exports even of traditional commodities when economic rents make continuing production at least possible. Credit rationing and implicit subsidies to capital goods imports result in the use of capital-intensive techniques and in the failures of productive employment opportunities to increase even in countries in which rapidly growing labor forces make such employment growth a political necessity.

Several lessons are clear, then. The first is to avoid making big policy mistakes. This dictum applies as much to large public sector infrastructure schemes as it does to the key macroeconomic variables set by governments. Although neoclassical economics may not be "right," it provides a reasonable guide for many purposes. The hallmark of successful developing countries that have made policy mistakes along the way has not been the perfection of policy but the avoidance of (and willingness to correct) large mistakes.

The second is that a foremost consideration for policymakers is to avoid letting a key policy instrument generate large conflicts between government regulations and private profitability. Government policies put in place to prevent profitable endeavors or to require unprofitable courses of action by individuals are likely to be ineffective. People are always ready to seize opportunities for evasion, whether legal or illegal, but they in turn generate additional government efforts at containment. The result is more complex administrative regimes and more profitable opportunities for bureaucrats and private agents. Thus, the exchange rate regime must be realistic enough to keep exchange controls and import licensing unnecessary or at least insufficiently restrictive. Too high a rate of inflation induces significant difficulties with regard to savings and often results in capital flight. Suppression of producer prices in agriculture leads to urban food shortages and negative supply responses. Credit rationing, where effective, leads to incentives for the use of capital-intensive techniques for those to whom credit is allocated and large decreases in the efficiency with which new resources are employed. And encouragement of infant industries with high walls of protection and the conferral of monopoly positions induces monopolistic behavior, including a mismatch between consumer demand and types and varieties of output offered, inattention to quality, and pricing outputs that lower levels of demand.

Implicit in these lessons, but important enough to mention in its own right, is the growing appreciation of trade and trade policy to further development. High walls of protection not only fail to induce sustainable rapid growth (for the reasons cited above) but also become a stronger disincentive to the development of exports than was earlier recognized. For most developing countries, development of exports is perhaps the most promising path for rapid growth: it permits them to use their scarce capital and abundant labor to concentrate on the production of those goods (industrial and otherwise) that they can produce relatively efficiently; and given their relatively small domestic markets, the international marketplace becomes a competitive environment that simultaneously permits rapid expansion of efficient entrepreneurs, encourages plants of adequate size to allow economies of scale, and spurs all to better performance.

That much said, there are many areas where understanding is still highly imperfect. A first concern is how to achieve better governmental performance in those areas, such as infrastructure, where government has a clear comparative advantage. Here, the key, perhaps, is understanding the types of institutional arrangements that induce behavior consistent with good performance. When government officials derive power and income from the ability to withhold or delay valuable licenses and permits, they are likely to be less concerned with the growth objectives intended by the policymakers. An important question, then, is how to create incentive frameworks more consistent with the underlying objectives. Research is greatly needed for answers. In fact, our understanding of how effective institutions arise and are maintained is still very limited.

A second major area of concern relates to the "economics of transition": granting that we know a reasonable amount about an appropriate policy framework for development, how does one design a policy for transition? To what extent can the dislocations associated with adjustment be minimized, and how costly and long-lasting are such adjustments? When politicians are unwilling or unable to reform all policy instruments simultaneously, are there particular policies that require reform before others? Although some insights have come from research and experience (see chapters 12, 13, and 14), reform efforts continue to flounder.

Analysis of lessons learned to date cannot, however, await further developments. Thus the implications of the lessons thus far learned for aid and aid effectiveness are discussed in chapter 3.

3

Toward a Theory of Development Assistance

ANNE O. KRUEGER
AND VERNON W. RUTTAN

In chapter 2 the development process is treated primarily as the domestic response to a developing country's economic and trade policies when international financial and other resource flows are largely determined by market forces. In this chapter the focus is primarily on the economic effects of economic assistance.[1] Thus the two chapters provide the framework for our subsequent discussion of the policies of aid donors and recipients and for our review of the empirical evidence thereof.

Development Assistance Defined

The analysis and discussion in this study focus on "official development finance," or what the public and press typically call foreign aid. The basic characteristic of these flows is that they come from official sources and have as a primary objective the promotion of the recipients' economic development. Specifically excluded are transfers of private funds from voluntary agencies,[2] assistance provided by the International Monetary Fund (generally considered short-term financial transactions, not development assistance), military assistance, and official export credits. Although these flows often are also called foreign aid, they either are not from official sources or are provided largely for reasons other than the promotion of the recipients' development. Hence, consideration of their development impact or effectiveness was outside the scope of this study.

Official development finance as used here includes three major components:

1. Concessional flows to developing countries from individual donor countries, *bilateral official development assistance (ODA)*. To qualify as ODA, the flows, in addition to being official and developmental, must be highly concessional (i.e., they must have a grant element of at least 25 percent).

2. Concessional flows from multilateral development institutions, *mul-*

tilateral ODA. This includes funds from the International Development Association (IDA) and by the "soft window" of the regional development banks, the assistance provided by development agencies of the United Nations, such as the U.N. Development Program (UNDP) and the World Food Program (WFP), and the concessional assistance provided by limited membership multilaterals established by the European community and by members of the Organization of Petroleum Exporting Countries (OPEC).

3. Near market term loans provided by multilateral development institutions, *nonconcessional multilateral flows*. This assistance includes lending by the World Bank and by the "hard windows" of the regional development banks and the "limited membership" multilaterals.

As noted above, official development finance may consist, at one extreme, of a loan at or near market rates of interest and, at the other, of an outright grant of convertible currency. One method of comparing assistance flows with widely different terms and conditions is to calculate the difference between the amount received and the discounted present value of the repayment stream as a percentage of the original face value (Pincus, 1963; Schmidt, 1964). In calculating these "grant elements" the Development Assistance Committee (DAC) of the Organization for Economic Cooperation and Development (OECD) has adopted the convention of using a 10 percent discount rate, which is supposed to reflect broadly donors' opportunity cost of capital. By this convention, loans at 10 percent interest have a grant element of zero, while grants have a grant element of 100 percent (OECD, *Development Cooperation*, 1987, p. 110).

Aid is provided in a variety of forms from convertible foreign exchange (U.S. dollars, Japanese yen, French francs), which the recipient can use to cover a wide range of foreign exchange requirements, to much more specific and more restricted forms, such as food aid, technical assistance, or "tied aid" (according to which the donor requires the recipient to spend the aid in the donor's own market). While it is recognized that the value to the recipient of these more restricted forms of aid is likely to be less than that derived from untied forms of aid (see chapter 5), in practice the fair market value of the tied aid or food shipments is usually not estimated; instead, the donor's accounting of the costs of the aid is the reported aid figure. The result can be an overestimate of the value of the aid flow, for example, when food assistance is valued at farm support prices that are well above world prices (Bhagwati, 1970b) or when equipment purchased in the donor country with tied aid funds is more expensive than that available in other countries.

Another complication can be the classification of loans at market rates of interest that carry maturities longer than could be obtained commercially. When the market rate for such a loan is not observable, the true grant component is difficult to identify, but clearly it would be wrong to treat such a loan as entirely nonconcessional. Recognition of the underlying concessionality of such loans is potentially important when evaluating the role of donors such as the World Bank, which provide or facilitate such flows.

Although financial and commodity transfers account for the major share of recorded development assistance, donors also provide assistance in a number of other forms, some recorded as aid, others not. For example, both bilateral and multilateral agencies have supported substantial technology transfer and institutional and human capital development programs. These activities are sometimes incorporated in programs involving financial flows to developing countries; for example, a loan for a water resource development project may include components for training personnel and for research. At the other extreme are funds provided by a bilateral assistance agency to an educational or research institution in a donor country for technology transfer or training. While the funds for training and research in the first example would be included in official aid statistics, in the second example only the official support for individual fellowships to developing country students to support study and training would typically be included in the aid statistics.

Development Flows

Development assistance is fundamentally a post–World War II phenomenon. Initially, the United States was the only major provider of economic aid, marked most dramatically by the Marshall Plan, enacted in 1948, which was followed in the United States by the Point Four program in 1951, the Development Loan in 1957, and the United States Agency for International Development (US/AID) in 1961. During this period assistance was increasingly extended to former colonial territories by the United Kingdom, France, the Netherlands, and Belgium. The list of donors expanded to include most members of the OECD during the 1960s. The extent of this increase in the role of other donors is illustrated by the decrease in the proportion of total aid provided by the United States: from almost 60 percent of total bilateral ODA by members of the DAC in the early 1960s to only 30 percent by the mid-1970s and only 21.5 percent in 1987 (see table 3.1).

On the multilateral side, the World Bank (formally the International Bank for Reconstruction and Development, or IBRD) was created in 1944. This was soon followed by the establishment of specialized agencies of the United Nations which provided assistance to developing countries. The late 1950s and the 1960s saw the appearance of several other multilateral assistance organizations: the Inter-American Bank, the first regional bank (1959); the IDA, the concessional affiliate of the World Bank (1960); and in 1956 three other regional development banks—African, Caribbean, and Asian—which promoted economic development in their respective regions.

Table 3.2 shows the net financial receipts of the developing countries

Table 3.1. Net Disbursements and Burden Sharing of ODA by DAC Member Countries (Current $U.S.)

	1960			1970			1975			1980			1987		
	ODA ($b)	Share (%)	ODA as % of GNP	ODA ($b)	Share (%)	ODA as % of GNP	ODA ($b)	Share (%)	ODA as % of GNP	ODA ($b)	Share (%)	ODA as % of GNP	ODA ($b)	Share (%)	ODA as % of GNP
Australia	0.6	1.3	0.38	0.20	2.9	0.59	0.55	4.0	0.61	0.67	2.5	0.48	0.63	1.5	0.33
Austria [a]	—	—	—	0.02	0.3	0.05	0.08	0.6	0.17	0.18	0.7	0.23	0.20	0.5	0.17
Belgium	0.10	2.1	0.88	0.12	1.8	0.46	0.38	2.7	0.59	0.60	2.2	0.50	0.69	1.7	0.49
Canada	0.08	1.7	0.19	0.35	5.1	0.42	0.88	6.4	0.58	1.08	4.0	0.43	1.89	4.5	0.47
Denmark	0.01	0.2	0.09	0.06	0.9	0.38	0.21	1.5	0.58	0.48	1.8	0.74	0.86	2.0	0.88
Finland	0	0	0	0	0	0	0.05	0.4	0.18	0.11	0.4	0.22	0.43	1.0	0.50
France	0.85	18.1	1.38	0.95	14.0	0.63	2.09	15.1	0.62	4.16	15.2	0.63	6.53	15.7	0.74
Germany	0.24	5.1	0.33	0.60	8.8	0.28	1.69	12.2	0.40	3.57	13.1	0.44	4.39	10.6	0.39
Ireland [a]	0	0	0	0	0	0	—	—	—	0.03	0.1	0.16	0.05	0.1	0.20
Italy	0.08	1.7	0.22	0.15	2.2	0.14	0.18	1.3	0.11	0.68	2.5	0.15	2.62	6.3	0.35
Japan	0.11	2.3	0.24	0.46	6.8	0.21	1.15	8.3	0.24	3.35	12.3	0.32	7.45	17.9	0.31
Netherlands	0.04	0.9	0.31	0.20	2.9	0.60	0.61	4.4	0.75	1.63	6.0	0.97	2.09	5.0	0.98
New Zealand	0	0	0	0	0	0	0.07	0.5	0.52	0.07	0.3	0.33	0.09	0.2	0.26
Norway	0.01	0.2	0.11	0.04	0.6	0.32	0.18	1.3	0.66	0.49	1.8	0.87	0.89	2.1	1.09
Portugal	0.04	0.9	1.45	0.03	0.4	0.58	0	0	0	0	0	0	0	0	0
Sweden	0.01	0.2	0.05	0.12	1.8	0.38	0.57	4.1	0.82	0.96	3.5	0.78	1.38	3.3	0.88
Switzerland	neg	neg	0.04	0.03	0.4	0.14	0.10	0.7	0.18	0.25	0.9	0.24	0.55	1.3	0.31
United Kingdom	0.41	8.7	0.56	0.45	6.6	0.32	0.90	6.5	0.37	1.85	6.8	0.35	1.87	4.5	0.28
United States	2.70	57.5	0.53	3.05	44.8	0.29	4.16	30.0	0.26	7.14	26.2	0.27	8.95	21.5	0.20
Total	4.70	100.0	0.52	6.81	100.0	0.32	13.85	100.0	0.36	27.30	100.0	0.37	41.53	100.0	0.35

Source: OECD, *Development Cooperation*, various issues.
[a] 1960 data for Austria and 1975 data for Ireland were negligible but positive.

Table 3.2. Total Net Resource Receipts of Developing Countries from All Sources, 1960–1987

	Constant 1983 $U.S. Billions					Average Annual Growth Rates (%)		
	1960–61	1970	1975	1980	1987[a]	1960–86	1970–80	1980–87
I. Official development finance	20.3	24.0	35.4	40.6	42.2	2.9	5.4	0.6
A. Concessional	19.5	22.2	31.6	36.1	37.0	2.4	5.0	0.4
1. Bilateral ODA	18.6	19.4	25.9	28.8	29.3	1.6	4.0	0.2
DAC	15.9	14.8	14.6	17.0	23.1	1.2	1.4	4.5
OPEC	2.7	1.0	8.4	8.2	2.5	—	23.4	−15.6
CMEA[b] and other donors[c]	0.9	3.5	2.9	3.6	3.7	1.1	0.3	0.4
2. Multilateral ODA	0.9	2.8	5.7	7.3	7.7	8.7	10.1	0.8
IDA	—	0.6	1.7	1.4	2.7	—	8.8	9.8
UN	—	1.3	2.0	2.3	2.5	—	5.9	1.2
EEC	—	0.5	0.9	1.0	1.3	—	6.3	3.8
Other	—	0.4	1.0	2.6	1.2	—	20.5	−10.5
B. Multilateral nonconcessional flows	0.8	1.9	3.8	4.6	5.2	8.3	9.4	5.2
World Bank	—	1.5	2.6	3.0	3.5	—	7.1	2.2
Regional development banks	—	0.3	0.8	0.9	1.4	—	13.3	6.5
Other	—	0.1	0.4	0.7	0.3	—	21.5	−11.4
II. Private voluntary contributions	—	2.3	2.0	2.2	2.7	—	−0.4	3.0
III. Export credits	4.8	7.0	8.4	12.7	−0.5	−4.1	6.1	−37.0
IV. Private direct investment	6.5	9.7	16.9	9.9	15.4	1.6	0.2	6.5
V. Private lending[d]	2.2	8.6	18.5	47.3	4.2	4.6	18.6	−29.2
VI. Other[e]	0.7	1.5	3.6	5.4	4.5	8.2	13.7	−2.6
VII. Total flows (I+II+III+IV+V+VI)	34.8	53.1	84.6	118.1	68.5	2.7	8.3	−7.5
Memo item: IMF purchases (net)	—	0.9	4.8	2.5	−3.6			

Source: OECD, *Development Cooperation*, various issues.

[a]Figures obtained by converting 1987 data in current dollars presented in 1988 review to constant 1983 dollars.

[b]Council for Mutual Economic Assistance, which comprises Bulgaria, Cuba, Czechoslovakia, the German Democratic Republic, Hungary, Mongolia, Poland, Romania, Vietnam, and the Soviet Union. Albania is a nonactive member.

[c]The bulk of the assistance in this category is provided by CMEA countries.

[d]Private lending includes bond lending and international bank lending, which in recent DAC reports takes into account short-term debt. For 1980 the total bank lending figure provided in the 1985 DAC report was used in place of the bank sector lending figure to make the estimate compatible with current DAC reporting of private lending.

[e]Includes official bilateral nonconcessional flows. The DAC, however, now includes such flows as part of official development finance.

between 1960 and 1987 from all sources. This table highlights a number of important characteristics and changes in financial flows over this period:

— ODA doubled in real terms (constant prices and exchange rates), with much of this growth occurring during the 1970s.

— In the 1970s members of OPEC became important sources of development assistance, with their aid rising from $1 billion in 1970 to $8 billion in 1975.

— There was a significant increase in the level and relative importance of multilateral assistance, both concessional and nonconcessional. The shift toward multilateral aid can also be seen in the changing share of donors' total aid allocated to multilateral institutions, which increased from only 6 percent in 1965 to 32 percent in 1977–78.

— Private bank lending increased dramatically in the 1970s, rising in real terms from $9 billion in 1970 to $47 billion in 1980. This in turn led to a drop in the share of total net financial receipts accounted for by aid flows. In 1960–61 aid represented 60 percent of developing country receipts; by 1980 they had dropped to 35 percent of the total.

— Since 1980, ODA flows have effectively stagnated in real terms. Underlying this overall trend was a relatively strong growth in DAC donors' aid, very modest growth in multilateral ODA flows (with the notable exception of IDA), and a dramatic fall in OPEC aid.

— The rapid growth in nonconcessional multilateral flows experienced in the 1970s continued (albeit at a somewhat reduced rate) into the 1980s as the World Bank in particular was called upon to address the serious adjustment problems of the heavily indebted middle-income countries.

— Despite the stagnation of overall aid flows between 1980 and 1987, the precipitous fall since 1980 in net export credits (from $13 billion to minus $0.5 billion) and private bank lending (which fell to only $4.2 billion in 1987) has meant that aid flows again represent over 60 percent of developing countries' net financial receipts.

The importance to different countries of official assistance, and in particular ODA, varies considerably. As a group, low-income countries have extremely limited access and ability to service nonconcessional flows; hence, they depend heavily upon development assistance. Table 3.3 shows that ODA in 1983 accounted for 87 percent of the total net capital flow of the least developed countries, 76 percent for the low-income Sub-Saharan African countries, and 66 percent for the low-income countries. As one would expect, as the level of development increases, the ability to obtain private flows increases and, correspondingly, the dependence on aid flows decreases. In 1983 ODA flows to lower-middle-income countries accounted for 29 percent of their net financial receipts. For upper-middle-income developing countries the figure was only 14 percent.

Table 3.3. External Financial Receipts of Developing Countries, by Source for Selected Years (in percent)

| | ODA | | Official Non-concessional Flows | | Export Credits | Private Flows | | Other[b] | Total[c] | Total ($billion in 1986 prices & exchange rates) |
	Total	Bilateral	Total	Multi-lateral		Direct Investment (OECD)	Financial Markets[a]			
Least developed countries										
1979	76	53	3	2	7	6	2	6	100	11.2
1983	87	59	5	1	4	1	−3	6	100	11.8
1986	86	58	1	−1	2	1	4	6	100	12.6
Low-income countries										
1979	66	48	5	4	9	12	3	5	100	32.3
1983	66	47	8	5	7	6	8	5	100	38.3
1986	61	44	7	4	5	10	11	6	100	46.2
Low-income Sub-Saharan Africa[d]										
1979	60	49	9	6	16	13	3	x	100	8.8
1983	76	64	19	8	−3	2	6	x	100	7.7
1986	85	75	13	3	−5	3	4	x	100	7.5

Lower middle-income countries									
1979	26	21	11	7	11	8	38	6	100	19.9
1983	29	24	17	15	10	10	31	3	100	19.9
1986	48	42	25	17	1	10	9	8	100	13.4
Upper middle-income countries									
1979	14	12	4	3	16	15	48	4	100	76.1
1983	14	12	6	7	7	14	58	2	100	57.7
1986	39	35	24	17	−12	30	2	16	100	20.4
Western Hemisphere									
1979	8	6	3	3	7	17	59	6	100	53.1
1983	17	14	8	10	8	13	52	3	100	33.2
1986	32	27	30	21	2	17	5	13	100	18.5

Source: OECD, Financing and External Debt of Developing Countries, 1987 Survey (Paris, 1988).

a International bank lending and bond lending.

b Grants by non-governmental organizations, private business transactions, estimates of unreported bond lending, and direct investment by non-OECD countries.

c May not total 100 due to rounding.

d Excludes unallocated ODA, grants from non-governmental organizations, and other private flows.

Table 3.4. ODA as a Percentage of Recipients' GNP

	1960–61	1970–71	1983–84	1986–87
All developing countries	1.7	1.2	1.1	1.5
Sub-Saharan Africa	1.9	2.9	5.0	6.5
Low-income countries	2.5	3.6	10.1	14.3
Lower-middle-income countries	0.6	1.4	0.9	1.1
Upper-middle-income countries[a]	3.7	15.5	9.6	10.1
North Africa and the Middle East	4.2	1.2	1.3	1.2
Low-income countries	4.6	2.1	5.1	9.0
Lower-middle-income countries	6.4	3.9	2.6	3.2
Upper-middle-income countries	3.9	0.7	0.8	0.7
Asia	1.6	1.3	0.8	1.4
Low-income countries	1.5	1.4	1.0	1.8
Lower-middle-income countries	0.7	0.7	0.9	1.6
Upper-middle-income countries	4.1	1.5	0.1	0.1
Latin America	0.5	0.6	0.5	0.8
Low-income countries	3.1	2.6	6.9	9.0
Lower-middle-income countries	0.3	0.9	2.7	4.3
Upper-middle-income countries	0.5	0.5	0.2	0.3

Source: OECD, *Development Cooperation,* various issues.
Note: The income and regional groupings in this table are those defined by the DAC for analytical purposes.
[a] The high ratio of this set of countries reflects primarily the very large aid flows relative to
GNP provided by France to the French Overseas Department and Territories (DOM-TOMs)
included in this grouping, coupled with the fact that the grouping includes only two non-DOM-
TOM countries.

The table also illustrates an apparent anomaly in the flow of capital to
low-income African countries during the 1970s. Many of these countries,
such as Kenya, Sudan, and Zaire, despite their low level of income and relatively limited capacity to service commercial debt, were able to obtain substantial export credits and other loans at market or near-market terms. But
this relatively extensive use of short-term commercial credit, coupled with the
often inefficient or nonproductive use of the funds and distorted domestic
policies increased their debt burden without a commensurate increase in their
capacity to repay. The result was that with the rise in real interest rates and
worldwide recession in 1980–83, a serious debt crisis arose in many of these
countries. The table also highlights the dramatic fall in private lending to the
middle-income countries in the mid-1980s.

The importance of aid flows is further illustrated in table 3.4, which
compares the level of ODA flows with the recipients' GNP. Three character-

istics and trends stand out from the table: (1) aid flows on average have been modest in comparison with developing country GNP and had declined until recently. Their increase to 1.5 percent of the developing world's GNP since 1983–84 is due to weak growth in these countries in recent periods; (2) for Sub-Saharan countries, however, the role of the ODA has increased dramatically over the last quarter century to a level of 6.5 percent of their GNP, 14.3 percent for the low-income African countries; in contrast, for low-income Asia ODA has been far smaller relative to GNP.

International Financial Assistance

A surprising amount of intellectual effort has been required to clarify the contribution of aid to the resources available to a recipient country. In the 1950s critics of aid programs urged a policy of "trade, not aid" (Kaufman, 1968). An attempt by Harry G. Johnson to clarify the contributions of both trade and aid policies led to what at that time was the clearest articulation of the contribution of international financial transfers: "As a first approximation aid serves two functions. First, it provides real resources additional to what can be extracted from the domestic economy, increasing the total available for investment; second, since the resources are foreign, it averts the real income loss to the country involved in transforming domestic into foreign resources" (Johnson, 1967, pp. 55, 56).

Johnson pointed out that increased trade can raise real incomes, first, by making possible a fuller utilization of domestic resources, and second, by realizing the gains from the specialization or scale economies associated with trade. The opening up of additional opportunities to trade differs from the provision of additional aid by providing a less developed country with the opportunity to realize efficiency gains from the conversion of domestic into foreign resources (Johnson, 1967, p. 56). There may, of course, be some offsets to the gains. It has been argued that Johnson did not adequately take into account the dynamic externalities associated with trade, such as technology transfer and learning by doing (Thirlwall, 1976; Karunaratne, 1986). Furthermore, critics of foreign aid have noted that the transfer of financial resources, unless well managed, can be expected to cause an appreciation of the foreign exchange value of the recipient's currency (Krauss, 1983, p. 157; McKinnon, 1986).

THE TWO-GAP MODEL

Beginning in the early 1950s considerable effort was devoted to attempting to estimate the appropriate magnitude of assistance flows. An expert committee of leading development economists (Alberto Baltra Cortez, D. R. Gadgil, George Hakim, W. Arthur Lewis, and Theodore W. Schultz) appointed by the secretary-general of the United Nations (1951) recommended that the developed countries transfer approximately $10 billion annually in loans and grants with the objective of achieving an increase in the annual rate of growth of per capita income of 1.5–2.0 percent. Yet the primary criterion for determining the size of aid flows employed by assistance agencies during the 1950s was whether projects could be found that generated a sufficiently high rate of return to meet conventional financial criteria. While financial resources were often transferred on "soft terms," they were expected to fund "hard projects." As a consequence, the size of aid flows would be determined by the results of individual project analysis.

The most ambitious attempt to make operational the advances in conceptualizing the relationship between financial transfer and economic growth was the "two-gap" planning model approach developed by Hollis B. Chenery and several collaborators during the early and mid-1960s.[3] In the simpler version of the model (see chapter 2) an assumed capital output ratio is used to derive the investment rate needed to achieve a targeted output growth rate. A fixed relationship between imports and growth of output is also assumed, and export growth is taken as exogenous, which permits a derivation of the level and rate of growth of import requirements. A savings gap occurs when the domestic savings rate is below the level necessary to permit the investment required to meet the output growth target. Even if savings are adequate, a trade gap may emerge when the level of imports that can be financed through export earnings is less than the level needed to achieve the targeted rate of growth of output. The role of financial assistance is to remove both the savings-investment and the import-export gaps by matching whichever is the larger of the two gaps (Bruton, 1969).

Two-gap models employ an implicit phase, or regime, approach to economic development. In the first phase, growth accelerates as rapidly as is permitted by skill constraints or other limits to absorptive capacity, as measured by investment growth. Although capital transfers during this phase are relatively small, technical assistance for project design and implementation can be productively employed to partially offset the constraints imposed by limited absorptive capacity. In the phases that follow, the structure of the economy is modified in order to effectively absorb more external capital.

Critics of the two-gap approach generally have interpreted the work by Chenery and associates as employing a second stage in which growth is limited by the import-export gap (Fei and Ranis, 1968; Bruton, 1969). Chenery and Strout insisted, however, that there is no logical necessity for the sequence of savings-investment and trade gaps: "It is not the sequence in which the savings constraint and trade constraint become binding but the fact that there is not an automatic mechanism to equate the two gaps in the short run that lies at the heart of our analysis" (Chenery and Strout, 1968, p. 915). Furthermore, they presented a modified version of the two-gap model in which the "gap between the gaps" is reduced or eliminated by assuming a more flexible economy and better policy coordination (Chenery and Strout, 1966, pp. 697–701). This second model has been largely ignored by the critics and by development practitioners.

The two-gap approach was fully consistent with the dominant perspective on assistance policy during the 1950s and early 1960s (Millikan and Rostow, 1957; Rosenstein-Rodan, 1961). The two-gap models were developed at a time when the resources available to US/AID and other bilateral and multilateral assistance agencies were expanding rapidly. Acceptance of the two-gap approach to implement assistance policy was facilitated by Chenery's role as director of the policy staff at US/AID during the mid-1960s.

The major criticism of the intellectual perspective that dominated aid policy in the 1950s and 1960s and, hence, of the two-gap model is based on the excessively strong focus on the volume of resource flows and the scant attention to the incentives for efficiency in resource use (Michalopoulos, 1975).[4] The responsiveness of exports to changes in real exchange rates was not taken into account. Accordingly, in implementation a single factor— scarce foreign exchange—was treated as the most important constraint on development. Finally, the focus did not adequately take into account the magnitude or duration of the investments in human capital that were necessary to employ large inflows of financial assistance productively.

Despite the qualifications that can now be made, the two-gap approach remains the most ambitious attempt—even if flawed—to integrate a theory of foreign economic assistance and economic development. The two-gap and, sometimes, even one-gap models continue to be used by the World Bank to estimate long-term needs for capital inflows (Khan, Montiel, and Haque, 1986; see also chapter 15). Although the shift in emphasis to more policy-based lending has made the two-gap model increasingly inappropriate, it is not hard to discover an implicit two-gap approach in a good deal of current discussion about development policy (Michalopoulos, 1987).

IMPERFECT CAPITAL MARKETS

The professional criticisms of the two-gap model during the 1960s centered primarily on its limitations as a guide to the programming of financial transfers by the bilateral or multilateral assistance agencies. During the 1970s other bodies of thought questioned the size of the effect that might be expected from financial transfers and the desirability of external financial assistance.

Arnold C. Harberger argued that it would not be unreasonable to expect project loans to developing countries to generate average real rates of return above 10 percent—more than double the approximately 4–5 percent employed by the United States in its domestic project analysis. If the 10 percent rate were applied to U.S. assistance over the 1946–68 period, he went on to argue, we would find that the only countries in which our foreign aid may have caused a substantial percentage increase in national income were those where political and military motives had resulted in exceptionally high per capita aid levels (Harberger, 1972, pp. 634, 635).

A second set of criticisms, advanced in a series of articles and books by Peter T. Bauer (1972, 1981, and 1984), focused on the role of international capital markets. Bauer argued that external assistance has never been necessary for the development of any society. To the extent that investment funds are required for development, they may be obtained by commercial borrowing. But those who viewed private capital markets as an effective substitute for aid did not address the problem of imperfections in international capital markets. These markets, even among the developed countries, are not perfect, and the imperfections are magnified in the markets that link developed and developing countries.[5] Even in situations in which international commercial capital is available and projects would yield the necessary returns, in some circumstances it would not pay anyone in a recipient country (including the government) to undertake a project at commercial terms. Most analysts of aid have focused on two reasons: (1) the gestation or payout period of projects (e.g., education projects) is too long; and (2) the investor cannot fully capture the stream of returns (e.g., investments in roads, ports, and power stations) (Krueger, 1986, pp. 65–66; chapter 8).

If a project's repayments stream is not matched to the earnings stream it generates, an investor would not undertake the project unless there were other earnings streams (or borrowing possibilities) to service the obligations in the project's early years. One might ask, of course, why the country could not refinance (or borrow more) to cover debt-servicing obligations in the years prior to high returns. In reality, commercial capital flows to developing countries typically have had a maturity structure of ten years or less (implicitly even less in the late 1970s, when the inflation premium in the nominal interest rate rose). Thus, poor countries may be unable to borrow at or near commercial terms to finance much of their infrastructural investment, despite the prospect of adequate real rates of return in the long run. A second and related difficulty is that many investments in the early stages of development entail public financing of activities that have significant externalities and for which user charges may not be appropriate.

These considerations appear to have most relevance for the very poorest countries, those with high levels of illiteracy, rudimentary transport and communications systems, and low savings rates. It must be emphasized that this case for concessionality is based on the productivity of these particular investments in these countries and is additional to the case based on need or humanitarian motives.

An unanswered question from critics who argue for the sufficiency of private capital markets is whether official flows on commercial terms can improve the welfare of both donors and recipients (Mikesell, 1968; Krueger,

1986). The answer hinges on whether imperfections in the private international capital market preclude it from equalizing (risk-adjusted) rates of return between donor and recipient. If returns were higher in developing countries, the welfare of both donor and recipient could be improved through official flows. The recipient could service its debt and nonetheless have a higher future income stream than would otherwise be possible. Simultaneously, the donor could obtain a rate of return equal to or greater than that obtainable on other assets.

Consider the maximization of world welfare in the context of a simple two-factor neoclassical model. Even if the usual conditions for economic efficiency were met within individual countries, free trade might fail to equalize factor returns in the absence of capital flows. Gains in world efficiency, even under these conditions, would require the development of institutions to facilitate the flow of capital from low-return to high-return countries.[6]

A first conclusion, therefore, is that official flows on commercial terms could hardly reduce world welfare. Indeed, normally they would be expected to increase world welfare. This conclusion is based on the assumption that development assistance permits incremental investments with real returns at least as great as the return to the donor. Another underlying assumption is that behavior in a borrowing country is not influenced, at least not negatively, by the receipt of official development assistance. Subject to these qualifications, official flows on commercial terms would not reduce welfare but would increase it if the flows encouraged improved policies or if private markets failed, despite the higher real rates of return, to supply the capital (see chapter 6).

A second conclusion is that international financial assistance can be particularly important in sustaining development momentum during a period of financial stress. Debt "overhang" can severely limit a developing country's ability to use the private international capital market. For some developing countries, current debts are so great relative to existing income that increases in future earnings must be tapped to finance their existing obligations. Because the private capital markets correctly perceive this claim on future income, they will not make loans even for new projects that would yield acceptable returns (Guttentag and Herring, 1984). This inability to insulate new claims from existing debt puts countries in a vicious circle: they cannot restore creditworthiness without growth, and they cannot grow until creditworthiness is restored. Thus the private capital market may fail despite the rational behavior of all participants (see Krueger, 1987a and 1987b, for a fuller discussion).

In the decade of the 1970s there was increasing concern that achievement of higher rates of GNP growth did not translate into widespread improvements in well-being. This focused attention on the definition of minimum standards of consumption of goods and services essential to meet basic needs in such areas as food, water, and shelter and on the identification of target groups of poor within countries whose consumption levels fell short of the minimum. Concern about the persistence of unequal income distribution and widespread poverty in the face of rising overall incomes also led to the development of aid programs aimed at targeting assistance to the poor (chapter 9).

This burgeoning interest in income distribution and poverty in both development and aid literature came to an abrupt halt in the early 1980s as the emerging international crisis forced adjustments that resulted in substantial reduction of overall incomes and output in many countries. Only recently has attention started to shift back on the implications of domestic adjustment programs supported by external assistance on poverty and income distribution.

Also, during the 1960s and 1970s a new literature, drawing on the theory of investment in human capital and the implications of that theory for technical and institutional change, implied a much more optimistic view of the impact of development assistance. The next two sections review the thinking on the role of technical assistance and policy-based lending.

Technical Assistance to Poor Countries

A continuing argument within both bilateral and multilateral assistance agencies concerns the appropriate role of assistance for investment in physical and human capital. In US/AID an intense confrontation took place throughout the 1950s and early 1960s between the advocates of capital assistance and the advocates of technical assistance—between those advocating aid intended to raise output by increasing the supply of capital (often termed "commodity") assistance and those advocating aid intended to raise output by changing the methods of production (technical assistance) in recipient countries (Wolf, 1960, p. 61).

The distinction between aid in the form of financial flows or commodities, designed to increase the factors available for production, and aid in the form of technical services, designed to change the methods of production and enhance the productivity of factors, is conceptually clear within the framework of neoclassical production economics. In practice, however, it tends to be somewhat misleading.

> In theory, technological change implies a possibility of increasing the productivity of existing factors of production. In practice, raising the productivity of existing factors frequently requires substantial amounts of new factors as well. Technical assistance, viewed as services only, may change production possibilities in the static sense of what is known without providing the means to change what is done. . . . Similarly, the impact of capital, without technical assistance, may raise output by less than would be pos-

sible given knowledge of improved methods of using capital. (Wolf, 1960, pp. 61, 62)

The answer, of course, is to view technical assistance and capital assistance as complements rather than alternatives.

Not until well into the 1960s, however, was a clear intellectual foundation established for the role of technical assistance. Early programs tended to be dominated by a naive "know-how, show-how"—what today would be termed a "technology transfer"—perspective. Projects were initiated on an ad hoc basis, with little sense of priority or strategy. In the late 1950s substantial advances were made in our understanding of the role of technical change in releasing the resource constraints on economic growth (see chapter 2). By the mid-1960s a well-articulated theory of technical assistance began to emerge. The core of the theory was what Harry G. Johnson termed a "generalized capital accumulation approach" (see chapter 2).

The generalized human capital approach has provided an intellectual foundation for a much broader perspective on the sources of the productivity gains—the new income streams—that could be realized by a wide range of investment in human capital and institutional development. A conceptual foundation was established for assessing the relative priorities and the economic gains from technical assistance. Conceptualizing assistance to education as an investment in human capital opened up the issue of variations in the rates of return among different levels in the education system. Public health and medical care could be conceived of as an industry concerned with the maintenance of human capital. Institutional arrangements for supporting and rewarding fundamental and applied research could be considered an investment in the production of intellectual capital. It became possible to view technical assistance for the reform of public finance in terms of institutional innovations that would enhance the rate of return in both material and human capital investment.

These insights were followed by a large body of research that documented rates of return to agricultural research (Ruttan, 1982, pp. 237–61), agricultural extension (Huffman, 1978), formal and nonformal education (Lockhead, Jamison, and Lau, 1980; Psacharopoulos and Woodhall, 1985), and health (World Bank, 1980a). Even in areas in which quantitative estimates were unfeasible or unavailable, by the late 1960s the human capital perspective began to exert a pervasive influence on the thinking of development practitioners and policymakers. Activities formerly viewed as not directly productive were now perceived to be appropriate areas for both development lending and technical assistance. The generalized human capital approach also shifted attention from the earlier naive technology transfer perspective to a more serious concern with assistance for the development of capacity to generate the human capital and to design the new technology needed to sustain technical and institutional change.

The research on institution building and assistance for institutional development (see chapter 2) was also a product of the generalized human capital perspective. (A number of such efforts are examined in greater detail in chapters 10 and 11.) However, our knowledge of the process of institutional design and innovation is far less advanced than our understanding of the effects of investment on physical and human capital. Consequently, our ability to draw on this knowledge to enhance the productivity of either financial assistance or technical assistance remains underdeveloped.

THE COSTS OF TECHNOLOGY TRANSFERS

A careful study by Teece of the costs of technology transfer by multinational firms (1977) provides many useful insights into the specific contributions of human capital investment. Earlier, it was conventional to view the transfer of technology among countries as almost costless. Teece attempted to identify the costs of transferring the relevant "unembodied knowledge" over and above the transfer of the material capital by considering four cost categories: (a) preengineering technological exchange; (b) engineering costs associated with the transfer of process design and engineering; (c) exchanges of research and development personnel; and (d) pre-start-up training and debugging costs. All four cost categories reflect intensive inputs of human capital. He also identified several institutional characteristics that influence the cost and the success of the transfer: (a) the extent to which the technology is completely understood by the transfer personnel of the firm that is the source of the technology; (b) the age of the technology and the extent to which it has stabilized; (c) the number of firms, and hence the diversity of experience, with the technology; and (d) the level or intensity of research and development of physical and institutional infrastructure in the host country.

Costs are larger when the technology transfer does not involve the close institutional collaboration within the multinational firms studied by Teece. They will be further magnified if, as suggested in the induced innovation literature, the technology must be redesigned or even reinvented (due to different resource endowments, factor prices, and market opportunities) to make the technology economically viable in the host country (Thirtle and Ruttan, 1987). These costs may be reduced, but not eliminated, by the technical assistance that is often rendered within the framework of capital lending by the multinational banks or bilateral assistance agencies.

INVESTMENT IN HUMAN CAPITAL

A primary rationale for bilateral and multilateral technical assistance is that many investments in human and institutional capital have a substantial public goods component. Only part of the gains can be captured by the firm that must pay for the technology transfer or will be retained by the country to which the new technology is transferred. Mansfield estimated that in the United States the private rate of return to industrial research and development is equal to only about half the social rate of return (Mansfield, 1977).

The full gains from more generic investments in education, nutrition, and health are difficult to capture by individual households or even by individual countries. There is strong evidence that the social rate of return in education substantially exceeds the private rate of return (Schultz, 1971, pp. 132–88). Owners of scarce personal assets do not have exclusive private use of these assets; it is the value of the assets in a large and complex economic system that makes them most valuable. Significant gains to social interaction are found above and beyond what individuals can achieve on their own (Arrow, 1983, p. 188; Lucas, 1988). The growth of global and political interdependence implied a decline in the significance of national boundaries. Inasmuch as national boundaries are not coextensive with the scope of economic interdependence, they do not limit the gains of sharing benefits of economic growth from investment in human and institutional capital. For example, the export-oriented policies pursued by Japan, Korea (chapter 13), and several other East Asian countries have generated much higher rates of return to human capital investment than would have been generated by more inward-looking policies, and these gains have been shared with the rest of the world in the form of lower prices.

Clarification of the intellectual foundations of investment in human and institutional capital broadened the scope of grant and lending activity by both bilateral and multilateral assistance agencies in the late 1960s and early 1970s. The World Bank made its first national educational development loan to Tunisia in 1962. In the following decade the Bank's support of investment in human capital and institutional development (e.g., health, education, agricultural research, and urban and rural development) increased rapidly (Heyneman, 1985; Measham, 1986).

Investment in human capital by bilateral and multilateral donors has declined since the early 1980s, however. Assistance agency practice has been viewed as less effective in implementing projects to strengthen the institutional infrastructure than in implementing projects to strengthen the physical infrastructure.[7] Also, the forms of human capital, the professional manpower that is essential for technology and institutional transfer, have risen in economic value. As these costs have risen, technology transfer activities that make intensive demands on developed country human capital have been reduced by both bilateral and multilateral assistance agencies. A third factor has been a rise in the major demand for financial transfers associated with the slower growth of the developed countries and the debt crisis in a number of developing countries in the early and mid-1980s. The tension between the theory and practice of the transfer of financial and material resources and assistance for the development of human capital and institutional capacity that was so intense in the 1950s has not yet been fully resolved.

The New Assistance Package and Policy-based Lending

Although so far financial flows and technical assistance have been discussed separately, in practice they may be provided as a bundle. Technical assistance for project design has usually been included as part of a major infrastructure project or as part of a loan to strengthen a recipient's higher education system (Lethem and Cooper, 1983).

Since the early 1980s, technical assistance has focused increasingly on institutional development and policy reform at both the sector and macroeconomic levels. Perspectives on lending in support of institutional developmental and policy reform have varied over time. In the 1960s US/AID engaged in intensive bilateral discussions about macroeconomic policies with, for example, India, Brazil, and Turkey (Nelson, 1986; chapters 12 and 14). In the 1970s, however, US/AID narrowed its focus and concentrated on sector and project lending. By the early 1980s the World Bank was assuming a much more extensive role in policy-based lending than in the 1970s. Evidence was growing that poor policies were a major source of poor economic performance in many developing countries.

The greater emphasis on institutional development and policy reform in the 1980s also reflects advances in our understanding of the role of institutional innovation and policy reforms (see chapter 2). It has become increasingly clear that very substantial gains in economic performance often are available as a result of institutional innovations and policy reforms in the areas of macroeconomic trade and price policy. The performance of financial and banking institutions is frequently critical to the success of macroeconomic reforms. Sorting out the areas that are appropriately organized as public or private sector activities is particularly important, and the development of markets that provide the incentives necessary to efficiently mobilize and direct the efforts of individuals and firms has often paid high growth dividends. (The experience with policy-based lending in the 1980s spearheaded by the efforts of the World Bank is discussed in chapter 6.)

The broader perspective on the appropriate elements in a package of assistance leads to a more positive evaluation of the potential contribution of economic assistance to a recipient country's economic development. The view that emerged from the evolution of thought on financial transfers emphasized the limited growth that could be realized from the simple transfer of financial resources. Opportunities to achieve much higher rates of return occur when financial transfers are complemented by productivity-enhancing investment in human capital and in the institutional infrastructure. Thus, the potential rate of return—the potential new income streams—becomes much larger than it could in a situation characterized by simple financial and technology transfer. When technical assistance is extended for the development of recipient capacity for policy analysis and institutional design, constructive dialogue between recipients and donors can further enhance the productivity of donor resources (see chapters 4–6).

Nevertheless, the intellectual or technical capacity of assistance agencies and national governments to make effective project decisions is substantially limited even when the policy environment is favorable. Beginning in the 1960s, the project-planning staffs of both the donor agencies and the recipient governments have tried to incorporate into practice a series of new planning and decision tools: social benefit-cost analysis, sector analysis, and computable general equilibrium models. The assistance agencies have contributed to these developments. The World Bank, for example, has invested very substantial resources in the development of social benefit-cost analysis (Harberger, 1987; Lal, 1987). Evaluation units have been established in both multilateral and bilateral assistance agencies to analyze and feed back into the planning and design process the lessons from development assistance.

In practice, however, sector priorities reflecting national or donor development strategies often have tended to dominate project rate of return calculations. Experience suggests that project lending has been most effective when both donor and recipient policies have been guided by long-term development considerations (Leff, 1985; Traxler and Ruttan, 1986 and 1989). The results of evaluation studies have carried less weight than anticipated by donor evaluation staffs in influencing project design and operation (Cassen, 1986, pp. 104–80).

The debt crisis of the 1980s also has imposed unexpected constraints on the objectives-of-policy dialogue. In addition, the slow growth of the world economy has provided a less favorable environment for policy reforms than the more buoyant environment of the 1970s. The policy reforms involving deregulation of domestic markets and an export-oriented trade regime are still important, but because the world economic environment is less favorable, the growth generated by the reforms may be smaller in the 1980s than in the 1970s (Bhagwati, 1986).

The new economic environment in which the assistance agencies have found themselves has forced them to deal with a series of new issues and complications. The synthesis that emerged with respect to development assistance theory and practice in the mid- and late 1960s appears less adequate from the perspective of the late 1980s than it did in the late 1970s. And the new synthesis that has begun to emerge is still incomplete. There continues to be general agreement about the relevance of the policy lessons of the 1970s—the desirability of maintaining an appropriate real exchange rate, effective incentive structures, a high rate of domestic savings, and responsible fiscal and monetary policies. There is also agreement on the need for policies designed to enhance investment in human capital and the capacity to generate productivity growth in both the agricultural and industrial sectors.

But agreement is still lacking in theory or practice as to how to approach medium-term macro-adjustment processes. We understand a good deal about the macroeconomic policy environment that is consistent with supply side growth policies. Still, our understanding of the domestic and external economic and political forces that induce institutional innovation and reform remains deficient (chapter 2). The knowledge to prescribe or support the policies needed to achieve a transition from the massive disequilibrium that characterizes both national and international economic relations represents a particularly serious gap in our understanding. The experience of the 1980s has made it clear that macroeconomic imbalances that lead to rapid inflation have much more detrimental effects on long-run growth prospects than had earlier been appreciated. But the linkages between inflation and growth are not yet well understood.

A new synthesis that can adequately accommodate the insights of development theorists and practitioners has yet to emerge. We will return to this issue in the final chapter.

Part Two

DONORS AND RECIPIENTS

4

Recipient Policies, National
Development, and Aid Effectiveness

ANNE O. KRUEGER
AND CONSTANTINE MICHALOPOULOS

In Chapter 2 it is argued that the economic environment of developing countries is of overriding importance in determining the success of development efforts. Three major interrelated components of this environment are identified: the macroeconomic policy framework, the microeconomic incentive structure, and the physical, institutional, and human infrastructure. Chapter 3 discusses how aid could in principle contribute to the improvement of this economic environment. The purpose of the present chapter is to summarize the evidence of the interaction between aid and national economic policy in the promotion of development based on the country studies and other developing country experience. The focus is on the interactions between aid and macroeconomic policy and between aid and the microeconomic incentive structure.

Economic Policy Experience: A Summary View

The country studies presented later in this volume show significant differences in the extent to which a developing country's macroeconomic and incentive policies effectively support the pursuit of development objectives. It is hardly surprising that the effectiveness of aid has also varied considerably. Policies have differed both among countries and for the same country over time. With respect to macroeconomic policy, the country experience ranges from the high inflation, deficit spending, and financial instability of Ghana in the late 1970s and early 1980s to the relative economic stability and low budget deficits experienced by India and Korea in the last few years. In comparison, since the 1950s Turkey has itself experienced several cycles of deficit spending, inflation, and massive external imbalances followed by periods of stabilization and adjustment. In many respects, the experience of the five countries studied is representative of the experience of a large number of developing countries in the postwar period. Countries as diverse as Argentina, Chile, and Nigeria have exhibited this pattern of expansion, inflation, and stabilization at several points during the last twenty-five years. In other countries, such as Tanzania, the combination of ineffective macroeconomic policies and distorted patterns of domestic incentives has led to long-term economic stagnation.

This boom-bust syndrome frequently has its origins in the developing country's own drive to stimulate development through public sector investment. Ambitious but poorly designed investment programs are usually launched without the necessary increase in domestic savings and appropriate exchange rate management. The effect has frequently been inflation, an appreciating real exchange rate, and shortages in foreign exchange availability, all leading inevitably to a balance of payments crisis, devaluation, monetary and fiscal retrenchment, and so on.

In recent periods, excessive absorption and inflation in many developing countries has been linked to large government deficits. These deficits are sometimes related to excessive central government investment expenditures, but most frequently they result from inflated government payrolls, as well as government subsidy programs. Government subsidies either are explicit (e.g., the general food subsidies provided by Sri Lanka to the *entire* population through most of the sixties and seventies) or result from central government support to public sector enterprises, which for a variety of reasons are often operated at a loss.

In Argentina, losses in the over three hundred state-owned enterprises are estimated at $2 billion annually. These enterprises hold $11 billion of the country's $46 billion foreign debt and are a major cause of persistent government budget deficits (Choksi, 1986). In Egypt, state-owned enterprises account for 45 percent of total fixed investment. Most have sustained large and growing deficits, low rates of capacity utilization, and inadequate financial rates of return. These deficits account for about one-third of the national fiscal deficit (World Bank, 1987, box 7.5).

At times, major changes in the international environment have produced major and often rapid shifts in the economic conditions confronting the developing countries. In some cases these changes have been positive, as in the case of the commodity price boom of the early 1970s. In other cases the changes have been highly adverse: the oil price increases of 1973–74 and 1979; the economic recession of the early 1980s; and the rise in real interest rates and the decline in commodity prices during the 1980s. Again, the macroeconomic performance of individual developing countries in the face of such economic shocks has depended critically on their own policies of adjustment to the international environment (Krueger, 1987a and 1987b).

With regard to the complex set of policies affecting the incentives for production for the home market or for exports, a fairly regular pattern evolved early on for most developing countries. In most instances policymakers re-

jected the notion of comparative advantage in favor of efforts to pursue industrialization via import substitution, necessarily involving significant protection through trade controls.

Some protection was initially introduced following a balance of payments crisis. But even then protection often proved not to be temporary, as
costs failed to decline over time and industries remained high-cost and un-
competitive. Policymakers in developing countries were then quickly confronted with overvalued exchange rates, usually because they maintained a
fixed nominal exchange rate while domestic prices increased more rapidly
than international prices. The problem was often compounded by excessively
ambitious development plans and/or deteriorating terms of trade. Policymakers responded by adopting quantitative restrictions partly to foster domestic
industry but more importantly to restrain excess demand for foreign exchange. These quantitative restrictions increased protection well beyond the
range of products and levels warranted by any infant industry considerations.
Heavy protection on imports led to high-cost purchased inputs for exporters,
which, along with the overvalued exchange rate, served as a disincentive to
exporters, further confounding the problem.

Once in place, restrictions tended to become increasingly severe over
time, both because of the tendency for export proceeds to rise slowly and
because of tendencies for increasing currency overvaluation.[1] Since the demand for imports rose with efforts to stimulate development, and planners
tended to underestimate import demands, excess demand for imports also
increased with time. Instead of altering the exchange rate, authorities in most
developing countries chose to restrict imports further through increasingly
severe licensing restrictions (see, e.g., chapter 15 on Ghana).

The overvalued currency and restrictive licensing system not only discouraged exports but also conveyed higher and higher levels of protection to
domestic producers. This in turn created incentives for the domestic production of many goods, regardless of whether there was any prospect of reasonable economic efficiency at any later date. Many domestic producers enjoyed
virtual monopoly positions as competition from imports was prohibited and
restrictions on imports of intermediate goods precluded the entry of domestic
competitors (see chapter 12). Hence, even in industries in which there might
have been comparative advantage, the incentives for low-cost production were
relatively limited. As these policies continued, import substitution progressed
to ever higher-cost industries both because they were increasingly capital-
intensive and because the domestic market was too small to permit economically sized plants.

Parallel to, and in part as a consequence of, the heavy protection of
industry and the overvaluation of the exchange rate, agricultural production
has been heavily penalized in most developing countries (see World Bank,

1986a, chap. 4). Consumer prices of foodstuffs have been kept below world market levels, in part because of the desire to cater to the demands of powerful urban interests. This has necessitated either significant subsidies or keeping the prices to producers low, or a combination of the two. Where producer prices have been kept artificially low, governments have attempted to offset the problem by providing subsidies to fertilizer and other inputs. By and large these efforts at offsetting imperfections in the goods market have not been successful in achieving the intended results and in many cases have had unintended adverse income distribution effects. Subsidized credit and inputs have had to be rationed, and the benefits typically have accrued to large farmers.

Distortions have also been introduced by governments in the factor markets. Interest rates have been controlled in general or for specific sectors, such as public enterprises. Frequently interest rates have been negative. In a sample of nine developing countries examined in the 1987 *World Development Report*, on the average over the period 1970–83 eight had negative real deposit rates, and six had negative real lending rates (World Bank, 1987, box 7.6). As a consequence of cheap subsidized credit, the capital intensity of production has been encouraged, leading to wasting of scarce resources, as well as discouraging savings.

Distortions are equally frequent in labor markets. The main forms involve minimum wage legislation, limitation on laying off workers, as well as setting of public sector wages at higher levels than for comparable jobs in the private sector (Heller and Tait, 1983).

The degree of distortions in product and factor markets varies considerably among developing countries. Very few economies, such as Hong Kong, have maintained an open trade regime and a distortion-free domestic market environment. Some countries, such as Korea, Singapore, and Taiwan, originally started with a heavily inward-looking distorted policy regime but over the last two decades have moved progressively to a policy framework that, while not free of distortions, does not significantly bias production toward the domestic markets. Many other countries, such as Chile, Turkey, Mexico, Nigeria, and Indonesia, have been making significant efforts to reduce economic distortions and improve economic efficiency in recent years. But in far too many others serious reform efforts have yet to be initiated. In most cases, it appears that inward-oriented countries tend also to have significantly more distortions in their factor markets (see Krueger, 1983).

The consequences of ineffective macroeconomic policies compounded by microeconomic distortions on economic growth have been highly adverse. Because of the dislocations caused by increasingly severe balance of payments problems, rates of economic growth tended to slow down over time until corrective action was taken. Thus, many developing countries experienced "cycles" of growth.

First, a balance of payments crisis would force a slowdown in economic activity. Then the situation would become sufficiently desperate that the regime would be liberalized and the exchange rate altered to a realistic level in the midst of domestic recession and acute shortages of imports (often including essential intermediate goods such as petroleum). Then would follow a period of slow growth during which export earnings would increase and import demand would be relatively restrained because of the low level of domestic incomes. When foreign exchange reserves would start to accumulate, the authorities would relax the import regime and/or adopt more ambitious spending plans. Either way, imports would boom, domestic production would expand rapidly, export earnings would fail once again to keep pace with rapidly rising import demand, and another balance of payments crisis would ensue.

Second, the tendency toward production of ever-higher cost (relative to the international cost) goods, with increasingly capital-intensive techniques, meant a slowdown in growth as the incremental output-capital ratio fell. Thus, both a cyclical growth pattern and a secular tendency for the growth rate to decline came to be associated with highly restrictive, import-substitution-oriented trade regimes.

There is extensive evidence that countries with an outward trade orientation have achieved higher economic growth than countries with inward-oriented trade regimes (see Balassa, 1984; and Krueger and Michalopoulos, 1985). Recently these findings have been extended to a sample of forty-one developing countries (Greenaway, 1987). It has also been shown that outward orientation is positively related to such variables as growth in industrial output and employment, the rate of domestic savings, the output/capital ratio, and growth in total factor productivity. Similarly, in a sample of thirty-one developing countries over the period 1971–85 there was evidence that the greater the distortion in interest rates, the lower the industrial and aggregate economic growth (World Bank, 1987, box 7.5).

Perhaps nowhere is the contrast in the structure of incentives more vivid than in the comparison between Ghana and the Ivory Coast (chapter 15). With resource endowments similar to those of the Ivory Coast, Ghana pursued policies of heavy industrial protection with a bias against agriculture, which led to a series of crises and stagnant growth. In comparison, the Ivory Coast pursued a much more evenly balanced set of incentives and until recently showed a remarkably strong growth performance.

Korea, on the other hand, started with an import substitution regime but recognized its adverse effects on growth and was able to make a remarkable transformation in its economy (chapter 13). The required policy shifts included a move toward a realistic exchange rate (which was then maintained, at least with purchasing power parity, at a realistic level to provide adequate incentives to exporters), liberalization of the trade regime at least to a point where exporters were enabled to purchase their inputs from their preferred supply source at international prices, and a removal of the extreme bias in favor of import substitution activities. When these policy shifts were undertaken, the increase in the efficiency of economic activity was remarkable. Growth rates rose spectacularly, as did the rate of domestic savings. However, the prospective returns on investment were increased so much that additional capital, over and above domestic savings, was highly profitable. In the early stages of development much of this was provided by aid. As the economy progressed, commercial capital flows provided the main supplement to domestic savings.

The Interaction between Macroeconomic Policies and Development Assistance

It became apparent to governments in the 1950s and early 1960s, when the cumulative difficulties inherent in restrictionist trade regimes had not yet become evident, that their "foreign exchange shortages" constituted an effective constraint on their ability to undertake investment projects and permit rapid economic growth. In many instances, receipts of aid permitted significantly higher levels of investment in the short run than would otherwise have been possible, given available sources of foreign exchange. And given the distortionary macroeconomic and trade policies being pursued at that time, there can be little doubt that foreign aid permitted growth at rates in excess of what would otherwise have been attainable. However, since the dislocation associated with inflation, overvalued exchange rates, increasingly restrictive trade policies, and distorted product and factor markets inevitably implied a slowdown in growth rates, aid may have postponed the time when governments were forced to take corrective actions.

There have been some cases, such as Taiwan and Korea, in which country analyses have concluded that economic assistance made a large contribution to economic growth notwithstanding a less than optimal policy setting especially at the initial stages essentially because aid was provided in very large amounts (see chapter 13; and Jacoby, 1966). Indeed, in Korea it was only when it became apparent to the government that U.S. bilateral assistance would be substantially reduced that the government initiated a series of policy reforms that formed the basis for a subsequent successful economic performance. This does not mean that all foreign assistance during a period of macroeconomic disequilibrium is counterproductive. Many of the infrastructure projects undertaken in Korea during the earlier period of widespread distortions in macroeconomic policy were essential in permitting higher growth when the policy environment was improved. However, the ample availability of aid resources in the earlier period prolonged the existence of multiple exchange rates, rapid inflation, and a restrictive trade regime (see chapter 13).

There is also little doubt that the macroeconomic environment in some countries, such as Ghana and Tanzania, was so severely distorted during several periods of the 1960s and the 1970s that projects supported by economic assistance (as well as those not supported) were not especially productive and did not contribute significantly to economic growth (see chapter 15; and Lele, 1984). In Ghana, for example, the volume of cocoa exports peaked in 1965; thereafter, in the face of increasingly severe currency overvaluation and policies by the domestic marketing board that further penalized producers, they declined to half of that level by 1976 and fell an additional 25 percent by 1982. Prices received by producers were so low that little replanting was undertaken, and both yields and area under cultivation fell over time. In this environment efforts by donors to increase agricultural output were doomed to fail. In Tanzania the pressure of ineffective macroeconomic and incentive policies contributed to a substantial decline in output over a long period in the 1970s and 1980s. During most of this period Tanzania continued to receive considerable assistance, although there were disagreements both among the donors themselves and between major donors and the government over appropriate policy directions.

Donors usually tend to reduce resource levels and/or the scope of assistance when they perceive that the policy environment has become obviously distorted and there are no other overriding political objectives. Aid to Tanzania and Ghana in the late 1970s and early 1980s was ultimately reduced substantially because of weaknesses in the policy environment. Similarly, aid to countries such as Ethiopia and Campuchea has been concentrated primarily on food relief programs to help address famines. There are two reasons for such programs: (1) some aid programs, such as education or famine relief, can make a contribution irrespective of the policy environment; and (2) continued if limited assistance during periods of an ineffective policy environment can be used as an instrument of demonstrating continued interest in the recipient's development and as a vehicle for the conduct of a policy dialogue that over time could lead to a policy environment more conducive to development. Indeed, following substantial changes in policy direction in the mid-1980s a significant flow of aid resources resumed to both Ghana and Tanzania.

In practice, bilateral donors have sometimes terminated programs of assistance ostensibly on the grounds that the economic policies of the recipient were not supportive of development. These terminations have often been politically motivated—in the sense that neither the donors nor the recipients found it politically advantageous to maintain an aid relationship—usually following a coup or a revolutionary change in the recipient country.[2]

Implications of the Incentive Structure for Aid Effectiveness

The existence of severe distortions in the structure of incentives in developing countries has implications for aid effectiveness at various levels. At the macroeconomic level, a recent study by De Melo (1987) shows that in a general equilibrium setting the output-capital ratio—a crude measurement of productivity—was higher for countries with outward-oriented or neutral strategies than for countries pursuing heavily distorted inward-looking strategies. This finding is consistent with other evidence on this issue (World Bank, 1987). De Melo further shows, however, that the marginal productivity of foreign capital is highest in inward-looking inefficient regimes because in such regimes there is a very high premium on foreign exchange. This, of course, does not imply that priority should be given to providing assistance to such countries. Indeed, the opposite is the case: the overall effectiveness of a given aid inflow is highest when accompanied by a neutral set of incentives that do not distort resource allocation.

At the sectoral level, distortions have led to less efficient resource allocation and especially discrimination against agricultural production and export-oriented industry. At the project level, distortions have led to the undertaking of inefficient activities.

IMPLICATIONS OF THE INCENTIVE STRUCTURE FOR SECTORAL RESOURCE ALLOCATION

Distortions in the structure of incentives frequently have resulted in assistance to some key sectors being less effective than it might have been. A realistic exchange rate and trade policies are especially critical in the context of efforts to promote structural change involving increasing industrial exports. In the developing countries that pursued inward-oriented trade policies, in comparison with the newly developed import substitution industries the traditional export industries were generally at a disadvantage, despite the fact that the economic return from their expansion would often have been higher. Moreover, the potential that some import-substitution industries undoubtedly had to develop into export industries was not fully exploited, again largely because of skewed incentives. In many instances (again including India, where there was a special export promotion unit within US/AID to assist in the encouragement of industrial exports) aid projects were developed to encourage exports. Those projects would have been either more effective or unnecessary in the presence of a more realistic exchange rate.

Aid in support of agriculture has also been rendered less effective through the presence of an inappropriate incentive structure and inappropriate exchange rate policies. Because in the early stages of development such a large fraction of the population is engaged in agricultural production, and such a high percentage of the national income is generated by the agricultural sector, many aid programs have been heavily oriented toward raising agricultural productivity through a variety of means. Many aid projects were designed to increase production of selected key commodities by subsidizing inputs and credit in an effort to make production more profitable and hence more attractive (see chapter 9). However, the value of the subsidy entailed in these programs was frequently far less than the disincentive effect, or tax, inherent in an overvalued exchange rate. In addition, efforts to overcome distortions with subsidized credit programs have proven highly ineffective. For example, subsidized inputs and credit tend to go to larger, better-off farmers; subsidized fertilizer is not used well; and credit is not repaid (Virmani, 1986).

In India, for example, the overvaluation of the exchange rate in the early 1960s constituted a tremendous disincentive for producers to grow export crops (Bhagwati and Srinivasan, 1975). The relative domestic prices of these crops (including tea and jute) were so low that supply failed to grow as rapidly as it would have at more favorable prices and India's share of the world market fell sharply. Meanwhile, agricultural assistance projects were addressed to increasing the supply of these and other commodities. After the devaluation of the Indian rupee in 1966 a more realistic exchange rate prevailed. The success with raising production during the Green Revolution was partly attributable to aid programs and government efforts to stimulate agriculture; however, the additional incentives provided by the changing relative prices associated with devaluation were undoubtedly a precondition for success.

For many countries, especially in Africa, the failure of agricultural production to grow at satisfactory rates was to a significant extent due to the relatively low prices producers received for their outputs. That peasants are responsive to the incentives they confront and will alter their outputs in response to those incentives is one of the most important lessons from development experience to date (see chapter 9). Relatively low prices were in turn a reflection of the exchange rate, compounded by the high relative prices of manufactured goods encouraged by the trade regime. A more realistic exchange rate and outward-oriented trade policy would have provided substantially larger incentives to agricultural producers. Assistance to encourage agricultural production had a substantially higher payoff in the presence of realistic exchange rates and trade policies.[3]

EVALUATION OF PROJECTS

In the presence of price distortions arising from product and factor market imperfections, as well as from protection and exchange rate overvaluation, it is appropriate to use shadow pricing for factor inputs and "border" (or international) prices for evaluating the benefits and costs of individual projects. Shadow pricing of labor and capital inputs has been common practice among most donors evaluating potential projects. Even when donors are fully aware that domestic prices diverge from international prices, however, adjustment of estimated costs and benefits to take these divergences into account is difficult and employs the time of highly skilled individuals whose skills could be more productively employed elsewhere.

In the early aid experience even those adjustments were seldom attempted. Project evaluation, which is probably one of the areas where aid made a considerable long-run difference in improving the abilities of developing countries' governments to allocate their internal resources more rationally than had earlier been the case, was generally based on existing prices. Limited project analysis capability, as well as the desire not to antagonize recipient priorities, resulted in donor support for many projects, especially in the industrial sector, that were viable only under heavy protection and therefore allocated resources wastefully. Examples of such practices abound, but the waste was blatantly obvious in such capital-scarce countries as Tanzania and Ghana. Indeed, because highly protected industries could not withstand international competition, each new protected industry that emerged represented more political pressure for continuing protection and made liberalization of the trade and payments regime more difficult. In that sense, aid that went to financing high-cost production also went to building in pressures to maintain the uneconomic system.

Moreover, when projects that were socially worthwhile but financially unprofitable due to distortions were undertaken, governments had to use scarce financial resources to cover the shortfall. Regardless of whether the project was undertaken in the private sector (induced presumably by a subsidy) or in the public sector (which would then incur a loss to be covered by other budgetary sources), funding was necessary. There are real resource costs associated with such financing irrespective of whether the funding comes from diverting existing sources of revenue or from raising additional revenues.

Among the lessons that have been learned by almost all foreign assistance agencies is the importance of evaluating projects using shadow pricing and of using border or international prices. At the same time, it is increasingly widely recognized that if the exchange rate is permitted to become significantly overvalued for a protracted period of time and the exchange control regime is increasingly restrictive, project evaluation becomes subject to increasingly wide margins of error, and it becomes increasingly difficult to undertake socially profitable but financially unviable projects.

Facilitating Change in the Incentive Structure

Given the significant costs that a distorted structure of incentives generates, a possible productive use of aid can be to promote policy reform aimed at reducing distortions in the factor and product markets, including the trade and payments regime, so as to make resource allocation more efficient. The debt problems faced by developing countries in recent years have focused attention on the importance of reducing price distortions as a means of promoting structural shifts that favor increased production of tradables, as well as general improvements in economic efficiency and economic growth. Many donors, under the leadership of the World Bank, have emphasized the need for developing country reforms in the structure of their policy incentives and have provided assistance specifically aimed at encouraging such reforms.

Many areas of reform have been the focus of World Bank policy lending using sectoral and structural adjustment loans (see chapter 6). Particular attention is being devoted to pricing reforms in agriculture, energy, and public sector enterprises. Tax system, interest rate, and financial sector reforms have also been supported in several countries; but perhaps the most frequent target of support has been the reform of the trade regime (Michalopoulos, 1987). As already indicated, once high-cost import-substitution industries are in place, there are political pressure groups supporting the maintenance of policies that are uneconomic from the viewpoint of the country's long-run development interests. One of the most difficult political measures to be undertaken to which aid can contribute is the thorough reform of the trade and payments regime.

While the payoff from reform of the trade regime is high, there are significant difficulties involved in undertaking it. Those who will eventually gain do not necessarily realize it, while all those standing to lose can easily see that reform is not in their self-interest. In addition, there is a strong tendency to underestimate the general benefits and to fail to recognize the new opportunities that reform and more rapid growth will create. Moreover, policymakers must be able to provide visible proof that the new, liberalized policies will be sustained, or individual producers will be hesitant to respond to the new incentive structure for fear that it will be temporary. Finally, without some source of foreign exchange, policymakers cannot liberalize the import regime until exports respond to altered incentives, yet altered incentives cannot be achieved until the import regime is liberalized.

The first and second considerations point to the likelihood that there will be political opposition to liberalization and that the longer the benefits of liberalization are delayed, the greater and longer-lasting the opposition will be. The third point pertains to the need to provide assurances that the new set of incentives will be long-lasting. This need is especially important in countries where previous reform efforts have proved to be short-lived. The fourth aspect relates to policymakers' need to be able to liberalize the regime at a time when existing incentives have led to a shortage of foreign exchange—in a sense, there is a chicken and egg problem.

In the absence of support from abroad, reform is inherently risky. In order to liberalize imports, policymakers would have to suppress domestic demand, which in turn would result in a lower level of economic activity than would otherwise be desirable. Consequently, the resulting recession would strengthen the political forces opposed to the liberalization. Meanwhile, the absence of sufficient backing and available foreign exchange reduces people's willingness to believe that the new measures are likely to be long-lasting. When producers hesitate to alter their behavior, the period of uncertainty and transition is increased, which allows more time for political opposition to mount (Papageorgiou, Michaely, and Choksi, 1986).

Many of these considerations apply to reforms in other sectors where change is likely to encounter political opposition. The inherent difficulty of trade reform and its increasing riskiness in the absence of adequate foreign exchange backing, however, provides an exceptionally high-return aid endeavor (Cooper, 1971; Krueger, 1978). This indeed is one of the fundamental justifications for the emphasis on trade reform in the structural adjustment lending by the World Bank since 1980 (chapter 6).

Sufficient backing by the aid donor community can instantly increase the credibility of the reform effort; simultaneously it can permit a higher level of economic activity during the adjustment period than would otherwise be consistent with liberalized imports. These two factors together can serve to diminish substantially political opposition to aid and to accelerate producers' responses to the altered incentives. Added speed of adjustment, a higher level of economic activity, and the greater availability of imports can all be achieved through aid.[4]

It is important, however, that a government receiving aid for the purpose of trade liberalization proceed to carry out the reforms on which the aid is predicated. Otherwise the influx of foreign aid would simply permit the continuation of policies that support an overvalued exchange rate. Worse yet, there is evidence, especially from Africa, that increases in aid would result in an appreciation of the exchange rate (Van Wijnbergen, 1986). Such a development would then discourage exports and lead to further pressure on the balance of payments, leading to further demands for aid in a vicious cycle that can be stopped only through parallel trade reforms.

An outstanding example of the productivity of allocating foreign aid to facilitate policy reform is provided by the Turkish devaluations of 1958 and 1980–81. The realignment of policies in both cases was accompanied by an increased flow of imports. In the first instance, inflation was reduced from the double-digit range to less than 5 percent. Reduced inflation was also achieved in the second reform effort, but the end result was a reduction in the rate from 100 percent to 35 percent. In each instance, export earnings grew rapidly and the rate of economic growth exceeded 5 percent in the year following the change in policies. By contrast, the Indian devaluation of 1966 was accompanied by little liberalization of imports other than intermediate goods used in domestic production. The recession that followed (which was compounded by drought) intensified the political opposition to the move. As a consequence, the devaluation was not followed by other policy initiatives to change incentives and represented only a once-and-for-all change in relative prices rather than the beginning of a longer-term, sustained liberalization effort.

Conclusion

The above discussion suggests that implementation of sectoral or project-specific assistance programs must be undertaken only after a careful assessment of the recipient's overall economic policies. Not only is knowledge of the macroeconomic environment essential for appropriate project evaluation but assistance can have enhanced payoffs when undertaken in the context of appropriate domestic economic policies.

There is little question that appropriate relative prices and rewards for producers' economic activities represent the most important single inducement to rational resource allocation. That implies that foreign assistance devoted to facilitating increases in production in sectors where relative prices are depressed by domestic economic policies is far less effective than it would be were relative prices appropriately aligned. By the same token, an important role of economic assistance might be as a means of supporting policy reform that would improve the structure of incentives and thus the efficiency of resource use and the effectiveness of future aid.

5

Donor Policies, Donor Interests, and Aid Effectiveness

KEITH JAY AND CONSTANTINE MICHALOPOULOS

While economic development is often stated as the goal of donor economic assistance flows, donors in fact provide such assistance in pursuit of a wide variety of objectives. Not only is economic development of the recipient at times viewed by the donors as secondary to the pursuit of these other objectives but the two can directly conflict on occasion. These other donor objectives may include supporting a particular government; strengthening cultural ties between donor and recipient; or promoting the commercial, economic, or political interests of the donor. Humanitarian motivations, such as raising the consumption level of the poor or providing relief in the aftermath of a natural catastrophe, are another important and frequent rationale underlying donor assistance flows. While the pursuit of humanitarian objectives can contribute importantly to a country's economic development efforts, the two objectives are not identical and are often pursued through different aid instruments.

Several potential benefits may accrue to either the donor or the recipient as a consequence of the pursuit of these national objectives through economic aid. First, the donor or the recipient, or both, may obtain political, security, or other noneconomic benefits. Large amounts of economic assistance were provided by the United States to Vietnam in the 1960s and early 1970s and are currently being provided to Israel and Egypt in support of political objectives. Eighty percent of Soviet and Eastern European aid goes to Vietnam, Cuba, and Mongolia in support of friendly governments. The extensive French aid to education provided to former French colonies in Africa and the strong focus of OPEC assistance on Arab countries derive in part from cultural and political considerations. Second, the donor may obtain specific economic benefits through aid tying, mixed credits (where aid is combined with export credits), and similar practices, but at the cost of reducing the real value of the aid provided to the recipient. Third, the recipient may benefit because the volume of aid that donors are willing to extend in pursuing these nondevelopment objectives is higher than the amount they would have been willing to provide if the economic development of the recipient and improved world-wide allocation of resources were their sole objectives.

Pursuit of nondevelopment objectives—whether political, cultural, or commercial—through economic aid can potentially have a seriously detrimental impact on aid effectiveness by affecting (*a*) the country allocation of the aid or (*b*), given the country allocation, how effectively the aid is used. Aid effectiveness depends critically on the recipient's policies, but if a donor, for example, provides aid in order to promote mutual security objectives even where the economic policies of a recipient are not conducive to development, aid effectiveness is likely to suffer. The costs in terms of aid effectiveness that the pursuit of these objectives entails are difficult to quantify. Nonetheless, evidence of their presence can be gleaned from the experience of waste and inefficiency in aid programs that had been motivated primarily by the presence of nondevelopment objectives.

Donors have an opportunity to pursue national objectives much more openly and much more directly through bilateral than through multilateral assistance. Nonetheless, donors also may influence the aid practices of multilateral aid institutions, making them more supportive of the donors' overall foreign policy objectives.

In this chapter we first consider the allocation of assistance and its linkages to donors' interests as opposed to recipients' policies and needs. Subsequently we discuss how the pursuit by various donors of foreign policy and commercial objectives, primarily through bilateral assistance, tends to impose costs and constraints on the attainment of development objectives. This discussion focuses on the implications of aid tying and donors' pursuit of commercial objectives. Next, we examine the evidence that pursuit of nondevelopment objectives has helped augment the volume of official assistance. Finally we draw some conclusions about the implications for multilateral and bilateral aid of pursuit by donors of nondevelopment objectives through their aid programs.

Principles of Aid Allocation

Chapters 3 and 4 argue that aid effectiveness is affected by the quality of the economic policies of the recipient. In principle, therefore, if donors were interested in maximizing the development impact of their assistance, recipients' policies (present and future) should be an important criterion for aid allocation among countries. It has also been argued that on economic grounds, particularly in light of the limited availability of such flows, concessional assistance should be allocated largely to lower-income countries, provided of course that they are pursuing appropriate economic policies. If the allocation of concessional assistance does not conform to these criteria, then aid would be provided to countries that may not use it effectively or to countries where the relative need for scarce concessional flows is far less.

There is abundant statistical evidence however, that donor interests rather than general considerations of efficiency or recipient countries' policies and needs, have dominated the country allocation of bilateral assistance. Early analysis of the issue showed how historical relationships between donors and recipients, as well as domestic political factors in each country, influenced the allocation of assistance resources (White, 1974). Cold war considerations were an important factor in explaining per capita aid allocation for the United States in the 1960s, while trade ties were an important variable explaining French and British aid allocations (Wittkopf, 1972).

Similar conclusions were reached by McKinlay and Little (McKinlay, 1978; McKinlay and Little, 1977, 1978a, 1978b, 1979) in their investigations of the allocation processes of four major donors. They attempted to explain the country allocation of aid for the same four donors analyzed by Wittkopf (the United States, the United Kingdom, France, and Germany) during the 1960s, on the basis of two alternative models, one reflecting "recipient need" and the other "donor interest." The application of the recipient-need model yielded no statistically significant results for any of the four donors. By contrast, the donor-interest model, which contained such factors as strategic, political, and trade interests, yielded statistically significant explanations of aid allocation.

More recently, Maizels and Nissanke (1984) confirmed and extended these earlier findings. The two authors used again a recipient-need versus donor-interest, two-model approach for a larger number of countries, for two periods (late 1960s and late 1970s), and for both bilateral and multilateral aid. They found that recipient need does not provide an adequate explanation for the aid allocation by bilateral donors. However, the balance of payments variable in their model was significant. This would suggest that aid allocation by bilateral donors is responsive to short-term balance of payments problems of recipients. But clearly, while this might be helpful, it does not necessarily conform to the economic rationale for providing assistance for long-term development. If assistance for balance of payments support is not combined with appropriate conditionality with regard to policy reform by the recipient, it might permit continuation of the ineffective recipient policies that may have contributed to the balance of payments problems in the first instance.

The authors found that the donor-interest model provided a very good explanation of bilateral aid allocation for the period 1978–80 (but not for the earlier period). The key explanatory variables for bilateral aid as a whole were political and security interests, as evidenced by arms transfers and particular regional interests. For the individual donors, different self-interest variables were important. For the United States, strategic considerations were most

Table 5.1. Percentage Distribution of Total Assistance to Developing Countries, by Country Group for Selected Years (Three-Year Average)

| | Official Development Assistance[a] | | | | | | Other Flows[b] | |
| | OECD/DAC[c] | | OPEC[d] | | Multilateral | | | |
Per Capita GNP	1973–75	1982–84	1973–75	1982–84	1973–75	1982–84	1973–75	1982–84
Less than $400	44.4	39.3	23.2	32.8	50.7	68.8	4.4	3.9
$401–700	11.6	17.8	45.1	12.7[e]	14.4	12.2	14.1	10.2
Over $701	44.0	42.9	31.7	54.5	34.9	19.0	81.5	85.9
Total	100.0	100.0	100.0	100.0	100.0	100.0	100.0	100.0

Source: OECD, *Geographical Distribution of Financial Flows to Developing Countries,* various issues.

[a] Total ODA gross disbursements.
[b] Total net receipts minus total net ODA.
[c] Includes resources from the European Economic Community Fund.
[d] Includes funds from OPEC-financed agencies.
[e] The significant percentage decrease from the 1973–75 period largely reflects the major change in the OPEC aid allocation to Egypt. More recent estimates show little difference from the 1982–84 period.

important; for France, links with former colonies; and for Japan, links to countries with markets of importance to Japanese exporters.

Maizels and Nissanke (1984) showed that in contrast, the recipient-need model explained country allocations by multilateral aid agencies in both periods. Recipient need accounted for three-quarters of the variation in the level of multilateral assistance among countries in the 1969–70 period and almost all of the variation in the 1978–80 period. Table 5.1 shows that 81 percent of the multilateral concessional assistance was channeled to developing countries with a per capita income of less than $700 in 1983 dollars, compared with 57 percent for OECD bilateral donors and a little over 45 percent for OPEC bilateral donors. For the low-income countries (less than $400 per capita) the proportions are 69 percent, 39 percent, and 33 percent for multilateral, OECD, and OPEC, respectively. Among the multilaterals, IDA, which accounts for close to one-third of total concessional multilateral flows, allocates 95 percent of its total credits to these low-income countries.

This allocation of the majority of multilateral concessional assistance to the low-income countries is reinforced by a generally strong project selection process in these institutions that is designed to promote the effective use of the assistance allocated to a country. For example, in the World Bank, projects must yield at least a 10 percent rate of return before they are funded. While most major bilateral donors also carry out some appraisal of their aid projects, in many cases the analysis is less rigorous, the criteria are less quantitative or strict, and the final decision is influenced by a range of other noneconomic considerations.

These findings have important implications for aid effectiveness. If the country allocation of bilateral aid is determined primarily by donor interest, it would be purely accidental if such allocation resulted in the bulk of assistance going to countries where the economic justification for obtaining such assistance was strongest. In the first instance, when bilateral aid programs attach little importance to recipients' circumstances and needs in the allocation of aid, the likelihood is increased that concessional aid will be extended to countries for whom there is little economic justification for obtaining such assistance. It could be argued, of course, that despite the large influence of donor interests on their aid allocation, bilateral aid is nonetheless provided primarily to countries who are pursuing appropriate economic policies. There is, however, little evidence that this is the case. Furthermore, while an improved policy environment in the recipient country is a prerequisite for aid effectiveness—a prerequisite increasingly recognized by donors and recipients—most bilateral donors still find it difficult to engage in a meaningful policy dialogue with aid recipients (see chapter 6). Some donors continue to feel that their efforts to influence recipients' economic policies involve undue interference in the affairs of another sovereign nation, and some recipients would indeed argue that a policy dialogue with a bilateral donor is unwelcome for precisely that reason. Even those donors who are able and would like to carry out a policy dialogue—such as the United States—often find it difficult to do so because of the fear that disagreement over economic issues will threaten other, more important foreign policy objectives. (Evidence of the difficulties the United States faced in this respect in Turkey is discussed in chapter 13.)

A main reason for the significantly larger allocation of bilateral assistance to middle-income countries is political (e.g. U.S. aid to relatively advanced countries such as Israel, French aid to high-income former overseas territories). It is ironic that some of the donors who have shown the strongest concern about aid effectiveness in international fora, such as the United States, are also prone, because of the influence of a range of noneconomic objectives, to allocate bilateral aid to countries, under circumstances that might well undermine its overall effectiveness.

Promotion of Commercial Objectives through Aid

One of the most pervasive nondevelopment objectives pursued by donors through aid has been the promotion of their own commercial interests. Donor governments have sought to justify and elicit domestic support for their aid programs by arguing that aid serves domestic commercial interests. The promotion of long-term, broad-based economic development can serve donors' long-term economic and commercial interests, since development tends to increase the demand for products and services from industrial countries. Commercial interests, however, are often perceived by the donor in a much narrower and much shorter-term perspective and pursued through much more direct means. Donors have adopted a series of practices, such as direct and indirect tying of aid to procurement in the donor country and the extension of "mixed credits," aimed at increasing their exports of goods and services to aid recipient countries. Other aid practices often followed by donors have included the requirement that the assistance be used to finance imports as opposed to local costs and to fund capital as opposed to recurrent costs. These practices stem in part from donors' desire to promote their own commercial objectives and in part from legitimate development considerations. They have, however, a variety of implications for aid effectiveness in promoting development.

DIRECT TYING

The most direct and most obvious mechanism used by donors to increase the commercial impact of their aid programs has been the tying of assistance (a) by source, requiring the recipient country to use the foreign assistance to purchase goods and services in the donor country, or (b) by end use, specifying the project, product, or sector to which the assistance will be allocated. Often both forms of tying are used together and are combined with more indirect measures to promote donor commercial interests.

Aid tying by source has been used by all bilateral donors. Approximately 46 percent of DAC *bilateral* ODA provided in 1985–86 was tied, while another 7 percent was classified as partially untied. In 1976 the corresponding figures for tied and partially untied bilateral aid were 53 percent and 10 percent, respectively.

Table 5.2 indicates the extent to which each DAC donor reportedly has untied its aid program. It is generally believed, however, that some assistance technically classified as untied, effectively remains tied to the donor country in practice. In Germany, for example, only 26 percent of the bilateral assistance was classified as tied in 1981, yet the DAC estimates that 60 percent of German assistance was used to purchase German goods and services. Similarly, while only 16 percent of Sweden's bilateral assistance was classified as tied, it was estimated that almost half resulted in procurement of Swedish goods and services (OECD, *Development Cooperation*, 1983). By way of comparison, Germany captured only 10.5 percent of the total World Bank equipment procurement that was undertaken in developed countries over the fiscal period 1981–85 based on international competitive bidding; Sweden's share of this equipment procurement totaled 1.4 percent.

In contrast, since 1973, donor contributions to the multilateral develop-

Table 5.2. Percentage of DAC Assistance Classified as Untied

	Percentage of Donor's Total ODA Classified as Untied		Percentage of Donor's Bilateral ODA Classified as Untied	
	1973[a]	1985/86 Average	1976[b]	1985/86 Average[c]
Australia	45	63	81	52
Austria	83	29	47	4
Belgium	31	44	24	38
Canada	33	60	15	44
Denmark	53	71	45	62
Finland	56	71	18	60
France	31	42	42	40
Germany (Federal Republic)	51	63	79	64
Italy	60	31	19	12
Japan	32	70	26	41
Netherlands	33	63	44	59
New Zealand	8	73	96	66
Norway	78	84	60	74
Sweden	85	78	71	72
Switzerland	51	75	29	68
United Kingdom	20	37	21	25
United States	22	51	18	43
DAC average	34	55	37	46

Source: OECD, *Development Cooperation,* various issues.
[a] The 1973 figures for the United Kingdom and New Zealand may be understated, since a significant portion of their IDA was listed in this context as "status undetermined."
[b] The first year in which the data are provided in a bilateral and multilateral breakdown.
[c] Data for Austria, France, and Switzerland are for 1985 only; more recent estimates are available only for a few countries and show little change.

ment institutions and the subsequent lending by these institutions have largely been untied. As a result the increase in the proportion of donor aid channeled through multilateral institutions during the 1970s contributed to the decline in the *overall* portion of donor assistance that was tied.

Most donors also reinforce their source tying by specifying what the assistance will be used for. The effort to specify use can be based on sound developmental reasons, but it can also be abused in order to support commercial objectives. A donor may allocate assistance to specific sectors, subsectors, or projects that (1) involve the potential export of goods or services from its domestic industries that the donor believes are competitive or wants to assist; (2) will increase the supply of commodities that are important to the donor; or (3) provide the basis for significant future sales with or without future donor assistance.

These sectors or projects may not always represent the highest development priorities of the country. One example from the early 1980s was a proposed port development in Sudan at a time when Sudan was facing very serious financial problems. This proposed project was supported by a pledge of German assistance specifically linked to the port development. It was, however, viewed by most other donors and multilateral agencies to be of low priority because the additional port capacity would not be needed for many years and thus the rate of return on the project would be low. Only after extensive discussions did the Sudanese government agree to delete this project from the investment plan because of its low priority.

Another example is the Majes water diversion and irrigation project in Peru, started in the early 1970s. In 1977 it was estimated that the costs of this massive project exceeded U.S. $23,000 per hectare and over U.S. $30,000 per beneficiary family. Originally this project was turned down by both the Inter-American Development Bank and the World Bank on the grounds that it was not economically viable. The economic planning staff of the British aid agency likewise advised rejection, but pressure from other government departments resulted in their funding it because of the expected commercial benefits to a British construction firm. A subsequent evaluation by the British aid agency demonstrated few such benefits, however, and in a 1979 report, the World Bank identified this as one in a series of nonproductive public investments contributing to the growing financial deficit and inflation in Peru (Independent Group on British Aid, 1982, p. 14).

Germany in the late 1970s provided special support through its aid programs to its ship and railway equipment industries, which were then experiencing difficulties through a specific budget allocation representing 10–15 percent of its assistance budget (Arnold, 1982, p. 25).

The choice of the form of assistance can also affect the level and type of donor exports generated. An obvious example is food aid. Food aid programs have included among their multiple objectives the movement of surplus domestic agricultural commodities and the establishment of longer-term commercial markets for the donor.

There are few areas in development assistance policy more controversial than that of food aid impact. Criticisms have focused on four major points: (1) food aid can have direct price disincentive effects for local producers; (2) it may cause a change in long-run consumer preferences from local to imported goods; (3) it may encourage or enable the recipient government to neglect agricultural production and investment; and (4) it can create economic and political dependency. These points are most typically raised in the case of wheat and rice sales, which are seen as displacing (particularly in the face of distorted domestic farmgate prices) soybean, millet, and other domestically grown products (Isenman and Singer, 1977).[1] Others have argued that the volume and type of commodities shipped typically reflect donor availabilities and may not match the specific priorities and requirements of the recipient (Miyamoto, 1974). Similarly, it has been noted that despite the fact that such food shipments may derive from donor surpluses, the existence of donor price support programs, plus the requirement that the commodities be shipped on donor vessels, can result in raising the cost of such commodities to levels much higher than world market prices. In a study of aid to Indonesia, Miyamoto found that the cost of commodities provided under the U.S. PL 480 program over a three-year period was on average one-third more than if the same commodities had been purchased commercially from a low-cost producer. Other restrictions associated with food aid include the requirement that imports of food aid be additional to commercial food imports and that the funds accruing to the recipient country government from the sale of food aid commodities be assigned to designated purposes (Abbott and McCarthy, 1982). It should be noted, however, that while in principle restrictions associated with food aid can yield a net welfare loss to the recipient, available evidence suggests that donor restrictions are circumvented where possible by food aid recipients, so that the net effects of aid are not usually detrimental.

In the debate on food aid a broad, gradual shift can be discerned from an unqualified criticism toward a more positive analysis of conditions that must be met in order to avoid disincentives or to replace them with positive incentives. In their study on the impact of food aid, Clay and Singer (1982) note that it has at times faced a Catch-22 set of criticisms. For example, if food aid is given in the form of staple products actually consumed by the population, it is criticized for directly competing with local production. If different commodities are supplied (wheat or rice in place of traditional maize, millet, or sorghum), then food aid is said to wean people away from traditional domestically grown products and to create a demand for recurrent imports in the future.

Criticism of food aid is especially severe when the displacement of local production leads to a shift toward export cropping, which is said to result in neglect of domestic basic needs, increased instability, and greater dependency. Some studies have countered this criticism, arguing that more detailed and more empirical country work would show the advantages rather than the disadvantages of the production of foreign-exchange-earning crops in promoting overall development (Hillman, 1981). They also point out that although the shifts in taste away from traditional staple foods may go hand in hand with food aid, they are not necessarily causally connected. Finally, the discussion of disincentive effects on government policy often alleges urban bias or antisocial bias in government policy; it is by no means clear whether the criticism is of the impact of food aid as such or of food aid's being used in the framework of such policies. Here, it is interesting to note that concern with disincentives has broadened from the simple market effect on the local producer to the wider effect on government policies and priorities with a focus on effectiveness of aid.

The main conclusion that can be reached from this analysis of food aid is that such aid obviously can promote donors' commercial objectives while posing potential problems to the development objectives of recipients. But the development value of food aid depends crucially on the policies of the recipient governments, with countervailing incentive factors such as the long-run effect on productivity and demand and the impact of additional resources being important elements.

INDIRECT TYING

Donors shape their assistance programs in order to pursue commercial objectives in a number of additional less direct and less readily identifiable ways. Donors frequently require that technical services, involving, for example, teachers or consultants funded with aid funds, be obtained from the donor country. It can also create delays. Hendra (1987) cites the example of a Canadian agricultural project which was delayed more than two years while the Canadian aid agency searched for Canadians qualified to fill two positions on the project team. This component of the aid program has in fact been viewed by some as an employment service for the donor. Donor country technicians are often very expensive relative to similar experts available either within the country or from other sources. In recognition of this fact, most technical assistance is provided in grant form. Other services, including shipping and insurance, have also often been tied; for example, 50 percent of the goods procured in the United States under U.S. assistance programs must be shipped on U.S. vessels.

Project design work done by donor country experts and firms can be an advantage to these firms or other firms in the donor country even where the subsequent project or procurement may not be funded by or tied to the donor country. This advantage may result from the technical specifications incorporated in the design or from the contacts, name recognition, and so on, developed in these preparations.[2] If the tying of technical assistance results in an inferior project design, a bias toward capital goods, or the purchase of higher-cost or lower-quality inputs or encourages the undertaking of low-priority projects, it will correspondingly reduce the effectiveness of assistance.

Second, donors' allocations of bilateral assistance among countries may be dictated by commercial considerations (Cunningham, 1974). Donors who wish to use their assistance as a means of promoting their commercial interests may provide higher amounts than otherwise justified to countries that are not normally significant markets for their exports; or if a donor's assistance is untied, it may direct its assistance to countries that are normal commercial markets in an effort to increase the potential exports generated by the assistance. Country allocation can also be influenced by a donor's interest in access to specific imports. For example, access to imports of strategic minerals from Zambia and Zaire has often been mentioned in US/AID congressional testimony as one of the considerations in U.S. assistance allocations to these countries. Similarly, with its aid program, Japan has supported activities aimed at increasing the supply of raw material imports from East Asian countries.[3] The net result can be that the country allocation of the donor's assistance differs substantially from one based solely on a judgment of the best economic allocation of concessional assistance.

MIXED CREDITS

In recent years donors have engaged increasingly in the use of "mixed credits." These involve the combining of concessional assistance funds with commercial trade credits as a means of winning export contracts by reducing the financing cost of the transaction. In many respects mixed credits are a specific form of tied aid. Until the late 1970s, mixed credits were a very small part of the overall concessional assistance or export credit programs of most donors. A major exception was France, which used mixed credits as a standard aid mechanism. In the late 1970s and early 1980s, however, there was a proliferation of ad hoc as well as formal mixed credit programs as major donors started using mixed credits to promote export sales and to counter mixed credit offers of other donors.

Data on actual mixed credit transactions are incomplete and generally of poor quality, reflecting differing definitions and inadequate reporting. Available data do, however, point to a substantial increase in the use of mixed credits in the early 1980s. While mixed credits were estimated to total less than $250 million in 1975, during the three-year period 1983–85 a total of $6.7 billion in associated financing transactions was reported by twelve DAC donor countries.[4] The amount of ODA used in support of these associated financing transactions totaled $2.7 billion. France has been by far the largest user of this financing technique, accounting for 52 percent of the DAC total, followed by Italy with 11.5 percent and the United Kingdom with 10 percent.

Irrespective of motivation, this rapid expansion in the use of mixed credits has resulted in increased concern among donors regarding the justification of mixed credits and their impact on both trade and the development effectiveness of donors' aid programs (OECD, *Developmental Cooperation*, 1987, p. 68). Mixed credits can distort both international trade and development

assistance programs. The distortion of trade flows occurs when the more favorable financing terms, resulting from the combination of concessional aid
with the export credit, shift the contracting decision away from an otherwise
lower bidder or when the known availability of such financing discourages
other competitive suppliers from bidding.[5]

From a development perspective, since mixed credits are based largely
on commercial considerations (the prospect of a commercial sale and in some
cases the gain of a preferred market position), they can reduce the overall
development impact of a donor's program by shifting the allocation of aid
flows much as tied aid does. Commercial transactions and trade competition
are far greater in the more advanced developing countries. Pressures are therefore generated to extend mixed credits to middle- and high-income countries
and to shift aid allocations away from the low-income country recipients,
which tend to have the highest needs and greater economic justification for
obtaining concessional assistance.

The potentially distortive effects on aid allocation of engaging in mixed
credits are illustrated by the report by the Independent Group on British Aid.
This report concludes that the quality of British official assistance was diluted
by its support of mixed credits. The report cites specific examples in which
because of pressure from commercial interests, British ODA, was extended
to high-income countries, such as Mexico, that were not otherwise eligible to
receive British ODA, and commitments to mixed credit transactions were
made before any appraisal was carried out by the aid agency (Independent
Group on British Aid, 1982). The recent provision of concessional aid funds
by Japan to Turkey for a second Bosphorus bridge could also be argued to be
an example of a mixed credit resulting in the allocation of scarce concessional
resources to a high-income country.

Mixed credits can also result in a shift of funding away from priority
development activities to imports or projects having a lower development priority or, in some cases, to projects that are incompatible with a country's
resource endowments.[6] Mixed credits often involve capital- and import-
intensive projects such as transportation, telecommunications, and power
generation. While many such projects are undoubtedly economically sound,
the emphasis placed on these type of projects increases the potential that low-
priority projects will be undertaken because they happen to fall within these
commercially promising (for the donor) areas. For the same reason, mixed
credit financing tends to be biased against projects and programs with low
import content, such as rural development projects or primary health care,
and projects that involve a large component of local-cost financing. For example, on average for the period 1981–83, energy accounted for 30 percent
of mixed credit financing transactions, industry and transport for 20 percent
each, food and agriculture for 10 percent, and health and social infrastructure

for only 2 percent. Four recent mixed credits to Thailand involved an oil refinery, a national fertilizer company, railway modernization, and mass-transit buses (Ball, 1985).

Supporters of mixed credits argue that they promote development objectives by increasing the level of concessional assistance that their legislative bodies are willing to provide or by increasing the level of nonconcessional flows, such as export credits. They also argue that mixed credits can improve the quality of export credits by (1) bringing the judgment and monitoring of aid agencies to bear on export credits extended to developing countries and (2) providing more favorable financing terms for middle-income countries that are no longer major recipients of scarce ODA but to whom some concessional assistance flows are still justified. Opponents, however, argue that many of these effects could also be achieved more directly and more effectively through the direct provision of a limited amount of aid rather than through the use of mixed credits, which have the potential for distorting aid and trade. Furthermore, there is little specific evidence that ODA has been increased or "stretched" by this use.

QUANTIFYING THE COSTS OF TYING FOREIGN ASSISTANCE

The potential costs of aid tying have long been recognized. During the late 1960s and early 1970s a number of studies attempted to measure the cost of tying to the recipient (Haq, 1967; Bhagwati, 1970b; Bhagwati and Desai, 1970; Colaco, 1973; OECD, *Development Cooperation*, 1973 ; Miyamoto, 1974). India has received perhaps the greatest attention (see chapter 12). Most of these studies analyze the direct costs of tying in an individual country or for a series of individual transactions within a country or sector by seeking to measure the increase in the direct cost of procurement resulting from the tying requirements.

Indirect factors such as the proportion of total external resources available to a country whose aid is tied by source, the existence of monopolistic practices among suppliers in the donor country, and the availability and terms of financing in international capital markets can affect the overall cost of aid tying (Colaco, 1973). For example, monopolistic practices can produce additional shipping expenses for goods procured with tied aid.[7] Several authors have pointed to the importance of the administrative costs incurred by the recipient in implementing tying procedures (Bhagwati, 1970b). In India these costs have been seen by these authors as a potential contributing factor to the setting up of a costly exchange control regime. In many countries, including India, tying requirements have been seen as slowing aid disbursements (see chapter 11).

None of the studies provide an estimate of the global costs of tying. At most, the authors use the results of specific case studies as a foundation to speculate on the overall impact of the practice. The quantitative estimates are best treated only as suggestive of the magnitude of the costs of aid tying rather than as precise values. However, it is interesting to examine a few of the results.

One approach has been to try to identify the potential excess cost of tied aid by looking at the spread of bids on IBRD loans and IDA credits (Bhagwati, 1970b; Colaco, 1973). The hypothesis of these studies is that aid tying provides an opportunity for monopolistic pricing. If the range of bids, from the highest to the lowest, on international tenders is very large, the potential for abuse and higher procurement prices from a tied source is correspondingly large. Colaco found evidence that there was in fact a very wide range in the bids on individual tenders. He also found that prices paid for transformers financed with tied aid were close to domestic prices in the recipient countries, which are typically far above international prices because of the high protection prevailing in developing countries.

On the other side of the equation, the information gathered by Colaco indicates that suppliers are generally aware of the range of prices that their competitors will charge; as a result, the very existence of international competitive bidding can lead to cost economies. Bhagwati, however, noted that where the possibilities of substitution are very limited, even an international tender may be ineffective in getting the lowest rates.

Haq also looked at the potential of monopolistic pricing in tied aid projects. His study, which analyzed specific transactions in Pakistan, showed that the quotations offered by the suppliers were often higher if the suppliers knew that tied credit was involved and came down considerably once it was made clear that the supplies would be financed against cash or untied credits. In a sample of twenty development projects, a comparison was made between the lowest quotation from the tied source and the lowest quotation from international bidding. The overall result was that the weighted average price for those twenty projects was 51 percent higher from the tied source.

Basing their estimates on such analyses, some of the authors speculated that tying imposes a cost of 15–20 percent of the total aid provided to the recipient (Pearson Commission, 1969). The conclusion of Haq's study for Pakistan shows that the tying of foreign credits raised the average price of procurement for Pakistan by about 12 percent; but some results have shown very high costs, such as the commodity-specific studies for India, which estimated that the excess cost of nitrogenous fertilizers was as high as 80 percent (Haq, 1967).

Despite this evidence, there is some uncertainty regarding the actual success of the donors' tying efforts. A 1972 Overseas Development Council report (McKitterick and Middleton, 1972) directly questioned the degree to which aid-tying efforts in practice actually "tied" the aid and, correspondingly, the reported costs of such practices to developing countries. The report noted that to the extent that recipients have the capacity to shift procurement among alternative sources, they can mitigate much of the potential cost of tying by purchasing from the donor commodities that would normally be purchased from that donor in any event. In contrast, a 1972 Rand Corporation report found that "the current tying procedures are quite effective in generating additional U.S. exports from the various aid recipients. In 1969, approximately 90 percent of U.S. development loan assistance dollars came back to the United States in the form of additional exports. In fact, many countries spent more on additional exports from the United States than they received as aid. These results indicate that the tying program has been considerably more effective than was previously thought" (Cooper, 1972, p. iii).[8]

Recently there has been little quantitative analysis of the costs of tying. It could be argued that given the notable reduction over time in the proportion of donor aid that is classified as tied, it no longer constitutes a significant development issue. Nonetheless, donors continue to tie a considerable portion of their bilateral assistance, typically 40–60 percent; and as noted earlier, numerous indirect mechanisms are utilized by donors to effectively increase the extent to which their assistance is tied even where it is classified as untied.

Commercial and Foreign Policy Objectives, Aid Effectiveness, and Aid Volume

It is recognized that aid tying and the donors' pursuit of multiple foreign policy objectives through economic assistance introduce distortions that undermine the effectiveness of aid. But it is often argued that such practices should be tolerated because they result in a higher volume of economic assistance than would be forthcoming if the economic rationale discussed earlier were the sole reason for aid (see chapter 3). Thus recipients may get less development impact per dollar of nominal aid that they receive, but they get much more aid in total, and hence their development in the end is more adequately supported.

This argument does not imply that similar and even higher amounts of assistance may not have been justified in principle on economic grounds alone. Rather, support for economic aid by different segments of legislative bodies and ultimately the public is based on various and sometimes conflicting motivations—foreign policy, humanitarian, and economic. Political support from all of these groups is needed for approval of the overall package. As a consequence, the argument has been that if the only objective pursued through economic assistance were the economic development of the recipient, the level of assistance approved would be substantially reduced, despite the economic merits of the case.

There is no question of the importance of nondevelopment considerations in providing strong support for specific components of the donors' assistance programs. It is hard to imagine, for example, that in the absence of surplus disposal and market development objectives the volume of U.S. food aid would have been as high. At the same time, humanitarian motivations and the support of private voluntary organizations (PVOs) have been instrumental in the provision of substantial amounts of food aid and in the food distributed under Title II of the PL480 program which is distributed in developing countries by the PVOs. The volume of economic assistance channeled through the US/AID Economic Support Fund to countries such as Israel and Egypt, and before that to Vietnam, is much higher than could be justified on economic grounds alone. There is also some evidence that tying of assistance to domestic procurement has been important for sustaining support for significant levels of assistance in some donor countries, for example, France, Germany, and Japan.

It is, of course, difficult to determine what an appropriate level of economic assistance would be if one were to provide such assistance solely on the grounds of its desirability in furthering the development of the recipient, along the rationale discussed in chapter 3. This is a moot point because in practice, foreign policy and other considerations always play some part in affecting aid levels. Donor governments have tried to forge coalitions among groups with widely divergent motivations in order to muster the support needed for legislative approval of the overall economic assistance packages. The problem is that while initially such motivations might raise the total volume of assistance, they also tend to introduce considerations that reduce its effectiveness. When this becomes apparent, it undermines public support for all forms of assistance and over time may result in aid levels much lower than would otherwise result.

Financing of Local and Recurrent Costs

Over the last two decades the bulk of donors' aid has been extended to finance solely the foreign exchange component of programs or projects.[9] The foreign exchange funding limitation has been based on two major considerations in addition to commercial motivations. First, there is a perception that donors can more directly and effectively alleviate a foreign exchange constraint by funding the foreign exchange costs of the project or program. There is often also a desire by donors to ensure that the recipient has a serious commitment to a particular project. One way of demonstrating this commitment in the eyes of the donors has been to have the recipient contribute a share of the project costs, typically that portion involving financing of local costs.

Donors have also traditionally financed primarily the capital costs of projects and have provided only limited funding for recurrent costs. Donors view financing recurrent costs in general, and maintenance in particular, as financing for current consumption rather than investment. Also, as evidence of commitment to the project, the recipient is expected to assume the financing of recurrent costs upon program completion or after a specified period. This, plus the fact that recurrent costs, such as teacher salaries, road maintenance, and the like, involve primarily local cost financing, makes most donors reluctant to provide such financing. This donor preference for financing capital costs can foster excessive capital intensity especially in developing countries, where distortions in factor markets result in an excessively low price of capital relative to labor (Tendler, 1975).

Maintenance is a continuing problem faced by most developing countries, especially with respect to roads and other physical infrastructure (see chapter 8). Particularly severe problems have developed in many countries in Sub-Saharan Africa. In most cases these problems are the result of ineffective policies in the recipient countries. Many face substantial difficulties in raising revenues from general taxation. Often, user charges are not imposed or are not high enough even in cases where the services provided do not fall within the bounds of "public goods." Overambitious investment programs are often accompanied by inadequate provision for recurrent cost financing in central government budgets. For a variety of reasons, situations have arisen in Africa and elsewhere in which the government faces such a budget stringency that it is unable to finance the recurrent costs of existing development projects although the stream of future returns to recurrent inputs is much higher than that of new development projects (US/AID, 1982d).

Donors' priorities can contribute to this problem. First, donor emphasis on financing capital costs limits the flexibility of recipients, since for many recipients foreign aid is both a large proportion of new capital formation and greater than their own budgetary resources allocated to recurrent expenditures. This contributes to misallocation of resources if the expected return on recurrent inputs is higher than on new capital equipment. Second, the proliferation in low-income countries of capital projects, each of which calls for the government to finance the projects' recurrent cost requirements over time, can easily exceed any likely revenues available either through user charges or through general public revenues available to the recipient's government. The result is projects that are poorly maintained or poorly utilized or in some cases abandoned.

Making Foreign Assistance More Effective

Any attempt to make foreign assistance more effective in realizing development objectives will need to find ways to deal with the negative effects that the pursuit of other donor objectives has had on their aid program. Two actions that would help would be a further untying of bilateral aid and the reduction in the use of mixed credits. A shift of aid to favor multilateral assistance (which does not have many of these problems) would accomplish the same objective. Efforts have also continued over the course of the last two decades to reform foreign assistance. Progress, however, has been slow.

UNTYING AID

The costs associated with aid tying have produced repeated calls for international action to reduce and eliminate such practices (Task Force on International Development, 1970). Most donors, however, believe that tying represents an important aspect of their aid program in parliamentary and public debate regarding the merits of aid and aid budget levels. Therefore, a major reduction in aid tying has been seen by many donors to be politically feasible only in the context of a multilateral effort in which all major aid donors would agree to reduce mutually the incidence of tying in their aid programs. During the 1970s two separate efforts were undertaken under the auspices of the DAC to negotiate a multilateral untying agreement for bilateral aid. Both efforts, however, were unsuccessful.

While these multilateral negotiations failed, agreement was achieved in 1974 on a more limited form of untying which permitted the developing countries to be eligible sources for procurement under otherwise tied development loans. This represented a positive but small step in reducing the overall level of untying. Shifts in the nature of donor assistance programs, such as the increased direct funding of local costs and the increased provision of program-type assistance, including extensive use of cash grants by the U.S. aid program, have produced some reduction in the overall tying of assistance. In addition, bilateral donors through the DAC have continued to explore ways to improve the aid procurement process. In 1986 agreement was reached on a set of principles governing procurement practices for official development assistance (OECD, *Development Cooperation*, 1986, annex 1).

Given the political problems of visibly untying bilateral aid, the surest way to reduce the overall incidence and cost of tied aid may be to increase the share of multilateral assistance (which typically is untied) in the donors' overall assistance programs. In the early 1980s, however, there has been an apparent reversal in the previous trend toward increased multilateral aid.

REDUCING THE USE OF MIXED CREDITS

The concern over the potential impact that a proliferation of mixed credit transactions could have on both trade flows and development programs has led to a number of international actions. In the late 1970s the OECD established a set of basic guidelines governing the terms and conditions of OECD export credits. The basic focus of this arrangement was the reduction of the use of subsidized export credits. Some general provisions dealing with "tied aid credits" were also incorporated. The intent of these provisions was both to increase the transparency and to reduce the potential advantage of the mixed credit to the initial offering country and thereby discourage its use.

Reporting under this arrangement, however, remained incomplete, and some donors sought to avoid the requirements by structuring the transactions to fall technically outside the guidelines. Reflecting concerns over the increasing pressure to use aid resources to support mixed credits, in June 1983 the DAC adopted guidelines governing the use of "associated financing." [10] And in 1985 and again in 1987 the OECD further tightened the tied aid credit provisions. [11]

It is too early to assess whether these guidelines will have any significant impact on the level or type of mixed credits provided by donors. Nevertheless, one apparent result of these efforts has been the generation of an improved flow of information to the OECD on the mixed credit actions of donors.

IMPROVING OTHER DONOR PRACTICES

Donor practices with respect to financing only imports or capital costs are frequently well-intentioned, but as noted above, they have tended to limit the effectiveness of donors' assistance. In addition, with greater attention focused in the 1970s and 1980s on assistance to agriculture, health, education, and population—all sectors involving aid activities with significant local cost components—relaxation of donor local cost financing limitations has increasingly been seen as necessary. In 1977 the DAC developed guidelines for local cost financing in bilateral programs. According to the guidelines, donors agree to take measures to meet shortfalls for developing countries that desire to promote programs/projects with large local cost components but in spite of determined efforts are unable to mobilize all the required resources internally (OECD, *Development Cooperation*, 1977). The conditions under which local cost financing would be encouraged depended in part on evidence of self-help efforts by the recipient in the form of savings and tax revenues and in part on whether the activities focused on the "social" sectors, whose output could be expected to address the basic human needs of the poor.

Reflecting this understanding, donors currently are permitting more extensive financing of local costs than a decade ago. The pressures for tying of aid put some limits to this flexibility, however: instead of purchasing local currency directly, at times donors have developed mechanisms to provide imports through aid and then utilized the local currency proceeds from the sale of those imports to provide local cost financing for other, unrelated project activities. While the practice avoids some of the most obvious distortions that result from limiting funding to foreign exchange components of the aid-funded project, it also introduces administrative complexities and further complicates the policy dialogue with the recipient.

In recognition of the problems generated by financing only capital costs, some changes in donor policy either have been implemented or are under consideration. For example, in a policy paper on recurrent costs (US/AID, 1982d), US/AID indicated a willingness to fund a "portion of recurrent costs of host country projects through a variety of mechanisms at the project, sectoral or macro levels for a period up to ten years, provided the country agrees to shoulder an increasing share of total costs over this period" (p. 19). In addition, this policy also requires that these recurrent costs have a higher development impact than new investment, that the recipient be unable to undertake the recurrent cost financing, and that the recipient undertake a program of policy reform that would enable it to meet recurrent cost financing needs in the future.

The World Bank has also provided recurrent cost financing (1) by financing for a time the recurrent costs of projects it has helped undertake; (2) by financing projects intended to overcome the backlog of deferred maintenance and to improve future maintenance; (3) by special emergency or rescue operations associated with drought and other emergencies; and (4) as part of sector loans.

In addition to greater flexibility in the financing practices of individual donors, perhaps what is needed most to address this problem is improved donor coordination. Such coordination is necessary to assure that decisions about financing of individual projects are not taken in isolation and without regard to the overall implication of such projects for recurrent cost financing by the recipient.

Conclusions and Implications

This chapter suggests various ways whereby the pursuit of foreign policy objectives through bilateral assistance by various donors tends to compromise economic development objectives. Our analysis suggests that the more dominant political and commercial objectives are, the less effective economic assistance is likely to be. Although the evidence is open to some interpretation, it also points strongly to the conclusion that the pursuit of commercial interests does reduce the overall effectiveness of donor assistance programs. The size of this effect is not known, however, and will vary among donors, programs, and country-specific situations.

Bilateral donors have recently made significant improvements in their assistance programs by becoming more flexible in the financing of local and recurrent costs. Equally encouraging have been the recent efforts to limit the use of mixed credits. But in most donor countries the provision of bilateral assistance continues to be motivated by complex foreign policy and commercial objectives that tend to undermine its development effectiveness.

The multilateral assistance agencies have been much less affected by such considerations and are able to allocate the resources available more in keeping with the pursuit of development objectives. Moreover, multilateral institutions engage in international competitive bidding in the procurement of goods and services financed through their aid. This practice contrasts with the utilization of direct and indirect aid-tying mechanisms used by most bilateral donors in the pursuit of their commercial objectives. Thus, on these grounds, and other things being equal, this chapter suggests that aid through multilateral institutions would tend to be more effective than bilateral assistance in support of development.

6

Interaction between Donors
and Recipients

KEITH JAY AND
CONSTANTINE MICHALOPOULOS

The key conclusion of chapter 4, on the interaction of the aid process with development in recipient countries, is the crucial importance of "getting the policies right." As shown in that chapter, many aid projects and programs had their effect reduced or offset by policy incentives or structures inimical to development. In terms of growth prospects and performance, no amount of foreign assistance can substitute for a developing country's internal policies and incentives for increasing output and improving the efficiency of resource allocation. Similarly, in chapter 5, it is shown that donor aid policies also reduce the effectiveness of aid even when the recipients' objectives and policies are geared to promote development. Since the effectiveness of economic assistance is affected by both recipient and donor policies and since there is ample reason to believe that these policies, which almost always address multiple objectives, are not optimally designed to maximize aid effectiveness, in most cases there is an important role for donor-recipient policy dialogue to strengthen the effectiveness of economic assistance.

The need for a dialogue derives fundamentally from the fact that both donor and recipient governments are accountable for the funds transferred. That is, they usually have to demonstrate to their publics that the aid funds have been utilized effectively. In some extreme circumstances there may be no need for donor-recipient interaction over donor practices or recipient policies. For example, if donor practices were guided solely by the motivation to promote the economic development of the recipient, and the recipient's policies were known to be most favorable for the attainment of development objectives, there would be little need for donor-recipient dialogue aimed at improving aid effectiveness. At the other extreme, if donors were uninterested in the economic development of the recipient, and the recipient used the economic assistance provided inefficiently or to pursue nondevelopment objectives, there would appear to be little motivation for either to talk about aid effectiveness. But in most cases, given the need for accountability and the imperfections in policies on the part of both donor and recipient, there is a need for a dialogue.

How this dialogue is conducted and how effective it is depends on a variety of factors. The provision of official economic assistance is by definition an act involving sovereign governments directly or indirectly (through multilateral institutions). This implies that the process of determining what the aid will be used for, how closely it matches the donors' and recipients' objectives, and how effectively it is utilized involves a complex and delicate interaction between donor and recipient that depends on their power relationship and contains elements of collaboration as well as coercion. Political considerations obviously condition and frequently constrain both the donors' and the recipients' conduct of the dialogue. Furthermore, given the politically sensitive nature of the dialogue and the need for confidentiality, it is frequently very difficult to evaluate its effect on policy change in either the donor or the recipient country.

The discussion so far has focused on individual donors and recipients. In practice, there are a variety of donors each with a variety of objectives in providing assistance to individual recipients. Aid can be more or less effective depending on the extent to which donors coordinate their efforts in support of recipient development objectives. Uncoordinated aid efforts can lead to conflicting policy advice, wasteful duplication, and general confusion and inefficiency.

The first part of this chapter focuses on the conduct and constraints to the policy dialogue, drawing primarily on examples from the country studies. The second part discusses aid coordination both at the country level and more broadly.

Donor-Recipient Policy Interaction

Aid effectiveness needs to be measured in terms of results, that is, its contribution to stimulating economic growth and improving the welfare of the recipient. Whether official flows tend to promote these development objectives will depend in part on the recipients' policies. Donors have the capacity to influence recipients' policies through various means for better or worse.

INFLUENCE, LEVERAGE, DIALOGUE, AND CONDITIONALITY

The use of aid to influence the recipient country's economic policy implies an initial divergence of views between donor and recipient over various aspects of the latter's economic policy.[1] The objective of donor influence is the reduction or elimination of the initial disagreement so as to produce convergence in donor and recipient views. Note that in the course of a dialogue it is possible for *both* the donor and the recipient to change their views about the latter's economic policy. There is no presumption that donors know best, although in some cases the dialogue may contain a true technical assistance component when recipients have limited institutional capacity to analyze the implications of policies they do or could pursue.

Influence can be viewed as a continuum: at one extreme, the donor might have complete control and impose its will on the recipient; at the other extreme, the donor would have no capacity to affect the course of the recipient's policies. The concept of an influence continuum can be used to analyze the concepts of leverage and policy dialogue. "Leverage" is the capacity to have one viewpoint prevail over the other. This capacity may not always be the donor's: the recipient may get its way in areas of economic policy in exchange for a commitment that it will take some action favorable to the donor in some other area, for example, defense or security.

"Dialogue" is the process through which either or both viewpoints about the recipient's policies or the donor's practices may change to bridge the initial divergence between the two. The donor may convince the recipient through a dialogue that a policy change advocated by the donor is in the recipient's interest. By using leverage, the donor may induce the aid recipient to follow certain policies, not because the recipient concurs with the donor's views, but because if it does not, the donor might terminate aid, or if it does, the donor might extend additional aid.

Leverage is frequently exercised by the donor, contingent on the recipient's agreeing and adhering to certain conditions in the conduct of policy. "Conditionality" is thus understood to refer to the conditions attached to the extension of economic assistance and to the consequences for the flow of this assistance if the conditions are not met.

In some cases the recipient may agree to undertake certain policy steps that it would have taken anyway. This may be done to satisfy the donor's desire to have certain "conditions" attached to the lending or to address the problem of internal opposition to proposed policy action in the recipient country by shifting the onus for the possibly unpopular measure to the foreign donor. Cases of such "phantom" leverage are frequent.

In practice, it is difficult to distinguish between leverage and dialogue. Even in the most friendly and continuous policy dialogue the recipient may be conscious that in the event of disagreement the donor has the option to terminate assistance. On the other hand, explicit and strict conditioning does not mean that a dialogue that will produce a meeting of minds is impossible. Indeed, it is difficult to visualize a pure leverage case in which no dialogue has occurred.

Focusing attention on the availability of leverage and conditionality as a means of influence can be counterproductive. Potential leverage, usually linked to the possible size of the aid program, can facilitate policy dialogue but is neither a sufficient nor a necessary condition for its success. On the other hand, a good understanding of the determinants of economic policies in developing countries is a necessary condition for any policy dialogue to occur.

THE CONDUCT OF THE DIALOGUE: LIMITS TO DONORS' INFLUENCE

The effectiveness of donors' efforts to influence recipients' economic policies hinges critically on donors' understanding of why recipients' economic policies are ineffective. It would be far easier to correct policies if their shortcomings were due primarily to misinformation or ineffective design or implementation. But economic policies in most countries are responsive to a number of domestic political interests—agriculture, protectionist lobbies, labor unions—that make it impossible to adhere to such clear-cut efficiency and development objectives. In addition, most developing countries have memories of a colonial legacy under which the colonial powers determined domestic economic policies. Such a historical legacy has several consequences that must be borne in mind whenever the question of influencing domestic economic policies arises.

First, any attempt by foreign (and especially Western) countries to influence domestic economic policies is regarded with suspicion and resentment and can be viewed as tantamount to an effort to reassert colonial status.[2] Second, living standards did not rise appreciably during the colonial period in most colonies. Since the colonial powers generally did not pursue activist or interventionist economic policies, market-oriented policies advocated by donors concerned with the efficiency of resource allocation may be regarded as too laissez faire and thus as designed to prevent growth. Third, in many developing countries the predominant business group has historically been a minority—the whites and Indians in Africa, the Chinese in much of Southeast Asia. A major problem for policy formulation in many of these developing countries is that political power is in the hands of one identifiable national, racial, or ethnic group, while economic power is regarded as being held by another identifiable but minority group. Pursuit of policies that will enhance the productivity and profitability of the private sector is therefore often perceived as advocacy of minority interests. Regardless of the extent to which the "right" economic policies might in the long run benefit all groups in a particular society, the political sensitivities engendered by the minority-majority problems, and by memories of the colonial legacy, impart to economic policy a sensitive political dimension for which there is probably no counterpart in most developed countries.

To say that there are strong, and possibly emotion-based, political pressures surrounding economic policy formulation in developing countries is not to say that donors cannot or should not attempt to influence policies. However, as demonstrated by the Indian devaluation experience in 1966 (see below), there are limits—which may vary from country to country and from time to time—to the extent to which donors may influence recipient country policies. Furthermore, some efforts to influence country policy may be counterproductive.

Bilateral assistance, particularly by the larger donors, is sometimes provided under a tacit understanding or as an explicit condition for certain actions by the recipient outside the economic field, such as the provision of military bases. In such circumstances the potential for an effective policy dialogue with the recipient on economic issues can be for all practical purposes nonexistent. In other cases the volume of bilateral assistance is determined primarily on the basis of political considerations. For example, there is a tacit understanding about the relative size of U.S. economic assistance to Egypt and Israel. In such cases, the dialogue with the recipient, if there is one, is not over the size of the assistance that can be productively used but rather, given the size, over how it can best be allocated between sectors and uses. In such an environment the staff members of the donor assistance agency are in a weak position to conduct a dialogue about the effectiveness of assistance programs. This constraint has not always been prohibitive. There have been cases in which a significant policy dialogue has occurred, notwithstanding the basic prior commitment to provide the aid. The leverage, however, has been typically less.

It is possible that "correct" advice, either given in too strong a dose or pushed too far, can lead (or even force) policymakers to move in the opposite direction. Moreover, adoption of a "correct" policy can lead to the downfall of a politician or a government and bring into power political leaders whose policies are even more antagonistic to efficient resource allocation and growth than those prevailing when the initial policy advice was given. The recorded instances of such reactions are numerous. Among the countries included in the case studies in this volume, Ghana, with its 1971 devaluation, may provide the best example (chapter 15). By any economic criteria, a realignment of the relative prices of tradable (and especially exportable) and nontradable goods was probably called for, and the government was persuaded to devalue the cedi. The political reaction, however, was so strong that the government was overthrown, and the devaluation was reversed within a period of months.

India's 1966 devaluation is illustrative of more subtle and more problematic aspects of donor efforts to influence domestic economic policies (chapter 12). There can be little doubt that the rupee was overvalued in 1966. There is also no doubt that the government was essentially reluctant to devalue and decided to do so only under considerable foreign pressure, which was effective because there were significant amounts of concessional aid administered by a consortium of donors. The amount of the devaluation was apparently selected with a view to choosing the minimum amount that would satisfy the donor countries. That amount was probably smaller than would have been desirable on economic grounds; nonetheless, it was large enough to generate a domestic political reaction that seized upon "foreign interference" as a rationale for protest (Bhagwati and Srinivasan, 1975).

The vehemence of that protest left as a legacy the conventional wisdom in India that devaluation is not a viable political action in almost any circumstance. For present purposes, the lesson is really a question: Were donors wise to push for a devaluation, which in any event was probably too small to be optimal, under circumstances in which the government was reluctant, and whose unpopularity could be blamed on foreigners? There is no ready answer to that question, and country experiences vary widely. For example, at about the same time, donors engaged in a policy dialogue with Indonesia that resulted in a successful series of reforms, including the significant devaluation of the rupiah. Clearly, the Indian economy would have been significantly worse off in the short run had the rupee remained as overvalued as it was. The fact that there is no definitive answer to the above Indian devaluation question is illustrative of the difficulties surrounding policy advice determined in the context of a sensitive political environment.

Aid practitioners argue that receptivity of the host country government is a necessary condition for the use of aid to influence economic policies. Receptivity depends first on the validity of the economic advice; if the donor has little useful to say, a dialogue is not meaningful. Assuming that the donor has something to contribute, the effectiveness of the dialogue depends on its conduct, which by its very nature must be highly diplomatic.

Dialogue leads to an acceptance of policy advice as being in the recipient's own economic development interest. The potential for dialogue, however, is not well correlated to the strength of the potential leverage as measured by the size of the aid program. A large donor who has little useful to offer in terms of specific policy suggestions may find it difficult to engage in any significant policy dialogue. At the same time, economic policies adopted solely because large donors insist on them are not likely to be implemented forcefully and may well result in the recipient's failure to meet its commitments. Economic policy reform will be lasting only if the host government accepts and fully supports it.

A relatively small assistance program does not by itself rule out all possibilities of a dialogue over a country's policies. On the other hand, a minimum amount of aid is probably necessary before a recipient can be induced to listen to what a specific donor has to say. The aid program is a useful entry point without which a dialogue would be impossible to initiate or sustain.

It is thus desirable, in all circumstances and to the extent possible, that recipients reach their own conclusions and not feel that they are undertaking policy reforms under duress. In order to accomplish this, donors usually attempt to strengthen the position of host country advocates of specific policy measures. It is often assumed that this strengthening may tip the balance of whatever internal debate is going on in favor of the donor's advice. However, the opposite outcome is also likely, with resentment of the pressure by donors being channeled to their domestic "allies" even when the policy reform has the expected results. And when the policy change is adopted but fails to achieve its intended objectives, as in India's case, the internal position of those who supported the donor's view is badly compromised.

These thoughts on the conduct of macroeconomic policy dialogue apply to some extent in other areas as well, for example, in the context of sectoral policies or budgetary allocation decisions. There are important linkages as well as important differences, however. For example, dialogue over the conditions that would make a particular power project cost-effective may quickly lead to broader issues, such as those related to utility pricing policy, role of parastatals, or general energy policy. However, the symbolic importance attached to macrovariables, such as the exchange rate, often makes the dialogue on such macrovariable issues more sensitive politically than that on the smaller or less visible, but potentially important, sectoral policy issues or issues involving specific budgetary allocations. Donors' efforts in support of a sector or subsector can influence such allocations by strengthening a particular minister's hand in dealing with the ministry of finance or planning in the allocation of domestic resources for specified activities. While the fungibility of resources suggests that such influence may be illusory, claims are made frequently by aid administrators that they were successful in exerting such influence. Their typical argument is that budgetary resources, while fungible in principle, in fact are not. The weaker the ministry in charge of the budget, the less fungible the funds and the greater the donor's influence.

Bilateral and Multilateral Policy Dialogue

Some form of policy dialogue has been present in almost all donor-recipient relationships. Considerable use of leverage was introduced in the 1960s through a number of operations of the U.S. bilateral assistance programs. The most controversial one was the conditioning of resumption of U.S. and multilateral economic assistance to India on the devaluation of the rupee in 1966.

In India, the overvaluation of the exchange rate in the early 1960s constituted a tremendous disincentive for producers to grow export crops (Bhagwati and Srinivasan, 1975). The relative domestic prices of these crops (including tea and jute) were so low that supply failed to grow as rapidly as it would have at more favorable prices, and India's share of the world market fell sharply. Meanwhile, agricultural assistance projects were addressed to increasing the supply of these and other commodities. After the devaluation of the Indian rupee in 1966 a more realistic exchange rate prevailed. The success with raising production during the Green Revolution was partly attributable to aid programs and government efforts to stimulate agriculture; however, the additional incentives provided by the changing relative prices associated with devaluation were undoubtedly a precondition for success.

While the devaluation was much needed, it was ill-timed and undertaken in the face of substantial domestic opposition. The reform process was soon to be undone by both economic and political processes and to have a significant and lasting adverse effect on donor-recipient relationships.

Other early cases of donor-recipient dialogue, such as Colombia and Korea, were much more successful. Colombia achieved substantial development success in the 1970s, attributable to effective domestic policies supported by significant amounts of aid, and a constructive policy dialogue. Foreign assistance also made a contribution to the development of public sector institutions and economic policymaking (Currie, 1984). Similarly, in Korea the long-run policy dialogue between Korean officials and U.S. aid officials in the 1960s had a positive impact on the Korean government's willingness to formulate and implement development policy (chapter 13). Finally, the Ivory Coast, in sharp contrast to Ghana, is an example of a country that in the 1970s achieved substantial progress based on relatively effective and distortion-free economic policies supported by advice and assistance especially from France and the World Bank (chapter 15).

For a variety of reasons, multilateral institutions and, in particular, the World Bank have been urged by bilateral donors to take the lead in conducting a policy dialogue with aid recipients. Their nonpolitical nature, their comparatively stronger analytical capabilities on macroeconomic issues, and their command of significant financial resources have given such institutions opportunities to carry on an active policy dialogue with a number of aid recipients.

The World Bank's program of Structural Adjustment Lending (SAL) and Sectoral Adjustment Lending (SECAL) offers a number of recent examples of policy dialogue and foreign assistance lending involving policy conditionality. This program started in 1980 and has been developing rapidly (see table 6.1). By the end of fiscal year 1987, 121 adjustment operations, frequently called policy-based loans, to forty-two countries had been approved.

Policy-based loans have been extended to countries at various levels of development, some to low-income countries, such as Malawi, others to more advanced economies, such as Turkey and Mexico. The design of the reform programs was directly related to the current economic situation in these countries. The countries either were facing severe macroeconomic problems or had major problems looming on the horizon. All countries were finding it difficult to adapt to the changing international environment. Most were experiencing debt servicing difficulties resulting from a large debt overhang. These difficulties were often compounded by a whole range of country-specific do-

Table 6.1. Trend in Nonproject Lending Commitments by the World Bank
($ millions)

	FY 1979–80	FY 1985	FY 1986	FY 1987
All countries				
Total lending	10,746	14,384	16,319	17,674
Sector adjustment, program, and structural adjustment lending	403	1,638	3,100	4,118
As percentage of total	*3.8%*	*11.4%*	*19.0%*	*23.3%*
Low-income countries				
Total lending	3,430	5,931	6,261	6,913
Sector adjustment, program, and structural adjustment lending	153	371	650	658
As percentage of total	*4.4%*	*6.3%*	*10.4%*	*9.5%*
Highly indebted countries				
Total lending	4,114	4,993	6,251	6,690
Sector adjustment, program, and structural adjustment lending	76	745	2,050	2,382
As percentage of total	*1.8%*	*14.9%*	*32.8%*	*35.6%*

Source: World Bank.

mestic problems, including institutional inflexibilities, uncontrolled expansion of the public sector, and excessive protection of the industrial sector.

Although the structural adjustment programs varied considerably in the specifics of design, the underlying adjustment strategies were similar. They emphasized structural change in three critical areas: (*a*) improving the structure of incentives for exports in order to ease the adjustment process and contribute directly to economic growth; (*b*) greater use of market forces and more realistic pricing in domestic and foreign trade so as to improve the efficiency of resource use and enhance the competitiveness of producers; and (*c*) better management of public sector operations so as to raise economic and social returns on public spending and reduce public sector deficits. More recently, World Bank programs also are starting anew to pay much greater attention to the impact of these adjustment measures on the poor.

The experience with the Bank's policy-based lending is frequently too recent to evaluate fully. It is also difficult to disentangle the impact of Bank assistance from that of IMF credits, which also contained substantial conditionality and were frequently put in place in parallel with Bank assistance. Nonetheless, several lessons can be drawn. First, there has been some disappointment. In almost all operations reviewed the process of preparing, legislating, and executing policy reforms was difficult to implement. The capacity of governments to implement reform measures was usually inadequately assessed, and often the Bank was over optimistic as to the degree of the governments' commitment to and understanding of the reform measures. Another important element is the deterioration of the world economic environment in the early 1980s, with the result that the impact of the structural adjustment programs in many countries has been below expectations.

Second, in spite of the delays and difficulties, many of the loans have set in motion a worthwhile reform process, with significant impact on both the governments and the Bank. The reviews of past loans show that in most countries they have played a major role in focusing the attention of governments on structural problems and the links between various policy instruments. The Bank has helped borrowers to identify the nature of their problems and formulate strategies. This was particularly important in countries with limited analytical capability to perform that task themselves.

Third, and one of the most important lessons of the Bank's experience, the process of policy reform must be internalized in the country as quickly as possible so that the reform program is designed by the country itself and integrated into its longer-term development program. This can be done by seeking the active participation of relevant parties in diagnosing problems and seeking solutions. The experience has shown that results have been best where from the beginning the government's active participation was sought in designing the program and in formulating solutions, such as in Turkey or Chile in the 1980s (Michalopoulos, 1987; World Bank, 1988).

As many observers have also concluded, "the dialogue is most effective when the donor can persuade the recipient to move further along a path on which it already wants to go" (Cassen, 1986, p. 89; see also Nelson, 1986). A challenge to prevailing vested interests or political convictions can be implemented only when there is a crisis. But when the crisis abates, commitments tend to be abandoned if they are not internalized.

This review should not suggest that donors always know best. Indeed, the evidence, frequently from Africa, is quite mixed. In Tanzania donors provided the bulk of the resources needed for an industrialization effort undertaken in the context of seriously distorted incentives that led to significant waste and inefficiency (Lele, 1984). A study directed by Uma Lele notes "the relatively small role donor assistance seems to have played in the growth that has in fact occurred" in six African countries and attributes it to the fact that "a large amount of donor assistance was allocated with the best of intentions to types of activities that have little effect on growth." Many "new" donors have underemphasized the importance of investment in human capacity; and assistance has been characterized by unwarranted orientation to the food crop sector, where a balanced food and export crop approach is of critical importance (Lele, 1988, p. 117).

The Forms of Assistance That Facilitate Policy Dialogue:
Program versus Project Aid

One of the oldest dilemmas of foreign assistance centers around the question whether it should take the form of program or project aid. "Program aid" is provided as general support for a country's overall development objectives and thus is destined to finance additional imports, while "project aid" supports particular investment activities in the recipient country. There are also several mixed forms of assistance. Sector aid focuses on particular sectoral objectives but can be composed of a series of linked projects; or it can primarily involve nonproject assistance, such as budget support to a particular ministry; or it can be a mixture of both. Depending on its composition, sector aid can thus be more or less projectized. At present, according to the DAC, roughly 28 percent of bilateral donor assistance is identified as program-type assistance. By contrast, despite the increase in World Bank program-type lending noted above, only 11 percent of multilateral aid was classified as program-type assistance (see table 6.2).

There are, of course, significant variations in the level of program lending provided by individual donors (see table 6.3). The United States, for example, traditionally has provided a substantial level of its assistance in nonproject form, reflecting the significant role of food aid and security-related assistance. Only 37 percent of its aid is identified with specific projects. In contrast, Japan, Germany, and France provide 82, 81, and 77 percent of their aid in project form. In the case of France, this reflects in part the large proportion of the French aid program that funds French teachers in developing

Table 6.2. Percentage of Aid Commitments by Major Purpose, 1987

	DAC Bilateral ODA	Multilateral Assistance[a]
Social infrastructure	24.2	19.9
Education	10.6	4.3
Health	5.2	7.8
Economic infrastructure (Transportation, energy)	17.2	30.4
Production	21.6	36.6
Agriculture	13.2	23.2
Other	8.4	13.4
Program-type assistance (Program aid, food aid, debt relief, emergency aid)	28.1	11.1
Other (Administrative expenses, multisector, unspecified)	8.9	2.0

Source: OECD, Development Cooperation, 1988.
[a]Concessional and nonconcessional.

Table 6.3. Sectoral Allocation of Bilateral ODA Commitments, 1987

	Economic Infrastructure	Social Infrastructure	Agriculture	Other[a]	Sector-allocated Assistance as a Percentage of Total Bilateral Assistance
Australia	7.5	27.7	8.2	2.0	45.4
Austria	30.5	43.8	3.0	10.9	88.2
Belgium	13.9	46.2	11.7	8.3	80.1
Canada	13.9	15.5	18.8	8.3	56.5
Denmark	15.9	20.6	10.8	4.7	52.0
Finland	27.7	23.9	19.7	18.6	89.9
France	17.6	42.5	10.1	6.3	76.5
Germany	26.2	32.1	10.8	11.9	81.0
Ireland	0.4	46.9	17.2	5.5	70.0
Italy	21.8	21.4	18.3	8.5	70.0
Japan	37.3	18.5	14.2	12.4	82.4
Netherlands	17.0	18.9	23.3	6.8	66.0
New Zealand	4.8	44.0	10.9	2.9	62.6
Norway	17.8	39.2	13.9	12.8	83.7
Sweden	10.4	17.3	12.6	9.0	49.3
Switzerland	13.9	17.3	20.2	4.7	56.1
United Kingdom	19.2	26.8	10.2	17.0	73.2
United States	3.2	17.5	11.2	5.1	37.0
Total	17.2	24.2	13.2	8.4	63.0

Source: OECD, *Development Cooperation,* 1988.
[a] Industry and other production.

countries. In the cases of Germany and Japan, the large proportion of their programs allocated to sector activities reflects in part a strong emphasis on the funding of basic infrastructure activities.

These estimates are only rough indicators of the nature of the assistance given. Over time the distinctions between program and project aid have blurred. The World Bank, for example, has extended a variety of project loans for export development or with a sectoral orientation that has very clear non-project dimensions. Such loans are extended in support of broad economic policy reform, such as in interest rates, trade controls, and so on, and are fast-disbursing, since financing of current imports frequently accounts for a significant proportion of the total loan. In Sub-Saharan Africa at present the Bank has recognized the need for assistance in support of the maintenance and rehabilitation of existing capital projects rather than new projects. Such assistance may be packaged by donors as a sector loan or as a project, but it clearly involves significant nonproject elements.

Early thinking about assistance focused on the proposition that by financing particular projects, donors could influence the investment programs of a recipient country along preferred lines. The difficulties with this general defense of project aid lie in the fungibility of resources. Unless a donor finances a project that would not otherwise be undertaken, the donor's decision to undertake project A will simply permit the government to undertake whatever was the marginal project on its list of preferred investments. If a recipient country knows that the donor believes that more resources should be devoted to a particular sector—agriculture, for example—the recipient can simply cut down its own planned expenditure on that sector and encourage donor projects in it.

Another argument contends that many donor-financed projects have had an important component of technical assistance in them that could not have been transmitted in the absence of the projects. For that reason, project aid at times may be preferred to program aid. It is for this reason that recent World Bank program-type lending has often been accompanied by specific related technical assistance activities.

It can be argued that program aid, as an alternative, can be based upon an examination of the overall set of policies that a particular country undertakes. The difficulties with this argument are several. First, as already seen, there are often important political reasons why a donor (especially a bilateral donor) has an interest in good relations with the country; as a result, cessation of or severe cutbacks in assistance because of disagreement over economic policies are difficult if not impossible. Second, while donors can negotiate over a government's overall economic policy, the domestic political sensitivities discussed earlier are an important limit to such negotiation. Third, the judgment issues raised earlier become exceptionally important under program lending.

On the other hand, there are certain advantages to program-type aid in the context of influencing recipient macroeconomic policy. Program aid is a *flexible* instrument. It can be quickly disbursed, it can be increased or decreased at the margin or delayed in timing, and it can be released in tranches. One can therefore support economic policy changes as they occur, as well as monitor their implementation. Project assistance, by contrast, cannot be turned on and off easily, and its potential leverage on economic policies is correspondingly weaker.

Finally, program aid is more relevant to a discussion of macroeconomic policies or even of sector development strategy. It is much more difficult to develop a policy dialogue on macroeconomic issues on the basis of projects in individual sectors whose links to macroeconomic policy are tenuous however large the projects. Also, project aid tends to be administered by ministries with sector responsibility—for example, agriculture—but with very little responsibility for macroeconomic policy. In contrast, program aid negotiations typically involve ministry officials responsible for determining overall macroeconomic policy. Thus program aid is unquestionably the superior form if it is considered desirable to attempt to use leverage to change macroeconomic policy and condition assistance through time-related performance criteria. If influence is to be exerted primarily through discussion and exchange of ideas rather than through specific loan conditioning, the choice between project and nonproject aid is more equivocal. Also, there may be some policy issues of importance outside the macro sphere that could be addressed through the sector or project mode.

Some bilateral donors are devoting a significant portion of their resources to nonproject lending. In some cases, however, this is taking place without an effective policy dialogue. One reason for this failure to use this type of lending to promote a dialogue is that while a number of these donors have emphasized the importance of the policy dialogue in principle, in practice they have extended nonproject aid in support of broad political objectives and with little concern about policy conditioning.

There is probably no ideal balance between project and nonproject aid. Indeed, with the traditional program/project distinction blurred, it is hard to argue at present that program loans are in some way categorically better instruments in support of policy reform or that project lending is less fast-disbursing. Given the political constraints surrounding bilateral aid (and the technical assistance components of many aid projects), it may well be that a combination of program and project lending is appropriate, with program lending increasing in importance during periods when governments are undertaking genuine and sustained efforts at policy reforms. Clearly, in cases where the policy environment is very distorted only project assistance ought to be considered, and only in activities least affected by these distortions. In short, the appropriate mix depends to a large degree on the objectives pursued through the loan, the structure of the loan, and the policy dialogue between donor and recipient.

In the final analysis, donors are now moving in the direction of creating multiple and flexible assistance instruments that involve combinations of what traditionally were considered program, project, and technical assistance activities. And they are trying to tailor the combination to the relative needs of recipients, with technical assistance components emphasized in low-income countries and nonproject elements emphasized in circumstances where for a variety of reasons there is relatively greater need for such assistance compared with traditional project financing.

The Coordination of Development Assistance

"Aid coordination" is a broad and imprecise term. It can encompass activities from general discussions in international fora on broad principles of development cooperation and assistance policy, to country-level discussions between donors and recipients regarding development constraints and programs, to very narrow and concrete actions by several donors and a recipient concerning specific project or sector assistance. This lack of precision, coupled with the implicit positive connotations attached to the terms "cooperation" and "coordination," has meant that donors have traditionally expressed public support for the general concept of coordination. But practical interest in the issue by donors has varied greatly over time. Donors have had divergent views regarding the appropriate type, nature, or intensity of such cooperation, and at times there has been active resistance by some donors to anything but the most general nonoperational forms of coordination.

COORDINATION INSTITUTIONS

The first donor aid coordination group, led by the World Bank, was convened in response to a foreign exchange crisis in India in 1958.[3] Subsequently a permanent aid group was established for India, and a similar arrangement was made for Pakistan in 1960. Also in 1960 the leading industrial-country aid donors established the Development Assistance Group, reconstituted as the Development Assistance Committee (DAC) in 1961, as a forum for consultations among donors on major aid questions. One of the major issues at that time was burden sharing. The United States and the United Kingdom encouraged other developed countries to develop or expand their aid programs. A second concern was to improve aid effectiveness.

During the 1960s and 1970s the number of aid donors, recipients, and assistance activities expanded dramatically, as did the complexity of many of the development issues confronting both donor and recipient. This rapid expansion also brought with it the increased potential that the projects, programs, development emphasis, and policy advice provided by an individual donor would needlessly duplicate, be inconsistent with, or prove detrimental to the aid efforts of other donors and/or the overall development effort of the recipient (Pearson Commission, 1969). One response to this potential was the expansion of the number of aid coordination groups, although they remained basically limited to the larger developing countries, and the formation of a variety of other aid coordination mechanisms.

While improved aid coordination has become a standard agenda item in international discussions of development issues, it often has been one of low priority. In the last few years, however, the importance attached to effective aid coordination has increased, reflecting (1) the serious economic problems faced by the developing countries; (2) the increased importance attached to the implementation and maintenance of sound economic policies; (3) the slow growth and uncertain prospects about the future levels of economic assistance; and (4) increasing evidence of the costs associated with an absence of effective aid coordination, including the distortion of the recipient's investment program, a proliferation of donor projects, a rapid expansion in the recurrent costs required to support donor projects, an increased administrative burden on the recipient, and a failure to avoid conflicting or duplicative activities or the provision of contradictory advice.

Investment can be distorted as a result of a donor's desire to identify projects that match its own commercial interest or its own development emphasis. Even where the sector or project makes sense in isolation, a lack of coordination among donors can result in an imbalance in the distribution of investment if a large proportion of the donors decide independently to focus on the same sector or issue, as donors have also been caught up in development fads. This potential for distortion can be reinforced by a lack of control or coordination within the recipient's own government. Ministries in some countries have had fairly broad authority to work with individual donors to develop projects of special interest to the particular ministry with little effective review or screening of these ministry-supported projects against an overall investment plan for the country.

Rapid proliferation of projects, reflecting the preference by most donors to fund projects can strain the financial and human resource capacity of recipients to implement, monitor, and maintain these projects. This problem has been particularly severe in a number of African countries. For example, a review of donor programs in Kenya revealed that there were approximately 600 active projects by 60 donors on the books in Kenya. Similarly, the UNDP estimated that there were 188 projects by 50 donors in Malawi, 321 projects by 61 donors in Lesotho, and 614 projects by 69 donors in Zambia (Morss, 1984).

Recipients also often face a wide array of differing assistance procedures and requirements; for example, the project identification and selection process, the contracting procedures (including forms and specifications), and the monitoring and accounting procedures can differ significantly among donors. Recipients need to use scarce administrative talent to understand and comply with each donor's individual aid process.

Finally, a failure to coordinate can result in donors' supporting projects or programs that are in conflict, directly or indirectly, with those of another donor. For example, one donor may be supporting the increased production of a commodity that another donor is encouraging the government to diversify out of. It may also result in a failure to identify and undertake projects in which joint action would be highly desirable, given the differing resources of each donor, or projects whose scale exceeds the support ability of an individual donor. When a donor's project or program directly or indirectly involves a recipient's economic policies, a lack of communication can lead to conflicting policy actions.

BENEFITS FROM COORDINATION

Coordination of aid programs can serve a variety of purposes, including:

1. Facilitation and improvement of the flow of information. This can include the development and exchange of information on (1) the nature, level, and distribution of donors' assistance and their assistance policies; (2) basic economic and technical conditions that can assist in the identification, structuring, and implementation of development projects; and (3) the recipient countries' economic policies, performance, and development plans. The DAC has played a key role in developing and disseminating information on donor assistance programs, particularly those at the global rather than the project level, while the World Bank, along with the IMF, has played a major role in developing information on the economic constraints, policies, and prospects of individual developing countries.

2. Providing a mechanism for project-level coordination. Exchanging information on current and proposed assistance projects, as well as project experience (e.g., evaluation results), helps donors avoid problems and identify areas in which joint activity or cofinancing with other donors or the private sector may prove beneficial.

3. Stimulating and improving the dialogue on recipient country economic policy. An increasing number of donors are turning to coordination efforts as a means of assuring that policy issues are being addressed seriously and coherently and that the program, project, and policy advice from each of the donors supports needed policy improvements more effectively. This is seen as particularly important for bilateral donors, for whom the ability to engage individually in an effective policy dialogue may be very limited.

4. Increasing the quantity and quality of aid. On the recipient's side, an important outcome of the coordination process can be increased aid. It also can provide a country with an opportunity to lay its case before the donors. Coordination efforts may also reinforce peer pressure among donors, which may stimulate additional flows or agreements on improved aid policies and procedures.

5. Increasing the public support. On the recipient's side, coordination efforts may provide, via statements and actions by donors, a vehicle to generate support domestically for necessary but painful policy measures. On the donors' side, the demonstration that they are actively coordinating their assistance efforts can help build constituents' support for aid.

BARRIERS TO EFFECTIVE COORDINATION

Despite what might appear to be an area in which agreement would be easy, aid coordination has often been a controversial issue for both donors and recipients. Some developing countries view increased donor coordination as detrimental to their own interests. Furthermore, a recipient may view a lack of coordination to be in its interest if it believes that it can use this lack of coordination to (a) increase the level and quality of aid or (b) achieve an allocation preferable in its view to that which would likely occur through joint donor action (e.g., playing donors off against each other to achieve a better deal) (Arndt, 1979).

Some donors believe that aid coordination, particularly when it is related to policy dialogue, constitutes an unacceptable level of interference in the recipient's sovereignty. In other cases it is avoided because of basic disagreements among the donors regarding aid practices, policies, and philosophy. Donors may also be reluctant to share detailed project information, on the grounds that such information interferes with the achievement of their own commercial objectives. Finally, most donors are not willing to relinquish control over their assistance efforts.

Effective aid coordination requires both financial and human resources for the careful analysis of issues and to carry out the logistics involved in any coordination effort. These staff and financial costs fall on both the recipients and the donors. For some of the low-income countries, these human and financial costs may be viewed as a serious constraint. For many of the smaller and poorer developing countries, this, coupled with previous limited interest of many donors and recipients, has meant little country-specific coordination effort until recently.

It has often been argued that aid coordination is most effective when it becomes an ongoing, "on-the-ground" process. Most aid donors, however, do not have an extensive network of in-country missions staffed by personnel with in-depth country-specific knowledge. This makes the development of an ongoing process of in-country coordination that extends beyond the periodic consultative group meetings more difficult.

IMPROVING COORDINATION

Economic assistance policies, programs, and performance are discussed in a wide range of generalized as well as specialized fora. The most continuously and extensively involved has been the DAC. Aid policies and practices have been debated in other fora, especially the development organizations of the United Nations, but these debates have rarely involved specific practical aspects of these issues.

At the level of the individual country, the consultative groups (CGs) sponsored by the World Bank have constituted the main mechanisms for aid coordination. Since the first aid consortium group was established for India in 1958 close to forty countries have had one or more of these aid group meetings, and most of the groups are still active. In recent years in particular there have been both an increase in the frequency of CG meetings and significant expansion in the number of countries with CGs.[4]

The value of these efforts varies. On the positive side, the World Bank's economic analysis, the recipients' presentations of their development plans, and the donors' presentations of their current and prospective assistance efforts have often been valuable sources of information for donors and recipients alike. This exchange of information can be particularly valuable for smaller donors, who may have limited resources to undertake their own analysis.

Consultative groups nonetheless have not been immune from criticism including that they offer an opportunity for ganging up on recipients and force policy advice on recipients that is counterproductive. The experience of Bangladesh in 1971–72 is viewed by some as such a case. A number of Bangladeshi economists, including members of the planning commission, felt that donor representatives at the consortium, who had less experience and less expertise, were forcing the Bangladesh government to make unwise economic decisions—"too often exhibiting arrogance combined with authority derived from their being representatives of agencies and interests with large resources" (Faaland, 1981).

The other major country-oriented aid coordination mechanism comprises the UNDP-sponsored "roundtables." These are normally held in-country and generally have been less formal, had greater U.N. involvement, and been more focused on program and project issues than on overall economic problems, a major focus of many of the CGs. The roundtables, although not totally new, have only recently become a significant mechanism for country-level aid coordination. The increased role derives from a decision made during the 1981 U.N. Conference on Least Developed Countries that these countries, most of whom did not at that time have formal country assistance coordination mechanisms, should organize aid coordination groups to provide them the opportunity to present and discuss with donors their economic situation and development plans for the purpose of increasing donor support. Subsequently, there has been a significant expansion in both CGs and roundtables for these low-income countries. Reports on the initial set of these meetings were mixed. Not only was it a new process for many of the recipients but often the recipients and donors had different views regarding the purpose of these meetings. At least initially, many recipients viewed them as aid-pledging sessions, while most donors wanted the emphasis placed on the analysis of the recipients' economic policies and problems.[5]

In some circumstances the effective coordination of development efforts requires the coordination of aid activities in a number of countries within an area or region. These efforts have included not only the regular meetings of the regional multilateral development banks but also a number of specific regional consultative mechanisms, such as the Colombo Plan, the regional CGs for the Caribbean and Central America, and the Club du Sahel in Africa.

Increasingly, continuing "on-the-ground" coordination between donors and recipients is perceived as a particularly desirable form of coordination where it can be developed and maintained effectively. Reflecting the increased support for this on-the-spot coordination, agreement has been reached in a number of recent aid group meetings, particularly for Sub-Saharan African countries, to strengthen their existing in-country arrangements or establish new ones. The willingness of these developing countries to support this type of detailed and ongoing coordination effort points to a positive shift in the attitude of these governments toward aid coordination.

The tasks of these in-country groups vary depending on the specific circumstances. In Kenya, for example, until recently the focus was on the prolonged drought situation and its related food crisis, but attention has now been shifted to the formulation of a program to strengthen the country's national agricultural research system. In Mali the focus is on the health and population sector, although nonproject aid and structural adjustment are also receiving attention. In Senegal in-country coordination encompasses a large number of sectors, including agriculture, water supply, maritime fisheries, industry, education, and tourism. It is also interesting to note that in countries such as Malawi (transport and agriculture) and Sri Lanka (water supply and sanitation), coordination meetings have led to an agreed division of labor among donors, including co-financing of projects by donors.

The World Bank-led Special Program of Assistance for low-income debt-distressed countries in Sub-Saharan Africa initiated in late 1987 also illustrates this increased level of coordination. Some of its key features are: (1) the exchange of documentation among donors; (2) the participation of bilateral donors on selected World Bank missions; (3) regular biannual multidonor meetings as well as special meetings on individual countries and issues; and (4) work on standard procurement and disbursement procedures.

It is difficult to gauge the effect that aid coordination efforts have had on aid effectiveness. The foregoing discussion points to a number of general conclusions, namely, that the absence of aid coordination can seriously reduce the benefits of development assistance efforts; that the experience with aid coordination efforts has been mixed, and in some cases the efforts have been judged to have been of limited value; and that increased importance has recently been attached to improved coordination by both donors and recipients. Whether this focus on coordination is sustainable and whether it can overcome the resistance of both donors and recipients to move beyond the exchange of information to the effective coordination of programs and efforts to increase the development impact of donor assistance remains to be seen.[6]

Part Three

SECTOR ASSISTANCE

7

The Impact of Development Assistance: A Review of the Quantitative Evidence

CONSTANTINE MICHALOPOULOS AND VASANT SUKHATME

The economic impact of development assistance can be assessed at both the microeconomic and the macroeconomic level. At the microeconomic level the contribution of aid can be assessed by examining the rate of economic return of individual activities, usually specific projects, such as the building of a multipurpose dam or a highway financed by aid. There have been a number of studies using this approach. By and large these evaluations have shown that average rates of return on multilateral assistance projects have been rather high (see below).

As noted in chapter 3, aid can affect macroeconomic growth in several ways. At the simplest level, aid represents foreign savings. If these savings are additional to domestic savings, and if they are channeled to domestic investment, then in the context of a simple model of capital accumulation aid has the potential to stimulate growth. Foreign aid also provides access to imports of goods and services. As a result, it has been argued, aid can promote growth if growth is subject to a foreign exchange constraint (see chapter 3). Most of the studies of the impact of aid on growth focus on these rather simple notions.

Aid, however, is typically a small portion of domestic capital formation, savings and other macroeconomic variables in most countries. Thus it cannot be expected to have a significant impact on growth (Harberger, 1972). The small size of aid relative to other macroeconomic aggregates, as well as conceptual and empirical shortcomings in many of the analyses, has contributed to many inconclusive findings about the relationship of aid to growth.

The purpose of this chapter is to summarize these findings of past research on the relationship of aid to economic performance both at the micro and at the macro level. First, some of the findings of project-based analyses of aid effectiveness are reviewed. Next, the evidence of the relationship of aid to domestic savings is analyzed. This is followed by a discussion of analyses of aid's contribution to growth in the context of a foreign exchange constraint. Subsequent sections focus on some additional broad linkages between aid, capital formation, productivity, and output growth. The final section draws some tentative conclusions about the current understanding of the aid-growth relationship and explores some possibly useful areas for further analysis.

Rates of Return of Aid Projects

Rate of return analyses have been commonly employed in analyzing the effectiveness of aid resources both in the appraisal phase of potential projects that are candidates for receiving assistance and in the evaluation of completed projects. Since most foreign assistance has been extended in support of specific projects, donors, especially the multilateral institutions, wish to assure themselves to the extent possible that the resources they provide are allocated to activities with a positive and substantial potential rate of return. The World Bank, for example, will not normally finance projects with an ex ante calculated rate of economic return of less than 10 percent. Similarly, ex post evaluations of aid have tended to focus on the rates of return of projects financed in part or in whole by aid institutions.

Past empirical analysis strongly suggests that projects financed through multilateral aid in developing countries generally have yielded high rates of economic returns. The simple average real rate of return on the projects financed by IBRD loans in the 1960–80 period has been estimated to be 17 percent. Those undertaken through IDA credits show an 18 percent simple average rate of return. The weighted average rate of return on projects financed by IDA credits has been higher, about 21 percent (World Bank, 1982a). One possible explanation why larger projects have, on average, higher rates of return is that many smaller projects involve innovative or experimental activities. Typically, undertaking smaller projects involves greater risk, and their rates of return show greater variation and are smaller on average.

Other multilateral agencies have had similar experience with their projects. The Asian Development Bank (1984) reports that 97 out of 139 projects financed through its resources were generally successful in achieving their aims, and the remainder partially so. Projects financed by the Inter-American Development Bank (1982 and 1983) have had similar results.[1] Since the bulk of assistance from these institutions over the periods evaluated has been in the form of projects, it could be argued that the activities supported by assistance from these institutions have made a positive direct contribution to the recipients' development.

Less is known about the projects financed by bilateral donors. About 30 percent of such assistance consists of nonproject aid, and there have been fewer systematic evaluations of rates of return by projects financed by bilateral donors (see table 6.2).

A study by Peterson (1983) also examined the marginal rates of return on development assistance contributed by multilateral aid agencies, the

OECD, and centrally planned economies. He used a production function approach to estimate marginal rates of return on development assistance capital based on cross-sectional data for seventy-seven developing countries over the 1961–77 period. The capital stock data were divided into three components: capital financed from domestic resources, capital transferred from market economies and multilateral agencies, and capital transferred from centrally planned economies. The various land variables and the environmental variables were shown to be relatively unimportant in explaining total or per capita GNP growth. What was important was reproducible capital—both human and physical. Peterson computed a 56 percent marginal rate of return on capital acquired from market economies and multilateral agencies and a 15 percent marginal rate of return on capital financed out of domestic resources. In striking contrast, the rate of return on capital contributed by centrally planned economies was estimated to be negative.

It is tempting to use the results of these analyses of rates of return on projects, especially those financed by multilateral assistance, to support the conclusion that economic assistance has been successful in promoting economic growth in the recipient countries. Such a conclusion is not always valid. Project evaluations, ex ante or ex post, represent partial equilibrium analyses, based on the assumption that projects do not substantially affect behavior in the rest of the economy. Such an assumption may not be warranted. Moreover, rate of return analyses usually do not take into account externalities, both positive and negative, which may have important effects on overall development. Positive learning-by-doing effects of foreign aid projects on developing countries' human resources cannot be evaluated through this approach either. Finally, foreign-financed projects may have higher rates of return on average; but they might have been undertaken in any case, and foreign aid might simply have permitted the undertaking of other activities with much lower rates of return. Thus for a variety of reasons, it is desirable to explore the impact of aid in a wider setting.

Development Assistance and Savings

A number of writers examined the link between aid and savings by considering savings functions of the form $S = f(Y,F)$, where S = domestic savings, Y = gross national product, and F = foreign capital inflows. Then, using cross-sectional data from a number of countries, a regression equation relating Y and F to S is estimated using ordinary least squares.

The results of early cross-country regression analyses were conflicting (see table 7.1). They showed that a dollar of capital inflow in the early 1960s may have "led" to anywhere between a reduction of \$0.82 and a marginal increase in domestic savings. Areskoug (1969) and Griffin and Enos (1970) argued that foreign assistance contributed little, if anything, to economic

Table 7.1. Results of Cross-Country Regressions of Domestic Savings on GNP, Capital Inflows, and Exports of Developing Countries

Study	Number of Countries	Dependent Variable	Constant (K)	GNP (Y)	Capital Inflow (F)	F/Y	Exports (X)	R^2
Griffin, 1962–64[a]	32	S/Y	11.2			−0.73 (0.11)		0.54
Griffin, 1962–64[a]	13[b]	S/Y	16.1			−0.82 (0.52)		0.71
Griffin, 1960[a]	18[c]	S		0.1716 (0.005)	−0.6702 (0.204)			0.75
Weisskopf, 1957–63	17[d]	S		0.183 (65.9)	−0.227 (−5.3)		0.176 (4.6)	—
Rahman, 1962	31	S/Y	0.1427			−0.2473 (2.568)		—
Gupta, 1962	50	S/Y	0.1108 (0.0088)			0.0310 (0.0804)		0.06

Sources: M. Anisur Rahman, "Foreign Capital and Domestic Savings: A Text of Haavelmo's Hypothesis with Cross Country Data," *Review of Economics and Statistics* 50 (1968): 137–38; Keith L. Griffin, "Foreign Capital, Domestic Savings and Economic Development," *Bulletin of the Oxford University Institute of Economics and Statistics* 32 (May 1970): 99–112; Kanhaiya L. Gupta, "Foreign Capital and Domestic Savings: A Test of Haavelmo's Hypothesis with Cross-Country Data: A Comment," *Review of Economics and Statistics* 52 (May 1970): 214–16; Thomas E. Weisskopf, "The Impact of Foreign Capital Inflow on Domestic Savings in Underdeveloped Countries," *Journal of International Economics* 2 (February 1972): 25–38.

[a] Griffin does not specify whether the figures in parentheses are t-statistics or whether they are significantly different from zero.
[b] All in Asia.
[c] All in Latin America.
[d] A pooled sample.

growth and domestic savings. Griffin and Enos, on the basis of cross-sectoral evidence from fifteen countries in Latin America for the 1957–64 period, concluded that "the general tendency is that the greater the capital inflows from abroad, the lower the rate of growth of the receiving country" (Griffin and Enos, 1970, p. 318). Their explanation was that governments receiving aid often refrain from raising taxes but expand consumption after aid begins, and so do private entrepreneurs who receive loans from abroad (Griffin and Enos, 1970, p. 321). As a result, there is a decrease in domestic savings as a percentage of GNP. Similar conclusions were reached by Weisskopf (1972a and 1972b) using a two-gap model for seventeen developing countries. On the other hand, Gupta, in a cross-sectional study of fifty developing countries (1970), found no relationship between capital inflows and domestic savings.

Differences in the samples of countries examined caused substantial differences in the estimated coefficients, suggesting that the capital inflow-savings relationship may be different in different countries or different policy regimes. According to the Chenery-Eckstein study of savings behavior in sixteen Latin American countries in the 1950–64 period (1970), for instance, a dollar of foreign trade deficit "led" to between a $1.15 reduction in domestic savings in Panama and a $0.64 increase in Bolivian domestic savings.[2] These studies had limited implications for assistance policy, since they did not identify the structural factors or the policy regimes that resulted in the large variation in savings impact.

Analyses of the capital inflow-savings relationship for the same country over time have provided somewhat greater insight into the factors involved. Pakistan's experience with foreign aid in the 1951–70 period, discussed by Islam (1972), throws some light on the apparent instability of capital inflow-savings or aid-savings relationships in developing countries. Essentially, Islam concludes that the major influences on the savings rate over time were institutional reforms, changes in the terms of trade, and the government's fiscal policy rather than the volume of aid.

In the end, what does all of this effort to relate aid to domestic savings truly mean? Some of the early results should not be taken seriously as evidence of the impact of aid on development. First, they suffer from conceptual problems. In terms of the national income accounting identities, savings is defined as the difference between national income and consumption. A capital inflow, whether in the form of aid or private flows associated with an import surplus, increases available resources and can be expected to add to both consumption and investment. But an increase in consumption with national income given would imply lower savings. Similarly, to the extent that aid goes proportionally more to low-income countries, which have lower domestic savings rates, an inverse relationship between aid and savings based on a cross-country statistical analysis may reflect nothing more than donor decisions to assist the more "needy" countries, or countries with poor economic performance. Thus it may not be surprising when a simple analysis of the relationship between aid and savings yields a negative relationship between the two (Halevi, 1976).

In light of these conceptual shortcomings, it is not surprising that other studies using similar techniques showed that the inverse association between capital inflow and domestic savings is not a peculiarity of the aid-recipient countries. In a cross-country regression estimate of a savings function from a sample of sixteen developed and fifty-four developing countries, Singh (1975) found an inverse and significant correlation between savings rates and capital inflows. This should not surprise observers of recent U.S. experience, in which large foreign borrowing has been accompanied by low domestic savings rates.

In any economy, if aggregate demand exceeds domestic output or, equivalently, domestic savings is less than investment, there will be a current account deficit. The causality, therefore, could run from the direction of the domestic economy to the current account deficit or surplus, rather than the other way around. In a situation where capital inflows and domestic savings are simultaneously determined, it is very difficult to assert that one "causes" the other. This point is illustrated by a statistical analysis undertaken by Over (1975) based on the earlier work by Griffin (1970).

Finally, a savings function must explain savings *behavior* by both the public and the private sector. None of the functions estimated in the 1970s explain savings behavior. The theoretical foundation of such functions is especially weak, since savings or investment is seen solely as an alternative to consumption rather than as a way of redistributing consumption in a temporal sense.

In addition to these conceptual problems, the early analyses used the current account deficit as a proxy for aid—clearly a poor substitute when other capital flows are present as they clearly were in many of the countries considered. In the case of India, in which Weisskopf (1972a and 1972b) found a negative and significant correlation between capital inflow and savings, and Bhagwati and Srinivasan (1975) found a negative but statistically insignificant association, Chaudhuri (1978) found a marginally significant positive correlation between foreign aid and domestic savings.

In summary, most of the analyses of the relationship between aid and savings based on cross-country or time series data are conceptually flawed, and the empirical results are weak and contradictory. In our view they do *not* suggest that aid as such systematically leads to declines in the domestic savings effort of recipients. Domestic macroeconomic policies will be the primary determinant of how a capital inflow and aid are absorbed. Statistically this will show up as differences in the savings rate—but this is an ex post observation that may have little to do with the impact of the inflow itself on the domestic savings rate. A variety of macroeconomic policies would need to be investigated in order to trace the effect of aid on domestic savings and overall economic growth. It is extremely difficult to design meaningful econometric indicators for such policies that can be tested through cross-country models. In any case, the effect of aid may be small, because while aid can be an important component of domestic capital formation in some countries over some periods, on average it has been quite small.

Development Assistance and the Foreign Exchange Constraint

Given the extensive attention paid to the role of aid in relieving a foreign exchange constraint, especially in the 1960s, very little empirical evidence exists to support the hypothesis that development assistance indeed plays such a role. There are various reasons why any empirical testing of the foreign exchange hypothesis will yield inconclusive results. First, the foreign exchange constraint concept is fundamentally a planning one (see Chenery and Strout, 1966). Ex post, there is equality in the observed foreign exchange and savings gaps. This makes it methodologically difficult to test hypotheses about the impact of foreign aid in relieving one constraint or the other, whichever may have existed ex ante.[3]

Second, there are some cases in which large inflows of aid, essentially of a program type, have occurred in response to a perceived need to shore up the very shaky balance of payments position of a country in which a donor has a special foreign policy interest. Sometimes this shoring up has been done through bilateral aid, but more recently it has been done in the context of multilateral assistance to highly indebted countries. It could be argued that in such cases, the influx of assistance either permitted the implementation of an adjustment program with positive long-term growth effects or enabled a recipient to avoid a significant domestic retrenchment that would have adversely affected growth. But because assistance of this kind is frequently extended to countries with low overall growth, any positive effect that aid may have had in averting a crisis does not show up in cross-country analyses. Also, where aid was extended, sometimes in massive amounts, in support of donors' noneconomic objectives but in the absence of good economic policies in the recipient country, it tended to have little impact on growth either in the short or the long term.

Perhaps because these reasons are well understood, few efforts attempt to isolate the foreign exchange dimension of economic assistance and relate it to country economic performance. The only empirical analysis that we have discovered is an old effort by Massell, Pearson, and Fitch (1972). Their analysis was not strictly an evaluation of the role of economic assistance in relieving a foreign exchange constraint as defined in chapter 3. Instead, they simply distinguished three components of foreign exchange: exports of goods and services, net public foreign capital inflows, and net private foreign capital inflows. Using both lagged and current values of these variables, they concluded that the three types of foreign exchange receipts had markedly different effects on annual gross fixed capital formation, GNP, and aggregate imports of goods and services. In terms of overall impact, private foreign capital inflows were judged to have the greatest impact on all three of the above indicators of development. Public foreign capital (most of which was foreign aid) resulted in a smaller net increase in imports and in investment and was "quite ineffective in stimulating GNP."

These results, as noted earlier, are not strictly a test of the foreign exchange constraint hypothesis. The study also suffers from some of the same shortcomings as the early studies of the relationship between aid and savings, namely, an absence of a clearly specified analytical framework within which the statistical relationships are explored. The lack of relationship between exports and GNP and other domestic variables is rather surprising in light of the strong relationship uncovered in other, similar studies of the issue (see Michalopoulos and Jay, 1973 and Balassa, 1978). Finally, the strong link between private flows and GNP, in contrast to the absence of a link between public flows and GNP, may be due to the sample. Several countries in the sample were receiving significant amounts of foreign aid to shore up shaky balance of payments positions; a number of others did not rely much on aid but, because of their strong economic performance, were able to attract significant private capital inflows, which in that period were primarily in the form of direct private investment. Thus the direction of causality could again be in question. It is not necessarily true that private flows result in good performance; rather, strong economic performance attracts more private capital, while aid is sometimes used to bail out bad performers.

On balance, the obvious and hence popular links between foreign aid, foreign exchange availability, and economic development are difficult to demonstrate and indeed may not exist in many cases. In most countries, the size of economic assistance is small relative to foreign exchange availability; the countries' own policies are more important than aid in determining their balance of payments situation. In the light of all these difficulties, it would seem that other lines of inquiry that do not focus on the foreign exchange dimension may be more effective in gauging the impact of economic assistance on development.

Development Assistance, Capital Formation, and Growth

Paralleling the analyses of aid in the context of savings and foreign exchange constraints, another series of studies, similar in conception, has been undertaken that attempts to relate aid to capital formation and output growth in developing countries. Two sets of analyses can be distinguished: first, simple investigations that implicitly assume that if a positive relationship between aid and capital formation is found, aid can be presumed to make a positive contribution to growth; and second, broader studies in which output growth is related to capital formation, from domestic and foreign savings, as well as other variables, such as labor, export growth, and so on, in various combinations of cross-country and time-series analyses.[4]

Studies by Heller (1975) and Halevi (1976) are characteristic of the first set of analyses. In an econometric study of public fiscal behavior in eleven aid-recipient African countries in the 1960s, Heller found that on average $1.00 of official loans increased investment by $1.39.[5] Halevi examined the relationship between long-term capital inflow in the aggregate and in its components, private and public investment and consumption, for forty-four countries also in the late 1960s. When all variables were expressed in per capita terms, he found a positive and significant relationship between long-term capital in the aggregate and private and public capital inflows and investment. He also found that long-term capital was positively related to public consumption. He concluded that there was a significant link between long-term capital inflow, investment, and growth but that clearly such capital inflow also tended to increase public consumption.

It is useful to recall in this connection that while in national account terms aid and other foreign capital inflows are treated as additive to domestic savings, a good deal of aid is indeed provided with the intention of raising consumption, public or private. In a more recent cross-country study of the aid-investment relationship, Lavy (1985) argued that foreign aid falls into two general categories. A part of foreign aid is more unanticipated, transitory and of a "relief" nature, such as drought-related food transfers, medical and refugee relief, and balance of payments crisis support, which can be considered to augment consumption. The second category of aid is intended for development purposes, is more permanent, and is anticipated from previously negotiated commitments by donors. Using a cross-country estimate, he concluded that most anticipated foreign transfers tend to be invested.

Most studies in the second set of analyses examine the direct impact of capital inflows and aid on developing countries' growth in the context of a neoclassical framework, with growth in capital and labor inputs explaining output growth. However, they disaggregate between domestic and imported capital and other variables that aim to capture other aspects of developing country performance, especially those indicative of efficiency in resource allocation. The basic equation used in such models is $Y = f(K_d, K_f, L)$.

Michalopoulos and Jay (1973) showed in the context of such a model that labor inputs (L), foreign capital inflow (K_f), and capital formation from domestic savings (K_d) were positively related to output growth (Y) using cross-country analyses for thirty-nine developing countries in the 1960s. They also showed that the growth of exports was an important additional explanatory variable of GNP growth, even after the effects of labor and capital inputs were considered; they attributed this to the overall economic efficiency of countries with good export performance. These results were subsequently confirmed and extended by Balassa (1978) to cover a different range of countries and later periods. In both cases the indications were that the effect of capital inflow on output growth, while positive, was small, indeed smaller than the impact of domestic savings.

These results are similar to Papanek's (1973b) findings. He also used cross-country analyses to examine the relationship between GNP growth and aid, other capital inflows, and domestic savings. His analysis did not include labor inputs or other "efficiency" indicators; on the other hand, he distinguished between aid and other capital inflows. His conclusions were that savings and foreign inflows explained about one-third of GDP growth in his sample of Asian, African, and Latin American countries. Some interesting regional differences in the estimated equations were also observed. For example, "savings and foreign inflows, and especially aid, have the most unequivocal impact on growth in Asia and the Mediterranean countries . . . coefficients are distinctly lower for the Americas and barely significant" (Papanek, 1973a, p. 123).

Finally, in a survey article, Mosley (1980) attempted to determine whether the relationship between foreign aid inflows, income, and savings estimated using 1960s or earlier data would hold over different samples and different time periods, as well as whether a lag structure would improve the results. Using data from the 1970s, he estimated by two-stage least squares a model of lagged response of GNP to aid for a sample of less developed countries stratified by income level. The coefficients of determination for the equations where growth of GNP is the dependent variable were generally very low. Only "between 4 and 25 percent of growth in LDCs in the 1970's is explained by domestic savings and capital flows from abroad." "This poor explanatory performance is not surprising," he added, "given the number of other variables that can influence growth . . . but it does suggest that the investment/GDP ratio, once seen as an *over-ridingly* important determinant of growth in LDCs, must no longer be seen in this way" (Mosley, 1980, p. 82, emphasis in the original).

In a more recent investigation (Mosley, Hudson, and Harrell, 1987) using a cross-country specification reminiscent of those by Balassa (1978) and Michalopoulos and Jay (1973), no significant statistical relationship was found between GNP growth and aid as a percentage of GNP. There was little improvement in the results when various subgroups of developing countries or various subperiods were used. A positive relationship (statistically significant only at the 5 percent level) was shown for Asia in the 1970s and early

1980s, while a *negative* relationship for all developing countries was present in the 1960s.[6] Like the previous analysts, Mosley, Hudson, and Harrell found that export growth was the only factor that seemed to be consistently strongly correlated with developing country performance.

Productivity Growth and Policy Reform

The weakness of the results on the link between aid and growth obtained through cross-country analyses reflects the weakness of both the concepts and the data utilized, as well as the fact that aid in many cases is a small proportion of investment. An important additional reason for these weak results has been that the methodologies employed to examine the aid-growth relationship have been inadequate. Their inadequacy arises from their focus on a narrow range of characteristics of economic assistance, especially its role in augmenting savings, investment, and foreign exchange availability, a range that omits some important dimensions of aid that in theory could have significant effects on growth.

Two of these appear in principle to be of potential significance: aid's impact in raising total factor productivity, as well as its role as a catalyst in promoting policy change that leads to greater efficiency and growth. Growth in factor inputs typically explains only a small portion of many developing countries' growth. Improvements in factor productivity in many cases have been shown to play an even more significant role in promoting growth (Chenery, Robinson, and Syrquin, 1986).

Aid programs can and do aim to improve the recipient's factor productivity through the introduction and spread of new technology, through training, and through managerial and other improvements. Aid, of course, can also support or promote policies leading to inefficient resource allocation, with adverse effects on productivity.

In the past, analyses of aid have tended to treat all forms of aid as one and to treat all aid as capital inputs. In a sense, aid is that. But that treatment does not capture the effects of aid on productivity growth, and thus there is a presumption that on this count at least the benefits from aid have been underestimated. The important potential of aid in raising factor productivity was recognized in the recent study by Mikesell, Kilmarx, and Kramish (1983). They did not attempt to explore systematically the effect of assistance activities in raising productivity; to do this requires a disaggregation of aid by type.

Most aid programs consist partly of technical assistance efforts. The objectives of these activities are to raise productivity by introducing new, more productive technologies, training, and improvements in management, all of which can have an impact on improving productivity. While in theory these activities can have a significant positive impact on development, this impact is not readily measurable. This is in part because their effect is diffused among sectors, in part because they often are provided in the context of, or become a part of, a capital project.

There is substantial evidence that the technology transferred to developing countries through the technical assistance efforts of aid agencies in agriculture, especially in the introduction and spread of the high-yield varieties of wheat and rice, has greatly contributed to the rapid expansion of agricultural output (chapter 9). Similarly, recent information about the effects of the international effort to eradicate onchocerciasis suggests that this technical assistance activity can have significant long-term effects not only in improving health but also in raising the productivity of a significant portion of the population in Central and West Africa.[7] There are many such examples. However, there is a dearth of information systematically evaluating the effect of technical assistance activities in raising productivity in individual countries or in individual sectors across countries.

Training is another significant component of assistance programs. Economic returns to projects involving human resource development in developing countries typically have been shown to be quite high (Psacharopoulos, 1985). But there is limited information relating to the aggregate effect of training in raising productivity in the recipient nations.

It should be noted that some of the more vocal critics of aid implicitly suggest that aid has the effect of *reducing* rather than increasing productivity growth. The essence of one of Peter Bauer's (1968) main criticisms of aid practices is that aid has tended to strengthen the role of the public sector in development and to support public enterprises that have tended to be inefficient. Another argument has been that aid has tended to tilt the investment patterns of recipients toward sectors with long-term or lower payoffs (Griffin and Enos, 1970). This would also translate into reduced productivity growth.

There are, of course, many examples of individual public sector enterprises that are inefficient, some of which have been supported by aid agencies. The argument that aid activities directly result in lower rates of return does not stand up to systematic scrutiny, as shown, for example, by the IDA retrospective study (World Bank, 1982a).

In general, evidence about how aid promotes low efficiency and thereby lower productivity has not been compiled systematically. Nor has the evidence been analyzed with the objective of determining the effects that aid may have had in the same countries through technical assistance or through the introduction and spread of more productive technology, training, or other mechanisms that tended to raise factor productivity. It would appear that an important area of future inquiry on the impact of assistance should be its effects on productivity at the country level.

In addition to stimulating productivity growth directly, aid can also be a catalyst for improved policymaking that promotes growth of the recipient country; or it can provide the underpinning for the continuation of ineffective policies. Recipients' policies in turn may well be the most important factors differentiating good growth performance from bad (see chapter 4). Again, of course, this is a very difficult effect to quantify. In general, neither aid's contribution in raising total factor productivity nor its contribution to policy change is amenable to the simple cross-country or time-series analyses that have characterized investigations in this field.

The question of the catalytic effect of aid in promoting improved economic policies and more efficient allocation of resources lies at the heart of the controversy about its effectiveness in promoting growth. While there is unanimity on the preponderant role of developing country policies in determining growth, there is little agreement on whether aid practices have tended to play a positive or a negative role in promoting better economic policies and improved allocation of resources in recipient countries. On balance, World Bank experience in the 1980s suggests that aid has played a positive role: the economic performance of countries that received a number of adjustment loans which were conditioned on policy reforms, was on the whole better than the performance of countries which received no such loans—although the former faced substantially less favorable external conditions (World Bank, 1988a and World Bank and the UNDP, 1989).

Summary and Conclusions

Analyses of rates of return of projects financed by foreign assistance, in particular by multilateral institutions, provide clear evidence of aid effectiveness at the microeconomic level. This evidence, however, cannot be used to argue about aid effectiveness at the macroeconomic level. The cross-country evidence is ambiguous. At best it suggests that the macroeconomic impact of aid on growth has been positive but modest—a finding not unexpected given the relative importance of aid as a capital input in total savings and investment. This evidence is tainted by conceptual ambiguities and data shortcomings. On the other hand, there is certainly no systematic evidence that aid has been *detrimental* to growth.

The nature of aid's contribution depends on the nature of the aid provided. Most analyses suffer from the drawback of lumping all aid together, when it is well known that there are great differences between the potential impact of, for example, a road project, a loan in support of major policy reform, and a program of technical assistance designed to introduce a new technology. The lumping together of all types of aid has also focused attention on the role of aid as a capital input. This tendency has resulted in neglecting to evaluate aid's impact on raising productivity and, as such, has possibly led to a general underestimate of the positive effects of aid.

Finally, whether a country takes advantage of the potential that aid in its many dimensions offers clearly is a function of a country's own economic policies, as well as the limitations imposed by donor policies. Both the economic policies and the donor-recipient relationship are country-specific and can best be examined in a single-country context. It is only through intensive analysis of these issues that further insights on the macroeconomic effects of aid are likely to be developed.

8

Assistance for Infrastructure Development

CONSTANTINE MICHALOPOULOS

In the past three decades a significant portion of economic assistance to the developing world has concentrated on physical infrastructure, primarily transportation, power generation, and distribution, as well as irrigation and telecommunication. This emphasis was much greater in earlier periods. For example, roughly 75 percent of World Bank lending between 1946 and 1961 was for transportation and electric power generation; however, the proportion of World Bank lending to infrastructure fell to about 32 percent in 1985.

Emphasis on Infrastructure Development

The reasons for the earlier emphasis on infrastructure development can be found in a combination of theoretical perceptions about the development process and pragmatic aspects of international development cooperation and administration. On the theoretical side, it was thought that the absence of transportation, power, and other infrastructure was an important barrier to economic development for a variety of reasons: (1) a certain minimum of infrastructure is a precondition to any economic activity and essential to the transformation of subsistence economies to market economies; (2) infrastructure activities generate significant external economies and as such can provide stimulus to other economic production; (3) the presence of indivisibilities and scale economies in these activities made them attractive candidates for investment in the eyes of supporters of the "big push" doctrine, such as Rosenstein-Rodan.

Infrastructure activities were also considered appropriate targets of economic assistance by international donors. Since they were thought to require large amounts of capital for efficient operation, and in keeping with the early thinking about the role of capital in development (see chapter 2), it followed that external resources would be required to supplement those of the developing countries. Their import intensity made them attractive targets for international donors that normally financed only the import component of investment. And since they were usually in the public sector, it was easier for donors to obtain commitments on related local currency financing and subsequent maintenance.

The appropriate technology for the projects was thought to be available from international engineering and consulting firms, which could be relied upon to implement the projects efficiently. Finally, the projects appeared to lend themselves more readily to accurate economic calculation of their future costs and benefits.

The decline in the proportion of economic assistance devoted to infrastructure over time is owing to several factors. In the first instance, because a number of projects were financed, it was concluded that some of the developing countries' needs had been filled. Notwithstanding the significant infrastructure needs present in many parts of Africa and elsewhere, the developing world as a whole today has more developed infrastructure systems than thirty years ago. This is especially true of such sectors as multipurpose dams, railroad systems, or trunk roads. This is largely a result of the efforts of international donors. At the same time, the balance shifted because of changing perspectives about the nature of the development process and the priority to be attached to other sectors, for example, agriculture or human resource development. The balance shifted also because some problems arose in implementing projects, and there were resulting shifts in the nature of the infrastructure projects themselves. The lessons that can be drawn from this experience are outlined below.

LINKAGES TO OTHER SECTORS

The notion that infrastructure development would alone lead to expansion of economic activity was never seriously espoused in development practice. For example, aside from the historical experience in North America, which suggested that much infrastructure followed rather than preceded development, it was clear quite early that (1) a variety of other constraints (e.g., human capital, organization, technology) needed to be addressed simultaneously to stimulate the growth process; and (2) unless capital infrastructure was fully utilized, huge costs in capital—the very factor that was extremely scarce in developing countries—would be entailed.

The potential benefit of new infrastructure in stimulating development is undeniable. A US/AID evaluation showed that where new roads made transport possible for the first time, costs were greatly reduced. In one case, hauling prices were reduced by a factor of 15 (Anderson and Vandervoort, 1982). Similarly, new road projects substantially improved prices received by farmers and reduced prices paid for inputs such as fertilizer. Improved transport also permitted farmers to diversify cropping patterns to include more perishable cash crops and to increase the land area under cultivation. However, these improvements in agriculture would not have been as pronounced or even occurred at all in the absence of the complementary introduction of new technology through agricultural research and extension, the development of credit institutions, and the improved utilization of water resources.

Similar examples of linkages between other types of infrastructure projects and related productive activities can be listed. One of the key questions is the degree to which planning of sequences of investment decisions is necessary to maximize the efficiency of investment both in infrastructure and in related activities.

Complementarities put a premium on the design of integrated programs involving detailed sectoral plans of economic activities linked to the infrastructure projects. Over time the high expectations about the contributions of detailed planning to development have been tempered by two factors: (1) the realization that human resource limitations in developing countries place severe constraints on effective planning and (2) a greater appreciation of the importance of market signals in informing decisions about investment allocation. As a result, donors have tended to eschew the big, complex infrastructure projects or, where these have been undertaken (the Mahaweli project in Sri Lanka, for example), to phase activities so as to minimize capacity underutilization and to keep infrastructure development in step with expansion of other economic activity.

THE "BIG IS BEAUTIFUL" SYNDROME

The capital and import bias of infrastructure projects, especially in earlier periods, has been well documented (see Tendler, 1975). Imported components typically account for 60 percent of power project costs. Electric power generation, port facilities, railway systems, and trunk roads all tend to be subject to economies of scale over a significant range of output. They also tend to be capital-intensive. In earlier days of aid giving, distorted factor prices in developing countries that have tended to favor capital over labor combined with perverse incentives among donors and aid recipient administrators who have favored import-intensive and larger projects to produce a heavier emphasis on capital-intensive infrastructure than was warranted.

The capital-intensity bias and the size bias derive from a related set of factors: the technology developed by international engineering and consulting firms has usually been geared to factor proportions in developed countries and typically has been more capital-intensive than appropriate in a developing country context. Its incompatibility frequently has been disguised, however, by factor price distortions in developing countries. The bias extends both to factor proportions used in the provision of the service and to the technology used in construction. Furthermore, there is an administrative bias in aid giving toward large projects; the effort of organizing, obtaining the necessary internal approvals, and overseeing the implementation of a single $100 million power project is much smaller than the comparable effort required to fund ten $10 million projects.

The market distortions in developing countries and their impact on import-intensive development were discussed in chapter 4. On the donor side, as noted in chapter 5, aid regulations have frequently limited donors' contributions and financing solely to the import component of specific projects. Thus, for very different reasons, there has also been a coincidence of forces that has tended to bias project design toward import intensity in all projects and has been of considerable importance in infrastructure projects.

Over time these problems have received increased attention from the donor community and the developing countries. While some of the biases are still present, there have been considerable changes in the nature of donor assistance to infrastructure. The changes have moved projects in two broad directions: project modes that are less capital-intensive and more divisible have been given greater preference; and efforts have been made to adopt more labor-intensive techniques, especially in construction.

The shift to less capital-intensive and more divisible modes is manifested in (1) the reduction of the share of railway transport relative to roads in general (from 50 percent through 1961 to 6 percent in 1962); (2) the increase in the share of rural feeder roads relative to main arteries (for example, in 1975–77 the former represented 93 percent of the mileage built with World Bank assistance, compared with 38 percent in 1965); (3) greater emphasis on irrigation in secondary and tertiary canal building and water management and conservation as compared with headworks construction; and (4) experimental work in the development of mini-hydro projects and alternative sources of renewable energy.

The question of adapting and using more labor-intensive technology in construction has attracted considerable attention, especially in road transport projects. The possibility of labor substitution in other types of infrastructure, for example, power generation, has appeared to be quite limited, however. Labor-based construction methods can save costs of road building as well as help relieve the employment problem in developing countries. Starting in 1971, the World Bank initiated a research and application program for labor-based construction of civil works, especially roads in a number of countries, including, Kenya, Honduras, Chad, and Lesotho. The main conclusion of this effort is that labor-intensive methods are both technically feasible and economically justifiable for many construction activities. Its economic justification is affected by a variety of factors, including wage levels and technical specification, but a determining factor often is the attitude of a country's political and technical leadership toward labor-intensive technology (World Bank, 1978).

Though local conditions vary widely, the World Bank estimated in the 1970s that the general range for a wage below which highly labor-intensive techniques save money is $2.50 a day, and between $2.50 and $4.50 when a mix of labor and equipment emphasis is called for (Tendler, 1979a, pp. 1–2). US/AID projects in Kenya and Colombia that used such techniques were considered successful (Anderson and Vandervoort, 1982, p. 9). Even where some intermediate or mixed technology may be more appropriate to urban and arterial roads, labor-based construction is clearly appropriate to rural roads, partly because they are less likely to be paved and because they are shorter and thus more suitable for piecemeal and decentralized methods.

Cost savings are often offset by other factors. A US/AID summary evaluation reported four projects that had aimed to use labor-based methods, but two of these were scrapped when the high cost of maintaining schedules became evident. The delays were caused primarily by a lack of time and manpower needed to organize and supervise unskilled workers.

Equipment-intensive arterial projects are administratively "clean," that is, they usually are managed by a single contractor and cohere in space and time. Overhead on labor-intensive projects consists more often of training and supervision than of equipment. Many work teams or small contractors are likely to be involved, and schedules follow seasonal availability of labor rather than time costs of idle equipment (Tendler, 1979a). High use of staff from the development agency is considered a source of delay in changing to labor-using methods (Anderson and Vandervoort, 1982, p. 9). This is a general issue not limited to aid-financed activities. In a general analysis of labor-saving technology in Indonesia, Timmer found the constraint on staff time in the recipient government to be a source of bias toward capital-intensive projects whether or not aid was involved (Timmer, 1975).

Paved roads, usually technology- and capital-intensive, are not just administratively clean; they are technically clean as well. They are easier to maintain than unpaved roads, and they can generally accommodate any kind of traffic that might want to use them. The standards of curvature, gradients, alignment, and so on, by which they are built are often important for reasons of safety and vehicle operating costs.

When feeder roads are upgraded, the job is easier if they were originally built to standards appropriate to paved roads, but without the paving. Effort may be duplicated if they must be "rebuilt" when the time comes to pave them. In the case of the Tanzam penetration road, an estimated $2 million out of a total of $5 million in paving costs could have been saved by paving the road as it was built rather than later. However, even in a case of such "clear" savings, discounting future costs and benefits may lead to the conclusion that if the improvement is not needed now, the extra expense is not justified. In the Tanzam example, if the paving had been delayed by just three years and the discount rate were 15 percent, the eventual cost would have been less than the cost of the improvement.

Sometimes the stigma of low standards is attached to labor-intensive construction, whether donor-financed or local, since contractors, engineers, and—not incidentally—administrators inevitably will be more familiar with the equipment-using methods. The goal of fostering labor-intensive construction can thus become a task in institution building when capital-intensive methods are entrenched. New personnel may have to reach decision-making levels, and political support may need to be developed.[1] Tendler suggests that donors seek out institutional environments more compatible with the goals and means represented by labor-based technologies. "All the persuasion and technical assistance of donor organizations dedicated toward the adoption of labor-based techniques will count for little if there are no forces in the institutional environment which also dictate that approach" (Tendler, 1979a, p. 43).

It may be a good idea to turn to local entities, many of which are already familiar with labor-intensive methods and less exacting standards. This approach would also have the advantage of mobilizing local participation and local decision making, which could provide greater motivation, especially for much-needed future maintenance work. Or the responsibility can go to some national agency with nontechnical priorities. In either case, a new administrative apparatus may need to be developed, requiring many lessons and procedures to be relearned.

Postconstruction Issues

Problems of appropriate technology, design, and implementation in infrastructure projects are frequently overshadowed by issues that arise after the projects have been completed. The main difficulties arise in two areas that are in part interrelated: pricing of services and maintenance, and benefits to recipients.

PRICING

Several problems of pricing can be identified. First, there are problems of arbitrary pricing of services, resulting in prices that are usually too low to recover the cost of providing the service and cover the capital costs of the project as well. Second, there are problems of efficiency in resource allocation when countries consciously use pricing policies (especially of public utilities, including transport) to subsidize users either to stimulate a particular economic activity or to promote income distribution objectives. Third, there are general financial problems of institutions established with donor support whose low overall charges do not assure their financial viability. These problems spill over to the maintenance problems discussed below. They also have resulted in requests for supplementary donor assistance to shore up ailing institutions. Finally, there are technical issues surrounding the establishment of user charges for particular services in the context of rural settings.

Examples of inappropriate rates that have led utilities to financial difficulties abound. For example, in Uganda there were very strong debates within the Uganda Electric Board (UEB) when the World Bank required the UEB to raise its electric power rate in order to allow the UEB to meet its debt payments and achieve financial soundness. The Bank also required reforms to reveal the board's financial status accurately (Friedmann, Kalmanoff, and Meagher, 1966, p. 411).

In Latin America autonomous public corporations evolved, sometimes through donor pressure, to operate infrastructure and related sectors. "Such corporations have been favored because of their more businesslike attitudes and greater immunity from political pressure than regular government departments" (Friedmann, Kalmanoff, and Meagher, 1966, p. 439).

Public utilities are vulnerable to government regulation in times of rapid inflation, when the regulated sector may be a convenient place to hold down at least some price increases while the utilities' own operating costs are rising because of inflation. This was the case in Brazil, where the power company was foreign and so was particularly likely to draw fire. In other cases public corporations became convenient places to provide additional employment, irrespective of its effect on overall efficiency and costs.

Some glaring inefficiencies in differential pricing were demonstrated by the experience of railroads in the 1960s. In many developing countries the railroads had a monopoly on hauling and were used by the governments, to their advantage, for development and other political goals. Rate systems were often extremely distorted, and when competition from road transport became available, the traffic paying artificially high rates deserted, leaving the railroads with customers expecting the artificially low rates to continue. For political reasons, governments were often reluctant to remedy the rate distortions. Capital investments suffered, leading to further deterioration of the rail system and the seeking of additional assistance from international donors to shore it up.

The promotion of rural electrification and the importance of proper water management in rural areas have raised questions of metering and water charges. Disadvantages of electricity metering are its high cost and the utilities' weakness in the area of distribution. Flat rates, however, which are favored by developing countries, tend to result in an effective subsidy to the wealthier users by the poorer users, since the wealthier use more power. A possibility suggested by Tendler (1979b, pp. 7–9) is to base charges on appliances in the home or some other index that does not require constant monitoring.

The subsidization of rural enterprise by reducing electric rates is also controversial. The World Bank has opposed this practice on the grounds that the businesses affected spend only a small portion of their income on electricity and can afford to pay rates that cover costs (World Bank, 1975, pp. 27, 46). The World Bank also has opposed the use of declining block rates, especially in rural areas. It does, however, suggest pricing below average cost in the initial years of a project because as demand expands later, average cost will decrease, and the early below-cost pricing helps to promote usage during the first years of a project. Since costs are inevitably higher in less dense rural areas, prices should be higher there on average (World Bank, 1975, p. 52).

As a consequence of insufficient pricing and other practices, in the early 1980s a large number of public corporations in many developing countries faced mounting deficits, which contributed to the overall public sector fiscal deficits that characterized many developing countries during the period and especially those that were heavily indebted. For example, one study reported that "in Argentina, the 353 state-owned enterprises lose an estimated $2 billion annually and have borrowed about $11 billion of the country's $46 billion foreign debt; they are a root cause of the inflationary budget deficits. In Nigeria, by the beginning of the 1980s, there were around 70 non-commercial and 110 commercial federal public enterprises, many of which required extensive financial support to cover operating losses" (Choksi, 1986, pp. 8–9). The report goes on to argue that in these and other countries improved public enterprise performance in such sectors as railway, electric, and water utilities, port, and so on, should be an essential part of reforms aimed at restoring the growth momentum of these economies. Indeed, a number of World Bank structural and sectoral adjustment loans had been conditioned on such reforms (see chapter 6).

In recent periods, the World Bank and other international donors have generally stressed the importance of financial viability of all public enterprises, including public utilities providing infrastructure services. This means the introduction of user charges that cover both the fixed and the variable costs of the services provided. Whereas there has been general improvement in the practices of many developing countries as they relate to the financial viability of institutions providing infrastructure services, a lot remains to be done. Progress has been perhaps much more limited in the provision of irrigation services. Robert Repetto argued in a recent study that "financial discipline over investment decisions in public irrigation systems is structurally weak, farmer to international banker; because no party—except the general taxpayer—is seriously at risk. At the same time because rents are so large, the pressures for new investment (as opposed to efficient utilization or maintenance of existing resources) are strong" (Repetto, 1986, p. 21).

Repetto went on to argue that irrigation water is a saleable commodity and that segregation and measuring individual use is not so costly that water needs to be treated as a public good (p. 30). However, because of existing vested interests by farmers and public authorities, no effective systems of user charges have been implemented. As a consequence, there is a tendency both for overinvestment in new systems and for waste and inefficiencies in existing systems. Repetto also noted that some donors treat irrigation projects differently than other infrastructure. For example, US/AID does not demand that governments recover the capital costs of the project it helps finance. The World Bank, although it calls for recovery of capital costs attributable to irrigation, has not always insisted on user charges.

In summary, the current broader financial crisis facing many developing countries has brought greater attention to the question of efficiency in the use of the infrastructure investment that they have put in place—frequently with the assistance of external aid—and it has also raised questions about ways to improve both donor and recipient policies that have a direct bearing on the effectiveness of economic assistance provided in this sector.

MAINTENANCE

A related issue that impinges on the effectiveness of economic assistance to infrastructure is that of assuring proper maintenance of infrastructure projects once completed. This problem has been acute over the years, and impressions are that it is not improving significantly.

Typically, donors are loath to provide financing for maintenance or other recurrent costs over an extended period. While there is usually a provision for financing of some maintenance costs, there is a presumption that the recipient should pick up the financing of maintenance and other recurrent costs either upon completion of the project or after a specified period. This approach rests on the premise that this is the best way to assure the commitment of the aid recipient to the project. Donors also view financing recurrent costs in general and maintenance in particular as providing financing for current consumption rather than investment—something they like to avoid. Such financing also involves primarily local cost financing, which for a variety of reasons not all donors are willing to provide (see chapter 5).

On the recipient side, provision of maintenance funding is usually inadequate, notwithstanding commitments to donors. In cases where user charges can be used to defray costs, charges are frequently too low and thus put a squeeze on maintenance services; in cases where user charges are not readily feasible, funding from general revenues cannot be obtained because tax revenues are usually scarce and maintenance costs are given lower priority than construction costs. There are several hypotheses as to why maintenance is given lower priority than construction in developing country resource allocation although the benefit-cost ratio in such activities is often very high. First, new construction in general, and construction of roads in particular, is politically more attractive. Second, it appears that construction represents more technically challenging and interesting tasks for highway department officials and engineers.

As a consequence of both recipient and donor policies, infrastructure maintenance in many developing countries is in dire straits. The primary effect is the poor state of repair of many of the roads built with international assistance only a few years earlier. This is a frequent observation in evaluations and a usual complaint of communities in the areas served by the projects.

The secondary effects of poor maintenance vary. Sometimes aid recipients are led to "overbuild," paving roads before traffic warrants it because paved roads require less maintenance. And when they do deteriorate and begin causing problems, paved roads must often be "rebuilt," offering the chance to appeal for capital assistance and satisfying the bias of highway departments toward construction activity. On the other hand, underbuilding has also been a problem, perhaps traceable to the same roots. In a desire to maximize construction given available funding, developing countries may build many substandard roads and let those that turn out not to be useful simply fall apart. The inadequacies of those that are used can be justified politically for improvement—a construction activity (Tendler, 1979a, pp. 48, 50–51).

Donors have not yet found an answer to the maintenance problem. Perhaps the answer lies in finding institutional linkages that will tie maintenance to construction. In the case of road building, one way to do this is to have the community that benefits from a road be responsible and empowered for maintaining it. If the community also helps with construction, the skills needed to maintain it, as well as a sense of responsibility for it, can be fostered at the same time. Or a person who lives along the road may be put in charge of maintenance, given simple tools, and paid a monthly fee after verification that maintenance work is done. This "line-man" system was used in the past in presently developed countries.

Other policy recommendations (e.g., by US/AID) include making outside financing contingent on the country's maintenance of the project. The host country's maintenance capabilities would be increased by (1) including agencies clearly responsible for maintenance in the planning and evaluation processes, (2) including maintenance as a topic in the planning and evaluation processes, and (3) promoting increased community involvement (Anderson and Vandervoort, 1982, pp. 46–48).

In addition, it is clear that a lack of donor coordination in financing capital projects exacerbates the problem. A variety of donors in several African countries have agreed to undertake capital projects, each with an allegedly strong commitment by the recipient to finance recurrent costs upon the project's completion. In many cases, the total recipient commitments are so large as to exceed any likely available revenues either through user charges or through general public revenues to the recipient government. There is a need for a coordinated look at the balance between capital and noncapital assistance in individual countries in order to prevent significant deterioration of the infrastructure being put in place a few years hence.

The Distribution of Benefits

The relative capital intensity of many donor-financed infrastructure activities has made it quite clear that with some exceptions, such as the impact on agricultural production, infrastructure construction and the provision of services are of limited value in directly raising employment and labor incomes. Thus the direct impact of such investment in raising the standard of living of the poor, whose main income-generating asset is their own labor, is likely to be limited. Their benefits are expected to result indirectly from the economic activity stimulated by infrastructure investment. For example, the building of a dam is expected to stimulate increased agricultural production and rural incomes through irrigation. The construction of a road would decrease transport time to marketplaces, permit the expansion of perishable cash crop sales, and result in similar increases in agricultural incomes. In addition, some explicit efforts have been made over the years to improve the standard of living of the rural poor through rural public works and rural electrification programs.

In the 1970s, concerns were raised in developing countries and among donors that the benefits of growth in many developing countries were not spread widely and that limited progress was being made in addressing the basic needs of the poor. These concerns focused frequently on the distribution of the indirect benefits resulting from infrastructure projects. Results of recent evaluations on the impact of roads and rural public works and rural electrification that shed some light on this issue are discussed below. One consequence of these more recent evaluations is a more favorable perspective on the income distribution effects of rural infrastructure (Ahmed, 1988).

ROADS

Rural roads reflect the bulk of recent road building efforts by donors. Their construction is more labor-intensive, and to the extent that rural communities tend on the average to have lower incomes than urban centers, there may be a presumption that these roads tend on the whole to have a stronger direct positive effect on the poor than previous donor efforts focusing on major arterial construction. However, this is only a judgment, since there is no empirical evidence in support of it, especially evidence that evaluates the effects of major urban transport networks on farm income or on urban job creation.

The key issue that has been raised about rural roads is the extent to which the relatively better-off farmers capture a disproportionate share of the economic benefits of such transport because of their position in the local power structure and their better access to complementary inputs. The distributional impacts of several US/AID road projects generally depended on many other factors, such as land tenure and simultaneous government efforts to spread modern agricultural technology (Anderson and Vandervoort, 1982). The poor benefited from rural roads, but unless the communities reached by the roads had secure and stable land tenure, the well-off benefited more. In Honduras the roads were part of a package including land reform, cooperatives, agricultural services, and credit, and small farmers were the main beneficiaries. Similarly, the roads permitted better access to health care and increased the willingness of teachers to work in rural areas, thus resulting in direct benefits to the poor.

The analysis by Anderson and Vandervoort (1982) showed, however, that some compensatory effort may be required to keep projects from increasing income inequality. More affluent farmers are more able to take advantage of opportunities by changing more rapidly to the more advanced technologies, purchasing complementary inputs, and acquiring information, because (a) they are not as constrained by cash requirements and are perceived as more creditworthy and (b) they frequently exercise considerable control over local or central government administration.

Women benefited along with men from increased mobility. They may also have gained more freedom owing to access to the modern amenities. In Liberia, however, improved income opportunities at major resource centers drew men from their families, and increased cash cropping drove subsistence farming, often done by women, back from the roads into the bush.

Roads were universally seen as beneficial even by people displaced by subsequent results. This favorable view is easy to understand: immediately after road construction come more visitors, new things to buy, broadened opportunities, more exciting weekly markets, and, often, rising agricultural income. The harmful effects, such as accelerated deforestation and lower nutrition, often follow more slowly and are harder to connect to the roads; and roads symbolize development and progress to most people (Anderson and Vandervoort, 1982).

RURAL ELECTRIFICATION

The benefits of electrification are already largely available to urban consumers in developing countries. Projects in the past helped to provide the capacity to meet growing demand or to overcome shortages. In addition, there was considerable effort to increase rural electrification. Various rural electrification projects placed emphasis on different goals; some emphasized household consumer benefits, while others concentrated on stimulating economic activities (World Bank, 1975; Tendler, 1979b, p. 4).

US/AID programs, for example, focused to a greater extent than the World Bank on household consumer benefits. This orientation resulted mainly because US/AID's electrification projects were promoted and implemented largely by the National Rural Electric Cooperative Association (NRECA), which evolved its approach from experience with rural cooperatives in the United States in the 1930s. The consumer orientation was reinforced by the perceived success of the electrification of the countryside in the Philippines, a program that was intended to help the government resist subversive influences (Tendler, 1979b, pp. 4–5). It should be noted, however, that US/AID's evaluation of the Philippine project indicated that the expected economic benefits, even if realized (which they were not), would not alone have justified the project.

World Bank policy suggests that while some attention should be given to nonquantifiable benefits such as improvement in the quality of life, the benefits are likely to be less important in the case of electrification than in certain other sectors, such as water supply or education. Alternative sources of light and energy, though generally inferior, are available even in the poorest regions; thus electricity is not considered as much of a necessity as some of the other benefits.

Limited experience in some countries, for example, El Salvador, indicates that economic returns to rural electrification projects can be significant—with internal rates of return in excess of 10 percent. In this connection, it appears that village demand alone often is not sufficient to yield such a return. It is only when there are demands for farm uses and by agroprocessing industries that economic returns are substantial. This appears to be a critical factor in determining the economic returns of such projects.

RURAL PUBLIC WORKS

In an effort to promote more labor-intensive infrastructure development, several donors, including US/AID, have supported rural public works programs in a number of developing countries. Rural public works programs can be defined as public sector activities undertaken using labor-intensive techniques with two primary objectives: (1) generating new employment and income opportunities among low-income groups and (2) creating productive assets, usually in infrastructure.

Experience with such programs has been mixed. Thomas and Hook undertook an extensive review of developing country experiences in this area in a US/AID manual in 1977 (Thomas and Hook, 1977). They concluded that although rural works are useful means of alleviating unemployment and promoting rural development, they result in only temporary alleviation of these problems. Rural works can stimulate and augment agricultural and rural development programs, but they are not substitutes for them. Also, rural works programs can be more useful in some developing countries than in others.

The common characteristics of countries that have used works programs successfully are:

— High population density relative to arable land. Countries such as Indonesia, Bangladesh, and Korea have used these programs effectively, while in much of Africa and the Middle East population densities are too low for successful implementation of these programs.
— Agricultural dependence and instability of agricultural output. In Tunisia and Morocco rural works made a major contribution when carried out in the context of fragile economies and yearly fluctuations in grain output.
— Availability of administrative competence. Where administrative competence has been lacking, for example, in Afghanistan with its Provincial Development Program in 1971–72, programs have suffered from poor administration and low-quality projects.

Thomas and Hook suggest that in general, well-financed, effectively administered programs might succeed in absorbing up to approximately 10 percent of estimated rural unemployment (depending, of course, on the size of the program and the number of unemployed). Cost-benefit studies of rural works programs show that they can be productive in rigorous economic terms. They can also become inefficient, as a result of poor planning and implementation. Experience suggests that even though rural works programs generally are not capable of any major redistribution by themselves, they can have moderately redistributive effects in conjunction with other redistributive efforts.

Conclusion

In many developing countries aid has made significant contributions in helping create much needed infrastructure. In some countries, such as Korea and India, aid-assisted infrastructural development has led to the establishment of substantial national capacity to construct and manage infrastructure. This capacity has indeed permitted these countries to compete internationally and become exporters of engineering and construction services.

During the last decade numerous studies have documented the strong positive impact of rural infrastructure investment on both the level and distribution of income in rural areas. Part of the positive impact is due to the direct impact on agricultural production; part is due to the more efficient functioning of input and product markets; and part is due to the multiplier effects of the income generated both during the initial construction phase and later through the impact of agricultural production and marketing on the demand for labor.

Early problems with the use of inappropriate technology in aid-assisted infrastructure development have abated significantly in recent years. Despite recent progress, pricing problems however, continue in many countries. They are especially worrisome in the area of water charges because of the importance of effective water management for both agricultural development and environmental protection. Finally, maintenance issues continue to be of importance especially in Africa and require greater coordination between aid donors and recipients.

9

Assistance to Expand Agricultural Production

VERNON W. RUTTAN

Development assistance programs have made major investments in African, Asian, and South American countries with the objective of directly expanding agricultural production. The evidence that can be drawn from the literature on the effect of such investments is reviewed here.[1] Particular attention is given to land and water resource development, agricultural research, agricultural extension, land tenure reform, and agricultural credit markets. In addition, the implications of the macroeconomic sector policies pursued by the governments of developing countries to expand agricultural production and the efforts of donors to influence those policies are discussed.

Land and Water Resource Development

During the 1950s and 1960s, investment in land and water resource development was given a major claim on the budgets of many developing countries and apportioned a significant share of the investment portfolios of the bilateral and multilateral assistance agencies. A strong presumption in the development literature of that period was that investments in transportation, communication, power, irrigation, and related physical infrastructure were a necessary precondition for economic growth (chapters 2 and 8).

Since the early 1970s the assumptions underlying the concentration of investment in large infrastructure projects have been under continuous attack. The view that a short period of intensive investment in physical infrastructure and basic industries was a prerequisite to self-sustained growth was replaced by emphasis on human capital, institutional innovation, and policy reform (see chapter 2). Nevertheless, support for land and water resource development by assistance agencies expanded rapidly during the 1970s and is expected to rise even more rapidly during the 1985–2000 period (Cassen, 1986, pp. 124–28; Repetto, 1986).

Land and water resource development projects fall under three general headings: (*a*) irrigation, (*b*) new lands, and (*c*) intensification. A review of the aid experience in each area follows.

By the late 1960s the World Bank had participated in the financing of approximately fifty projects having a substantial irrigation component. The most dramatic were a series of "big dam" gravity irrigation projects, such as the Gezira scheme in Sudan; the Aswan High Dam in Egypt; the Indus Basin Project in Pakistan; the Lower Mekong River scheme, involving Thailand, Cambodia, Laos, and Vietnam; and the Bhakra Nagal project in India (Otten and Reutlinger, 1969).

The early experience with gravity irrigation projects was disappointing. Otten and Reutlinger's study of the eight ongoing irrigation projects in the late 1960s indicated that implementation took longer and was more extensive than originally anticipated (Otten and Reutlinger, 1969, pp. 5–6). By the mid-1960s it appeared to be increasingly difficult to find projects that met even the "soft" benefit-cost criteria employed by the multilateral and bilateral assistance agencies (Clark, 1967; President's Science Advisory Committee, 1967). Many completed projects were not generating sufficient benefits to cover even operating and maintenance costs (Small, Adriano, and Martin, 1986, p. 45).

More recent irrigation development evaluations suggest a somewhat more positive perspective than the earlier evaluations. In a number of countries, including Korea, India, Mexico, Pakistan, and Turkey, the big dam irrigation projects constructed in the 1950s and 1960s facilitated the rapid diffusion of the Green Revolution rice, wheat, and maize technology (Hertford, 1970a and 1970b; Traxler and Ruttan, 1986; chapters 12, 13, and 14). In Asia, it is estimated that irrigated land now under cultivation plus newly irrigated land will account for one- to two-thirds of the growth in agricultural production from 1985 to 2000 (Repetto, 1986, p. 3). World Bank evaluations of more recent irrigation projects have shown both low costs of employment generation and high rates of return (Cassen, 1986, p. 125).

A second area in which assistance agencies have been active has been the opening up of new lands for settlement. Such projects often have been conceived as a method to reduce the population pressure on older settled areas. In Peru, development of the interior areas on the eastern slope was undertaken to reduce the population pressure on the Andean highlands. In Indonesia, transmigration to the outer islands was undertaken to reduce the population pressure on Java. Such projects usually required the substantial commitment of aid for credit and technical assistance.

The experience with new settlement projects typically has been quite unsatisfactory. When a series of twenty-four new land development schemes carried out in Latin America during the 1950s and 1960s was analyzed, the author concluded: "Few spheres of economic development have a history or reputation for failure to match that of government sponsored colonization in humid topical zones" (Nelson, 1973, p. 265). The record was one of consistent discrepancy between initial projections and results and of grossly overestimated internal rates of return. In Africa, where land settlement projects frequently were coupled with tractor mechanization schemes, there was also a consistent record of failure (Eicher, et al., 1970). In spite of over three decades of experience, the most recent evaluations conclude that land settlement projects have been costly relative to the number of persons settled, continue to suffer from low productivity, and are often characterized by high rates of desertion (Oberai, 1988, p. xv). More recently, land settlement schemes have come under increasing scrutiny not only because of their poor economic performance but also for their environmental impact (World Commission on Environment and Development, 1987).

A third pattern of land and water resource development, the intensification of production on lands already being cultivated, has meant investment at the individual farm or local community level in land leveling, drainage, pump irrigation, and other improvements leading to more effective soil and water management. This pattern of development, which has emphasized improved productivity on lands already cultivated, has been relatively successful. A particularly interesting example is the rapid expansion of tube well irrigation in both East (Indian) and West (Pakistan) Punjab (Falcon and Gotsch, 1968). Initially, tube-well development proceeded less rapidly in East Punjab because of constraints on the drilling of tube wells in canal command areas. When these restraints were lifted and the policy was directed toward a system of coordinated ground water–surface water development, there was a rapid growth in the number of private tube wells. Falcon and Gotsch estimated that the additional water accounted for about half the increased output in West Punjab and more than one-third of the increase in crop output in East Punjab between 1953–54 and 1965–66.

Experience with attempts to achieve greater intensification on currently cultivated land offers some useful guidelines for land and water development to assistance agencies and national governments. One lesson is that the performance of public systems can be improved if incentives are built into the design of project management. When, for example, operation and maintenance revenues are returned directly to the irrigation agencies or to the water-user associations that purchase water in bulk, performance levels tend to improve. A second lesson is that greater efficiency in water use results with the introduction of an efficient area-based or volumetric pricing system that relates user costs to the cost of supplying the water (Bowen and Young, 1986).

The Indus Basin Project in Pakistan is a useful illustration of a development that involved the three elements discussed above: major infrastructure investment, new land development, and intensification of production. It also depended upon continued collaboration of the two major development assistance agencies, the World Bank and the US/AID. The realization of the potential for benefits to the project was delayed as a result of problems that had not been fully appreciated during the initial design and construction phases.[2]

The Bank played a major role in negotiating the treaty that settled the disputes between India and Pakistan over rights to Indus Basin waters. The treaty was followed with commitments by donors and the government of Pakistan of over $2.5 billion for construction of the project. It became apparent in the 1950s that these irrigation investments were not realizing the projected benefits. The irrigation infrastructure design and water management practices were oriented toward maximizing the area irrigated rather than toward achieving optimum crop yields through more intensive water application. Water loss through canal seepage and evaporation was excessive.

To correct the waterlogging and salinity problems, US/AID and the World Bank supported a number of major efforts to improve water management. The initial effort in the 1950s was a US/AID-sponsored Salinity Control and Reclamation Project (SCARP); it used large public tube wells to lower the ground water level by pumping water up and returning it to the surface canals.

By the early 1970s it was clear from the more accurate measurement of the sources of water loss that the SCARP approach was much less effective than early judgments had indicated. Even more water was being lost in the water delivery system than had been anticipated. These findings led to the support by US/AID of a major program to upgrade the quality of water delivery and to improve crop and water management practices. These efforts were quite successful: water losses were significantly reduced, cropping intensity increased, and crop yields were improved. Yet crop yields on irrigated land in Pakistan continue to remain low, even by Asian standards. Among the responsible factors appear to be the limited success in the development of replacement varieties of wheat and rice; the persistence of commodity market and land tenure institutions that dampen incentives to produce; the failure to develop efficient water pricing mechanisms; and the failure to invest in the education and health of the rural people.

During the 1970s a distinct shift occurred in land and water resource development efforts by the aid donors. They increased attention to efficiency and equity in project implementation and management and required more careful analysis of both the technical and the economic aspects of (*a*) the transmission of water to farmers' fields, (*b*) the allocation of water among farmers, and (*c*) the efficient on-farm use of water. For example, the World Bank's standard package for improving water delivery in India, which traditionally emphasized improvements in delivery structures, now shows greater concern for how the main systems are actually being managed (Wade, 1982, p. 171). A similar shift in emphasis has been made by US/AID. Several recent US/AID and World Bank irrigation evaluations have cited management as the major limitation on project effectiveness (Berry, Ford, and Hosier, 1980;

Steinberg et al., 1980; Benedict et al., 1982; Wade, 1982). Thus US/AID has placed greater emphasis on training for irrigation system managers and on more efficient performance of existing projects.

The importance of effective management for system efficiency is illustrated by US/AID project evaluation studies in Korea and Sudan. The Korean project was an attempt to achieve efficient and equitable delivery of water to farms in an intensively cultivated area (Steinberg et al., 1980; chapter 13). The following factors were important to the success of the project: (1) the project had available to it an effective Korean engineering and management staff; (2) the organization of institutions supplying inputs and services was effective; and (3) the farmers were organized into strong Farm Land Improvement Associations that were able to take responsibility for managing water distribution and collecting irrigation fees and, furthermore, to bring pressure to bear on their members for efficient water use and on system management for effective performance.

In contrast to the Korean project, the Rahad Project in Sudan exemplifies a project with many problems. It was undertaken to develop underutilized water resources and to extend intensive crop production into an area that had not been farmed intensively in order to expand the production of export crops. In 1982 farmers in the Rahad Project had just completed their fourth growing season; the record shows that cotton yields declined with each year and incomes were lower than those required to break even. Among the causes for the decline identified by the evaluation team were inadequate administration; labor shortages; highly mechanized production, which weakened the linkage between worker incentives and farm management decision making; and insufficient or inappropriate delivery of water (Benedict et al., 1982, pp. iii, 17, C-5).

The importance of effective farmer representation in planning and managing irrigation systems has been emphasized in recent literature (Small, 1982; Wade, 1982). When farmers did not get water in Rahad, they had no effective mechanism for dealing with the inefficient system management. In Korea, on the other hand, a strong farmer organization acted to reinforce effective management. Farmers' experiences contain valuable information that cannot be duplicated by expensive engineering personnel; furthermore, the opportunity cost of farmers' resources is less than that of civil service technical staff.

The response by assistance agencies and national governments to the poor performance of land and water development projects often has been attempts to strengthen design and construction performance and to improve project technology and management. These efforts are important, even though poor project performance frequently is due more to deficiencies in public policy that encourage rent seeking by contractors, project bureaucracy, and project clients (Repetto, 1986). Thus the solution to poor performance should have priority at the level of institutional innovation and reform, an area in which assistance agencies have not demonstrated great success.

Agricultural Research

The capacity to develop and manage agricultural technology is recognized as one of the most important variables accounting for differences in agricultural productivity among nations.[3] The returns to investment in land and water resource development typically are low unless it is accompanied by efforts to advance the technology of crop and livestock production. Countries that rely primarily on borrowed agricultural technology rarely develop the capacity to manage the borrowed technology in a manner capable of sustaining agricultural development.

Unfortunately, the location-specific nature of agricultural technology, particularly the biological and chemical technology required to sustain intensive crop and livestock production, was not widely recognized in the agricultural assistance programs of the 1950s. Support for improvement in agricultural production technology was dominated by an "extension," or "technology transfer," orientation.

THE EMERGENCE OF THE INTERNATIONAL INSTITUTE MODEL

Between the mid-1960s and the early 1970s the international research and training institute model emerged, in the perception of the international aid agencies, as the most effective way to organize the scientific capacity needed to generate technical change in agriculture in developing countries. The international institute model drew on the experience of two historic traditions: that of the great tropical research institutes, which played an important role in increasing the production of such export commodities as rubber, tea, sisal, and sugarcane; and that of the Rockefeller Foundation and the Ford Foundation in Mexico and the Philippines.

The complex of international agricultural research institutes evolved directly from two organizations: the International Rice Research Institute (IRRI) and the International Center for Improvement of Maize and Wheat (CIMMYT), established by the Rockefeller Foundation and the Ford Foundation in 1960 and 1966, respectively (see table 9.1).

During the late 1960s the two foundations collaborated again to establish the International Institute of Tropical Agriculture (IITA) in Ibadan, Nigeria, and the International Centre for Tropical Agriculture (CIAT) in Palmira (near Cali), Colombia. With these two new centers, it became apparent that the financial requirements of the system would soon exceed the capacity of the foundations. As a result, consultations among the Ford and Rockefeller foundations, the World Bank, the Food and Agriculture Organization, and the United Nations Development Program (UNDP) in 1969 and several informal

Table 9.1. The International Agricultural Research Institutes

Center	Location	Research	Coverage	Date of Initiation	Core Budget for 1988 (000,000)
IRRI (International Rice Research Institute)	Los Banos, Philippines	Rice under irrigation, multiple cropping systems; upland rice	Worldwide, special emphasis on Asia	1960	25.7
CIMMYT (International Center for the Improvement of Maize and Wheat)	El Batan, Mexico	Wheat (also triticale, barley); maize (also high-altitude sorghum)	Worldwide	1966	24.3
IITA (International Institute of Tropical Agriculture)	Ibadan, Nigeria	Farming systems: cereals (rice and maize as regional relay stations for IRRI and CIMMYT); grain legume (cowpeas, soybeans, lima beans); root and tuber crops (cassava, sweet potatoes, yams)	Worldwide in lowland tropics, special emphasis on Africa	1967	21.8
CIAT (International Centre for Tropical Agriculture)	Palmira, Colombia	Beef; cassava; field beans; swine (minor); maize and rice (regional relay stations to CIMMYT and IRRI)	Worldwide in lowland tropics, special emphasis on Latin America	1968	24.1
CIP (International Potato Centre)	Lima, Peru	Potatoes (for both tropical and temperate regions)	Worldwide, including linkages with developed countries	1971	15.3
WARDA (West African Rice Development Association)	Monrovia, Liberia	Regional cooperative effort in adaptive rice research among 13 nations with IITA and IRRI support	West Africa	1971	4.6

Center	Location	Research focus	Coverage	Year	Budget
ICRISAT (International Crops Research Institute for the Semi-Arid Tropics)	Hyderabad, India	Sorghum; pearl millet; pigeon peas; chickpeas; farming systems; groundnuts	Worldwide, special emphasis on dry, semiarid tropics, non-irrigated farming. Special relay stations in Africa under negotiation	1972	24.6
ILRAD (International Laboratory for Research on Animal Diseases)	Nairobi, Kenya	Trypanosoiasis; theileriasis	Mainly Africa	1973	13.1
IBPGR (International Board for Plant Genetic Resources)	FAO, Rome, Italy	Conservation of plant genetic material with special reference to crops of economic importance	Worldwide	1974	6.0
ILCA (International Livestock Center for Africa)	Addis Ababa, Ethiopia	Livestock production system	Major ecological regions in tropical zones of Africa	1974	17.4
IFPRI (International Food Policy Research Institute)	Washington, D.C.	Food policy	Worldwide	1975	8.3
ICARDA (International Centre for Agricultural Research in Dry Areas)	Lebanon; Syria	Crop and mixed farming systems research, with focus on sheep, barley, wheat, broad beans, and lentils	West Asia and North Africa, emphasis on the semiarid winter precipitation zone	1976	18.7
ISNAR (International Service for National Agricultural Research)	The Hague, Netherlands	Strengthening the capacity of national agricultural research programs	Worldwide	1980	6.5

Sources: John G. Crawford, "Development of the International Agricultural Research System," in *Resource Allocation and Productivity in National and International Agricultural Research,* ed. Thomas M. Arndt, Dana G. Dalrymple, and Vernon W. Ruttan (Minneapolis: University of Minnesota Press, 1977), pp. 282–83; and for 1988 budget data, the Secretariat for the Consultative Group on International Agricultural Research, World Bank, Washington, D.C.

meetings in January 1971 led to the formal organization in May 1971 of the Consultative Group on International Agricultural Research (CGIAR). The initial membership comprised the World Bank, FAO, and UNDP as sponsors, nine national governments, two regional banks, and three foundations. By the mid-1980s membership had grown to over forty.

The leadership of the Consultative Group is now centered at the World Bank, which provides the chairperson and the secretariat. Technical guidance is supplied by the Technical Advisory Committee (TAC), which was established by CGIAR. FAO provides the TAC secretariat. Technical matters, such as new institute initiatives and program changes at existing institutes, are referred to TAC for review before action by CGIAR. TAC develops draft policy statements on priorities within the system for CGIAR's consideration; it has the authority to initiate investigations and to suggest program changes to CGIAR. Since 1976, TAC has been charged with the responsibility to organize comprehensive quinquennial reviews of the programs of the several international research centers and with the periodic analysis of programs that have common elements, such as cropping systems or mechanization research. CGIAR-supported expenditures rose from only $34.5 million in 1974 to over $200 million in the mid-1980s.[4]

STRENGTHENING NATIONAL AGRICULTURAL RESEARCH SYSTEMS

By the mid-1970s it was clear that the productivity of the international agricultural research system was severely constrained by the limited research capacity of many national systems and that the adaptation and dissemination of the knowledge and technology generated at the international institutes was dependent on the development of effective national systems (Evenson, 1977).

The outreach programs of the international institutes, even when working through networks, such as those in international wheat research and the inter-Asian corn program, did not have the capacity to strengthen national systems. The regional commodity networks played an important role in enabling institutes to conduct research and to test materials and methods under diverse ecological conditions, but they could not assume a larger role without diverting effort from the institutes' research programs. By the mid-1980s only a few national systems (e.g., in India, Brazil, and the Philippines) had developed the managerial and professional capacity to effectively absorb, transmit, and adapt the knowledge and technology that were becoming available through the international institutes and developed countries' research systems and the stronger developing countries' institutions.

With the emergence of a consensus on the importance of strengthening national agricultural research systems, serious weaknesses have become apparent in the donor agencies' methods of supporting the development of national research systems and in the policies pursued by national governments to develop their national agricultural research systems. Among the problems are the following: (*a*) excessive investment in research facilities development relative to scientific staff; (*b*) excessive administrative burden, combined with inadequate identification of priorities; (*c*) experiment station location decisions based on political rather than scientific consideration; (*d*) lack of congruence between research resource allocation and economic importance of commodities in regions; and (*e*) cycles of development and erosion of capacity in a number of national systems (Ruttan, 1981 and 1986b).

RETURNS TO INVESTMENT IN AGRICULTURAL RESEARCH

The results of a large number of studies of the contribution of research to productivity growth from both developed and developing countries are shown in table 9.2. Some skepticism has been expressed about the results of the rate of return estimates. The presentation of the early hybrid corn and sorghum studies in the form of "external" rather than "internal" rate of return estimates resulted in considerable confusion in the interpretation of the estimates. The review of literature summarized in table 9.2 impresses one

Table 9.2. Summary of Studies of Agricultural Research Productivity

Study	Country	Commodity	Time Period	Annual Internal Rate of Return (%)
Index number				
Griliches, 1958	United States	Hybrid corn	1940–55	35–40
Griliches, 1958	United States	Hybrid sorghum	1940–57	20
Peterson, 1967	United States	Poultry	1915–60	21–25
Evenson, 1969	South Africa	Sugarcane	1945–62	40
Barletta, 1970	Mexico	Maize	1943–63	35
Barletta, 1970	Mexico	Wheat	1943–63	90
Ayer, 1970	Brazil	Cotton	1924–67	77+
Schmitz and Seckler, 1970	United States	Tomato harvester, with no compensation to displaced workers	1958–69	37–46
		Tomato harvester, with compensation of displaced workers for 50% of earnings loss		16–28
Ayer and Schuh, 1972	Brazil	Cotton	1924–67	77–110
Hines, 1972	Peru	Maize	1954–67	35–40[a] 50–55[b]
Hayami and Akino, 1977	Japan	Rice	1915–50	25–27

Table 9.2. Summary of Studies of Agricultural Research Productivity (*continued*)

Study	Country	Commodity	Time Period	Annual Internal Rate of Return (%)
Hayami and Akino, 1977	Japan	Rice	1930–61	73–75
Hertford et al., 1977	Colombia	Rice	1957–72	60–82
		Soybeans	1960–71	79–96
		Wheat	1953–73	11–12
		Cotton	1953–72	0
Pee, 1977	Malaysia	Rubber	1932–73	24
Peterson and Fitzharris, 1977	United States	Aggregate	1937–42	50
			1947–52	51
			1957–62	49
			1957–72	34
Wennergren and Whitaker, 1977	Bolivia	Sheep	1966–75	44
		Wheat	1966–75	−48
Pray, 1978	Punjab (British India)	Agricultural research and extension	1906–56	34–44
	Punjab (Pakistan)	Agricultural research and extension	1948–63	23–37
Scobie and Posada, 1978	Bolivia	Rice	1957–64	79–96
Pray, 1980	Bangladesh	Wheat and rice	1961–77	30–35
Regression analysis				
Tang, 1963	Japan	Aggregate	1880–1938	35
Griliches, 1964	United States	Aggregate	1949–59	35–40
Latimer, 1964	United States	Aggregate	1949–59	n.s.
Peterson, 1967	United States	Poultry	1915–60	21
Evenson, 1968	United States	Aggregate	1949–59	47
Evenson, 1969	South Africa	Sugarcane	1945–58	40
Barletta, 1970	Mexico	Crops	1943–63	45–93
Duncan, 1972	Australia	Pasture improvement	1948–69	58–68
Evenson and Jha, 1973	India	Aggregate	1953–71	40
Cline, 1975 (rev. Knutson and Tweeten, 1979)	United States	Aggregate	1939–48	41–50[c]
		Research and extension	1949–58	39–47[c]
			1959–68	32–39[c]
			1969–72	28–35[c]
Bredahl and Peterson, 1976	United States	Cash grains	1969	36[d]
		Poultry	1969	37[d]
		Dairy	1969	43[d]
		Livestock	1969	47[d]

Table 9.2. Summary of Studies of Agricultural Research Productivity (*continued*)

Study	Country	Commodity	Time Period	Annual Internal Rate of Return (%)
Kahlon et al., 1977	India	Aggregate	1960–61	63
Evenson and Flores,	Asia—	Rice	1950–65	32–39
			1966–75	73–78
	Asia—international	Rice	1966–75	74–102
Flores, Evenson, and Hayami, 1978	Tropics	Rice	1966–75	46–71
	Philippines	Rice	1966–75	75
Nagy and Furtan, 1978	Canada	Rapeseed	1960–75	95–110
Davis, 1979	United States	Aggregate	1949–59	66–100
			1964–74	37
Evenson, 1979	United States	Aggregate	1868–1926	65
	United States	Technology-oriented	1927–50	95
	United States	Science-oriented	1927–50	110
	United States	Science-oriented	1948–71	45
	Southern United States	Technology-oriented	1948–71	130
	Northern United States	Technology-oriented	1948–71	93
	Western United States	Technology-oriented	1948–71	95
	United States	Farm management research and agricultural extension	1948–71	110

Sources: Robert E. Evenson, Paul E. Waggoner, and Vernon W. Ruttan, "Economic Benefits from Research: An Example from Agriculture," *Science* 205 (1979): 1101–7, copyright 1979 by the American Association for the Advancement of Science; Yujiro Hayami and Vernon W. Ruttan, *Agricultural Development: An International Perspective,* 2d ed. (Baltimore: Johns Hopkins University Press, 1985), pp. 63–66.

[a] Returns to maize research only.

[b] Returns to maize research plus cultivation "package."

[c] Lower estimate for thirteen-year and higher for sixteen-year time lag between beginning and end of output impact.

[d] Lagged marginal product of 1969 research on output discounted for an estimated mean lag of five years for cash grains, six years for poultry and dairy, and seven years for livestock.

with the increasing sophistication displayed by the authors of more recent studies in response to the limitations of some earlier studies. The effects of more careful model specification, more complete measurement of costs, and greater caution in estimating benefits appear to have resulted in a downward bias in a number of recent studies (see Ruttan, 1982, pp. 252–54).

Despite the deficiencies in research organization and management noted above, almost all the studies indicate high rates of return to investment in agricultural research, well above the 10–15 percent (above inflation) that private firms consider adequate to attract investment. It is hard to identify many private or public sector investments that generate more favorable rates of return.[5]

Agricultural Extension

Publicly supported agricultural research systems were firmly established in a number of European countries and in North America and Japan during the latter half of the nineteenth century. Extension services to transfer new agricultural technology to farmers were set up somewhat later, typically during the first quarter of this century.

Research and extension services also were established by national governments and colonial regimes before World War II in a number of countries in Latin America, Asia, and Africa. The extension services often were quite different from the North American model. In many colonial countries they were directed to the needs of the expatriate-managed plantation sector. They often performed regulatory functions as well as educational and related technology transfer activities.

THE CHANGING ROLE OF AGRICULTURAL EXTENSION IN DEVELOPMENT ASSISTANCE

When the United States became involved in development assistance during and after World War II, developing or strengthening extension programs became a major focus (see chapters 12 and 14). U.S. development assistance personnel and many U.S. scholars were convinced that inefficient resource allocation among "irrational, tradition-bound" peasants who were "burdened by the yoke of custom and tradition" was a major constraint on agricultural development. There was also a perception that the enormous differences in levels of productivity between developed and developing countries could be overcome by technology transfer. These perspectives led to an "extension bias" in agricultural development assistance policy during the 1950s.[6] This bias was particularly strong in the early U.S. development assistance programs in Latin America (Mosher, 1957; Rice, 1974).

By the mid-1960s considerable disillusionment with the impact of agricultural extension programs had set in. Agricultural technology was much more location-specific than had been anticipated. And a new generation of scholars began to look upon peasants in developing countries as "poor but efficient" (Schultz, 1964). The attention of development assistance agencies and administrations and the flow of development assistance funds shifted from support of agricultural extension programs to agricultural research.

Concern with the effectiveness of technology transfer programs linking the new knowledge and the new technology emerging from agricultural research resulted in renewed attention to the problem of agricultural extension by the mid-1970s. This shift was reinforced by a new set of concerns with equitable access to technology and the need to strengthen communal institutions.[7]

A NEW FOCUS ON EXTENSION

By the early 1980s the World Bank had replaced US/AID as a major source of assistance for strengthening national agricultural extension systems. This focus on agricultural extension by the Bank owed much to the imagination and energy of the Israeli extensionist Daniel Benor. From the initial successful effort in the Seyhan Irrigation Project in Turkey (see chapter 14), Benor evolved the "training and visit" (T&V) extension model. Programs modeled on the T&V system were implemented in Bangladesh, Burma, Indonesia, Nepal, Sri Lanka, and Thailand with World Bank support.[8]

The basic technique employed in the T&V method is "a systematic program of training of the Village Extension Worker (VEW) combined with frequent visits by him to farmers' fields" (Benor and Harrison, 1977, p. 19).[9] A highly regimented schedule requires the VEW to be involved one day each week with intensive training related to the specific information that he or she must convey to farmers. The VEW is responsible, in turn, for visiting each relatively small group of contact farmers once a week for a half-day or once a fortnight for a full day.

Although support for the T&V system has often been enthusiastic, the system has not escaped criticism (Lowdermilk, 1981). Typically, the criticisms have focused on (a) organizational constraints, including the organization and training requirements of the system and the rigidity of the T&V model; and (b) the contact farmer, regarded by some critics as a major source of bias in the distribution of benefits from the system. Despite the extensive experience with the T&V system, it has only recently begun to receive the kind of thorough evaluation accorded earlier assistance for the development of the agricultural extension programs.

RETURNS TO INVESTMENT IN AGRICULTURAL EXTENSION

To assess the effect of extension programs, particularly as they influence the development process, some significant differences should be noted between the extension investment patterns in LDCs and DCs. Extension pro-

Table 9.3. Trends in Numbers of Research Scientists and Extension Workers, 1959–1980

Region/Subregion	Research Scientists[a]			Extension Workers			Ratio of Extension Workers to Research Scientists		
	1959	1970[b]	1980	1959	1970[c]	1980	1959	1970	1980
Western Europe	6,251	12,547	19,540	15,988	24,388	27,881	2.56	1.94	1.43
Northern Europe	1,818	4,409	8,027	4,793	5,638	6,241	2.64	1.23	0.78
Central Europe	2,888	5,721	8,827	7,865	13,046	14,421	2.72	2.28	1.63
Southern Europe	1,545	2,417	2,686	3,330	5,704	7,219	2.16	2.36	2.69
Eastern Europe and Soviet Union[d]	17,701	43,709	51,614	29,000	43,000	55,000	1.64	0.98	1.07
Eastern Europe	5,701	16,009	20,220	9,340	15,749	21,546	1.64	0.98	1.07
Soviet Union	12,000	27,700	31,394	19,660	27,251	33,454	1.64	0.98	1.07
North America and Oceania	8,449	11,688	13,607	13,580	15,113	14,966	1.61	1.29	1.10
North America	6,690	8,575	10,305	11,500	12,550	12,235	1.72	1.46	1.19
Oceania	1,759	3,113	3,302	2,080	2,563	2,731	1.18	0.82	0.83
Latin America	1,425	4,880	8,534	3,353	10,782	22,835	2.35	2.21	2.68
Temperate South America	364	1,022	1,527	205	1,056	1,292	0.56	1.03	0.85

Tropical South America	570	2,698	4,840	2,369	7,591	16,038	4.16	2.81	3.32
Caribbean and Central America	491	1,160	2,167	779	2,135	5,505	1.59	1.84	2.54
Africa[d]	1,919	3,849	8,088	28,700	58,700	79,875	14.96	15.25	9.88
North Africa	590	1,122	2,340	7,500	14,750	22,453	12.71	13.15	9.60
West Africa	412	952	2,466	9,000	22,000	29,478	21.80	23.11	11.95
East Africa	221	684	1,632	9,000	18,750	24,211	40.72	27.41	14.84
South Africa	696	1,091	1,650	3,200	3,200	3,733	4.60	2.93	2.26
Asia[d]	11,418	31,837	46,656	86,900	142,500	148,780	8.55[e]	7.28[e]	5.06[e]
West Asia	457	1,606	2,329	7,000	18,800	16,535	15.31	11.71	7.10
South Asia	1,433	2,569	5,691	57,000	74,000	80,958	39.80	28.80	14.23
Southeast Asia	441	1,692	4,102	9,500	30,500	33,987	21.54	18.03	8.29
East Asia	7,837	13,720	17,262	13,400	19,200	17,300	1.71	1.40	1.00
China	1,250	12,250	17,272	—	—	—	—	—	—
World total	47,163	108,510	148,039	177,521	294,483	349,337	3.87[e]	3.06[e]	2.67[e]

Source: M. Ann Judd, James K. Boyce, and Robert E. Evenson, "Investing in Agricultural Supply: The Determinants of Agricultural Research and Extension Investment," *Economic Development and Cultural Change* 35 (October 1986): 77–113, tables 1 and 2.

[a] Research scientists estimates include only workers with advanced degrees. An attempt has been made to include only research workers engaged in production-related agricultural research; research on postharvest technology, for example, is not included in these estimates.

[b] 1970 data are an average of 1968 and 1971 data.

[c] 1974 data are used when more recent data are not available. In other cases, the 1980 data are averages for 1974–80.

[d] Data for extension workers are estimated.

[e] Excludes China, for which data on extension workers were not reported.

Table 9.4. Summary of Returns to Extension Studies

Study	Country	Time Period	Type of Study	Conclusion
Patrick and Kehrberg, 1973	Brazil—eastern	1968	Production function	Extension (number of direct contacts of farmers with extension agents during the study year) had positive but generally not statistically significant effects on value added in farm production.
Evenson and Jha, 1973	India	1953–54 to 1970–71	Productivity change	Extension (index of maturity of extension program) contributes significantly to agricultural productivity change only through interaction with research programs. Investment in extension programs yields a 15–20 percent social rate of return.
Huffman, 1974	United States—Corn Belt	1959–64	Allocative efficiency, production	Extension (days, average for 1958 and 1960, allocated to crops by agents doing primarily agricultural work) and education are substitutes in inducing optimal nitrogen fertilizer usage on hybrid corn. The marginal value of extension time on this one decision is estimated at $4.48 per hour of extension agent time allocated to crops, or a social rate of return of 1.3 percent. Total social return from enhanced decision making suggested to be in excess of 16 percent.
Mohan and Evenson, 1975	India	1959–60 to 1970–71	Productivity change	The Intensive Agricultural Districts Program (presence vs. absence) contributed to more rapid agricultural productivity change. The social rate of return realized on the investment was 15–20 percent.

Huffman, 1976	United States—Iowa, North Carolina, Oklahoma	1964	Production function	Extension (agent days allocated three years earlier to crops and livestock activities by agents doing primarily agricultural work) contributes significantly to level of agricultural production. The marginal product of extension is $1,000–3,000 per day.
Mooch, 1976 and 1978	Kenya—Vihiga (a western division)	1971	Production function	An index of crop-related extension contact with male and female farm operators during the last year contributes significantly to corn (maize) yields. Extension and education are substitutes in corn production; extension interacts positively with the rate of nitrogen fertilizer application on male-operated farms (1978).
Halim, 1977	Philippines—Laguna Province	1963–73	Production function	An index of extension contact with farms, derived by weighting frequency of contact over previous five years, contributes positively and significantly to agricultural production. Marginal products imply a "relatively high return of extension contact."
Huffman, 1977	United States—Corn Belt	1959–64	Allocative efficiency	Same as for Huffman, 1974, except marginal value of extension time on this one decision is estimated at $600 per day of extension agent time allocated to crops, or a social rate of return of 110 percent.
Evenson, 1978	United States	1949–71	Productivity change	Extension (expenditures on applied farm management research and on applied agricultural engineering research are combined with expenditures on extension activity and deflated by number of commodity subregions) interacts negatively with education and positively with applied research. The internal rate of return on extension expenditures is 110 percent.

Table 9.4. Summary of Returns to Extension Studies (*continued*)

Study	Country	Time Period	Type of Study	Conclusion
Huffman, 1978	United States— Iowa, North Carolina, Oklahoma	1964	Production function	Extension is measured as days allocated to crops, livestock, and planning and managing farm businesses and as days allocated to the separate components. Emphasis is placed on holding constant factors that may be correlated with the extension variables. Marginal product of extension is sensitive to output mix (livestock vs. crop), ranging from very large to negative values. Crop extension performs better than other components.
Pudasaini, 1981	Nepal—Bara and Gorkha districts	1979–80	Production and profit functions	Extension (contacts with farmers during the study year—in rice, wheat, sugarcane, or total farm in modernizing Bara; in rice, wheat, maize, or total farm in more traditional Gorkha had positive or negative but generally not statistically significant effects on the individual crop output, value added, gross revenue, or profits of the farms of both districts.
Feder, Lau, and Slade, 1987	T & V system in northwest India	1979–80 to 1982–83	Production function; output supply and input demand functions	Rate of return of approximately 15 percent to incremental investment in extension.

Source: Wallace E. Huffman, "Assessing Returns to Agricultural Extension," *American Journal of Agricultural Economics* 60 (December 1978): 973. Updated and adapted for this study by Vernon W. Ruttan.

grams have expanded at a much slower rate than research programs in the most highly developed geographic regions but at relatively high rates in Africa, Latin America, and Asia (Judd, Boyce, and Evenson, 1986, p. 4). The developing countries spend more on extension than on research, whereas the developed countries spend much more on research than on extension (see table 9.3).

Evidence on rates of return to extension is much less adequate than in the case of research. Table 9.4 summarizes the findings of major studies of rates of return to extension. In general the results suggest modest but positive rates of return. While the estimated rates of return to extension are below those to research, this should not be interpreted as negating the importance of public extension programs. In many cases, the high rates of return to research would not have been realized in the absence of effective extension programs. The low rates of return to extension do emphasize the importance of continuing experiments in the organization and management of extension programs. This area is one in which institutional innovation may have a relatively high payoff.

Land Tenure Reform

Tenure reform has been viewed as essential to the mobilization of labor resources and the generation of productivity growth in both liberal and Marxist development perspectives. In the early post–World War II period economic logic and economic history combined to produce a remarkable unity in doctrine that a predominant owner-cultivator system allocates resources more efficiently and makes a greater contribution to national economic growth than does any other system.

The analytical support for this position drew on a tradition that extends back to the classical economists and was confirmed by Marshall (Jaynes, 1984). It was reexamined again within the framework of the Hicksian neoclassical theory of the firm in the 1940s and early 1950s (Schultz, 1940; Johnson, 1950; Drake, 1952; Georgescu-Roegen, 1960). The resulting major conclusion on the relation between tenure and productivity was that "there is no substitute, from the standpoint of sheer productivity, and irrespective of sociological considerations, for an owner-operated agricultural system" (Drake, 1952, p. 549).

This perspective led to the major emphasis on land reform by the international development assistance agencies after World War II. The U.S. commitment to land reform as an instrument of political and economic policy was carried out in Japan in 1947 under the authority of the Supreme Commander for the Allied Powers (SCAP). Its success was an important factor in U.S. support for land reform in other countries of East Asia in the early 1950s and in Latin America, under the Alliance for Progress, in the 1960s.[10]

During most of the post–World War II period the analytical deductions were consistent with historical experience. The land reform instituted in Japan, Taiwan, and Korea has been widely interpreted as supporting the proposition that an agrarian structure of extremely small owner-cultivator family farms could be economically viable, reasonably efficient, and capable of sustaining rapid increases in agricultural productivity. Contemporary experience in developing countries outside Asia, however, did not provide the same degree of support for the historical generalizations (Ruttan, 1969).

THE NEW LAND TENURE ECONOMICS

The lack of consistency between the logical deductions and the empirical observations regarding the efficiency of alternative land tenure institutions gave rise in the late 1960s and 1970s to a "new land tenure economics," which attempted to explore the economic rationale for the persistence and relative efficiency of share tenancy. The catalyst for these economics was Stephen N. S. Cheung (1968 and 1969). His analysis led to the conclusion that tenure reform is both unnecessary and redundant; and he implied that a more appropriate approach would be to focus on the development and reform of property rights.

Cheung's work was followed by an explosion of literature cast within the new land tenure economics paradigm. These works, however, led to substantial qualification of Cheung's conclusions (Binswanger and Rosenzweig, 1984, p. 23).[11] The major implication of the literature on the land tenure concepts is that the persistence of sharecropping rests on a combination of factors, such as the difficulty of solving the labor and management incentive problems in a direct labor management system and the persistence of imperfections in input and product markets.

In the inferences drawn from the modeling exercises of the new land tenure economics what options are implied for improving the welfare of workers and tenants and the efficiency of the farming system? The answer is the development and reform of more effective land, credit, and other factor markets. The models also confirm that in an environment characterized by underdeveloped factor, credit, and product markets, a land reform leading to an owner-operator system will contribute to greater efficiency in production than other tenure forms. Thus, the formal analysis brings us back full circle to the more intuitively derived policy implications of the pre-Cheung "old land tenure economics."

LAND REFORM IN LATIN AMERICA

The literature on the new land tenure economics has a peculiarly Asian flavor. Land reforms were carried out in Asia with the expectation that reforming labor and tenure relations through elimination of intermediaries, regulations of rental arrangements, and transfer of ownership rights to the tiller would achieve both equity and productivity objectives.

A very different flavor characterizes the literature on land tenure reform that has risen out of the Latin American experience.[12] Neither the practice nor the theory of land tenure reform in Latin America has given much weight to the achievement of productivity objectives through the transfer of land ownership to the tiller. Instead, land transfers have been looked on as a means to satisfy the land hunger of the peasants and thereby to reduce the threat of social and political instability in the countryside. Growth in production was expected to be achieved through the modernization of property rights, investments in physical infrastructure, and the development of market institutions. These reforms continue to be directed primarily at converting the hacienda or estate sector into a modern, large-scale farming sector.

Clearly, in a large number of Latin American countries the land reforms have successfully removed some of the most obvious sources of inefficiency and exploitation associated with the traditional hacienda system. There appear to be relatively few areas, however, where the land reforms have been accompanied by the policies needed to sustain productivity growth in the small-scale peasant sector and even fewer areas where the reforms have succeeded in resolving the problems of equity in the agrarian structure.

FUTURE DIRECTIONS OF ASSISTANCE FOR LAND REFORM

The dramatic transformations in land tenure relations instituted in Asia and Latin America since World War II have largely been completed. Even so severe a critic of Latin American agrarian structure as de Janvry conceded that "today, procapitalist estates with rent in labor services have, for all practical purposes, disappeared in Latin America. Those with rent in kind remain important only in some Central American countries and parts of Brazil. . . . As a result . . . these transitional reforms . . . can be considered successfully terminated . . . but the publicized goal of expropriation and redistribution toward formation of a reform sector has generally been held to a minimum. . . . Since large-scale farms in the commercial sector, with the full backing of state services, tend to be highly efficient . . . the family or cooperative farms created by expropriations of these lands will generally not be able to ensure delivery of an equivalent net surplus on the market . . . without a drastic redesign of agrarian policy toward servicing peasants" (de Janvry, 1981, pp. 221, 222).

The situation in Asia is quite different. Societies there had no choice but to look to small-scale family farms as the source of future productivity growth. Even the larger farms, outside of a very limited plantation sector, tend to be small by international standards. Very little land has been left in large enough units to support a redistributive reform; thus the technical and institutional infrastructure must be so developed that it is capable of sustaining productivity growth on small farms.

In most Asian countries the model of agrarian development that is evolving in response to demographic pressures and economic growth seems likely to resemble the system that has emerged in Japan, Taiwan, and Korea since World War II. Latin America seems most likely to follow the pattern that emerged in the U.S. South, in which a plantation system evolved into a modern farming sector and the surplus labor was absorbed by a growing industrial sector. In both patterns of development the evolution of a more efficient system of property rights, if pursued, could continue to make a modest contribution to the enhancement of equity as well as efficiency in agricultural production.

Agricultural Credit Markets

The development of agricultural credit markets and the provision of agricultural credit have been major activities in agricultural development programs by US/AID, the World Bank, and the several regional development banks. Prior to the 1970s a large share of the development assistance devoted to agricultural credit programs was directed to Latin America. Since the early 1970s the support of the development of agricultural credit institutions has been directed more heavily toward Asia and Africa. In this section I review some of the lessons from the experience of the 1950s and 1960s and then discuss the implications of the large programs of the 1970s.

CREDIT PROGRAMS OF THE 1950S AND 1960S
Funds for credit activities made up a relatively large part of externally financed agricultural programs in Latin America.[13] "In the ten years 1960 to 1969 the Agency for International Development (AID), the Inter-American Development Bank (IDB), and the World Bank group (IBRD) provided . . . agricultural credit worth approximately $915 million in Latin America" (Adams, 1971, p. 163). In the case of US/AID, over half the total direct assistance to agriculture in Latin America went into credit activities. In addition, US/AID helped to channel to agricultural credit institutions substantial amounts of "counterpart funds" and "local currencies" resulting from program loans and PL 480 sales in several countries. IBRD stressed livestock loans; IDB tended to support colonization and farm settlement programs; and US/AID emphasized technical assistance to credit institutions, supervised credit to family-size farms, and general expansion of loans to agriculture.

During this period, the organization of rural credit markets in Asia and Africa differed sharply from that of rural credit markets in Latin America. Studies of credit markets in Asia and Africa indicated that informal credit systems (private individuals, moneylenders, and merchants) provided a large part of the total rural credit, perhaps over 80 percent in many areas. The data suggested a much smaller role for informal credit in Latin America.

During the mid- and late 1960s the data and analysis that became available raised serious questions concerning the assumptions on which the credit programs of the 1950s and 1960s had been based (Bottomley, 1963; Blitz and Long, 1965; Long, 1968a and 1968b; Adams, 1971; Bottomley, 1975). Elasticity of supply or savings in rural areas tended to be grossly underestimated. Savings and capital formation by peasant farmers were shown to be responsive to profitable investment opportunities. In the Philippines, for example, capital formation was more rapid in areas of new settlement and on farms engaged in the production of commodities experiencing rapid growth in productivity (de Guzman, 1964). Taiwan was quite successful in the 1950s and 1960s in mobilizing voluntary savings by raising interest rates. This experience was repeated in Korea in the late 1960s (Adams, 1978).

The most obvious effect of the failure to maintain positive real rates of interest in credit markets was the exaggeration of credit needs and the erosion of the purchasing power of credit portfolios. Other effects include the concentration of credit in the hands of relatively few users; the failure of fragmented financial markets to allocate financial resources efficiently; the undermining of the vitality of financial markets; and the politicization of financial markets.

The experience of the Associação de Crédito e Assistencia Rural (ACAR) in Brazil illustrates some of these effects. ACAR was established in 1948 under the joint sponsorship of the state of Minas Gerais and the American International Association.[14] In 1960 ACAR became an independent and solely Brazilian agency. It began as an experimental effort to test the conviction that a program of supervised credit, similar to that developed by the U.S. Farm Security Administration, would lead to both better living conditions in rural areas and increased agricultural production. During the first few years the program included four activities: supervised credit, general farm and home extension education, medical care and health education, and distribution of materials. Approximately 80 percent of the total activity in the early years was accounted for by supervised credit and general extension.

A 1957 evaluation by Mosher concluded that the ACAR program had exerted a substantial impact on the levels of living and the agricultural resources of the families with whom it had worked. The program had not, however, had a measurable impact on agricultural production in Brazil, the state of Minas Gerais, or "even the Municipalities (counties) in which the program has operated" (Mosher, 1957, p. 71). Later evaluations by Wharton (1960) and Riberio and Wharton (1969) confirmed the contribution of the ACAR program to the welfare of the individual families who participated in it. It was particularly effective in reaching small farmers, and it established an enviable record for effective administration and flexibility in response to the changing needs of the farmers it served. As an example of a combined package of supervised credit and extension the ACAR program was clearly one of the models in the developing world.

At the same time, the performance of the ACAR program as an instrument of agricultural development was disappointing. Part of the difficulty centered on the issue of concessionary credit. The nominal interest rate charged on ACAR loans ranged from 6 percent to 8 percent. The annual rate of inflation in Brazil fluctuated between 15 percent and 25 percent in the 1950s and averaged slightly more than 30 percent during the 1960s. Given such rates of inflation, persons securing ACAR loans were, in effect, receiving very substantial income transfers through the negative real rates of interest in the formal credit market. The interest rate subsidy reinforced the incentive resulting from exchange rate distortions for ACAR farmers to overinvest in capital assets.

The ACAR program illustrates three important problems that have continued to plague credit development programs: (1) The policies that were adopted to reduce the cost of credit to farmers were inconsistent with the development of institutions capable of mobilizing savings in rural areas. (2) The policies designed to give more equitable access to credit have induced lenders to bias their lending activity toward the more affluent of the eligible clientele. (3) Research on similar supervised credit programs suggests that the costs of extending and servicing users' loans often run upwards of 20 percent of the value of loans extended; defaults and inflation add further to the erosion of the financial resources allocated to supervised credit programs.

AGRICULTURAL CREDIT PROGRAMS IN THE 1970S

Selective credit programs directed toward particular sectors, regions, or classes have been an important component of national development and donor assistance programs (Fry, 1988, pp. 398–418). Support for the development of agricultural credit systems has been an important component of donor assistance portfolios. US/AID support for agricultural credit programs since the early 1970s has leveled off or possibly decreased. During this same period agricultural credit has become more important in the portfolios of the World Bank.

Until fairly recently, surprisingly little research was directed toward evaluating the results of agricultural credit programs. US/AID's very comprehensive *Spring Review of Small Farmer Credit* (USAID, 1973b) contained about sixty papers describing credit programs. However, no paper systematically assessed the effect at the farm level of the credit programs. Since the mid-1970s the number of impact studies has increased. A critical review by David and Meyer (1980) identified several common features of the credit programs: "Borrowers had larger farms than non-borrowers. . . . Operating expenses and investment per hectare were higher for borrowers, but production differences were less marked. Moreover, net farm income per hectare, when reported, was roughly the same" (p. 207).

CREDIT SYSTEM VIABILITY

During the 1980s interest in evaluating the viability of the specialized farm credit institutions (SFCIs) supported by external donors has grown. A common feature of these programs has been the provision of credit to farmers at subsidized rates of interest and access to concessionary rediscount lines from central banks. This practice has driven a wedge between the mobilization of rural savings and the provision of credit on favorable terms to farmers. Thus the specialized farm credit institutions are dependent on the continuation of donor or national government support for their existence (Bourne and Graham, 1984). When such support is withdrawn, the capacity of the agency erodes. A "natural history" of the performance pattern of specialized farm credit institutions developed by Von Pischke (1980) is outlined in figure 9.1.

It is quite remarkable that the lessons learned from the more recent farm level and credit system impact studies tend to confirm the lessons learned from the 1950s and 1960s studies of the ACAR program. Among these lessons are the following:

— Credit is fungible. Subsidized production credit can be and is used to sustain current consumption levels, to invest in consumer durables, and to invest in land and relatively low-productivity capital inputs.
— When credit is made available at below-market interest rates (sometimes at negative real rates), it must be rationed by lenders. When credit is rationed, it flows to the larger borrowers. Programs designed to subsidize credit for the poor end up making loans less available to them than if a market rate of interest were charged.
— Subsidized credit projects often contribute to a decline in the viability of agricultural credit institutions. If agricultural credit institutions are to be viable, they must solve both the problem of credit mobilization and the problem of credit access. Excessive concern with the issue of credit access has made it impossible to solve the problem of mobilizing voluntary financial saving.

Why, if these lessons have been apparent for so long, have both bilateral and multilateral assistance agencies engaged in such rapid expansion of support of specialized agricultural credit institutions during the 1980s? The answer must be found in the economics and politics of development assistance (Adams and Graham, 1981; Kane, 1984). From the donor's perspective, less effort and less skill are needed to transfer money at below-market rates to national agricultural credit institutions than to provide almost any other form of development assistance; it is technical assistance–*extensive* rather than

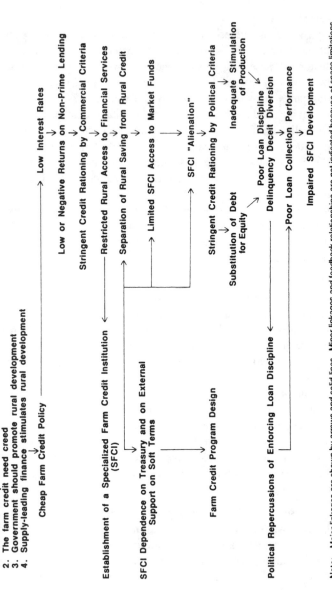

Fig. 9.1. A performance pattern of specialized farm credit institutions in low-income countries. Source: J. D. Von Pischke, "The Political Economy of Specialised Farm Credit Institutions," in *Borrowers and Lenders: Rural Financial Markets and Institutions in Developing Countries*, ed. John Howell (London: Overseas Development Institute, 1980), p. 84.

Note: Major linkages are shown by arrows and solid lines. Minor linkages and feedback relationships are not indicated because of space limitations.

technical assistance–*intensive*. Similar advantages exist from the perspective of the recipient country. Because money is fungible, it provides the recipient country with foreign exchange with very few effective constraints on its use. Furthermore, lending money at below the market rate of interest, particularly when it can be divorced from a simultaneous savings mobilization effort, also requires relatively little skill by LDC institutions. And the political advantages of concentrating benefits in the hands of larger borrowers may out number the disadvantages: the benefits of the subsidy are highly concentrated, and the costs are both hidden and diffuse.

Macroeconomic and Sector Policy

The success of assistance to expand agricultural production is strongly influenced by the macroeconomic and agricultural sector policies pursued by the governments of developing countries (see chapter 5). Production decisions by farmers in most developing countries typically are influenced by a complex matrix of input subsidies, product market interventions, and biased exchange rates. Often, irrigation water, fertilizer, and pest control chemicals are subsidized, and product prices are held below international market levels by parastatal or state trading organizations, export taxes, or subsidized food imports. The monetary and fiscal policies pursued by many developing countries often have resulted in severely overvalued exchange rates, which discourage exports and encourage the import of agricultural commodities (Hayami and Ruttan, 1985, pp. 383–88; Killick, 1985; World Bank, 1986b, pp. 61–109; Bautista, 1987. See chapter 15 for a discussion of the effects of a combination of bias in sector policy and distortions in monetary, fiscal, and trade policy in Ghana).

During the 1980s the bilateral and multilateral assistance agencies have made modest progress in encouraging reforms in macroeconomic policies that have corrected some of the worst distortions in exchange rate bias against the agricultural sector (chapter 7). It has been much more difficult to use either policy dialogue or leverage to influence reform in the prices of inputs or products. The gains from distortions in input and product markets are often so deeply embedded in the political structure that the political cost of reforms is high (Bates, 1981). This does not mean that modest progress cannot be achieved.

In Pakistan, for example, the World Bank used the dialogue that preceded the signing of a 1982 structural adjustment loan to obtain an agreement to phase out fertilizer subsidies. Implementation has been slow, however, because of disagreement over how to calculate the degree of subsidization. Nevertheless, fertilizer prices have been raised, and the cost of the subsidy has been reduced. The Bank and US/AID also have encouraged the formation and supported the organization of an Agricultural Prices Commission. It is responsible for providing the data and analysis needed to support agricultural commodity price policy. The commission is an attempt to institutionalize the economic information and analytical capacity needed to set input and output prices more systematically, in relation to domestic and international market forces, rather than a step toward true liberalization of agricultural commodity markets (Traxler and Ruttan, 1989).

Some Conclusions

In reviewing the literature on the impact of assistance to expand agricultural production through programs and investments in (a) land and water development, (b) agricultural research, (c) agricultural extension, (d) land tenure reform, and (e) agricultural credit markets (the development of product market institutions, including cooperative marketing organizations, and price support or stabilization programs are not discussed), perhaps the most striking observation that emerges is that of the continuous cycling of program priorities and thrusts. Most program areas experienced one or more such cycles. Extension programs, for example, were emphasized in the 1950s, were deemphasized in the 1960s, and emerged as a major area of development assistance again in the 1970s. Assistance for agricultural research emphasized the building of national systems in the 1950s and 1960s, the development of the international system in the 1970s, and a new emphasis on strengthening national systems in the late 1970s and 1980s.

A second striking feature of the programs is the failure to learn from failure. Credit programs are one striking example; the failure to achieve effective articulation between the engineering aspects and the management and policy aspects of irrigation is another.

Despite these problems, the rates of return to several areas of investment, when effectively carried out, are very high. The payoff to agricultural research typically has been very high, and the payoff to land and water development, particularly in situations where rapid technical change is also under way, also has been high at times.

The reform of land tenure arrangements and the development of effective rural credit institutions are important for agricultural development. Both areas are subject to severe program distortions resulting from the bias in the distribution of political resources. Opportunity for effective assistance by external agencies in these areas is highly dependent on indigenous demand for economic and political reform.

A major theme that emerges from the review of assistance to agricultural development in this chapter and in the several country studies (chapters 12–15) is the dynamic interrelationship of technical and institutional change. Technical changes capable of generating large new income streams at relatively low cost have been an essential condition for the success of agricultural development programs. Similarly, investments in physical and institutional infrastructures have been essential to enable countries to realize the contributions to economic growth opened up by advances in agricultural technology. In the absence of technical change, incentives for physical and institutional infrastructure investment have been weak. Unfortunately, development assistance agencies have given inadequate attention to the institutional design needed to assure political as well as economic viability of infrastructure investments and institutional reform; this continues to represent a major source of failure in assistance for agricultural development.

10

Improving the Quality of Life
in Rural Areas

VERNON W. RUTTAN

Programs designed to improve the quality of life in rural areas are a continuing concern for national governments and development assistance agencies. Prior to World War II, programs to raise living standards in the developing world were initiated by private voluntary agencies, the health and labor agencies of the League of Nations, and national and colonial governments (Mosher, 1976; Holdcraft, 1978; Moris, 1981). Since World War II, external assistance to improve the quality of life in rural areas has gone through two cycles. During the 1950s, programs were organized under the rubric "community development"; they gave way during the 1960s to programs designed to support expansion of agriculture; then, with the 1970s, assistance returned to the earlier emphasis on programs of "integrated rural development" and activities directed to meeting "basic human needs."

The rise and decline of these two program thrusts are traced in this chapter. The accomplishments and the limitations of the community development movement of the 1950s and the rural development and basic needs orientation of the 1970s are identified, and some lessons from this experience are drawn for the programming of development assistance.[1] Other contributions to rural development are discussed in chapter 8 (infrastructure development) and 9 (agricultural production). Population assistance programs, examined in chapter 11, also have important implications for the quality of life in rural areas. The programs discussed in this chapter differ from those in other chapters in that they focus more directly on meeting the basic needs and improving the quality of life of rural people.

The Rise and Decline of Community Development

The objectives of the community development programs initiated in the early post–World War II period were both economic and political. They held forth the promise of building grass-roots democratic institutions and contributing to the material well-being of rural people, but "without revolutionary changes in the existing political and economic order" (Holdcraft, 1978, p. 14).

Community development was viewed as a process that (*a*) requires the direct participation of people, (*b*) employs democratic processes, and (*c*) activates and/or facilitates the transfer of technology to community residents to enable the more effective solutions of common problems. The process of realizing community goals was itself important. It was "rooted in the concept of the worth of the individual as a responsible, participating member of society . . . [and] was designed to encourage self-help efforts to raise standards of living and to create stable, self-reliant communities with an assured sense of social and political responsibility" (Holdcraft, 1978, p. 10).

A project initiated in 1948 in Etawah District in Uttar Pradesh, India, was the model and inspiration for many other community development projects and programs.[2] Multipurpose village-level workers were employed by the project to initiate self-help approaches to increasing agricultural production and strengthening rural infrastructure. In 1952 the Indian government used the Etawah model as the basis for a major national rural development effort. Unfortunately, the national government did not have the technical or bureaucratic capacity to adopt "the painstaking approach to developing a participative administrative structure able to respond to bottom-up initiatives which had been the key to the Etawah project's success" (Korten, 1980, p. 3).

The community development movement expanded rapidly during the 1950s. By 1960 over sixty nations in Asia, Africa, and Latin America had launched national or regional programs. By the mid-1960s, however, community development was being deemphasized by both development assistance agencies and national governments. The decline in support was due to disillusionment when political leaders in the developing countries and officials of assistance agencies found that community development was unable to meet either economic or political development objectives. The programs were criticized for failing to improve the economic and social well-being of rural people. A related criticism, one that was seldom stated explicitly, however, was that successful programs set in motion political forces that could not be easily controlled by center authorities.

The global food crisis triggered by crop failures in South Asia in the mid-1960s shifted the attention of both national governments and development assistance agencies away from community development to a narrower focus on enhancing agricultural production. This shift was reinforced during the late 1960s when the potential of the new seed-fertilizer technology became apparent. Thus bilateral and multilateral assistance agencies redirected their support toward strengthening agricultural research, extension, credit, and input supply systems (see chapter 9).

Integrated Rural Development

After a decade of relative neglect, rural development again emerged near the top of the development assistance agenda in the early 1970s. A major symposium, Agricultural Institutions for Integrated Rural Development, was convened in Rome by FAO in 1971, and in 1973 the president of the World Bank pledged that organization's resources to improving the productivity and welfare of the rural poor in the poorest countries (McNamara, 1973). Integrated rural development now became an increasingly important focus of efforts in bilateral and multilateral development assistance programs.[3]

The integrated rural development approach drew on a complex of often mutually contradictory intellectual and ideological perspectives: Even rapid growth of income in rural areas did not assure either availability of social services and amenities or equitable access to them. "Systems thinking" about institutional design and program implementation came to the fore with the recognition that rural development depends on the interaction of a large number of interrelated activities. And disillusionment with technocratic and bureaucratic approaches to rural development led to reemphasis on local participation and to the resource mobilization themes of the earlier community development movement.

A common assumption of both the bureaucratic and populist approaches to development programs in the 1970s was complementarity among the several sectoral components of development. Widely different definitions of integration were adopted. By some definitions, the integrated delivery of materials (seeds, fertilizer), credit, and extension, as in the Puebla project in Mexico, was sufficient. But it was the inclusion of "equity components" in the integrated approach that distinguished the "new style" rural development programs from the more traditional programs, which had been designed to increase agricultural production. To fit the new concerns with rural poverty, agricultural production projects were often modified by including new activities, such as rural education, farm-to-market roads, potable water, health services, and family planning (Tendler, 1982). A number of observers found Moshers's (1976) classification useful for developing a typology of rural development projects (see fig. 10.1).

The village development program pioneered by the Bangladesh (formerly Pakistan) Academy for Rural Development at Comilla was a particularly influential model for other rural development programs.[4] The academy was established in 1959 as a training center for public officials who were responsible for rural development programs. The program evolved out of an effort by the staff to understand rural development processes in Comilla District, where the academy is located, and to use development activities in Comilla villages as a training laboratory. The program involved (*a*) developing a two-tiered village and *thana*, or township, cooperative system; (*b*) inducing

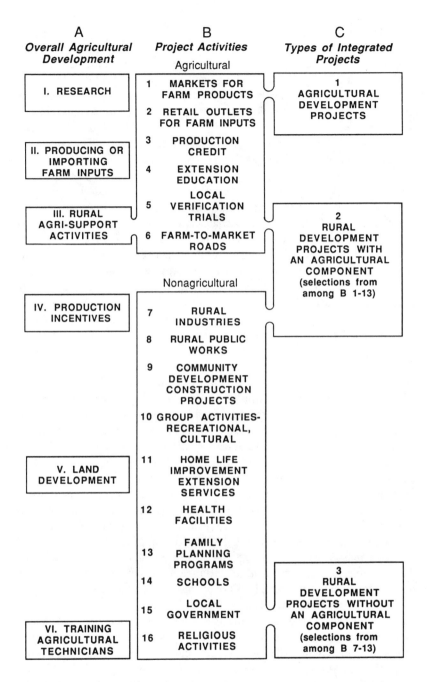

A *Overall Agricultural Development*	B *Project Activities*	C *Types of Integrated Projects*
	Agricultural	
I. RESEARCH	1 MARKETS FOR FARM PRODUCTS 2 RETAIL OUTLETS FOR FARM INPUTS	1 AGRICULTURAL DEVELOPMENT PROJECTS
II. PRODUCING OR IMPORTING FARM INPUTS	3 PRODUCTION CREDIT 4 EXTENSION EDUCATION	
III. RURAL AGRI-SUPPORT ACTIVITIES	5 LOCAL VERIFICATION TRIALS 6 FARM-TO-MARKET ROADS	2 RURAL DEVELOPMENT PROJECTS WITH AN AGRICULTURAL COMPONENT (selections from among B 1-13)
	Nonagricultural	
IV. PRODUCTION INCENTIVES	7 RURAL INDUSTRIES 8 RURAL PUBLIC WORKS 9 COMMUNITY DEVELOPMENT CONSTRUCTION PROJECTS 10 GROUP ACTIVITIES- RECREATIONAL, CULTURAL	
V. LAND DEVELOPMENT	11 HOME LIFE IMPROVEMENT EXTENSION SERVICES 12 HEALTH FACILITIES 13 FAMILY PLANNING PROGRAMS 14 SCHOOLS 15 LOCAL GOVERNMENT	3 RURAL DEVELOPMENT PROJECTS WITHOUT AN AGRICULTURAL COMPONENT (selections from among B 7-13)
VI. TRAINING AGRICULTURAL TECHNICIANS	16 RELIGIOUS ACTIVITIES	

Fig. 10.1. Elements in various integrated projects of agricultural or rural development. Source: Arthur T. Mosher, *Thinking About Rural Development* (New York: Agricultural Development Council, 1976), p. 54.

cooperation among public agencies in labor-intensive resource development activities, particularly irrigation, drainage, and roads; and (c) developing the capacity of local governments to coordinate and direct the departments responsible for civil administration and development (agriculture, water, health, education, etc.).

The Comilla program was clearly successful when it was evaluated in terms of diffusion of more productive agricultural technology, mobilization of local resources for village improvement, and development of cooperative institutions. The latter proved to be capable of generating modest savings and were successful in partially replacing traditional moneylenders as a source of credit. They also became effective channels of technical information on rice production practices, health practices, and farm and cooperative management between the villagers and technicians at the thana center. Many cooperatives also became capable of managing capital investments, such as tube wells; handling the distribution of inputs, such as fertilizer, insecticides, and seeds; and organizing such services as tractor plowing. Roads, irrigation, and drainage were improved. In the areas where such changes occurred the value of farm output increased, incomes of owner- and tenant-cultivators grew, and land values rose in response to the greater productivity and higher incomes. Furthermore, the experience gained in the Comilla thana influenced rural administration and development in a number of other thanas in East Pakistan. After independence the government of Bangladesh announced that the Comilla project would become the model for a national rural development program. The program that was actually implemented, however, is described more accurately as "cooperative development" than as rural development.

The Comilla experience and similar experiences in other countries have led some observers to question why it is so easy to identify a number of relatively successful small-scale or pilot rural development projects but so difficult to find examples of successful rural development programs, or of programs in which pilot projects have made the intended transition into general practice (Caiden and Wildavsky, 1974; Ruttan, 1975).

One reason that pilot projects tend to be reasonably successful is that they are able to draw on a level of professional resources and political and bureaucratic support that simply is not available when they are generalized to the regional or national level (Sussman, 1982; Wunsch, 1986; Cohen, 1987). Furthermore, when successful projects are extended on a regional or national scale, they often become mechanisms for imposing centrally mandated programs on communities rather than instruments to enable communities to mobilize their own resources for development. Few projects listed in table 10.1 made a sustained effort to strengthen that capacity of local governments. Part of this failure was due to the lack of understanding by assistance agency personnel of the difference between deconcentrated administration and decentralized governance—between locating the administrative offices of center

Table ... Examples of Integrated Rural Development Projects

				Project Components or Activities[a]								
Project	Country	Time Period	Sources of Outside Assistance	Credit	Extension	Marketing	Infra-structure	Inputs Supply	Health	Education	Family Planning	Other
Bicol River	Philippines	1975–	US/AID	y		y	x		Proposed w/nutrition	y	Proposed	Resettlement Tenure reform
CADU	Ethiopia	1967–	Swedish International Development Agency	x	x	x	x	x	y	x		Research; water
Comilla	Bangladesh	1959–65	Ford Foundation	x	Trained selected villagers	x	x	x		x	x	Research
Hellmand Valley	Afghanistan	1946–74	US/AID (1952)				x		x	x		Irrigation; research and housing
Invierno	Nicaragua	1975–	US/AID	x	x	x	x	x	y	y	y	Nutrition
Kigoma	Tanzania	1974–	World Bank; United Kingdom	x	Trained selected villagers	x	x	x	x	x		Water; resettlement
Lilongwe	Malawi	1968–78	World Bank	x	x	y	x	x	x	x		
Puebla	Mexico	1967–73	CIMMYT; Rockefeller	y	x	y		y				Research; crop insurance
Vicos	Peru	1952–67	Cornell University	x	x	x		x	x	x		Land tenure
Vihiga	Kenya	1970–76	US/AID and others	x	x		x	x			x	Rural; industry

Source: John M. Cohen, "Integrating Services for Rural Development" (Harvard University, Lincoln Institute of Land Policy and Kennedy School of Government, September 1979, Mimeo).

[a] x = project provides these components; y = project coordinates these inputs, which come from outside sources.

ministries at the provincial or district level and strengthening the capacity, particularly fiscal and administrative, for governance at the local level (Rondinelli, 1982; Mawhood, 1983, pp. 1–5). Local governments rarely become fully effective instruments of development if their powers are restricted to enforcing laws, collecting taxes, and administering programs mandated at higher levels of government.

The Basic Needs Perspective

In 1973 the U.S. Congress instructed US/AID to direct its efforts to meeting the basic needs of the poorest people in the developing countries (U.S. Congress, House of Representatives, 1973). In 1974 the United Nations World Food Conference adopted a declaration calling for the eradication of hunger and malnutrition by 1985 (United Nations, 1975). There followed specific program design proposals by the International Labour Organization (ILO) at the 1976 World Employment Conference (International Labour Office, 1977). These proposals and their program implications have been elaborated by staff members of the ILO, the World Bank, and US/AID.[5]

The basic needs approach was a radical departure from conventional development strategy. Growth objectives were replaced by consumption targets (Streeten and Burki, 1978). And the consumption targets were translated into specific program goals, such as a life expectancy of sixty-five years or more; a literacy rate of at least 75 percent; an infant mortality rate of fifty or fewer per thousand births; and a birth rate of twenty-five or fewer per thousand population (Grant, 1978).

Advocates of the basic needs approach did not argue that either material or nonmaterial needs can be improved easily. They held that achieving basic needs would require intervention by national governments to redirect both production and consumption goals and to reorder the content and direction of development assistance agencies' activities. But they also insisted that a basic needs strategy could contribute more to efficient growth than traditional assistance programs and that expenditures on education represent an investment in economic growth. Furthermore, they insisted that expenditures directed to improving nutrition and health and to reducing population growth rates also should be viewed as high-payoff investments (Johnston and Clark, 1982) and that intervention to raise both the material and nonmaterial components of consumption improves the well-being of the poor more efficiently than do the slower processes of technical assistance and institution building (Streeten and Burki, 1978, p. 139).

A fundamental premise of the basic needs approach is that high levels of basic needs achievement can be realized at relatively low levels of per capita income. The experiences of Cuba, China, Kerala, and Sri Lanka frequently have been cited as successful. In Sri Lanka, life expectancy at birth rose from 46 in 1945–47 to 64 in 1973–75; infant mortality declined from 182 per thousand in 1945–49 to 65 per thousand in 1965–69; and literacy increased from 68 percent in 1953 to 81 percent in 1969. These improvements were achieved in an economy in which per capita income was below $200 (1974–76 U.S.) (Grant, 1978, pp. 16–26).

Boutras-Ghali and Taylor's (1980) attempt to model the implications of a basic needs strategy for Egypt helps to clarify some of the implications of moving rapidly toward the achievement of basic needs objectives. Their analysis suggests that a basic needs strategy would be less capital- and import-intensive than policies presently being followed; that meeting basic needs in rural areas would be less capital- and import-intensive than in urban areas, although a further shift of resource use toward the service and government sectors would be required; and that prices of capital goods and agricultural commodities would rise relative to the general price level. To achieve basic needs program objectives without substantially sacrificing economic growth objectives, over half of Egypt's foreign exchange requirements would have to be supplied by foreign donors' and workers' remittances.

Efforts to model the implications of basic needs strategies in the Philippines and Korea produced a rather surprising conclusion: improvements in the domestic terms of trade for agriculture were more powerful than some direct consumption interventions in shifting the distribution of income and consumption to favor the poor (Adelman et al., 1979).

How did the basic needs perspective influence the organization of rural development programs? In the case of the projects supported by the World Bank and other donors, the effect was to include more of the activities listed in the lower half of figure 10.1.

One problem faced by the World Bank rural development projects in East Africa after the early 1970s was that they were more complex in design and objectives than earlier projects; they included many more productive and social service activities than had been considered feasible at earlier stages (Lele, 1979, p. 234). Lele also noted that their targets were often so ambitious they could not be supported within the existing technical and administrative capacity, and successful projects were difficult to replicate when governments and donors attempted to expand them into national programs. The Bank responded to these difficulties by allocating more resources to support rural development training and planning and by giving greater attention to monitoring, implementing, and evaluating project accomplishments.

A second problem faced development assistance agencies attempting to incorporate basic needs objectives into rural development programs, namely the difficulty of reconciling (*a*) a commitment to the objectives of mass participation in local decision making and of building institutions capable of mobilizing local resources for development with (*b*) the donor objectives of achieving measurable improvements in basic needs indicators within the relatively limited time span between program initiation and evaluation. The result frequently was that the participation and mobilization goals were supplanted by bureaucratic approaches to program delivery (Soedjatmoko, 1978; Cernea, 1979; Uphoff, Cohen, and Goldsmith, 1979).

A third issue has been the opportunity costs—the opportunities forgone—as a result of the basic needs and rural development reorientation in aid programming. A serious negative effect of the "new directions" mandate in Africa was US/AID's decline in support for the development of advanced training and for agricultural research. In the 1950s and 1960s a very promising beginning was made to organize faculties or build colleges of agriculture in Nigeria, Kenya, Tanzania, Malawi, Sierra Leone, and Uganda. During the 1970s US/AID support for higher education was reduced or discontinued.[6] Support for the development of agricultural research capacity was also adversely affected. The reorientation of assistance programs must bear some responsibility for the absence south of the Sahara in the late 1980s of the agricultural training and research capacity that is needed to sustain the growth in agricultural production demanded of agricultural producers.

There is a danger in overemphasizing the conflict between equity and productivity in program objectives or between efficiency in program design and delivery and mobilization of local economic and political resources for development. They are among the most difficult problems for any society to resolve.[7] Indeed, the capacity of a society to resolve these contradictions is a relatively sure indicator of political development.

Evaluating Rural Development Programs

How effective have efforts been to deliver integrated packages of services to rural communities? Because the integrated rural development and basic needs perspectives and programming are relatively recent, reliable empirical measures of the effectiveness of such programs are scant. Since the early 1980s, however, US/AID has engaged in an intensive effort to evaluate a number of programs. In this section, then, the assessments of a number of projects designed to improve rural roads, rural water supplies, and rural health are reviewed.[8]

RURAL ROADS

An important set of development projects in which activities have been directed away from primarily providing services in favor of mobilizing local resources has occurred in rural road building and upgrading. In 1982 US/AID completed a three-year study of the effectiveness and influence of rural road projects that it had sponsored in Asia, Africa, and Latin America (US/AID, 1982e). Project effectiveness was judged by two standards: (*a*) actual length of the road constructed, its cost, and time required, compared with projections; and (*b*) the degree of sustainability of project activities in terms of maintenance and continued rural road construction after US/AID dispersed all project funds. Project influence was measured by "the degree to which the project attains broader project purposes and goals" (p. iv), as well as any other intended or unintended effects (i.e., social, political, economic, environmental).

Although most rural road projects studied by US/AID evaluation teams were still operational, maintenance was generally neglected as a result of both donor and host country policies. Often, overoptimistic estimates of costs and completion time led to cost overruns. Many critical effects on land tenure, agricultural production and pricing policies, environmental quality, and the transport industry were overlooked. In particular, it was found that the "engineers who ran highway departments . . . were more attached to roadbuilding . . . than to maintenance" (p. v). Furthermore, "where road selection was centralized, there was a tendency to specify uneconomically high design standards and to overemphasize primary roads at the expense of rural roads" (p. 7). Tendler (1979, pp. 42–43) found that placing the road selection decisions at the local level produced a higher ratio of unpaved to paved roads, and the design standards were more appropriate to the low-traffic volumes found on rural roads.

In the evaluations of US/AID projects in Sierra Leone, Colombia, Liberia, Jamaica, the Philippines, Thailand, Honduras, and Kenya only one clear-cut case of success based on project sustainability was found: the Accelerated Rural Development (ARD) program in Thailand, begun in the early 1960s to foster internal security through economic development. Typically, in an ARD project, seasonal cart tracks are upgraded into all-weather dirt roads to link villages and small towns to the national road network, and potable water and minor irrigation works are developed. The three complementary efforts contribute to the development of the basic physical infrastructure needed for the development of rural communities.

In the Thai ARD program administration was decentralized. The local institutional development necessary for project sustainability was encouraged. Donor grants provided equipment and training directly to provincial organizations. The national ARD office contributed to the planning, design, construction, and maintenance of rural roads and village water facilities. Provincial organizations were also supported, under the leadership of their provincial governors, in the development of staff to coordinate the planning and implementation of rural development programs within the provinces. Road project guidelines provided for continuing maintenance of rural roads by local ARD organizations until traffic levels exceeded the engineering capacity of their organizations. At that time arrangements were made for the maintenance responsibility to be taken over by the national highway department (US/AID, 1980a).

RURAL WATER SUPPLY

In community water supply projects, more so even than in rural road projects, the systems evaluated as most successful were those built by mobilizing local resources and maintained and supported by local associations of users. Various technologies, from hand-dug wells with locally manufactured hand pumps in Tanzania to diesel pumps and gravity systems in Kenya, Thailand, Tunisia, Peru, and Panama, were found to be reliable in the evaluation study conducted by US/AID (1982b, p. 16). These evaluations focused on the relations between reliability and the beneficial effects of water systems. Equity of access, distribution of benefits, and interrelationships between water supply quality and health were major concerns. The evaluations demonstrated that a system tended to be more successful when communities contributed to its costs (US/AID, 1982b, pp. 24–26, 33, 37–38). When the users paid the full costs of operation and maintenance, no system was found to be unreliable. Furthermore, participation by the majority of a community tended to ensure equitable access.

The following conditions were found to be associated with project success: (a) tariff structures and payment schedules that resulted from discussions and where acceptable to the community; (b) the formulation of a local users group to set management policies and determine local priorities; and (c) a water supply organization able to support and maintain the equipment used. Also, projects were most likely to succeed when (a) the technology chosen represented an incremental improvement over the existing level and could offer the prospect of further step-by-step progress; (b) technologies used for projects did not exceed the logistic and technical support capability of the institution; and (c) diversity of equipment, which makes for problems in procurement and supply of parts, was limited (US/AID, 1982b, p. 37). It was noted as well that when institutional support was inadequate, project success could be assured if private sector sources of equipment, supplies, and expertise to service communities were available. Furthermore, the evaluation teams concluded that providing a method for insuring community contribution and involvement in the maintenance of the system was important to project success.

HEALTH PROGRAMS

Evaluating of health care activities in developing countries is more difficult conceptually and methodologically than evaluating the effects of rural roads or utility projects. The earlier view of expenditures on health as welfare was superseded by the view that improved health and nutritional status contribute to the quality of a society's human resources and to national goals of economic and social development (Johnston and Meyer, 1977; Schultz, 1980; Johnston and Clark, 1982, p. 117; chapter 2). Very substantial disagreement remains, however, over the methodology that is most appropriate for evaluating the operation and performance of programmatic health projects.[9]

The available reviews of health program effectiveness permit a few generalizations about program organization and effect.

1. Health and nutrition are intimately related. Programs designed to achieve health objectives are likely to be ineffective in those communities in which a substantial proportion of the population is malnourished. Successful and sustained programs of nutrition intervention are difficult to achieve, however. Supplemental feeding programs that cannot be sustained from domestic or even local resources rarely result in more than a temporary reduction in malnutrition. In rural areas the most effective instruments for improving nutrition are the agricultural research, extension, and marketing programs that expand the availability and reduce the prices of basic staples and generate higher incomes for agricultural producers. In both rural and urban areas, sustained increases in nutrition are difficult to achieve without programs that simultaneously generate growth in employment and income.

2. Mass campaigns (e.g., those that led to the dramatic decline in malaria and the virtual elimination of smallpox) have enabled developing countries to achieve significant improvements in health status and declines in mortality rates at very low cost. The widespread diffusion of the oral rehydration techniques for reducing infant death rates from diarrheal disease is a dramatic example (Johnston and Clark, 1982, pp. 126–34). However, few opportunities remain for rapid gains from the use of diffusion techniques in mass public health or immunization programs. Opportunities depend on new advances in biomedical research. Although the application of genetic engineering may speed the rate of advance in new disease control techniques, it is unlikely that the gains will be as rapid as they were during the 1950s and 1960s, when techniques used in the developed countries could be readily transferred to developing countries.

3. The incremental gains in health that will become available, whether donor-assisted or based primarily on national resources, depend on the development of more effective community health care systems. Evidence indicates that the viability of such systems is greatest when the programs can draw on effective community participation and local resources. In a number of countries, the capacity to organize health services to take advantage of low-cost paramedical and village-level health workers has been an important factor in putting the costs of health services within reach of urban and rural communities. Unfortunately, the "physician-hospital" fundamentalism of the medical profession often prevents or hinders the duplication of successful demonstration or pilot projects (Korten, 1975, p. 26). Evidence exists that the integrated delivery of nutrition, health, and family planning services enhances the potential for simultaneously achieving reductions in child mortality and im-

provements in family health (Taylor et al., 1975; Johnston and Clark, 1982, pp. 148–54), but the addition of family planning to ongoing public health services has reduced the effectiveness of family planning at times because it is given low priority in integrated programs that are dominated by traditional health ministry administrations (Simmons and Phillips, 1987).

Strengthening Local Organizations

The preceding review of community and rural development programs indicates that success depends largely upon the degree to which the energies and supports of the local communities are mobilized. This observation is not new: a century and a half ago Alexis de Tocqueville noted that "the art of associating together" was an important factor in the economic and political vitality of American communities. The mobilization of resources for rural development requires the strengthening of three interrelated sets of local organizations: the fiscal and administrative autonomy and capacity of local governments; local membership organizations; and local political organizations.[10]

The body of doctrine derived from the experience of local development programs poses severe problems for external development assistance agencies. The planning and management instruments developed for the more efficient delivery of bureaucratic services are in direct conflict with the approaches that are most useful in the development of institutional capacity to mobilize local resources. The literature is replete with examples of the destruction of local institutional capital by program and project designs—of well-functioning systems for local resource management institutions that were replaced by inept and often corrupt bureaucratic resource management or program delivery systems (Esman and Uphoff, 1984, pp. 239–46).

The unresolved contradictions between central management and local development are compounded by the conflict between central governments and local communities over access to the limited resources available for development. It is frequently asserted that local physical and institutional infrastructures—rural roads, rural water, schools, and health services—are too costly for central governments to maintain. Yet when we examine how the governments allocate resources, we must question whether the problem is in fact the costs of rural development programs. Even in societies that have achieved relatively high levels of development, the services needed to generate higher incomes or to improve the quality of life in rural communities often rank relatively low among national priorities.

Some Conclusions and Lessons

Perhaps the most striking impression that emerges from this review of the literature on rural development is the cycling of both intellectual perspective and program content (Rondinelli, 1985). The shift of doctrine has been more extreme than that of program content. Community development programs of the 1950s differed from the rural development programs of the 1970s by the doctrinal shift to "basic needs" and "integrated" approaches. However, what was hailed as the panacea in the 1970s came under criticism by the development assistance agencies in the 1980s.[11]

The personnel of development assistance and national planning and development agencies exhibit remarkable creativity in transforming enthusiasm for "new directions" into incremental changes in program activities. There has been a continuing tension between the proponents of physical infrastructure development and institutional infrastructure development; between the designers of programs to supply commodities and services to rural communities and the designers who emphasize institutional innovations that will enable rural communities to mobilize their own resources of development. The advocacies of alternative approaches within the development agencies—"seeds and fertilizer" versus "health and sanitation"—rise and decline in response to external rhetoric and political pressure.

A clear inference from the literature is that the efficient delivery of bureaucratic services to rural communities is very dependent on effective organization at the community level. Rural communities, operating either through the formal structure of local government or through informal or voluntary institutions, must be able to (a) interact effectively with the central institutions that are responsible for delivering services to local communities; (b) provide feedback to the agency management on program performance; and (c) mobilize sufficient political resources to provide incentives for effective bureaucratic performance (Korten, 1982; Swanberg, 1982; Montgomery, 1988).

The success of many rural development pilot projects has been due to relative intensity in the use of human resources for organization, management, and technical assistance. This intensity could not be sustained, however, when attempts were made to generalize the pilot projects to national or regional development programs. Directors of pilot projects tend to have access to the higher decision-making levels of government and to have the administrative freedom to tailor programs precisely to local resource endowments and capacities. These advantages frequently are sacrificed to administrative convenience when the projects are generalized (Sussman, 1982, pp. 29–68). A highly centralized administration usually is not receptive to uncontrolled experiments with program content and delivery methods to meet the diverse needs of individual rural areas.

The attempt to interpret recent development experience leads to a series of four generalizations that are essential to the viability of any large-scale rural development effort:

1. Rural development program activities must be organized around activities and services that have relatively well-defined technologies or meth-

odologies and objectives.[12] It is important that such activities and services become simultaneously available to the rural communities but not necessarily administratively integrated.

2. Rural development program activities must be organized to use the relatively low-quality (and inexperienced) human resource endowments that are available in the areas. The use of high-cost human capital must be extensive rather than intensive.

3. Effective implementation of rural development programs is dependent, to a substantial degree, on developing the institutional capacity to mobilize the available limited political and economic resources in rural communities. In societies in which rural administration has a strong control orientation, the political and economic conditions necessary for rural development rarely will be met.

4. Welfare in the rural areas of most developing countries is at least as much a problem of the level of output per person as of distribution. The search for new sources of income growth must continue to be sought in both technical and institutional change.

The structural characteristics of most rural communities, and of the societies of which they are a part, continue to prevent them from obtaining access to many development opportunities that are potentially available. In a society in which the distribution of political resources is strongly biased against rural people it is difficult to mobilize the bureaucratic resources needed to make rural development programs effective.

The authoritarian political systems in many developing countries, together with the urban elites that support them, often are so caught up in accumulating and husbanding the available limited political resources at the center that they are unable or unwilling to risk the emergence of multiple centers of political power that might result from the more effective organization and mobilization of rural development. The characteristic that distinguishes such states is not the intensity of effort with which they attempt to bring rural people into the political process but the skill with which they maneuver to keep them out (Esman and Uphoff, 1984, pp. 35–38; Rondinelli, 1985, p. 235). In such societies, institutional innovation is strongly biased toward reinforcing the existing distribution of economic and political resources.

11

The Impact of International Population Assistance

GAYL D. NESS

International population assistance is a relatively recent phenomenon. It resulted from concern with the high rate of population growth in the Third World and has been aimed primarily at reducing growth through fertility limitation policies and programs. The assistance has been limited in amount, narrow in scope, and highly controversial, and its effect has varied. In global terms, the influence of this assistance can be judged to have been substantial on population policy and marked but varying on family planning programs. The effect on fertility itself has been mixed and only indirect. In specific bilateral cases, population assistance activities show some of the most striking successes and most smashing failures to be found in the field of foreign assistance.

Population Assistance

A general description of the character and amount of international population assistance is a necessary prelude to considerations of its effects. Evaluating the performance of population assistance programs, however, is perhaps more difficult, both conceptually and empirically, than evaluating other sectoral programs. Nevertheless, the indications are that a general positive judgment is warranted.

RECENCY
International economic development assistance has been prominent on the world scene since the end of World War II. During these four decades the world's industrial nations have channeled billions of dollars in grants, loans, and technical assistance to virtually all the world's less developed countries for economic, education, and social development.

Population assistance is a much more recent activity. The International Planned Parenthood Federation, the Population Council, the Ford Foundation, and the Swedish government began to provide small amounts of assistance for population activities only in the late 1950s. Neither the United States nor the United Nations provided funds for population activities until 1966. Even then, the assistance was modest in amount and limited to a few nations. A notable expansion in funds and activities has occurred only since the mid-1970s. Thus the experience in population assistance has been far less than in all other sectors.

AMOUNT

Since its very small beginnings, total international population assistance from the mid-1950s through 1985 amounted to about $5.6 billion. It currently runs just under $500 million per year. By contrast, total economic assistance (ODA and OPEC) through 1985 amounted to over $550 billion and currently is about $35 billion per year. Thus population assistance constitutes only about 1.5 percent of total annual economic assistance.[1]

Population assistance has grown rapidly since 1975. Before then, total assistance amounted to only about $1.5 billion. Another $1.8 billion was added in the next five years, and then the amount jumped to about $2.3 billion for the five-year period 1981–85. Thus about three-quarters of all international population assistance was allocated in one decade, roughly, with as much as half in the last five years. An assessment of the effect is difficult, consequently, because not enough time has elapsed to judge how mature programs work in various settings and what effect they have had.

The sources of population assistance follow the general patterns of overall development assistance. The United States has been the largest single donor, but its proportion of total assistance has gradually declined over the past decade or more. As with the rest of development assistance, the majority of funds have come from less than a dozen industrial countries. Between 1965 and 1980 the United States provided about 55 percent of all population assistance. Sweden holds second place with 10 percent. Seven other countries that together provided about one-quarter of the total are, in descending order of contributions, Norway, Japan, the United Kingdom, Canada, the Netherlands, West Germany, and Denmark (Ness, 1979; Herz, 1984). More recently, Australia increased its population assistance substantially, and in October 1982 Italy announced that it would allocate 1 percent of all its development assistance to population activities.

The relatively small number of countries providing population assistance simplifies some of the accounting problems. First the OECD and more recently the United Nations Fund for Population Assistance (UNFPA) have undertaken annual assessments of all population assistance. The UNFPA has been especially effective in developing a standard accounting framework, but it has not solved the problem of determining exactly what population assistance is conceptually. Basically, we are left with accepting whatever donor nations record it to be. Some years ago the OECD recommended a more precise accounting of the amount and impact of population assistance by counting the funds received by the host countries (Hankinson, 1972), but as yet there is no systematic procedure for this accounting.

SCOPE

About two-thirds to three-fourths of all international population assistance in the less developed countries has been used to support national family planning programs and the provision of equipment (e.g., vehicles and surgical instruments), contraceptive supplies, and some recurring program costs (e.g., staff salaries, training, and international travel). Biomedical research (the search for better contraceptive methods), basic data collection (support for national population censuses and population surveys), and information, education, and communication activities have accounted for most of the rest of the assistance. Small amounts have been allocated consistently to basic social science research (especially on the determinants of fertility) and to conferences and promotional activities aimed at producing more effective population policies.

The goals of population assistance have been somewhat broader and hence a source of some controversy. The US/AID Office of Population, when it was under the direction of Dr. R. T. Ravenholt, tended to focus on the narrow goal of contraception distribution and fertility limitation. The UNFPA mandate is much broader and includes raising awareness of population problems and assisting member nations to carry out whatever population policies they adopt. The narrower goal makes assessment of effects somewhat easier because one can ask what assistance has done to reduce fertility; the broader goal makes such assessment much more difficult. All international programs engage in many varied activities. The mix of specific donors for these activities also varies.

The mix of activity support has followed trends determined largely by the stage of policy development in each host country. The external funds of countries with official antinatalist policies have gone largely to support national family planning programs. The assistance of countries without such policies has gone for data collection, social science research, and policy analysis.

These conditions have varied markedly by region. For example, Asia developed antinatalist policies and family planning programs prior to the surge of international assistance. Thus, family planning has absorbed most population funds since the beginnings of assistance programs to Asia. In most Latin American countries, before antinatalist policy decisions in the early 1970s, assistance went largely to data collection; by mid-decade, family planning accounted for more than half of all population assistance. Until the early 1980s the majority of assistance to Africa was for data collection, population censuses, and surveys on which to base fertility limitation policies.[2] From 1980 to 1985 both the amount and scope of population aid to Africa expanded greatly, with substantial increases to both private and public family planning programs.

One deviation from this pattern is the case of China. Antinatalist policy was proposed in China following its first Communist census of 1953. For the next twenty years the policy vacillated between anti- and pronatalism, following the ideological swings from economic growth to revolutionary aims (Ness and Ando, 1984, chap. 3). Since the early 1970s China has pursued a vigorous program of fertility limitation, all without international population assistance. Only recently has China become a major recipient; a major item of current support is a population census.

Although the major emphasis on support for family planning programs facilitates the assessment of the effect of foreign assistance, the distinct regional differences in the mix of activities and goals caution against any simple global evaluation.

Controversy and Ambivalence in Population Assistance

International population assistance always has been embedded in a great deal of controversy. Until 1966 key Western nations blocked the inclusion of population in U.N. technical assistance programs, and the U.S. government refused to provide assistance for fertility limitation during the same period (Symmonds and Carder, 1973). Even after the United Nations and the United States decided to assist population activities, controversy continued and even increased occasionally. It surfaced clearly in the 1974 Bucharest World Population Conference: Third World nations resisted the family planning programs promoted by Western nations and argued that "development is the best contraceptive." What was needed to address the problem of rapid population growth was a New International Economic Order rather than family planning programs (Isaacs, 1981).

By the time of the 1984 Second International Conference on Population in Mexico City this line of controversy had largely subsided, but another rose to take its place. For the most part donors and recipients now accepted the argument that socioeconomic development and family planning programs have complementary roles in reducing fertility and population growth. The official U.S. position at Mexico City in 1984 represented a radical reversal from its position at Bucharest a decade earlier (Finkle and Crane, 1975 and 1985). The new U.S. position held that the effect of population on economic growth is neutral; where its effects are considered detrimental, they can be reduced through more rapid economic development. The new U.S. prescription for solving the population problem was for governments to remove subsidies and controls and get out of the way. Furthermore, U.S. population assistance has come under attack from the New Right, which opposes abortion, despite the fact that U.S. population assistance does not include abortion assistance and deliberately distances itself from abortion aspects of the national family planning programs that it does support. Nonetheless, this new opposition forced the United States to withdraw assistance to the International Planned Parenthood Federation, the leading private international organization in this field. By 1986 the position hardened further, leading the United States to withdraw all funding to the UNFPA.

Controversies over population assistance programs also arise in recipient countries with multiethnic populations. Political tensions arise when different ethnic groups fear that fertility limitation policies are aimed at altering ethnic balances.[3] International assistance programs inevitably become involved in such domestic controversies.

These patterns of controversy and ambivalence present a generalized obstacle to international assistance programs and inevitably determine the level and type of effect assistance programs can have. That is, other things being equal, it can be expected that population assistance programs will have a greater positive effect in homogeneous than in multiethnic populations and that they will have a greater effect where the controversies are less, rather than more, salient politically. Although brief, this discussion illustrates the difficulties in assessing the effect of foreign assistance. Unforeseeable, exogenous conditions affect all forms of international assistance, but they are especially troublesome in population assistance, owing to the controversial nature of the problem.

Population Program Evaluation

The evaluation of international population assistance programs presents a number of thorny conceptual issues. On the input side is the question what should be included as population assistance. For example, we could include the full range of economic assistance: health, education, agriculture, and industrial development assistance programs all can be seen as affecting population.[4] On the output side is the question what population conditions programs are intended to affect. Population planning, for example, may include policies and programs related to fertility, mortality, migration, or population distribution (Finkle and McIntosh, 1980).

MEASURING THE INPUTS

Some simplification is necessary if we are to understand the scope of the problem. As a start, we can focus on the influence of donor-defined international *population* assistance on those current national policies designed to limit fertility. But even this limited approach does not eliminate all problems. There remain accounting problems on the input side, conceptual problems on the output side, and logical problems in determining effects. The lack of standardized accounting practices also means the presence of errors in counting population assistance resources. A few examples must suffice to illustrate the range of problems.

Prior to the establishment of international population assistance programs, resources often were provided for population censuses, but they were not counted as population assistance. Now they constitute a distinct accounting category, and in some cases the amounts are substantial. The links between census assistance and the desired outcomes on which effects are assessed are not at all clear, although the census assistance is part of the data on which judgments are based. It does not seem likely, for example, that the census assistance currently provided to China will directly affect fertility limitation programs or fertility, but those funds still will be counted as inputs for assessment purposes. In Africa the situation is quite different: the massive flow of funds to census activity there probably will lead to formal policy decisions on programs to limit fertility.

A similar inflation of population assistance is seen in the World Bank loans for population activities in the 1975–85 decade. For the most part these loans were for the construction of primary health care facilities supporting a range of activities not all of which affect population programming directly or significantly. If these funds are counted in the assessment, assistance programs will appear far less cost-effective. There are many similar accounting problems on the donor side, all of which argue for some caution in the use of simple causal models to assess the effect of international population assistance.

In order to understand the influence of foreign assistance on the output side, fertility limitation programs must be disaggregated into three major components: (*a*) the process of *policy formulation*, marked by the adoption of an antinatalist, or fertility limitation, policy;[5] (*b*) the organizational *implementation* of that policy, marked not only in the formation of national family planning programs but also in such legal changes as removing restrictions on contraceptive imports and distribution or changing the legal and actual age of marriage; and (*c*) the *effect* on fertility, which usually is assessed in any of three ways. Family planning programs work by first recruiting acceptors for the new contraceptive methods. Program acceptors, along with acceptors of nonprogrammatic methods (either market distributions or use of some traditional fertility limiting behavior),[6] affect the prevalence rate, or the proportion of eligible couples who actively practice contraception. Finally, there is the effect on fertility itself, which can be assessed by various statistics, such as the decline of the crude birth rate or of the total or age-specific fertility rate.

All these steps in the implementation process vary in such factors as timing and strength, and foreign assistance can be assessed against any or all of them. The steps in the process are causally connected theoretically and empirically. Thus the effect of any one step can be expected indirectly to affect steps further down the line. That is, an effect on policy can be expected to have indirect effects on both program formation and fertility decline, and an effect on programs alone can be expected indirectly to affect fertility decline as well. The connections between the steps are not fixed, however, and there is much room for variation. A strong policy statement may be followed by very weak programmatic action, or a strong program may turn out to have little new or independent effect on actual fertility.

The causal connections, however, are theoretically clear and empirically established. Policy decisions affect large-scale public health programs as well as some aspects of private market distribution. An official decision for an antinatalist policy opens both networks to the flow of modern contraceptives; a negative decision keeps these networks more or less closed. When a decision is made for an antinatalist policy, it becomes possible for administrators to construct programs and for foreign governments to engage in direct technical assistance for the programs. Thus policy formation makes a difference. Another implication is that foreign assistance that helps to establish a fertility-limiting policy also can be credited with some indirect effect on whatever fertility decline ensues.

The linkage between family planning programs and both prevalence rates and fertility decline has been the subject of much ideological and methodological debate and of some measurement (World Bank, 1984b; chapters 6 and 7). The demand side argument is that the effect of economic development on such factors as child survival, the value of children, and the economic alternatives for women is that people want fewer children. When they desire fewer children, they will find ways to limit fertility. Without broad economic changes, the demand for children remains high, implying a low demand for fertility limitation. Under such circumstances, family planning programs or the mere provision of services has little effect.

The family planning, or supply, argument holds that there is already a substantial unmet demand for fertility limitation and that meeting this demand will essentially increase the desire for further assistance.[7] Supply-side proponents acknowledge that economic conditions tend to have greater weight in fertility determination; but they still hold that the evidence supports the argument that programs have an independent, significant effect on fertility decline. A major mechanism by which programs work is to reach populations that are isolated by terrain, poverty, or ignorance. A striking case for the family planning argument comes from Matlab Thana in Bangladesh, where a model program has reduced fertility in the absence of any other effective economic development (World Bank, 1984b, pp. 144–45).

The logical problem is how to establish the causal link from foreign assistance to population policy adoption, program implementation, or fertility decline. It is not sufficient, for example, to show that family planning programs affect fertility and then to argue that foreign donors should be credited with some positive influence because they assisted the programs. A brief example illustrates the dangers of this not uncommon line of reasoning. Rosen-zweig (1981) reviewed microlevel studies in India and Columbia that indi-cated that where family planning is present, fertility *and* child mortality are reduced. Before foreign donors take comfort from this conclusion, however, the Population Council experience in Bohol in the Philippines should be re-viewed (Williamson, 1982). An integrated family planning and maternal and child health project there had no effect on fertility and was even associated with an increase in infant mortality. Inasmuch as this program was almost completely foreign-designed and funded, it is possible to conclude that for-eign assistance did not affect fertility and actually increased infant mortality. Although I do not accept this conclusion, it cautions me to focus specifically on the link between foreign assistance and population programming in assess-ing the effect.

ASSESSING THE IMPACT

Very few serious attempts have been made to examine the influence of foreign assistance on the overall process from policy formation to fertility decline. The OECD has provided a series of excellent reviews of international population assistance, beginning with the results of an international confer-ence in 1968 (OECD, 1968; Wolfson, 1983). The reviews discuss overall problems of such assistance with sensitivity and clarity, but they do not un-dertake systematic and comprehensive assessments of its effects. The Austra-lian National University's Development Studies Center published a volume on international aid in which Gavin Jones (1979) explored international popula-tion assistance. He gave a historical review of the controversies and of the flow of assistance, and he made a spirited defense of such assistance; he did not, however, provide a systematic assessment of the effect of that assistance on population processes. A series of more critical assessments of population assistance were put forward by Demerath (1976) and Bondestam and Berg-strom (1980), but these works are more ideological than systematic attempts to assess effects.

Ness and Ando (1984) developed a path-analytical model of the policy-program-fertility process for twenty-one Asian countries and addressed the issue of foreign assistance influence. Some of their results are shown in the path diagrams in figures 11.1 and 11.2. They first developed what they call a "political-ecological perspective" on the process of population change in Asia, which leads to the assessment of both political and ecological influences on the three-part process: policy formation, program implementation, and fertility decline. They argued that for Asia this process was driven largely by internal national conditions, with little direct pressure from foreign assistance. Figure 11.1 shows the outcome of the statistical estimation of their hypothe-sized process. It supports the view that the strength of the political-adminis-trative system combines with population density to affect the timing of the

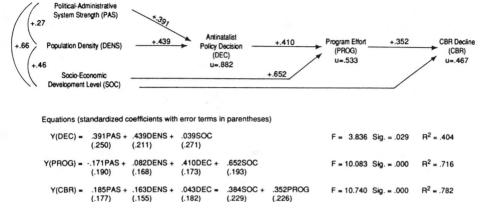

Equations (standardized coefficients with error terms in parentheses)

Y(DEC) = .391PAS + .439DENS + .039SOC
          (.250)   (.211)   (.271)   F = 3.836 Sig. = .029   R² = .404

Y(PROG) = -.171PAS + .082DENS + .410DEC + .652SOC
           (.190)   (.168)   (.173)   (.193)   F = 10.083 Sig. = .000   R² = .716

Y(CBR) = .185PAS + .163DENS + .043DEC = .384SOC + .352PROG
          (.177)   (.155)   (.182)   (.229)   (.226)   F = 10.740 Sig. = .000   R² = .782

Fig. 11.1. Path diagram of the determinants of crude birth rate decline, family planning program effort, and antinatalist policy decision for twenty-one Asian states, 1960–1975.

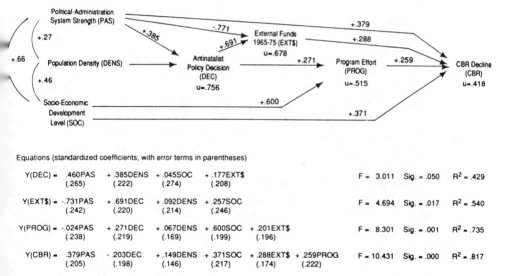

Equations (standardized coefficients, with error terms in parentheses)

Y(DEC) = .460PAS   + .385DENS + .045SOC   + .177EXT$
          (.265)   (.222)   (.274)   (.208)   F = 3.011   Sig. = .050   R² = .429

Y(EXT$) = -.731PAS + .691DEC   + .092DENS + .257SOC
           (.242)   (.220)   (.214)   (.246)   F = 4.694   Sig. = .017   R² = .540

Y(PROG) = -.024PAS + .271DEC   + .067DENS + .600SOC   + .201EXT$
           (.238)   (.219)   (.169)   (.199)   (.196)   F = 8.301   Sig. = .001   R² = .735

Y(CBR) = .379PAS   - .203DEC   + .149DENS + .371SOC   + .288EXT$ + .259PROG
          (.205)   (.198)   (.146)   (.217)   (.174)   (.222)   F = 10.431 Sig. = .000   R² = .817

Fig. 11.2. Path diagram of the determinants of crude birth rate decline, family planning program effort, external financial assistance, and antinatalist policy decision for twenty-one Asian states, 1960–1975.

antinatalist policy decision.[8] The strength of the family planning program or policy implementation was determined by the timing of the policy decision combined with the level of socioeconomic development.[9] Finally, the rate of fertility decline was determined by the strength of the family planning program combined with the level of socioeconomic development.

Into this basically closed-system, national model Ness and Ando added a measure of foreign population assistance—the total amount of population assistance per capita received from all donors between 1965 and 1975. The results of this estimation (fig. 11.2) support the following interpretation: Strong political systems in Asia came to antinatalist decisions largely from internal efforts to promote economic development and social justice. They mobilized resources internally and had a substantial influence on the direction of reducing fertility and population growth. The weaker political systems relied more on external assistance, which flowed more freely after the nations themselves made their antinatalist policy decisions. The foreign assistance also had some direct effect on fertility decline, although how this actually worked is still uncertain. Foreign assistance had a positive but quite weak influence on family planning program strength. (The regression coefficient from foreign assistance to program strength in fig. 11.2 is positive, not statistically significant.)

A more extensive study of twenty-four Asian countries from 1952 to 1980 showed similar results (Ness, Johnson, and Bernstein, 1983; Ness, 1984). Annual per capita population assistance from 1960 to 1980 shows no significant statistical relation to contraceptive acceptor or user rates or to rates of fertility decline. Another step in this analysis used program efficiency ratios (acceptors or users per staff or per funds) to indicate the level of program performance. When the level of socioeconomic development was controlled, per capita foreign population assistance showed no statistically significant relation with this measure of program performance. In that same study, individual countries showed great variance in the relationship between foreign assistance and fertility decline. Indonesia and Thailand, for example, had high levels of foreign assistance, rising efficiency ratios, and rapid fertility decline, whereas the Philippines had high foreign assistance, declining efficiency, and low fertility decline. In essence, country conditions were more important than the simple volume of foreign assistance in determining outcome.[10]

In Asia, then, it appears that foreign population assistance supported whatever the stronger political systems already were doing in the way of fertility reduction, and the assistance helped the weaker systems to do what they were not fully capable of doing themselves. This is, to be sure, only one of a number of possible interpretations of the results of the multiple regression analysis, but it is supported by the more detailed examination of cases identified as multivariate outliers. The interpretation cannot be taken as fully conclusive, although it is one of the few attempts to develop a theory of foreign assistance and population planning and to test the theory with quantitative data.

Other assessments of the effect of international assistance rely more on specific case analysis. They tend, however, to focus on the more successful cases, showing how they have been successful, rather than on the causes of the equally impressive failures. Two studies in Southeast Asia illustrate the positive side of this argument (Haaga, n.d.). A US/AID evaluation of the Indonesian program (Heiby, Ness, and Pillsbury, 1979) was specifically concerned with the US/AID influence on that program. The evaluation accepted the general evidence that the Indonesian program indeed had a positive impact on contraceptive use and a depressing effect on fertility, primarily in East Java and Bali. It found that US/AID had developed a low-profile program in Indonesia that supported the efforts of local elites to move the program out from its clinic base to the villages. US/AID's major contribution was to develop an administrative process that moved money rapidly from Jakarta to the provinces, thus stimulating local leadership to adapt the general aims of the program to local conditions. For various reasons that now appear to be largely historical accidents, US/AID was able to support strong local initiative to build an effective program.

US/AID also undertook an assessment of the Thai family planning program (US/Aid, 1980b), in which it found distinct positive effects from the foreign assistance. In this case, apparently US/AID's decision to finance contraceptive supplies at a level at which they could be provided free to the rural poor was largely responsible for the positive effect. Knodel and Bennett (1984) were able to show that the provision of free contraceptives tapped a new clientele and did not simply lead previous contraceptive users to shift to the free supplies.

Two points should be noted from these two evaluation reports:

1. There was no cumulation from one to the other. That is, the findings of the Indonesian evaluation could have been treated as hypotheses to be tested in Thailand, but they were not. The Thai case constituted a separate evaluation, focused on itself. The reports permit inferences to be made, but they missed the opportunity for a cumulative and continuous assessment of the manner in which foreign assistance can affect fertility and fertility decline.

2. Perhaps more important, each evaluation shows that the foreign assistance encompassed various activities, including long-term training of local staff, support for local planning, operational and research institutions, and program support closely tailored to the immediate needs of each country. Both countries had the advantage of having foreign and local staff who were technically competent and strongly committed to producing success in program performance. In neither case was the support short-lived, nor did it produce quick results. Further, in both cases population assistance was merely

one element in a large program of support for development activities, although the support for family planning was of a special type.

A similar evaluation of the family planning program in the Philippines (Family Health Care, 1977) produced less hopeful results from the perspective of foreign assistance. Again, the cumulative and comparative potential of the evaluation was not realized because the evaluation focused only on the Philippines. It found that the family planning program itself was deficient in leadership, management, and influence on the rural poor. It also could have noted, however, that this failure occurred *despite* the massive amounts of foreign assistance received for population planning. Ness and Ando (1984), for example, found that between 1965 and 1975 the Philippines received more absolute funds and far more per capita funds than either Thailand or Indonesia. The contrast between the failure in the Philippines and the successes in Indonesia and Thailand has gone unanalyzed in the agency's evaluation studies. The findings from the three countries do, however, fit the theoretical arguments and empirical analysis by Ness and Ando. In effect, they argued that foreign assistance has little if any real initiative power; it can help strong programs that are supported by political leaders (Thailand and Indonesia) but cannot produce either program strength or program support by itself (the Philippines).

The Philippine program provides additional evidence on the conditions of both success and failure in international population assistance. US/AID was among many donors that often urged the Philippines to move their program from the clinic out to the villages. Lessons from Indonesia and Thailand were in this case being deliberately transferred by a donor to the Philippines. The external stimulus supported some Filipino elites who also were convinced that services should be provided at the village level. The result was an outreach program modeled on the successful Indonesian program. Put in place in 1977, the outreach program has shown some striking successes (Laing, 1981; Herrin and Pullum, 1981). Service provision was overcoming barriers of distance, cost, fear, and ignorance among the rural poor. Contraceptive prevalence rates increased in many areas, and where they were not rising the methods were shifting from less reliable to safer contraceptives. Foreign donors paid a large share of the cost of the outreach program.[11] After fifteen years of assistance, foreign assistance appeared to be showing a substantial influence on Philippine population growth rates.

Success proved elusive, however. In the early 1980s political and administrative changes in the Philippines turned out to be decidedly antipathetic to family planning.[12] From 1982 on, the budget of the Population Commission was cut, drastic leadership changes proved highly disruptive, and serious attempts were made to turn the orientation from family planning service provision to primary- and secondary-level population education programs. The new government of President Corazón Aquino has proclaimed itself almost pronatalist. Foreign donors can claim some credit for the advances in policy and program made during the last half of the 1970s, but it would be inaccurate to hold them responsible for more recent setbacks.

AN EVALUATION AGENDA

Lacking more comprehensive and more detailed analysis of the effects of foreign population assistance, we can only suggest the ways in which this assistance can influence the three stages of population planning. If definitive statements are not produced, at least a set of questions or an evaluation agenda that would move in this direction can be established.

The first problem is to promote the formulation of an antinatalist policy decision. There has been a great deal of relatively modest and inexpensive activity in this direction. Support for international organizations, such as the United Nations, with its full schedule of conferences, constitutes one of the most effective types of policy promotion activities. Even the internal decisions that were made in Asia were strongly supported by international assistance to development planning activities in general and to the regional organizations that convened conferences and technical meetings on the planning process (the Economic Commission for Asia and the Far East [ECAFE] and the Economic and Social Commission for Asia and the Pacific [ESCAP]). As development planning matured, it almost inevitably produced decisions for fertility limitation activities. This has been true in capitalist, socialist, and mixed political economies.

Before the United Nations and the United States became major population donors, the role of promoting policy decisions was played with intelligence and sensitivity by several private foundations. The Ford and Rockefeller foundations, the Population Council, and the International Planned Parenthood Foundation all played active roles. They convened small meetings of national elites, produced papers identifying the implications of rapid population growth, and provided support for decision makers from high-fertility nations to travel and study. Comparable roles are being played today by international agencies in US/AID's Rapid project and the U.N. Parliamentarians project. They are part of various travel, conference, and training projects that primarily influence the current and future elites of the high-fertility nations. The funds involved are small, but the influence appears to be substantial. It should be noted, of course, that the influence now only *appears* to be substantial; we have no systematic evaluation of the processes of policy formation to establish the type and amount of influence coming from international population assistance.

A more definitive assessment of the effects of foreign assistance on policy formation is complicated by the strong two-way relationship between foreign assistance and policy formation. Foreign assistance to strategically placed elites has produced some policy decisions, but those decisions have also produced or increased the flow of foreign assistance to the recipient countries. Modest support for travel and information flows can help to produce policy decisions. Then, when the policy decisions are made, the way is open for a larger flow of foreign assistance to support program activities with much larger absorptive capacities.

Foreign assistance also can strengthen existing family planning programs. The most visible form of this support is through commodity provision. Contraceptive commodities constitute a substantial cost for any national program, and the shortage of supplies is often an obstacle in weak programs or weak political-administrative systems. In such cases, international population assistance has had a positive influence. It is only a slight exaggeration to say that today no national program need experience shortages of contraceptive supplies. The world community or the major population donors appear to be ready to meet virtually any need, either for imports or to assist in establishing local production capacities. Here again, the foreign support is available but can be realized only when a national program management sees the need and makes the proper requests.

In addition to commodity support, foreign assistance helps to build facilities (especially World Bank loan assistance), train personnel, provide specialized technical assistance (for activities from warehousing to service statistics), purchase needed equipment, and sometimes even to pay staff salaries. It should be relatively easy to assess the influence of international population assistance in this area. We need only ask how much financial support has gone to family planning programs and for what kinds of activities and then determine whether there is any relationship between this type of support and the strength of the individual family planning programs. There are, to be sure, intractable problems in distinguishing the effect of foreign assistance from that of domestic support.

Although major donors in the population field are few, their numbers and diversity still present a difficult problem in assessing the effects of assistance. In individual field situations, there is often a great deal of cooperation and collaboration among donors and, at the same time, competition and lack of coordination. In either case, with more than one donor, distinguishing which specific donor actions have been responsible for either the successes or failures of a given program is often difficult. The Indonesian and Thai evaluations (see above) noted the cooperative action of donors but did not go beyond general statements of relative effects.

Finally, the links from foreign assistance to fertility limitation are especially difficult to identify in a systematic manner. Many indirect effects are readily apparent. Assistance to education tends to raise female school attendance, which raises the age of marriage, supports the acceptance of contraceptives within marriage, and thus tends to reduce fertility. The task is long and tortuous, however, and many of the elements are only loosely connected. Much the same can be said for health assistance, especially for the type that attacks infant mortality. Assistance for sewage, for clean and abundant water supplies, for increased agricultural production, or for specific nutrition programs often leads indirectly to the decline of infant mortality and, in turn, tends to increase the demand for contraceptives. This, too, is a long and tortuous task with many loose connections, rendering it almost impossible to undertake a reasonable assessment of the effect of assistance on fertility.

Conclusion

In the assessment of international assistance on population, and especially on family planning and programming, much confusion, uncertainty, and controversy reigns. There is little hard and systematic comparative analysis that could provide more effectively grounded, if not definite, answers. It is possible, however, to make a number of tentative summary judgments, partly impressions from observations of a number of cases, partly suggestions from the few systematic evaluations that have been made, and partly questions that remain to be answered.

1. Foreign assistance probably has been most effective in the formation of antinatalist policy decisions. Here, relatively modest funds supporting the information flows directed at national elites have helped to sharpen perceptions of the urgency of the population problem and to identify both its local dimensions and the points at which some effective leverage can be gained by creating national family planning programs.

2. Assistance to family-planning programs, or policy implementation, can be more massive and have a profound influence by making supplies and services available, especially to the poorest of the poor—poor rural women. Where family planning programs have been successful in producing widespread fertility decline, that success has been largely owing to their success in reaching the rural poor. If the political will and administrative capacity of the host government are high, foreign assistance can have a substantial influence; if both are low, even large amounts of foreign assistance may almost totally lack effect.

3. The effect of foreign assistance on fertility is far easier to identify when it flows through direct programs. Foreign assistance to general social and economic development or to sector programs in areas such as health, education, or agricultural production cannot yet be shown to affect fertility directly.[13] These are, of course, important aims in international development assistance in their own right, and they need not be defended by reference to

their influence on fertility. Support for agricultural development, for health, or for education has consistently been far greater in magnitude than support for population programs. But if fertility decline is a policy aim, the foreign assistance that will have the most directly discernible effect appears to be direct assistance to fertility limitation programming.

Part Four

———————————————————

COUNTRY CASES

12

Assistance to India

VASANT SUKHATME

India became an independent nation in August 1947. Soon thereafter its government embarked on a series of plans to achieve rapid economic growth and social justice. The country's overall pattern of growth has been strongly influenced by the series of plans undertaken since then. Although the nation provided most of its own developmental resources, foreign assistance played an important role. In evaluating the effect of foreign assistance the unique characteristics of the Indian economy, its size, and its political climate should be kept in mind.

At the inception of India's first Five Year Plan in 1950 the total population of the country was about 360 million. Per capita income and literacy and education levels were among the lowest in the world. Schools and educational facilities, roads and rail transport facilities, electric power and irrigation capacity, credit and finance institutions, and other components of the infrastructure were at an early stage of development.

Over the past forty years, however, significant economic progress has taken place. Growth in GDP has averaged between 3.5 percent and 4 percent per year. The average growth rate was more than twice that recorded in the fifty years preceding Indian independence, although it was less than the planned target rates and less than the growth achieved in most other developing countries. Between 1965 and 1980 and again between 1980 and 1985, India's growth rate was less than the average rate attained by the group of low-income countries, including China (see table 12.2). With a population growth of about 2.3 percent per year between 1965 and 1980 and somewhat less between 1980 and 1985, India's relatively low rate of long-run growth has meant a slow increase in per capita income.

Phenomenal changes have occurred in India's enormous agricultural economy. Foodgrain production has shown a sustained upward trend, yet the annual rate of growth—about 3 percent per year between 1950 and 1980—was below that for China, Pakistan, and many other countries in Asia. The record of India's agricultural performance has been marked by periods of rapid growth and other periods of relative stagnation. Great change has also occurred in the industrial economy of India, but the growth rate of 4.1 percent per year between 1965 and 1980 and 5.4 percent per year in 1980–85 has lagged considerably behind the average for all low-income countries. Efforts have been made to promote industry by imposing stringent controls on the growth of industrial capacity and on imports, but the results are, essentially, a high-cost industrial structure with considerable inefficiencies.

India's slow overall rate of growth has meant little progress in eliminating poverty or reducing income inequalities. The country is still poor. Income shares of the bottom 20 percent and the top 20 percent of households have changed little since the early 1960s, but they are no worse than those in many upper-middle-income countries. Yet life expectancy at birth in India (in 1985, fifty-six years) is higher than the average for all low-income countries, excluding China, which is an increase of more than ten years in the last two decades. The infant mortality rate has fallen by more than 40 percent in the last two decades and is now lower than the rate in Pakistan or other low-income countries but higher than the rate in China.

The story of India's economic performance and its interaction with foreign economic assistance is complex. The primary purpose of this chapter is to consider certain selected aspects of the entire development assistance activity in India, such as magnitude, sources, types, and terms, in order to understand and assess the role of foreign assistance in the country's overall economic development.

The History of Aid to India

Early observers of and early participants in assisting India usually cited various reasons for the aid. They included the sheer size of the country, the great poverty and low levels of living among most of its population, the high infant mortality rates, and the low education levels. Much of this literature recognized the geopolitical aspects of the aid program, such as the economic rivalry with China, and how the aid served the foreign policy interests of the Western powers in Asia.

From a relatively modest beginning at the start of its First Plan, India has received more aid, in aggregate, from more countries than any other developing country. Scholars who studied the role of foreign assistance in India provided some data on the magnitude of the aid in rupees and in dollars (Narain and Rao, 1963; Streeten and Hill, 1968; Bhagwati and Desai, 1970; Harberger, 1972; Bhagwati and Srinivasan, 1975). The choice of currency units is somewhat arbitrary and depends on the data sources; the important point, however, is that it is difficult to give accurate totals when the list of donor countries and agencies exceeds two dozen and credits and loans have been provided in a number of different currencies. It is also difficult, given the changes in the exchange rate between the rupee and other foreign currencies and the changes in the terms and conditions of the aid, including the extent of aid tying, to construct a unique price index to calculate the purchasing power of aid rupees. However, it does seem clear that aid reached a purchasing power peak in the years 1964–66 (Lipton, Toge, and Cassen, 1984, p. 7).

During India's First Plan, external assistance authorizations were made by the United States, the Soviet Union, Canada, Australia, New Zealand, Norway, and the United Kingdom. India used about Rs 2 billion in assistance—a little less than 6 percent of the total investment in India during that period.[1] The U.S. share in total aid used by India was nearly 70 percent. During the Second Plan, the U.S. share fell to 54 percent, but it rose to nearly 60 percent during the Third Plan. The Soviet Union's share was insignificant during the First Plan period but increased to just over 5 percent during the Second Plan and to over 8 percent during the Third Plan. In the period 1966–69 members of the Aid India Consortium[2] provided over 90 percent of the total aid used by India during that period, whereas the Soviet bloc's share was about 6 percent. In the Fourth Plan period (1969–74) the Soviet bloc's share was about 8 percent, and consortium members still provided over 90 percent of the total aid used. Between 1974 and 1979 the share of the consortium members fell to about 76 percent when there emerged a new group of donors: Iran, Iraq, Kuwait, Saudi Arabia, and the United Arab Emirates. Between 1979–80 and 1982–83 the Soviet bloc's share fell to less than 2 percent and that of the consortium rose to over 90 percent of the total aid flowing into India.

Table 12.1 shows the relative importance of foreign assistance in India. The utilization of aid is given as a percentage of India's net national product, gross domestic capital formation, imports, and central government capital expenditures. In the early years of development foreign assistance represented a small percentage of India's net national product, but by the mid-1960s it had risen to over 4 percent; in recent years it has been about 1.5 percent. In the early 1960s aid utilization was over one-third of central government capital expenditures; this ratio fell to about one-sixth in the early 1980s.[3]

Several observers pointed out that on the basis of per capita foreign assistance India ranked at just about the bottom of the list of recipients. In terms of aid relative to existing levels of national income per capita, India fared a little better. Implicit in the use of deflated measures of aid is the view that if aid, suitably deflated, is low, its economic impact can be expected to be low. I. G. Patel argued that there are "many special characteristics about India which imply that the role of foreign aid in Indian economic development is likely to be particularly limited" (1968, p. 19). Among the "special characteristics" were India's size, political makeup, and uneven economic progress among the various states and regions of the country. Alone among contributors in this area, Arnold Harberger made an explicit attempt to estimate the additions to income that occur in aid-receiving countries from projects fi-

Table 12.1. Utilization of Aid in India, 1961–1962 to 1982–1983

| Year | Utilization of Aid as a Percentage of | | | |
	Net National Product	Gross Domestic Capital Formation	Imports	Central Government Capital Expenditures
1961–62	2.42	13.89	33.67	27.40
1962–63	3.00	15.05	40.72	30.00
1963–64	3.48	17.34	47.94	32.90
1964–65	3.62	17.78	53.64	33.69
1965–66	3.74	17.44	54.80	36.10
1966–67	4.74	21.05	54.45	42.00
1967–68	4.26	21.43	59.54	48.31
1968–69	3.16	15.43	47.28	38.51
1969–70	2.71	13.10	54.13	31.96
1970–71	2.31	10.78	48.43	26.63
1971–72	2.28	9.89	45.70	24.18
1972–73	1.65	7.43	35.68	17.40
1973–74	2.05	9.12	35.05	24.60
1974–75	2.21	8.76	29.08	27.48
1975–76	2.97	10.87	34.96	30.93
1976–77	2.40	9.05	31.51	26.49
1977–78	1.71	6.95	21.43	18.56
1978–79	1.50	5.29	17.84	13.91
1979–80	1.53	5.18	14.80	17.21
1980–81	2.04	7.08	17.21	21.00
1981–82	1.55	5.32	13.88	16.68
1982–83	1.68	—	15.67	—

Sources: Government of India, *Economic Survey, 1975–76* to *1984–85* (New Delhi: Government of India Press, 1976–85); idem, *Basic Statistics Relating to the Indian Economy, 1975* to *1984* (New Delhi: Controller of Publications 1975–84).

nanced by aid transfers. He argued that even if aid dollars were attributed "a rate of social yield more than twice [that] which is applied in the evaluation of our own federal programs and projects," the contribution of aid to the national income of the aid-receiving countries would be expected to be relatively small (Harberger, 1972, p. 635).

Aid flows to India were small relative to its population and its income. But aid was and continues to be important to the nation's development: it financed a significant though declining share of gross domestic capital formation, imports of plant and machinery, and central government capital expenditures; it permitted significant imports of foodgrains during years when India's own food production was tight; it contributed importantly to the agricultural sector's ability to generate new knowledge and techniques to enhance the food production capability. I show later in this chapter, however, that the effectiveness of the aid was blunted by the trade and industrialization policies that India adopted.

U.S., Soviet Bloc, and Other Aid to India

The U.S. government provided its first technical assistance to India in 1950. In 1951 the United States made an emergency wheat loan of about $190 millon (repayable in dollars) to help alleviate food shortages caused by the widespread crop failures of 1950. But the beginning of a broad-based program of U.S. economic and technical assistance dates to the Indo-U.S. Technical Cooperation Agreement of January 1952 (Hendrix and Giri, 1970, p. 142). Under this and supplemental agreements extending to 1970, the United States provided economic and technical assistance to more than 150 projects in agriculture, industry, transportation, education, health, and other fields—nearly all sectors of the Indian economy.

The following brief description of the sectors and projects aided conveys the scope of the U.S. contribution. Between 1950 and 1971 it was greater than the combined contribution from all other sources. Slightly over 50 percent of the total of about $4.5 billion was for food assistance. After the U.S. "tilt" toward Pakistan in the 1971 India-Pakistan conflict, U.S. development assistance to India fell sharply. Even so, between 1972 and 1985 the total new obligations entered into amounted to about $2.7 billion, of which food aid represented about $1.8 billion (US/AID, *U.S. Overseas Loans and Grants*, various issues). From 1982 to 1985 U.S. development assistance to India amounted to less than $100 million annually.

The United States financed fertilizer plants (Trombay); irrigation projects (Hirakud in Orissa, Kosi in Bihar, Nagarjunasagar in Andhra Pradesh); thermal power units (Bandel in West Bengal, Chandrapura in Bihar, and Satpura in Madhya Pradesh); locomotives, wagons, and coaches for the Indian railways; improvements in India's national highway system; airplanes for India's international airline; and numerous other industrial projects. In addition, funds were provided for the purchase of laboratory and scientific equipment for several institutions of higher education (e.g., the Indian Institute of Technology at Kanpur [Uttar Pradesh] and the All India Institute of Medical Sciences in New Delhi) and the establishment of agricultural universities.

The bulk of U.S. aid went to the Indian public sector, which led at least one observer to note that "such aid has increased the resources of the public sector relative to the private sector and has enabled the government to pursue policies which have tended to restrict the activities of private investment and have tended to discourage a larger inflow of foreign private capital" (Tansky, 1967, p. 113). However, the Indian private sector was not neglected: the

United States assisted several private sector firms under the provisions of the Cooley amendments to the use of PL 480 counterpart funds. The proportions of public and private sector aid were determined largely by the industrial policy that India adopted and the role assumed by the public sector in the industrialization strategy.

In contrast, Soviet aid went predominantly for projects in the heavy industrial sector, such as steel plants at Bhillai (Madhya Pradesh) and Bokaro (Bihar); an antibiotics plant at Rishikesh (Uttar Pradesh); a coal mining machinery plant at Durgapur (West Bengal); a thermal power plant at Neyveli (Tamil Nadu); oil refineries at Barauni (Bihar) and Koyali (Gujarat); and a heavy electrical plant at Ranipur (Uttar Pradesh). All were in the public sector. Inasmuch as Soviet bloc aid never rose significantly above 8 percent of the total aid to India, it is unlikely that Soviet assistance resulted in any state sector growth over and above what the domestic economic policy would have accomplished. Nonetheless, it is noteworthy that Soviet assistance also went to such sectors as petroleum and pharmaceuticals, which in the early years of Indian planning were dominated by the private sector. Further, Soviet aid was provided in areas for which Western assistance was not forthcoming (e.g., the steel plant at Bokaro).

A few other major projects also are identified with specific aid givers. A steel plant at Durgapur (West Bengal), a fertilizer plant at Naharkatiya (Assam), and a paper mill at Hoshangabad (Madhya Pradesh) were among the major projects receiving British assistance. Japanese assistance, which began in the Second Plan period, included two major activities: the fertilizer project at Baroda (Gujarat) and the Kiriburu (Orissa) iron ore project. Among nongovernment aid givers, the Ford Foundation played an important role in establishing the Uttar Pradesh agricultural university and the Indian Institute of Management at Ahmedabad (Gujarat), and the Rockefeller Foundation supported the Indian Council of Medical Research and the Central Rice Research Institute.

The World Bank and India

The first World Bank loan to India was made in August 1949 for the Indian railways and was followed soon after by a loan for the importation of agricultural machinery for a land reclamation project. In 1952 the Bank made the first direct loan to a private sector firm—the Indian Iron and Steel Company. Two years later the Bank participated in the formation of the Industrial Credit and Investment Corporation of India (ICICI), with a loan of $10 million. By the end of the First Plan the Bank had loaned India about $120 million. After the Aid India Consortium was organized in 1958, Bank lending to India rose quickly; and the entire Bank Group's commitments to India expanded rapidly again after the founding of International Development Association (IDA) in 1960.

Mason and Asher, in their monumental history of the World Bank, argued that India influenced the Bank as much as the Bank influenced India. Within the Bank, the thinking on how economic development takes place and how development can be assisted was influenced by the Bank's lending experiences in various countries and regions. The lending experience in India, where the economy was becoming mired in extensive controls on agricultural prices, interest rates, external accounts, and protection to domestic industry, pushed these development issues more to the forefront of the Bank's thinking on its role in the development process (Mason and Asher, 1973, pp. 457–73). The creation of IDA was due, at least indirectly, to the search by India and several other developing countries in the 1950s for an international agency to provide long-term credits to poor countries. Several other observers also noted that India played an important role in liberalizing the World Bank's outlook on two major aspects of development assistance strategy: the project versus program lending issue, and the private sector–public enterprise debate (Jha, 1973, p. 99; Veit, 1976, p. 176). I. G. Patel, an important figure in Indian economic affairs, noted "the difficulties we had in the early 1960s, for example, in persuading the World Bank that rural electrification, even though not so economic in the short-run, was important and deserved World Bank assistance. Later, in the early 1970s, the World Bank had begun to criticize us for not devoting enough attention to rural electrification!" (1986, p. 215).

Its experience with India offers an important case study of the World Bank's attempt to use leverage to influence the economic policies of a borrowing country (see also chapters 5 and 6). Until 1963 or so the Bank's influence on India was not significant at the macroeconomic policy level, only in the technical, economic, and other aspects of particular Bank projects. Toward the middle of India's Third Plan (1961–66), however, the Bank proposed, and the Indian government accepted, a comprehensive study of the causes of the slow pace of Indian economic development. This was the report of the Bernard Bell mission to India, which was released in early 1966. The report was critical of some aspects of Indian economic policies, mainly in the areas of agriculture, quantitative controls on imports, and foreign exchange. Several policy discussions were conducted between Bank officials and their Indian government counterparts, although, as I. P. M. Cargill pointed out, several policy alternatives of the Bell report already had been formulated and considered by the Indian government (1973, p. 91). The devaluation of the Indian rupee in 1966 (see below) was said to have followed pressure by the Bank. But here again Cargill noted (p. 92) that the Indian government had considered devaluation and related changes in trade and exchange policies before the Bell report. Nevertheless, the Bell report underscored the need for measures to improve the economic environment facing the Indian agricultural sector.

The Bank also played an important role from 1951 on in resolving the dispute between India and Pakistan over waters of the Indus River system (Mason and Asher, 1973, pp. 595–610) and reaching a settlement among all parties in 1960 after long and protracted negotiations. Both Mason and Asher (1973) and Veit (1976) commented that the Bank's leverage was strengthened by the promise of substantial funds to both countries to exploit the water resources. Shortly after the Indus Water Treaty was signed, and then again in 1966 and 1968, the Bank and IDA financed further development of the river water system.

Until the end of 1985 total Bank loans to India amounted to $6.8 billion, and IDA credits, to $12.7 billion (Government of India, 1985, p. 20). The government report on external assistance stated cryptically that program assistance "has been totally stopped since 1976–77 and since then the entire assistance from the World Bank Group is tied to projects" (p. 21). The projects financed were in nearly all sectors of the Indian economy: agriculture, irrigation, dairy development, rural and urban drinking water supplies, population and nutrition programs, fertilizer, oil, gas, railways, and telecommunications. At the end of 1985 a total of 130 projects were in progress. The magnitude of lending and the number and variety of projects financed obviously is not irrelevant to the leverage issue. At the project level, as opposed to the broad framework of macroeconomic policy, the Bank's influence has ensured efficient conduct. But there also have been disagreements on projects; for example, the Bank's technical standards on road projects were unacceptable to India (Jha, 1973, p. 100).

The Bank Group has played an important role in India in institution building to serve development. IDA support to India's urban planning and development agencies (e.g., the Calcutta Metropolitan Development Authority) was important in strengthening the nation's ability to cope with urban growth. Since the mid-1970s the Bank has supported the "training and visit" extension system (T&V) to replace the community development–derived system of multipurpose village-level workers (see below). The World Bank and IDA are now the biggest donors to India, contributing about 60 percent of the total assistance in 1982–83.

The consortium led by the World Bank was a useful institutional innovation from the point of view of the donors as well as from that of India, even though it did not completely replace bilateral aid relations. The Consortium members expected that "their aid to India would be put to good use" and that the Indian government would pursue effective policies to promote growth; from the Indian side, there were expectations that "so long as reasonably effective policies were pursued, the international community would continue with financial support of India's development program" (Cargill, 1973, pp. 90–91). Consortium members expected joint concerted action to influence Indian economic policies; in reality, however, aid leverage was never very large or onerous, and usually it was in line with Indian thinking.

Aid Tying Issues

In the early years of the foreign aid program the issue of tied aid, including project tying, source tying, and reverse tying, was frequently raised by various observers in India and other countries. Project aid, for example, is tied aid in that it is given to cover part or all of the foreign exchange cost of some identifiable undertaking. Nonproject or general-purpose aid comprises, for example, financing for purchases of spare parts and raw materials and, generally, support for the balance of payments; nonproject aid may be tied to purchases from a specific country source. Reverse tying occurs when the repayments of a loan from a specific source are made in the form of commodity exports to the country of the source. Aid from multilateral bodies is usually free from source tying because of their policies regarding global tendering. Project and source tying may occur when donors judge that the condition will lead to quicker and more efficient use of the aid and, simultaneously, enable the project so financed to be identified with the donor. When aid is used to finance the import content of new projects, the pattern of imports can become biased toward capital goods for new projects (see chapters 4–6).

The issue of aid tying generally has been approached in terms of costs to the recipient countries. Several authors concluded that these costs were high (see, e.g., Bhagwati and Desai, 1970; and Chaudhuri, 1978). The true extent of resource transfers was about one-fifth less than the nominal amounts of the transfers. Unfortunately, the lack of available information makes it difficult to give an accurate historical account of the extent of aid tying and, hence, of the actual transfer of real resources. However, some investigators have noted broad changes over time in the extent of source tying by donors in relation to total aid flows. About two-thirds of the bilateral loans to India during the Second Plan period (1956–61) were source-tied, and this proportion increased during the Third Plan period (1961–66) to 83 percent (Balasubramanyam, 1984, p. 174). However, the long-term trend has been toward a gradual untying of aid. Of India's thirteen main bilateral donors, eight have untied 60–85 percent of their assistance; only Japan and the United Kingdom give less than 40 percent of their aid untied (Lipton, Toge, and Cassen, 1984, p. 18).

It is also difficult to document the consequence on the nominal volume of assistance arising from recipients' attempts to untie aid. T. W. Schultz provides one telling example: "Sweden recently offered India a generous training grant in forestry. After two years of negotiations, however, the Indian government was unable to eliminate the tied condition that Sweden insisted upon, and the grant was for that reason not accepted. Weaker countries do not do what India did" (1981, p. 132).

The early years of the foreign aid program in India were marked by concerns with the rather long lags between authorization of aid and its use (Narain and Rao, 1963; Streeten and Hill, 1968; Bhagwati and Desai, 1970). These lags arose essentially because much of the aid was project-tied and source-tied, and India's much vaunted administrative service was not adequately prepared for detailed project preparation, programming, and scheduling, a task that became bigger with the increasing assumption of public control and ownership. Aid utilization rates are affected by a number of factors, among them the availability of complementary factors and inputs, the use of import licenses for capital goods, and the length of the gestation periods during project design.

The rate of utilization of external assistance has not been uniform. Bhagwati and Desai estimated the rate to be in the range of 26 percent to 53 percent during the Third Plan period. In the Fourth Plan years (1969–74) utilizations outpaced authorizations, and during the Fifth Plan (1974–79) aid authorizations reached Rs 98.4 billion but utilization was only Rs 72.6 billion. From 1979 to 1983, utilization of external assistance amounted to about two-thirds of the total authorizations of Rs 114.9 billion (Government of India, *Economic Survey, 1983–84*, 1984, table 7.1, p. 152). Unfortunately, it is difficult to ascertain with any confidence to what extent recent trends in the rate of aid utilization are due to the relaxation of donor practices on aid tying and to what extent they are due to improvements in project procedures, changes in Government of India policies on imports of capital goods, or changes in project composition.

A Macroeconomic Perspective on Development Assistance to India

The impact of development assistance depends on various factors, among them the share of foreign aid in the receiving country's total investment, although assessing the contribution of aid to productive capacity is difficult. The efficiency with which aid is used depends fundamentally on the economic environment within which it is employed. An assessment of its effect can be attempted only in conjunction with an assessment of the receiving country's economic policies.

India's formal planned development began in 1951. The development strategy, at least in industry, was basically in place by the beginning of the Second Plan (1956–61); it was to use publicly sponsored industrialization to achieve self-reliant growth. The Industrial Policy Resolution of 1956 very carefully defined the various spheres of public and private sector activity. Much of heavy industry and equipment, rail and air transport, electricity generation, mining, shipbuilding, and telecommunications became the exclusive responsibility of the public sector.

The policy also included the use of controls and licensing to allocate raw materials, increase industrial capacity, allocate foreign exchange, and control imports. The exclusion of private enterprise from large areas of industrial activity and effective exchange controls were principal deterrents to the inflow of private foreign capital. These administrative controls have undergone considerable refinements and adjustments, even periods of relative liberalization, but they still pervade nearly all spheres of economic activity.

India's inward-looking industrialization strategy led to a diversified industrial structure. This does not mean that the full implications of the development strategy were understood by the policymakers in India or, for that matter, by the aid givers abroad, however. The government recognized to some extent that the development of the capital goods industries was not likely to provide substantial direct labor employment. To compensate, it decided to develop the cottage and small industries sector. The policy has not been entirely successful, however. According to Krishna, "The volume of unemployment keeps growing, contrary to an important objective of Indian policy" (1980, p. 81). That this policy was not likely to succeed was noted early by several critics of Indian planning, most notably Milton Friedman. Peter T. Bauer quoted an unpublished 1955 memorandum prepared by Friedman for the U.S. International Cooperation Administration in which he concluded that the large investment in heavy industry as well as in cottage industry "threatens an inefficient use of capital at the one extreme by combining it with too little labor, and an inefficient use of labor at the other extreme by combining it with too little capital" (Bauer, 1961, p. 59).

Since the beginning of the First Plan the Indian economy has recorded an average growth rate of between 3.5 percent and 4.0 percent per year. Year-to-year fluctuations have occurred, but the rate has not risen or fallen on any sustained basis. Table 12.2 compares Indian economic performance with that in selected developing countries for the periods 1965–80 and 1980–85. In relation to the economic performance of those other countries, India's performance on savings and investment has been much better than on aggregate or per capita income growth. Gross domestic savings as a percentage of gross domestic product showed a steady upward trend, from about 10 percent in 1950–51 to 14 percent in 1965 and 21 percent in 1985. The public sector's share in gross domestic savings was 18.9 percent in 1950–51, 23.2 percent in 1960–61, 17.6 percent in 1970–71, and about 21 percent in 1981–82. The rate of gross domestic investment as a percentage of GDP also has risen over the past three decades. Although the ratio of added capital to increases in output rose steadily, investment in the public sector has had a very low rate of return, essentially because of inefficiency.

Table 12.2. Some Economic Indicators: India and Selected Developing Countries

Country	Per Capita GNP (1985 $)	GDP Growth Rate (%)		Agriculture Growth Rate (%)		Manufacturing Growth Rate (%)		Gross Domestic Savings (% of GDP)		Gross Domestic Investment (% of GDP)		Percentage of Labor Force in			
												Agriculture		Industry	
		1965–80	1980–85	1965–80	1980–85	1965–80	1980–85	1965	1985	1965	1985	1965	1980	1965	1980
India	270	3.8	5.2	2.8	2.7	4.4	5.6	14	21	18	25	73	70	12	13
China	310	6.4	9.8	3.0	9.4	9.5	12.4	25	34	25	38	81	74	8	14
Pakistan	380	5.2	6.0	3.3	2.1	5.3	10.1	13	5	21	17	60	55	18	16
Sri Lanka	380	4.0	5.1	2.7	4.0	3.2	5.5	13	13	12	25	56	53	14	14
Philippines	580	5.9	−0.5	4.6	1.7	7.5	−1.2	15	13	21	16	58	52	16	16
Turkey	1,080	6.3	4.5	3.2	2.6	7.5	7.9	13	16	15	20	75	58	11	17
Brazil	1,640	9.0	1.3	4.7	3.0	9.8	1.2[a]	27	22	25	16	49	31	20	27
Mexico	2,080	6.5	0.8	3.2	2.3	7.4	0.0[a]	21	26	22	21	50	37	22	29
South Korea	2,150	9.5	7.9	3.0	6.3	18.8	9.0	7	31	15	30	55	36	15	27

Sources: World Bank, *World Development Report, 1987* (New York: Oxford University Press, 1987); idem, *World Development Report, 1988* (New York: Oxford University Press, 1988).
[a] 1980–86.

The increases in saving and capital formation did not result in rapid economic growth, however. Strict licensing and controls on the growth of industrial capacity and direct quantitative controls on imports bred considerable inefficiency in the use of scarce resources. There is some evidence of declines (over the period 1959–79) in total factor productivity in several industry groups (e.g., metal products, petroleum products, wood and cork manufactures, rubber products, chemical products, and nonelectrical machinery) and of rising capital output ratios in nearly all industry groups (Ahluwalia, 1985, pp. 131–32).

Development Assistance and the Foreign Trade Regime

Bhagwati and Srinivasan (1975)[4] examined the Indian government's interventions in the foreign trade sector from 1950 to 1970 and the methods by which scarce foreign exchange was allocated in order to ascertain the static efficiency effects of the foreign trade policies and their effect on growth. The investigators concluded that the basic strategy of industrialization (detailed industrial targeting and licensing, coupled with strict import licensing) was detrimental to the growth of the economy "by adversely influencing export performance, by wasteful inter-industrial and inter-firm allocation of resources, by permitting and encouraging expansion of excess capacity and by blunting competition and hence the incentives for cost-consciousness and quality-improvement" (p. 245). The industrialization and trade policies reinforced each other by effectively eliminating domestic and foreign competition and, hence, the incentives for efficiency.

With its low ratio of exports to national income throughout the 1950s and 1960s, India's share in total world trade fell as exports remained heavily biased toward "traditional" items (e.g., tea, jute manufactures, and cotton textiles). Because these commodities were believed to have poor export growth prospects, the government's policy of import-substituting industrialization was reinforced despite the rising capital intensity of the policy.

The first severe foreign exchange crisis occurred soon after the Second Plan (1956–61) began. Although significant amounts of aid flowed into India, exports continued to stagnate, and the resulting foreign exchange crises led to the imposition of a quantitative-restrictions regime. The government made some tentative attempts to promote exports, but very little was accomplished. The large inflows of foreign aid became a painless substitute for foreign exchange earned via exports, and India was able to maintain a higher rate of investment than would have been possible if aid flows had been smaller.

Beginning in the early 1960s the government followed a policy of export subsidies and licensing preferences that reflected selective intervention with little economic rationale. However, the subsidies reduced the average degree of overvaluation of the Indian rupee. Export subsidies and increased use of

Table 12.3. Some External Sector Indicators: India and Selected Countries

| Country | Merchandise Trade, 1985 ($ millions) | | Manufactured Exports ($ millions) | | Average Annual Growth Rate (%) | | | | Total Long-term Debt Outstanding, 1985 | | Long-term Debt Service as % of Exports, 1985 |
| | | | | | Exports | | Imports | | | | |
	Exports	Imports	1965	1985	1965–80	1980–85	1965–80	1980–85	$ Millions	% of GNP	
India	10,260	14,608	828	5,890	3.7	4.6	1.6	2.2	29,743	15.0	12.7
China	27,327	42,526	1,021	13,380	5.5	8.8	8.0	17.6	7,020[a]	2.6	7.8[b]
Pakistan	2,740	5,890	190	1,731	4.3	2.4	0.5	3.9	10,707	31.7	30.0
Sri Lanka	1,333	1,832	5	398	0.5	7.3	−1.1	1.5	2,914	49.2	14.7
Philippines	4,629	5,459	43	2,534	5.7	−2.1	2.9	−5.9	16,559	52.1	19.5
Turkey	8,255	11,035	11	3,849	5.5	25.3	7.8	10.1	18,180	35.4	32.1
Brazil	25,637	14,346	134	8,911	9.4	6.6	8.3	−9.1	91,094	43.8	34.8
Mexico	21,866	13,459	165	7,129	7.7	10.1	5.7	−11.3	89,010	52.8	48.2
South Korea	30,283	31,129	104	27,669	27.3	13.0	15.2	9.8	35,756	43.0	21.5

Sources: World Bank, *World Development Report, 1987* (New York: Oxford University Press, 1987); idem, *World Development Report, 1988* (New York: Oxford University Press, 1988).
[a] Public and publicly guaranteed only.
[b] 1986.

import duties led to a gradual de facto devaluation that culminated in the formal devaluation of the Indian rupee in June 1966. This move effectively rationalized and unified the multiple exchange rates that had emerged from the myriad subsidies and controls on exports and imports. It was the beginning of a new phase in which export subsidies were eliminated and import duties were reduced.

The political fallout from the devaluation was heavy. Within India it was viewed as an attempt by the Aid India Consortium to influence policy, hence the aid relationship with the Western aid donors deteriorated. Yet the Indian government had thoroughly considered the devaluation of the rupee and the related changes in trade and exchange rate policies before the Bell report. If anything, "the actual timing of the devaluation came as a surprise to the World Bank" (Cargill, 1973, p. 92).

The devaluation and other export promotion measures of the late 1960s contributed importantly to Indian export performance from 1970 to 1985. The oil price increases of the early 1970s and the drop in external aid made an export drive imperative. Between 1970 and 1975, exports grew, in current prices, over two and one-half times, and they more than doubled between 1975 and 1982. Yet the quantum index of exports in 1980–81 was only 80 percent above the 1970–71 figure. In fact, India's share in total world exports fell steadily after 1970 to only 0.4 percent in 1981.

To a large extent, the growth and composition pattern of Indian imports has been determined principally by development strategy, particularly the policy of establishing an adequate indigenous capacity in the basic industrial sectors (e.g., machinery and transportation equipment). Consequently, the import share of mineral fuels and lubricants increased rapidly after 1970 with the rise in oil prices. Periods of liberalized trade have been brief and tentative at best, relying heavily on quantitative restrictions. Currently, a cumbersome scheme of export subsidies, quotas, and licenses as the main instruments of import control continues to characterize the trade regime, and India remains a relatively closed economy with slow economic growth.

Table 12.3 provides some comparative external sector data for India and a number of other countries. The data reflect the outcome of an inward-looking development strategy that has resulted in both export and import growth at much lower rates in India than in most other countries in the comparison group. India's debt situation also reflects India's reluctance in the past to borrow from private capital markets abroad. What is more important, however, in the light of recent attempts at trade liberalization and relaxation of controls on investment, there is potential for India to accelerate its growth by increasing borrowings in private capital markets abroad, which should also permit greater capacity utilization of existing plant and equipment and fuller use of India's skilled and unskilled labor resources.

Agriculture and Rural Development

At the time of independence Indian agriculture was in a sorry state. Total foodgrain production was stagnant, use of modern inputs was low, and the quality of rural life held little hope for most of the population. Since then, some regions of the country have been completely transformed. Agriculture still dominates the country's economy, accounting for about one-third of the gross domestic product in 1985. The percentage of the total agricultural labor force is about 70 percent, not much lower than it was in 1965. About 70 percent of total crop production is in foodgrains: nearly 40 percent in rice and about 33 percent in wheat.

Foodgrain production has risen over 3 percent per year, from about 50.8 million tons in 1950–51 to about 150 million tons in 1985–86, which ranks favorably with the growth rates achieved in the developed world, yet the per capita increase was only about 1 percent per year. From 1965 to 1980 the rate of growth of Indian agricultural output exceeded that of all low-income countries except Pakistan and China. During 1980–85 the growth rate in India was at the level of the earlier period and was less than one-third that of China but higher than that of Pakistan and even that for lower-middle-income countries (World Bank, 1987, p. 204). Foodgrain production grew largely as a result of increases in acreage during the 1950s but as a result of yield increases during the 1960s. Net irrigated area grew about 26 percent between 1950–51 and 1965–66 but about 44 percent between 1965–66 and 1980–81. Irrigation increased the wheat area over fourfold between 1950 and 1980, and the rice area, about 60 percent. Fertilizer consumption (in kilograms of plant nutrient per hectare of arable land) more than tripled between 1970 and 1982.

Growth rates of agricultural output for various subperiods depend, of course, upon the selected end years. For example, T. N. Srinivasan (1979) found that food output grew more or less uniformly between 1950 and 1978, with no evidence of either acceleration or deceleration after 1967–68. Bardhan (1984, p. 11) noted that despite impressive gains in wheat output and yields after 1967, the overall rate of growth was not accelerated after the Green Revolution of the late 1960s. The pace of oilseed and fiber production slowed after 1967, and the output of pulses, an important source of protein, was essentially stagnant between 1970 and 1982.

The government and international donor agencies devoted substantial resources to agriculture; the ultimate effect has been to alter the economic, institutional, and technological environment of Indian farmers. Agriculture is in the private sector in India in the sense that day-to-day decisions rest with millions of farm families. Neither the Indian government nor aid givers have had a systematic, long-term view of the conditions essential to effecting agricultural modernization. The presumption was that investments in physical infrastructure were not only necessary but sufficient to generate and sustain

economic growth, a view that is partly attributable to the inadequate understanding, from our current perspective, of the economic modernization process. Even so, the U.S. and other bilateral and multilateral assistance to India's agricultural sector was fundamental to the growth of that sector.

Like the industrial sector, the agricultural sector in India received aid
from various sources; however, the aid to agriculture was more specialized.
The United States and, to some extent, Canada financed food and fertilizer
imports as well as a large number of agriculture programs and projects,
whereas other countries concentrated on narrow areas within agriculture. Development assistance from Australia, New Zealand, Denmark, Switzerland,
the Netherlands, and Hungary went largely to animal husbandry, including
dairy development and processing of animal products; Norway, Sweden, and
Finland aided primarily forestry and fisheries; West Germany contributed significantly to area development programs; Japan aided agricultural extension;
and the Soviet Union assisted a large mechanized farm in Suratgarh. Sizable
assistance was also provided by the World Bank and IDA and by nonofficial
sources, such as the Ford and Rockefeller foundations.

IDA commitments for agriculture and rural development between 1961
and 1982 totaled nearly $4 billion, about 40 percent of total IDA agricultural
commitments. The credits went to nearly every segment of agriculture (e.g.,
irrigation, flood control, agricultural credit, food storage, and research and
extension), with the majority going to irrigation and agricultural credit. The
Indian seed industry, both public and private sector firms, was supported by
IDA, and with FAO and the World Food Program, IDA played an important
role in the phenomenal growth of milk production between 1970 and 1985.

India's government has devoted substantial resources to agriculture, from
Rs 7.2 billion in the First Plan to over Rs 61.3 billion in the Fifth Plan and
Rs 97.5 billion in the Sixth Plan, in current prices. The allocation of resources
has fluctuated among the various plan periods but consistently has been over
20 percent.

Even before substantial investments were made in irrigation to increase
the productive capacity of the land, a principal emphasis was on altering
people's motivations and attitudes toward change. Implicit in India's rural
development policy was the view that farmers are tradition-bound, economically unresponsive people who lack the motivation and ability to efficiently
use the resources at their disposal. The first, and by far the most ambitious,
effort to tackle the tremendous task of raising income, productivity, and quality of life in the rural population was the community development program
(see also chapter 10). Begun in October 1952, the program was a multipurpose, broad, frontal attack on every aspect of village life: agriculture, physical
infrastructure (e.g., roads and wells), education, health, cottage industry, cooperative organizations, the role and status of women, emancipation of the
"untouchable" class, and land reform. The U.S. government and the Ford

Foundation provided more than $100 million for the community development program between 1951–52 and 1960–61 (Brown, 1971, p. 5). In terms of resources, the outlays for the program were only about one-fifth of those for major irrigation works.

Several observers of the community development program concluded fairly early on that a rapid increase in agricultural production could not be achieved by relying on available agricultural technology. A U.S. Technical Co-operation Mission recommended in 1953 that the Indian government reallocate some community development funds away from demonstration-based extension activity to agricultural research on new agricultural technology. This recommendation was also stressed in 1955 by a Joint Indo-American Team on Agricultural Research and Education and in 1958 by the government's own Nalagarh Committee. Although the output and productivity gains due to the community development program were small, the program went a long way toward improving village environments and establishing certain administrative structures that still function.

The focus of policy shifted in the early 1960s with initiation of the Intensive Agriculture District Program (IADP), created to increase output rather than improve conditions of rural life. The IADP demonstrated how to achieve rapid increases in production in certain areas by concentrating scarce resources (fertilizers, pesticides, water, credit, technical and farm management assistance, etc.) in the more responsive districts, that is, those more likely to succeed. The IADP was assisted by the Ford Foundation, the United States, and the Japanese government. The Indian government and the state governments provided more than $30 million for the first five years of the program (Brown, 1971, p. 14). Evenson and Kislev (1975, p. 106) estimated that a total of about $100 million was spent on the program up until 1975, about one-half the amount directed to research activities for improving crop production in the entire country during the 1960s.

In the IADP experiment the use of modern inputs (especially fertilizer) expanded, yet the increase in output was small. The reason is that no new biological sources of growth in production had been generated by the Indian agricultural research system, which in its infancy focused research on ways to reduce the risks arising from drought and pests, for example, rather than on raising yields. Increased use of fertilizer and other modern inputs did not yield large increases in output until new seed varieties that could effectively respond to new chemical nutrients became available. New biological technology could not be brought in from abroad because of the location specificity of such technology. India's relatively undeveloped agricultural science capacity constrained the adaptation and development of more appropriate technology. Further, significant differences in soils, weather, and environmental conditions limited the possibilities for using new plant technology across different geoclimatic zones even within India.

Simultaneously with the IADP program there was under way an important institution-building program that was to lay the foundation for a science-based agriculture in India. This program received substantial assistance from the Rockefeller Foundation, the Ford Foundation, the U.S. government, and other agencies that provided scientists and technicians, financed the foreign training of Indian scientific personnel, and laid the basis for a growing and vigorous research establishment. The technological capacity to produce new sources of permanent income was achieved by a combination of critical political leadership in India and a long-term commitment of financial and human resources from donors (Lele and Goldsmith, 1989). The physical facilities for agricultural research and the scientific capacity to produce a steady stream of scientific knowledge and methods applicable to Indian conditions are an important prerequisite for sustaining agriculture (see chapter 9). The program has made rapid progress.

The Indian agricultural research system has been characterized as one of high caliber relative to those of most other developing countries and even those of some developed countries. Ruttan described the system as "clearly one of the half-dozen most significant national agricultural research systems in the world in terms of resources employed and level of scientific activity" (Ruttan, 1982, p. 95). The Indian Council of Agricultural Research coordinates and guides the country's agricultural research and education; thirty-two central research institutes and seven soil conservation research and training centers are under its jurisdiction. There are now twenty-one agricultural universities, seventy-three agricultural colleges (including those at the agricultural university campuses), and twenty-one veterinary colleges. During the 1960s six U.S. universities under US/AID-financed contracts assisted in developing the teaching, research, and extension programs in the agricultural universities; the first such university started functioning in Uttar Pradesh in 1960.

In a general sense, scientific personnel and capital and current expenditures are the inputs for the agricultural research system. The output is new knowledge. Whether it is embodied in new but conventionally defined production inputs or whether it serves to alter existing input combinations, the knowledge must be treated as a production input that affects the productivity of agriculture. The outstanding achievement of the agricultural research establishment has been the attainment of food self-sufficiency by India. Most of the increase in the production of cereals occurred after 1965, mainly owing to the introduction of the high-yield varieties of wheat, rice, and maize and their adaptation to Indian local environmental conditions. The agricultural scientists "were not the mere recipients of this (plant) material but they improved it significantly" (Randhawa, 1979, p. vi). The investments in Indian agricultural research have yielded very high returns in terms of agricultural productivity (see chapter 9).

The cumulative effect of the government's commitment to providing inputs, agricultural credit, the timely distribution of modern seed varieties, and the management of water resources, along with its price policy, is a relatively promising outlook for Indian agriculture. Foreign assistance played a crucial role in the development of the agricultural research system and of the infrastructural support for agriculture in India; it is one of the great success stories of the international donor community.

Food Aid Impact

Bilateral and multilateral aid to India for agricultural and industrial development was considerable, but it did not generate the kind of controversy or debate that food aid did. During the First Plan India imported significant amounts of food only during the first year, 1951–52. Foodgrain prices were stable during that period. From the beginning of the Second Plan (1956–61), however, India's food imports began to increase. The trend of agricultural production was upward, but fluctuations occurred; consequently, in the absence of adequate stocks of food or foreign exchange, the government entered into an agreement with the United States for assistance for the import of foodgrains.

The era of food aid opened with the U.S. Agriculture Trade and Adjustment Act of 1954 (PL 480). As PL 480 was originally enacted, food could be provided to recipient countries under three titles: Title I shipments were sold to recipient countries for local currency, which was accumulated by the United States in the recipient country and used to meet U.S. expenses there; Title II covered food donations for school meals and work programs; and Title III allowed the barter of U.S. food for strategic goods needed by the United States. For India, Title I shipments amounted to nearly 90 percent of all PL 480 shipments. Between 1955 and 1976 India received the most food aid of any country under PL 480: over 50 million tons of agricultural commodities, only slightly less than the combined shipments to Pakistan, South Korea, South Vietnam, and Egypt (Shenoy, 1974, p. 32; Isenman and Singer, 1977, p. 231; Tarrant, 1980, p. 247). The commodities included wheat, rice, maize, milo, cotton, dairy products, tobacco, and soybean oil. Wheat shipments dominated the program. U.S. food aid to India was about $2.4 billion between 1950 and 1971, about 53 percent of all U.S. aid to India during that period. From 1972 to 1985, U.S. food aid to India was about $1.8 billion, about 69 percent of total U.S. aid to India in that period (US/AID, *U.S. Overseas Loans and Grants*, various issues).

The nature and magnitude of these shipments, especially in the mid-1960s, and their effect on the development of the agricultural sector and on the overall economic development of India, especially whether food aid imports acted as a disincentive for domestic producers by depressing the price below the price that would have ruled in the absence of the aid, have been studied extensively. A related focus was whether the availability of food imports reduced the recipient's efforts to improve its agricultural situation by causing a misdirection of investment away from agricultural improvement.

T. W. Schultz (1960) was the first to express some concern with the possible negative effects of agricultural commodity aid on recipient countries. He provided the classic argument that other things remaining unchanged, food aid imports, by adding to domestic supplies, lower the price and hence, given a positively sloping supply curve of agricultural products, lower agricultural output. Others disagreed with him: they denied that production responded to changes in price; if such responsiveness *was* present, it was small (Mann, 1967; Streeten and Hill, 1968; Rogers, Srivastava, and Heady, 1972; Srivastava et al., 1975; Isenman and Singer, 1977). Isenman and Singer found little systematic evidence of the detrimental effect of that food aid on yields.

Between 1956 and 1960 Title I food aid amounted to about 3 percent of India's gross domestic production of foodgrains. The largest shipments occurred from 1965 through 1967, when food aid amounted to nearly 9 percent of India's own production of foodgrains (Isenman and Singer, 1977, p. 231). Food aid to India was tied aid: India could not untie it by shipping out the food. Food aid was repayable in rupees if not in dollars. Its grant equivalent was not the same as its nominal value, which was itself distorted because of its valuation at U.S. domestic farm support prices, which exceeded world prices. Even so, food aid played an important role in providing resources to the government. Isenman and Singer (1977, pp. 235–36) estimated that food aid equaled 10 percent or more of gross investment in the Indian economy in the first half of the 1960s. At a time when the government's investment effort and nonagricultural output were increasing, the availability of food aid restrained wages growth and offset the risk that the investment program would worsen the food situation in the inevitable years of low rainfall.

The basic developmental strategy of the Indian government during the Second and Third plans, with its emphasis on import-substitution industrialization and the creation of infrastructure, was supported by the food aid India received. The aid, essentially a short-term solution to the problem of disastrous harvests caused by the weather, helped to feed millions of poor people. India was not neglecting a long view on food and agriculture. The share of agriculture in total plan outlays during the First Plan (itself somewhat overstated owing to the inclusion of projects begun earlier) was larger than during the Second or Third plan; over the long haul, however, the share of agriculture in plan outlays has not varied very much and has been consistently over 20 percent. Actual expenditures for agriculture, in nominal and in real terms, during the Second and Third plans were substantially higher than during the First Plan. Large investments were made in major and minor irrigation projects, flood control, fertilizer, rural electrification, and community development, undertaken to increase food output. Agricultural research and institution building also were under way. The Indian government and the donors could not have foreseen the development, adaptation, and rapid spread of the new rice and wheat varieties that were appearing during the years of the biggest food aid shipments. Ultimately, then, even in the absence of food aid, it is unlikely that the basic thrust of India's development strategy would have changed.

Conclusions

Foreign aid to India has been small relative to her population and compared with her GNP. But the aid financed significant shares of India's gross investment and imports, for example, over one-sixth of gross domestic capital formation and one-half of imports during the 1960s. Subsequently, the proportions dropped to around 6 percent of gross domestic capital formation and about 15 percent of India's imports. Foreign aid sustained the growth of both industrial and agricultural capacity in India, the food aid playing a crucial role during years when the food situation was tight.

Furthermore, foreign aid brought policy dialogue at the micro project or sector level and at the overall macroeconomic policy level. The policy leverage exerted by U.S. foreign aid was, in Indian eyes at least, heavy-handed. In fact, the devaluation of the rupee in 1965–66 generated considerable resentment toward the United States and other Western donors. Since that low point, the aid relationship has evolved to one of greater mutual understanding and respect.

India is now self-sufficient in food, and aid represents less than 2 percent of India's national income. The biggest donors are the World Bank and IDA. India has developed considerable expertise in formulating policy. There is increasing recognition that the effectiveness of aid can increase only with more meaningful dialogue between India and the Bank Group on both the sector and overall policy levels.

Although India remains a poor country, impressive growth has occurred in physical infrastructure and production capacity in many sectors, and the educational, research, and financial institutions are strong. In agricultural science, medicine, and general engineering both the institutions and the personnel are of high quality. It is true that most of the resources in education and research came from within India, but foreign aid had a key role in developing the infrastructure and the institutions necessary for economic growth. Still, given the industrialization and trade strategies pursued by India, the effect of the inflow of foreign resources was at best modest.

Economic assistance for agriculture and rural development financed massive investments in the rural infrastructure of irrigation, power, roads, and communications. These investments could not have yielded high returns without the complementary investments in education and research. Biochemical and, to a lesser extent, mechanical technology in agriculture is highly location-specific. Thus the increased use of fertilizers and other modern inputs did not yield large increases in output until new seed varieties became available. Similarly, massive investments directed to changing peoples' attitudes and motivations were ineffective as long as inadequate attention was paid to the development of new sources of income and economic incentives provided for the users of these new inputs. Aid for agricultural research and education was spectacularly successful because it was properly adapted to Indian conditions by Indian administrators. Here, again, the success that seems apparent now was less so earlier.

Much has been learned from the Indian experience by the Indians, the economics profession generally, and the donor agencies. The task remains to improve and strengthen institutions, raise productive efficiency, and provide employment opportunities for India's millions. Ultimately, India's future economic performance will depend upon its internal and external economic policies.

13

Assistance to Korea

ANNE O. KRUEGER
AND VERNON W. RUTTAN

In terms of overall development, South Korea is the most successful of the countries studied in this survey. It illustrates the extreme difficulty of assessing the influence of external aid on the development policies and achievements of aid recipients.[1]

Because of the uniqueness of the Korean experience and its lessons for the assessment of aid generally, this chapter focuses on the period 1953 to 1975, the years when aid was a very important factor in South Korean development and the economy was transformed from one that was dependent and relatively slowly growing, with numerous distortions in its incentive structure, into the most rapidly growing economy in the entire world. After briefly outlining the economy's structure and growth during and after the years under review, we describe the aid relationship and the lessons learned therefrom. In the following sections we discuss the relationship between trade and aid; and assistance to agricultural and rural development.

Economic Growth in South Korea

Korea was a Japanese colony until 1945, when it was liberated by the Allied military forces. The upheaval that followed was economically difficult. When Japan withdrew, the monthly rate of inflation was in excess of 100 percent. Most businesses were Japanese-owned, and normal trading ties were disrupted. These difficulties were worsened by partition of the Korean peninsula in 1945.

The 1945–50 period was dominated by reconstruction. Major resources were devoted to developing the Korean educational system. A relatively egalitarian land reform that transferred land to the tiller was successfully accomplished. The American military government and the U.S. Economic Cooperation Administration (ECA) were instrumental in accomplishing both the land and the educational reforms. By 1948–49 the South Korean economy was beginning to revive, because of the relatively large transfer of resources by the military government (until 1948) and by the ECA (after 1948).

By 1949 the future of South Korea, and of economic assistance, was hotly debated in the U.S. administration and Congress. The debate ended in late spring 1950 with the beginning of the Korean War. The United States provided massive assistance throughout the war years (until 1953), most of it in military equipment and supplies (including food) essential to waging the war. The end of hostilities in August 1953 found the Korean economy even more devastated than it had been previously. Most of the progress between 1945 and 1950 was undone, and the economy's infrastructure—roads, ports, and schools—was severely damaged. Among the longer-term legacies of the war were a high rate of inflation (in excess of 50 percent per year from 1953 to 1957) and an elaborate system of exchange control and multiple exchange rates.

The reconstruction period in South Korea started with an extreme macroeconomic imbalance that was partly offset by sizable inflows of U.S. aid during the 1950s (see below). Suh (1986) estimated that between 1954 and 1959 approximately 70 percent of all reconstruction investment was financed by foreign assistance primarily from the United States. Three structural features were particularly important for the dramatic difference in the Korean economy during the 1950s and the 1960s:

1. Like the economies of most developing countries, the Korean economy was predominantly agricultural in the 1950s. In 1954 the primary sector accounted for over 50 percent, and manufacturing for only 5.3 percent, of GNP (table 13.1).[2] Even in 1962 the primary sector accounted for 45.3 percent of GNP, and manufacturing for only 9.1 percent. In short, despite some change in the relative importance of primary and secondary industry during the 1950s, structural transformation was relatively slow.

2. Private consumption accounted for 80 percent of GNP in 1954, while investment accounted for only 11.9 percent. The domestic savings rate was low. Foreign savings, primarily aid, accounted for 5.3 percent of GNP. Indeed, net domestic saving was negative in 1956 (see Krueger, 1979, table 52). The situation was still relatively unchanged by 1962: domestic savings were lower—3.3 percent—and foreign savings higher as a percentage of GNP than in 1954 (table 13.1).

3. Foreign aid was very important. Imports doubled in relation to GNP between 1954 and 1964, reaching 15 percent of GNP by the early 1960s, while exports rose from only 0.8 percent to 2.0 percent.

Thus, despite the opportunities for rapid growth in the postwar reconstruction period, Korean economic growth from 1954 to 1962 was relatively slow. The inefficiencies associated with the foreign exchange shortage and the multiple exchange rate system, with the inevitable corruption surrounding its administration, diverted resources from the export sector, and consequently

Table 13.1. Major Indicators of Korean Economic Growth, 1954–1982

	1954	1962	1972	1982	Average Annual Growth Rate (%)			
					1954–62	1962–72	1972–82	1962–82
1. Population (millions)	21.8	26.5	33.5	39.3	2.5	2.4	1.6	2.0
2. GNP (1975 constant billion won)	2,319	3,071	7,366	15,509	3.6	9.1	7.7	8.4
Primary industry	1,186	1,391	2,150	2,976	2.0	4.5	3.3	3.9
(Share of GNP, %)	(51.1)	(45.3)	(29.2)	(19.2)				
Manufacturing	123	279	1,538	5,304	10.8	18.6	13.2	15.9
(Share of GNP, %)	(5.3)	(9.1)	(20.9)	(34.2)				
Social overhead and services	1,010	1,401	3,677	7,229	4.2	10.1	7.0	8.6
(Share of GNP, %)	(43.6)	(45.6)	(49.9)	(46.6)				
Per capita GNP (1975 constant won)	106,376	115,887	219,881	394,631	1.1	6.6	6.0	6.3
Per capita GNP (1975 constant dollars)	220	239	454	815	1.1	6.6	6.0	6.3
Per capita private consumption (1975 constant won)	84,775	100,114	166,388	260,359	2.1	5.2	4.6	4.9
3. Exports and imports[a]								
Commodity exports, f.o.b. ($ millions)	24	55	1,624	21,853	10.9	40.3	29.7	34.9
Commodity imports, c.i.f. ($ millions)	243	422	2,522	24,251	7.1	19.6	25.4	22.5
Share of manufactured exports in total (%)[b]	—	27.0	87.7	93.7				
Ratio of commodity exports to GNP(%)	0.8	2.0	16.4	31.8				
Ratio of commodity imports to GNP(%)	7.2	15.6	23.7	36.5				
4. Investment and savings[a]								
Share of gross domestic investment in GNP(%)	11.9	12.8	21.7	26.2				
Share of manufacturing investment in total fixed investment (%)	17.5	20.6	19.4	15.3				
Domestic saving rate(%)	6.6	3.3	15.7	21.5				
Foreign saving rate(%)	5.3	10.7	5.2	4.8				

Source: Kwang-suk Kim and Joon-kyung Park, *Sources of Economic Growth in Korea: 1963–1982* (Seoul: Korea Development Institute, 1985).
[a] Based on current price data.
[b] The Ministry of Commerce and Industry's estimates reported in Economic Planning Board, *Major Statistics of Korean Economy* (Seoul, 1982), p. 217.

export earnings failed to grow significantly. Instead, resources were drawn to the import-competing sectors, where the margin of domestic over foreign prices was sizable.

Starting in the late 1950s a series of policy reforms were undertaken. The first step was the general tightening in 1958 of macroeconomic policies—monetary and fiscal—in response to reduced aid levels. A pronounced slowdown in the rate of inflation ensued from an average of 36 percent for the 1953–57 period to 3.8 percent for the years 1958–60 (Mason et al., 1980, table 19).

The second step was the liberalizing of economic policy (Balassa, 1985). A massive devaluation and a consolidation of the exchange rate system took place. The purchasing-power-parity effective exchange rate for South Korean exports rose from 223.8 won per dollar in 1955 to 319.6 in 1960, an increase of 42 percent in real receipts per dollar of commodities exported! The exchange rate reform was accompanied by the installation of additional export incentives (e.g., subsidies, access to subsidized credit, and rights to import goods duty-free). Although the South Korean government was unable initially to contain the rate of inflation, it maintained export incentives through changes in the subsidy rates between formal devaluations. Exporters were assured throughout the 1960s that whatever the domestic inflation rate, their real return on exports would be protected. After his election in 1963, President Park was almost single-mindedly committed to economic growth. The initial success of the export-oriented drive led him, and the entire government, to associate the reforms with the export successes.

Other policy measures should also be noted. In 1964 budgetary reforms substantially reduced the government's deficit from about 5.2 percent of GNP in 1962 to 0.6 percent by 1965. This drop, along with credit reforms, generated a markedly lower rate of inflation: about 10 percent annually, half the 1960–64 rate.[3] Interest rate reforms followed. Earlier the government's ability to direct credit had been an important instrument in subsidizing various producing sectors—initially farmers and import-subsidizing industries, subsequently export industries.

Conditions after 1965 cannot be described as those of a fully free market. Yet the rate of interest to domestic savers increased substantially—from 12 percent to 26.4 percent—and bank lending rates rose markedly. In each of the first three years after the interest rate reform, savings deposits in commercial banks doubled and the ratio of savings deposits to GNP rose from 3.8 percent in 1965 to 21.7 percent in 1969 (Suh, 1986). This rise, combined with the substantial reduction in the rate of inflation, significantly increased the cost of credit to borrowers and greatly reduced the subsidy element in loans from the banking system.[4]

Some of the other reforms that permitted the economy to grow rapidly were a liberalization of the import system and streamlining of the customs

Table 13.2. Indicators of Korean Growth, 1960–1970 (Average Annual %)

Year	Primary Sector	Industry	Services	Exports	GNP
1960	−0.5	6.7	2.8	54.1	1.9
1961	11.8	4.6	−1.1	22.7	4.8
1962	−5.0	14.0	8.9	30.0	3.1
1963	7.9	11.4	7.4	53.9	8.8
1964	15.3	12.6	3.0	36.7	8.6
1965	−1.6	20.4	9.9	47.0	6.1
1966	10.5	18.7	12.6	44.5	12.4
1967	−4.4	21.4	13.8	32.7	7.8
1968	2.3	29.5	15.4	45.8	12.6
1969	12.0	25.5	14.6	36.9	15.0
1970	−0.4	15.5	8.9	33.8	7.9

Source: Edward S. Mason et al., *The Economic and Social Modernization of the Republic of Korea* (Cambridge: Harvard University Press, 1980), table 12.

and other procedures surrounding export and import regulations and entitlements. The government itself was a major actor in the transformation, since it maintained the capacity of ports, communications, and transport to deal with the rapid increase in volume. Perhaps most significant was the government activity in the economic sphere: almost single-mindedly it facilitated the export drive, the hallmark of South Korea's dynamic economy.

Some indicators of the transformation are given in tables 13.1 and 13.2. The annual data (table 13.2) show that the first few years of the export drive were "successful" only in hindsight. Real GNP growth during the early 1960s was not significantly different from that of the late 1950s. The only real change apparently was in the rate of export growth. The overall rate of economic growth was adversely affected by the poor crops of 1960 and 1962. By the mid-1960s, however, the possibility of successful development and self-sustaining growth was beginning to be apparent. In most observers' minds the question still was how long the rapid rate could be sustained. As it turned out, it was sustained for more than twenty years and completely transformed the structure and performance of the Korean economy.

There was a dramatic change in economic structure between the early 1960s and the early 1980s. The share of the primary sector in GNP fell from 45.3 percent in 1962 to 19.2 percent in 1982 despite the fact that primary sector output grew at the very satisfactory rate of 3.9 percent annually. The share of manufacturing rose from 9.1 percent to 34.2 percent during the same period. Even more striking was the rise in the ratio of gross domestic investment, from 12.8 percent of GNP in 1962 to 26.2 percent in 1982. During the same period exports rose from 2.0 percent to 31.8 percent of GNP (table 13.1).

Productivity growth has been a greater source of economic growth in South Korea than in most developing countries. In their very careful study, Kwang-suk Kim and Joon-kyung Park found that growth in the conventional factors of production—labor and capital—accounted for 55.4 percent of the growth in output between 1963 and 1982, and the nonconventional factors—scale economies, advances in knowledge, and reallocation of resources from low- to high-productivity sectors and education—accounted for 44.6 percent (1985, pp. 166–67).

By any standard the South Korean story is one of success, to a degree previously regarded as unattainable. South Korea has few natural resources. The oil price increase and commodity price boom of 1973–74 affected the economy to a greater extent than in many other countries. The government, nonetheless, managed to pass on the price increases, encourage domestic saving, respond with new export activities (e.g., construction in the Middle East), and sustain the momentum of economic growth. The rate of growth of real GNP in South Korea was 9.1 percent between 1962 and 1972 and 7.7 percent between 1972 and 1982 despite some severe difficulties. In the late 1960s the real exchange rate was not maintained; in the 1970s the real interest rate and the premature decision to develop heavy industry created problems; and again in the late 1970s difficulties were associated with massive expansion of some heavy industries, the second oil price increase, depreciation of the exchange rate, and the political uncertainties following the assassination of President Park (Balassa, 1985). However, the real rate of growth exceeded 7 percent, and the rate of inflation averaged less than 4 percent in 1982–84 (Korea Development Institute, 1984).

The lessons for development assistance policy originate in the remarkable change in South Korean economic policies and economic performance between the late 1950s and the mid-1960s and in the role U.S. aid played in the process. The latter is the subject of the following section.

The Role of Aid in Korean Economic Growth

The roles played by foreign assistance in Korea are summarized in tables 13.1 and 13.3. U.S. economic assistance, which included both large resource flows and substantial technical assistance, was most important in the 1950s, when aid-financed imports accounted for 69 percent of total imports and aid represented about 77 percent of all savings (with foreign savings accounting for 88 percent of all savings). The period of rapid Korean growth in the 1960s was accompanied by a gradual reduction in the importance of aid, which made the returns from increasing domestic savings less than they would have been otherwise.

The early 1960s represented an important transition period in donor-recipient relations for Korea (Cole, 1980). Before 1961 the United States had

Table 13.3. Aid-financed Imports Relative to Total Imports, 1953–1975 ($U.S. and Percentage of Total Imports)

		Aid-Financed Imports							
		Total				U.S. Share			
		Grant[a]		Loan[b]		Grant[c]		Loan	
Year	Total Imports	$U.S.	%	$U.S.	%	$U.S.	%	$U.S.	%
1953	345	201	58			171	50		
1954	243	149	61			132	54		
1955	341	233	68			215	63		
1956	386	320	83			304	79		
1957	442	374	85			369	83		
1958	378	311	82			314	83		
1959	304	211	69			220	72		
1960	343	232	68			245	71		
1961	316	197	62			199	63		
1962	422	219	52			232	55		
1963	560	233	42			216	39		
1964	404	143	35	25	6	149	37	25	6
1965	463	136	29	2	0	131	28	2	0
1966	716	148	21	50	7	103	14	47	7
1967	996	152	15	80	8	97	10	38	4
1968	1,463	168	12	90	6	106	7	70	5
1969	1,824	155	9	169	9	107	6	71	4
1970	1,984	187	9	101	5	82	4	51	3
1971	2,394	126	5	193	8	51	2	34	1
1972	2,522	66	3	342	14	5	0	194	8
1973	4,240	23	1	224	5	2	0	123	3
1974	6,851	30	0	186	3	1	0	20	0
1975	7,274	37		348	5				

Source: Edward S. Mason et al., *The Economic and Social Modernization of the Republic of Korea* (Cambridge: Harvard University Press, 1980), p. 206.
[a] Total grant aid includes Japanese grant funds from 1965 on.
[b] Loan aid includes loans from international organizations and public bilateral loans.
[c] U.S. grant aid includes technical assistance costs in addition to commodity imports.

been the only major source of development assistance. The Park government made a successful effort initially to diversify its sources of donor support in part because of Korea's cool relationship with the U.S. government immediately following the 1961 coup. The U.S. government used aid leverage to induce Park to schedule elections in 1963 (Steinberg, 1985, p. 23). The currency reform of 1961 was initiated without consultation with the United States, and the 1962–66 Five Year Plan was formulated with only limited foreign advisory assistance. The joint U.S.-Korean Economic Coordination Commission did not meet from 1961 to 1963 (Steinberg, 1985, p. 24).

The World Bank made its first loan to Korea in 1962. The normalization of relations with Japan, vigorously opposed by student demonstrators, added Japan as a donor in 1965. The World Bank was encouraged to form a consultative group for Korea to coordinate donor support, and the group's first meeting was held in 1966. The Asian Development Bank became a donor in 1968. Subsequently, multilateral aid grew rapidly. Meanwhile, U.S. bilateral assistance to Korea, except for a small amount of PL 480 lending, was terminated in 1974.

A second major transition in donor-recipient relations occurred in 1984. Following its thirteenth meeting, the Consultative Group for Korea was dissolved because, as the official communiqué put it, "its role as a forum for aid coordination and enhanced mobilization of external capital for (South) Korea's development is now being fulfilled by the (South) Korean Government" (Ensor, 1984, p. 99).

The dissolution reflected substantial change in donor assistance to Korea. Most bilateral assistance had been phased out by the early 1980s (concessional loans from the International Development Association had been phased out earlier), and World Bank project-related loans had been largely replaced by structural adjustment and sector loans.

After its potential for rapid growth was amply demonstrated, South Korea was able to obtain increasing flows of foreign resources on the private international capital market and, thus, to enhance its growth rate by foreign borrowing. Even in the 1965–74 period foreign borrowing accounted for 42 percent of gross fixed capital formation, although capital formation as a percentage of GNP rose from 10.5 percent in the 1953–62 period to 22.7 percent over the 1965–74 period. Thus, South Korea could rely on the private external capital market for additional resources to exploit profitable investment opportunities beyond the level permitted by domestic savings and concessional foreign loans.

The South Korean experience sheds some light on two important questions: (a) If domestic policies are ill-advised, can foreign donors contribute in a manner conducive to economic development? and (b) What is the role of foreign donors in the dialogue on domestic economic policy? Given that foreign donors have a role only when they contribute aid, the second question is discussed first.

When the United States was a major donor of aid during the 1950s, the dialogue with the Korean authorities centered on appropriate levels of aid and Korean policy choices. The first economic plan, designed to promote recovery from the effects of the Korean War and to establish long-term growth and structural objectives and policies, was prepared with U.N. assistance by Robert R. Nathan and Associates. Subsequent plans, through the early 1960s, were based on substantial official U.S. technical assistance.

In the 1950s the American negotiators fully recognized and repeatedly pointed out the difficulties associated with the excess-demand, multiple-exchange-rate, and inner-oriented policies followed by the Rhee government. The negotiators gained limited concessions from the Rhee government (e.g., to devalue the won and to try to raise tax revenue or lower expenditures); however, the overall strategy of the Rhee government was to maximize the gap between domestic resources and expenditures for foreign aid to fill (Cole and Lyman, 1971, p. 79). Because the United States was politically committed to the maintenance of the South Korean government, U.S. bargaining power was relatively weak.

An observer might have concluded that U.S. aid policies in 1958 or 1959 were ineffective because of Korea's inappropriate economic policies. This view might have gained support from the 1960 policy reforms (after the overthrow of the Syngman Rhee government), which the Korean intelligentsia deemed necessary if the country was to have a reasonable future. The position announced at that time by the United States was that aid levels could not be expected to increase and, indeed, would gradually decline. Because Korea was dependent on raw material imports, that prospect threw into sharp relief the proposition that only the sustained growth of export earnings would permit rising levels of imports, a necessary condition for further growth of the economy.

These facts alone do not prove that aid donors, especially the United States, did not influence the policy changes that facilitated South Korea's success. Several considerations point in the other direction. In the immediate postwar period (to 1956) aid had been absolutely essential to the maintenance and subsequent recovery of the Korean economy. There is substantial evidence that economists with the U.S. aid mission participated in the discussions leading to the stabilization program of 1952–59, the precedent of the major reforms of 1960–64. U.S. assistance had financed the training of many Koreans in the United States, but their influence in the discussions is difficult to determine; certainly, the immediate impulse for policy change was internal Korean political discussions. The importance of the U.S.-Korean policy dialogue is further supported by the intimate involvement in the mid-1960s of American economists associated with US/AID. They collaborated with Koreans in working out the budget and credit reforms of 1965 (Mason et al., 1980, p. 330). Later tariff liberalization was accompanied by the same sort of collaboration between Korean policymakers and consultants provided by US/AID.

It is impossible to reach a firm conclusion on the degree to which donor influence contributed to the policy reforms. The forces favoring reforms clearly were strengthened by U.S. aid. Whether the reforms would have been undertaken in the absence of U.S. pressures is more problematic. The safest conclusions are that (a) U.S. aid in the 1950s did not reduce the likelihood of the policy reforms; (b) given the U.S. political interest in South Korea, it is remarkable that U.S. authorities took such a strong position on Korea's economic policies; (c) surely some donor influence on the intellectual atmosphere prevailed when a political consensus was finally reached; (d) a contemporary observer could not have perceived, from the vantage point of 1958 or 1959, U.S. aid influence on Korean growth policies; and (e) because U.S. aid officials already had experience in the Korean economy and understood some aspects of it, they were in a uniquely favorable position to assist in the continuation and furtherance of the policy reforms. While an attempt to analyze what might have been the fate of the reforms in the absence of significant external support would be purely speculative, the donor presence was certainly a positive factor in influencing their success. It is doubtful whether that influence could have been as constructively employed without prior experience in the Korean economy.

There remains the question of the value of assistance during the 1950s. It is almost unimaginable that political and economic stability could have been maintained without concessional assistance in 1953–55, when Korea was regarded as completely uncreditworthy in the private capital markets. The critical question, therefore, centers on the product of aid during the 1956–60 period. Undoubtedly, some aid had a very low return. Aid financing of imports led to distortions of various kinds. However, the considerable investment in infrastructure (see Mason et al., 1980; and below in this chapter) surely was valuable in paving the way for the successful export-oriented drive. This conclusion certainly is true of the educational reforms and assistance to education supported in the 1940s and 1950s by the United States. All observers point to the availability of a literate labor force as an important prerequisite for the degree to which Korea could capitalize on policy reforms. In the 1950s the rate of growth in the Korean economy was constrained by the availability of essential infrastructure (e.g., power, railroad and port capacity). Some of the infrastructure investments of the 1950s initially may have been less than optimally employed, but they certainly permitted a more rapid acceleration of growth in the 1960s than would have been possible otherwise. Furthermore, the experience gained in infrastructure construction in the 1950s and 1960s enabled Korea to become a major exporter of construction services to the Middle East in the 1970s and early 1980s (Kim, 1988).

If any lesson can be drawn from this experience, it may be that infrastructure projects enhancing a society's potentially productive resources probably are a wiser form of aid than program support when governments undertake ill-advised economic policies. But even this conclusion must be qualified. The policy dialogue in Korea in the 1950s centered on the level of program lending to support the import program, as well as on individual projects. Whether the same intangible influence on the climate of opinion could have been realized under project-only lending is an open question. In the absence of further evidence, possibly the safest policy prescription for a donor confronted with a recipient whose domestic economic policies are antidevelopmental is to support a higher proportion of project aid than one would for recipients whose domestic policies are deemed conducive to growth.

Trade and Aid in Korea

Korea's success is so intricately linked to the trade sector that much of the relationship between trade and aid has been discussed already. Certainly, the major factors retarding Korean growth in the 1950s were the excess demand associated with overall budgetary and monetary policy and the trade and exchange controls, which gave the wrong signals for resource allocation in the domestic economy.

Mason et al. (1980, table 29) calculated the fraction of output growth attributable to export expansion, import substitution, and domestic demand expansion for the 1955–63 and the 1963–75 periods. They estimated that import substitution accounted for about 26 percent of manufacturing output expansion in the earlier period and 7 percent in the latter period. By contrast, export expansion accounted for about 9 percent of (slower) growth in the former period and 39 percent in the latter. These results are confirmed by every other indicator of Korea's economic performance. In tradables, and especially in the manufacturing sector, resources were allocated in radically different directions in the import substitution years than under the export promotion strategy.

In the former period, foreign assistance actually substituted for foreign exchange earnings, especially when it was in the form of program aid. As such, it could not contribute as significantly to development prospects as would have been possible if more appropriate policies had been in place. In the latter period, foreign assistance (to an ever-decreasing degree) and, subsequently, foreign borrowing permitted Koreans to take advantage of highly profitable projects sooner than would have been possible otherwise. Consequently, despite the domestic savings rate, a higher rate of investment occurred in a highly productive manner.

Some Korean investments that had been financed through aid in the 1950s, especially those in import substitution sectors, such as cement, had very low rates of return. The lesson here is that one cannot divorce sectoral assistance programs, even those administered under project lending, from overall macroeconomic policy considerations. The assessment of individual projects must be undertaken only in the context of appropriate estimates of international prices (as opposed to domestic prices) of outputs of various alternative projects.

Another important lesson is found in the relationship of trade, concessional aid, and private capital flows. In the early stages of development countries are unable to borrow commercially because their general capacity to generate foreign exchange earnings is limited and the highly productive investments (e.g., in education, roads, and ports) have long gestation periods and cannot be financed readily by user charges. At this stage, concessional assistance may be the only way to lay the groundwork for later development. Yet later, when growth is centered on the tradable sectors of the economy, a country's ability to borrow commercially increases, and concessional aid no longer can contribute so much to the development process.

Agricultural Development

U.S. assistance to agriculture and rural development in Korea took several forms: supplies and money for reconstruction; the food the population needed; the design and implementation of land reform; and the provision of capital and expertise to rebuild damaged infrastructure. U.S. assistance also supported the import of essential agricultural inputs, such as fertilizer. When the Korean economy improved, U.S. assistance shifted to development and helped to finance a domestic fertilizer industry, to reclaim and improve land, to train people, to promote public health, to expand research and extension activities, and to create marketing and credit institutions.

At the end of the Korean War, the Rhee government helped to restore the economy by rebuilding the infrastructure, developing industrial capacity, maintaining a strong military, and improving private consumption levels within the limits of domestic production and available foreign assistance (Cole and Lyman, 1971, p. 164). Agricultural production and rural development were relatively neglected (Cole and Lyman, 1971, p. 79). Large shipments of PL 480 grains allowed the government to set rice prices below world market levels and even below production costs without too much concern with the level of production.

When the Park government tried to consolidate its political position after May 1961, it was impelled, at least initially, to adopt policies that were more favorable to the agricultural sector. Two major initiatives were undertaken in the early 1960s: government programs in the area of agricultural input supplies, commodity marketing, and agricultural credit were consolidated in a National Agricultural Cooperative Federation (NACF); and the research and guidance (extension) activities of the Ministry of Agriculture and Fisheries were combined in an Office of Rural Development (ORD).

In the early 1970s the Park government was motivated to adopt policies even more favorable to the rural sector. The PL 480 program had changed in the late 1960s from a grant program to a program of hard currency (through concessional) loans. The government responded in 1969 by initiating a two-price system for barley and rice. Farm prices were raised, and prices to consumers were subsidized.[5] These actions were not adequate to stem the rural areas' disenchantment with the Park government policies, however. When the 1971 elections confirmed the disaffection, the government initiated a series of new programs. Commodity prices were again raised, investments in rural infrastructure were increased, and the Saemaul (New Community) Movement was initiated (Steinberg, 1985, pp. 46, 47).

The Saemaul Movement was a highly organized, centrally directed effort to mobilize farmers on a national scale (Ban, Moon, and Perkins, 1980, p. 275). Following the election, Saemaul distributed three hundred bags of cement to each village in the country for community improvements. The enthusiasm elicited by the gesture was so great that President Park put the weight and prestige of his office behind the movement (Steinberg, 1982, p. 17).

Village improvement efforts intensified from 1972 to 1975, and increased emphasis was placed on improving agricultural productivity and rural incomes. Saemaul objectives were achieved with small amounts of external resources, considerable moral suasion, and overt political pressure. Both the ORD and the Ministry of Home Affairs (MHA) vied to mobilize local resources, and the MHA emerged as the coordinating agency of the Saemaul Movement. By the mid-1970s the agricultural and rural development programs had become so pervasive that they dominated almost every aspect of rural life. Early activities supported by US/AID, such as youth and community self-help projects, rural road improvements, extension of electricity and water supplies to rural areas, and better-quality rural education, were absorbed by the movement. However, neither the United States nor other donors assisted the Saemaul program directly.

In retrospect, Korea has achieved an exceedingly rapid structural transformation. In 1960, prior to the reforms in economic policy, 60 percent of the labor force was employed in agriculture; by 1980 that figure was only 35 percent. During this period, industrial policy became more export-oriented and agricultural policy became more protectionist. Nominal rates of protection for most agricultural commodities had been strongly negative during the 1950s, but the reforms of the early 1960s brought prices that on balance were relatively undistorted. By the early 1970s nominal protection levels averaged above 50 percent, and by the early 1980s, above 100 percent. This transition was interpreted by Anderson and Hayami (1986, pp. 21–24, 34–49) as a political response to the rapid structural transformation that dramatically lowered the agriculture sector's comparative advantage relative to the industrial sector in spite of rapid growth in both land and labor productivity (see fig. 13.1).

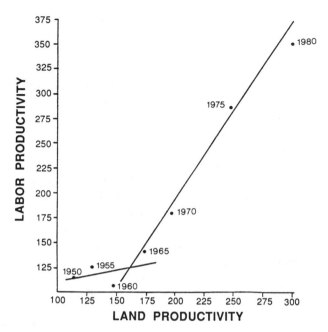

Fig. 13.1. Land and labor productivities in Korean agriculture, 1946–1980 (1946 = 100). Source: David I. Steinberg, Sung-Hwan Ban, W. Donald Bowles, and Maureen A. Lewis, *Korean Agricultural Services*, US/AID Project Impact Evaluation Report No. 52 (Washington, D.C., 1984), p. B–17.

In the following sections the role of aid in the evolution of the individual programs is described.

LAND REFORM AND LAND DEVELOPMENT

Between 1945 and 1953 the government of Korea, with technical and economic assistance from the United States, undertook a major land reform program. The first stage was the distribution of land that had been under Japanese control or ownership; the second stage, completed at the end of the Korean War, was the breakup of the larger Korean *Yangban* (gentry) estates. Thus, the number of families owning all or part of the land they farmed rose dramatically, from 48.4 percent in 1945 to above 90 percent after the reform (Ban, Moon, and Perkins, 1980, pp. 285–86).

However debatable the short-term effects of land redistribution and reform on production may have been, the political effects were clearly positive. In Korea, class tensions between rural landlords and tenants were diffused, and the distribution of income and wealth in rural areas became relatively equitable. By the early 1980s, however, the structure of land ownership that emerged from the land reforms had become an obstacle to growth in output and productivity in the face of a declining farm population and a smaller rural labor force.

U.S. assistance also played a major role in land and water resource development in South Korea. In the early 1960s the Korean government promoted a land development program that aimed at adding 15 percent more agricultural land to the country by reclaiming hillsides and tideland areas and by making irrigation and other improvements on existing farmlands (Cole and Lyman, 1971, p. 91). The land reclamation project was a labor-intensive effort supported by large quantities of U.S. PL 480 food aid. The latter was distributed as payment in kind to the hundreds of thousands of rural workers employed on the project. The newly developed land was divided among these workers or added to landholdings smaller than a certain size (Cole and Lyman, 1971, p. 91). PL 480 surplus food served as payment in kind to rural workers engaged in land reclamation and other agricultural projects (Ban, Moon, and Perkins, 1980, p. 80).

In general, the land reclamation project was relatively successful in meeting its objectives (employment generation and land reclamation) but less so, according to US/AID criticisms, in terms of management and benefit-cost criteria. There were also accusations of corruption and mismanagement (Ban, Moon, and Perkins, 1980, pp. 79–86). The result was the end of large-scale PL 480 assistance for new land development in 1967.

Donor experience with irrigation development support in Korea has been somewhat more successful. Between the early 1960s and the late 1970s the area irrigated increased from 682,000 to 1,122,000 hectares, and the ratio of irrigated to nonirrigated paddy land rose from 56 percent to above 85 percent. External support was provided by the World Bank, the Asian Development Bank (ADB), the U.N. Food and Agriculture Organization (UN/FAO), and US/AID. World Bank funding went primarily to multipurpose irrigation and hydroelectric projects, whereas US/AID supported smaller-scale projects primarily (Steinberg et al., 1980, app. H).

Early projects were characterized by substantial cost overruns stemming from inflation and exchange rate adjustments. However, by the mid-1970s Korea had achieved substantial capacity to plan, develop, and manage irrigation. A 1980 review of US/AID support for small-scale irrigation development during the years 1974–78 concluded that the primary contribution of US/AID was the resources to speed up the project's completion. The project, evaluated primarily in terms of meeting its rice production and farm income objectives, was regarded as a success by the review team even though no formal benefit-cost estimates were made. Two factors were considered to be particularly important in realizing the project objectives: (a) the growth of capacity by government institutions to design, supervise, and staff the subprojects and (*b*) the focus of the project on a single element—irrigation—in an environment in which other complementary elements were already in place (Steinberg et al., 1980, pp. 2–15).

MARKETING AND CREDIT INSTITUTIONS

When the first Republic of Korea government succeeded the U.S. military government in 1948, it inherited a system of compulsory grain collection, controlled farm and consumer prices, and food rationing. The administration continued these policies initially and assumed an active and interventionist position in agricultural input, commodity, and credit markets. The latter were a badly organized system of rural financial associations (Ban, Moon, and Perkins, 1980, pp. 201–4, 234–38). The administration's authority was enhanced by large imports of PL 480 grain throughout most of the 1950s. The food marketing and financial institutions were regarded by both domestic and foreign observers as plagued by inefficiency and corruption.

A series of efforts were made during the 1950s to reorganize and reform the marketing and credit institutions. Controls were relaxed, limited free market transactions were allowed, and the rationing system was modified. Additional reforms, based on U.S. mission recommendations, were carried out in the mid-1950s.

In 1961 the government under President Park took steps to reform and consolidate the agricultural supply, marketing, and credit systems. A National Agricultural Cooperation Federation (NACF) was established to merge the functions of the cooperative associations, which supplied production inputs and handled the marketing of agricultural commodities, and those of the Korean Agricultural Bank (opened in 1956), which extended credit to farmers. The new organization undertook to remedy such deficiencies as inadequate grain storage facilities, limited supplies and poor distribution of fertilizer and seed, and insufficient short- and medium-term credit (Steinberg et al., 1984, app. C).

The NACF was not a cooperative in the traditional Western sense. It was designed to control as well as to support the rural economy. The organizational structure permitted the government to participate in every aspect of commercial activity relating to agriculture. At the village level, the primary cooperatives were the only source of fertilizer, agricultural chemicals, and institutional credit. Farmers were required to purchase one or more shares in order to have access to the village cooperative services. Although the NACF corrected many of the abuses in the earlier system, excessive centralization contributed to the severe losses realized by the stabilization program during the 1970s.

U.S. assistance supported a series of reorganizations and reforms from the late 1940s through the early 1970s. Despite less than adequate documentation, the record suggests that US/AID participated in the funding of storage facilities, the organization and financing of credit programs, and the support of marketing activities; it also provided technical assistance and administrative personnel. The technical assistance seems to have exerted a significant impact on policy development and program implementation. In the following sections the input supply and commodity price policies pursued by the Republic of Korea and US/AID are discussed more fully.

THE FERTILIZER INDUSTRY

From 1945 into the 1960s U.S. assistance was the major funding source for the import of current inputs used in farming, such as pesticides, fertilizers, and new seed varieties (Ban, Moon, and Perkins, 1980, p. 100; Steinberg et al., 1984, app. B). Throughout the 1950s and into the early 1960s US/AID financed between two-thirds and three-fourths of all nitrogen fertilizer imports. An even greater proportion of the phosphorus and potassium inputs were provided through foreign assistance also (Ban, Moon, and Perkins, 1980, p. 104). In the 1960s five fertilizer plants were constructed. Three were operated by the public sector (Korean Government Chemical Company) and two by the private sector. The public sector plants were constructed using US/AID loans as a joint venture with U.S. firms, the other two with loan guarantees that attracted private sector investment. Although the industry initially was criticized as relatively inefficient, it aided agriculture, and perhaps more important, it became a source of trained personnel who later played an important role in the development of the Korean petrochemical industry. By the late 1960s Korea was a net exporter of nitrogen fertilizer. US/AID assistance for fertilizer imports terminated after 1969 (Ban, Moon, and Perkins, 1980).

The role of fertilizer and other technical inputs was critical in the expansion of agricultural production. Between 1946 and 1973 agricultural output grew at an annual rate of 3.41 percent. "For the whole period (1946–73) . . . about 57 percent of total production growth is attributable to the increase of inputs and the remaining 42 percent to improvement in productivity" (Ban, Moon, and Perkins, 1980, pp. 57, 60).

Some problems occurred with the distribution of aid-financed fertilizer imports. During the 1950s and well into the 1960s the government priced fertilizer well below the open market price, which made distribution through the free market impossible. Fertilizer was rationed, and distribution by the NACF was chaotic and undependable. Black market prices reached two to three times the official price level. In the 1960s US/AID encouraged the privatization of fertilizer distribution but with little effect. Reforms during the late 1970s brought prices closer to market levels and made distribution more effective; consequently, the black market in fertilizer was largely eliminated (Ban, Moon, and Perkins, 1980, pp. 108, 109).

AGRICULTURAL RESEARCH AND EXTENSION

Research to improve rice production was conducted throughout the Japanese colonial period (Steinberg et al., 1982, p. 4). Agricultural research and extension were neglected after World War II, partly because farmers and planners associated them with the coercive policies of Japanese colonialism. When US/AID provided assistance to the Ministry of Agriculture and Forestry to support agricultural extension activities as part of a broadly based community development program in the 1950s, a substantial amount of the aid was diverted to other purposes (Ban, Moon, and Perkins, 1980, pp. 269–71).

In 1962 the agricultural research and extension system was reorganized. The ORD was established as a separate, independent agency attached to the Ministry of Agriculture and Forestry, with the backing and financial support of US/AID. Its mission included both agricultural research and the extension or transfer of technology to farmers (Steinberg et al., 1982, p. G-2). The initial US/AID contribution was primarily for expanding and improving research facilities, creating a larger research network, and providing more training to both farmers and extension workers. In 1973 a new US/AID project supported additional overseas training of research personnel, resident and short-term expatriate advisory services, and strengthened library and computer facilities.

The ORD has evolved into a remarkably effective agricultural research and extension organization, what the Koreans called Rural Guidance. Its most dramatic achievement was the development, in cooperation with the International Rice Research Institute, of the high-yield, fertilizer-responsive Tong-il ("unification") rice variety. Tong-il was released in 1972, and by 1977 it was adopted in over half of the rice area in Korea. Rice yields rose from 3.3 metric tons per hectare in the early 1970s to over 4.5 metric tons per hectare in 1979 (Steinberg et al., 1982, app. C).

The effectiveness of the Rural Guidance system in promoting the rapid diffusion of the new Tong-il variety also contributed to a disastrous drop in rice production when Korea experienced colder than normal weather in 1979–80. The yield of the Tong-il variety declined from 5.5 metric tons per hectare to 4.9 metric tons per hectare in 1978 and 4.6 in 1979. In retrospect, a political commitment to self-sufficiency in rice production, combined with a highly centralized guidance and input supply system, clearly resulted in excessively rapid diffusion of the Tong-il variety into areas where it was ill-suited, as well as into areas where it had a clear advantage relative to other varieties.

At least two important lessons can be learned from the Korean research and extension system: (a) the integration of research and extension in a single administrative organization contributes to the effectiveness of both research and extension; and (*b*) a system in which decisions are centralized and little opportunity is provided for the feedback of farmers, extension workers, and scientists to influence program design can effectively disseminate inappropriate as well as appropriate technology (Steinberg et al., 1982; Burmeister, 1985).

Despite these qualifications, it is clear that in about twenty years Korea has developed an effective system for the generation and transfer of agricultural technology. During 1973–80 agricultural output grew at a rate of 5.4 percent per year. Total productivity—output per unit of total input—grew at 3.3 percent per year and accounted for approximately two-thirds of the growth of total output (Steinberg et al., 1984, p. B-16).

Clearly these gains were achieved as a result of complementary advances in agricultural technology, institutional development, and agricultural price policy. The effects of these developments on agricultural production and income in rural areas was largely realized after the assistance programs had been substantially reduced or phased out. The most convincing evidence of the success of the assistance programs has been the ability of the Korean government and the Korean people to carry out the reforms needed to sustain agricultural production.

Rural Development

U.S. assistance played an active role in developing the physical and institutional infrastructure for rural areas, especially roads, utilities, health, and education. They have had a direct influence on the quality of life in rural areas and an indirect effect on agricultural production and incomes.

RURAL ROADS

Before World War II only a small number of Korea's rural roads or major highways were paved. Overland traffic was both difficult and expensive. Assistance for road improvement was initiated after the Korean War in order to repair the roads damaged during the war. U.S. aid provided earth-moving vehicles, paving equipment, and technical advice. By 1960 the national and provincial highway system was restored to about the same level as at the end of World War II. From a long-term development perspective, the emergence of a construction industry with substantial technical and managerial capacity was perhaps of equal significance (Ban, Moon, and Perkins, 1980, p. 148).

Shortly after assuming office, the Park government initiated a massive highway construction program. In the 1970s this effort was complemented by intensive rural road construction and improvement to further the Saemaul Movement. US/AID was no longer supporting highway and road construction in Korea, but both the World Bank and the Asian Development Bank made substantial funding available. (The Seoul-Pusan expressway, however, was constructed against the advice of the World Bank and without World Bank assistance.)

The effects of the rural roads program on rural incomes and development were highly positive. Farmers were able to reach expanding markets for the more labor-intensive, higher-valued perishable commodities that were a result of rapid urban-industrial development (Ban, Moon, and Perkins, 1980, p. 154; Park, 1982, p. 67). The improved rural road network also facilitated education beyond the level of the village primary school, and transportation to middle and high school by bicycle and school bus became common (Steinberg, 1985, p. 12).

The road program has not been without critics, however. There have been frequent charges that the southwest region, a center of political opposition to both the Rhee and Park governments, was discriminated against in donor support for transportation, other rural infrastructure development, and industrial decentralization. Steinberg noted in his review of regional discrimination that donor lending was provided to "those areas that made sense economically. Such lending was designed neither to alleviate income differences nor to correct past deficiencies. And it accomplished neither" (1985, p. 52).

UTILITIES

The Japanese had developed the north, where most power was generated in Korea, as the major manufacturing region and the south as the food production region. Between 1958 and 1966 the power sector was the third largest category of US/AID grant project assistance in South Korea, comprising 11.5 percent of the total amount of grants (Cole and Lyman, 1971, p. 193). The provinces with the largest urban areas had the earliest and highest rates of rural electrification. Use of electricity in rural areas rose from negligible levels in the late 1940s to 25.2 million kilowatt-hours in 1962 and to 56.6 million kilowatt-hours in 1973. In 1964 only 12 percent of rural households had electricity (Ban, Moon, and Perkins, 1980, p. 144). A major objective of the Saemaul program was to raise the percentage of rural households with access to electricity to 90 percent by 1977 (Hasan, 1976, p. 108).

The push for rural electrification programs also came in part from the hope of establishing a rural industrial structure to provide employment opportunities. The Saemaul industrial program subsidized the location of factories in rural areas—over five hundred between 1973 and 1977. Within a few years one-third ceased operation and most of the others operated at less than full capacity. The failure of the program was caused by a lack of adequate attention to economic, as opposed to political, considerations in program design and location decisions. Industrial decentralization has been less successful in Korea than in Taiwan (Steinberg, 1982).

HEALTH

Japanese measures to improve public health during the colonial period included compulsory inoculation, enforcement of quarantines at major seaports, and establishment of public hospitals in each province and major urban area. Other measures to improve health conditions were the drilling of community wells and development of running water systems (Repetto et al., 1981, p. 198).

Between 1958 and 1966, 10.5 percent of US/AID grant project assistance to Korea was spent on health and sanitation (Cole and Lyman, 1971, p. 193). At first urban sanitation was a top priority, but as late as 1972 only 7 percent of all villages had a sanitary water supply system (Hasan, 1976, p. 163). A major effort was made during the 1970s through the Saemaul program to raise rural health through improvements in rural water supplies (Ban, Moon, and Perkins, 1980, p. 314); the objective was a sanitary water supply for all villages by 1981 (Hasan, 1976, p. 163).

Family planning, a low-priority item of the Korean government before 1960, was opposed by President Rhee personally (Steinberg, 1982, p. 32). In 1961, however, the administration formally initiated a family planning program. The influence of US/AID, Planned Parenthood, the Population Council, and the United Nations Fund for Population Activities (UNFPA) was high during the early stages of planning because these agencies supplied funding and technical expertise. Their role declined, but they continued to be key providers of contraceptive supplies, and to support research and advanced training in population and family planning (Repetto et al., 1981, p. 257). The crude birth rate declined from 43 per thousand population in 1960 to 23 per thousand population in 1982 (World Bank, 1984b, p. 257).

EDUCATION

Korea had a relatively high level of elementary education and literacy at independence, and the demand for higher education grew explosively. During the colonial period 45 percent of Korean school-age children had attended primary schools, but few had gone beyond that level.

The U.S. assistance program provided $100 million to build twenty-three thousand classrooms between 1952 and 1966 (Steinberg, 1982, p. 29). By the 1960s virtually all children in appropriate age groups were in primary schools, and increasing numbers were going to middle schools (Ban, Moon, and Perkins, 1980, p. 311). By 1974 almost 90 percent of the farm population was literate. For most village children, grade schools were within walking distance, but middle schools, high schools, or colleges were located only in urban centers. For many rural families the cost of boarding a child in the town or city was prohibitive. The increase in rural middle school education appears to have coincided with the rise in farm incomes in the 1970s (Ban, Moon, and Perkins, 1980, p. 311).

Much of the investment in Korean institutions of higher education has been generated by the private sector. Assistance by US/AID for the development of the College of Agriculture of Seoul National University, through a contract with the University of Minnesota in the late 1950s, was one of the few exceptions. In the 1950s and 1960s, however, US/AID sent large numbers of Koreans—nearly three thousand persons in education, the bureaucracy, and the business community—to the United States for training (Cole and Lyman, 1971, p. 279). Assistance agencies played an initial role in educational planning, but after that planning was done mainly by Koreans (Cole and Lyman, 1971, p. 204).

Few developing countries illustrate the contribution of human capital to economic growth more effectively than Korea (see chapter 2). Education and improvements in knowledge account for almost one-fifth of Korean economic growth between 1963 and 1982 (Kim and Park, 1985, pp. 165–75). Human capital investment has been particularly important in Korea's emergence, since the late 1970s, as a major exporter of capital goods and related services, including manufacturing plants and equipment, overseas construction, technology exports and licensing, and consulting services (Westphal et al., 1984).

Some Lessons from the Korean Experience

A number of issues in this review are not developed as we would have liked. For example, we concentrate very heavily on the period from Korean independence until the termination of U.S. assistance in the early 1970s, the period during which many of the preconditions for subsequent rapid development were established. Thus we largely neglect the later contributions of other bilateral and multilateral donors. Despite these omissions, a number of important lessons can be drawn from the experience of development assistance in the support of economic development in Korea.

One of the most important lessons is that it is a mistake to attempt the premature assessment of the effects of assistance. From the post–World War II and Korean War recovery periods until the early 1960s, external assistance was clearly essential to Korea's economic and political viability. In the early 1960s there was still considerable skepticism that Korea could emerge as an economically and politically healthy entity, even with continued U.S. assistance (Cole and Lyman, 1971, p. 1).

Another conclusion is that the long-run policy dialogue between Korean officials in policy, planning, and sector development and U.S. assistance agency officials and their consultants had a positive effect on the South Korean government's capacity to formulate and implement development policy. External advice was frequently rejected. The emergence of a professional elite with the capacity for policy analysis and dialogue and with confidence in its ability to mobilize domestic political and economic resources for development was partly a product of a dialogue that was both pervasive and continuous for almost a quarter-century. It contributed to the effective use of the even larger multilateral and private resource flows that became available after the mid-1960s.

The Korean experience also holds some lessons for the effectiveness of donor assistance during a period when a government persists in pursuing "wrong" economic policies. The substantial infrastructure investments that were made in transportation, communication, and land and water development sustained development until the policy environment became more favorable in the 1950s and the 1960s. Even during the 1950s, however, partial reliance on program lending was both an opportunity and an incentive for meaningful policy dialogue. When the policy environment changed in the 1960s and 1970s, both bilateral and multilateral donors found it productive to devote a larger share of their portfolios to sector and program loans.

A further lesson from the Korean experience demonstrates the efficiency of economic incentives to generate economic growth. The Korean approach to reducing investment, savings, and import constraints in the 1960s was a sharp departure from the conventional wisdom of that time. Private savers responded to high interest rates; farmers responded to the more favorable domestic terms of trade; and the industrial sector responded to the more realistically priced foreign exchange. A result was even more rapid mobilization of both domestic and foreign resources than had been anticipated. But the Korean experience offers no support whatsoever for the view that successful development can be achieved merely by freeing markets from the distortions caused by public intervention. The Korean government has continued to play an important role in institutional reform, technology development, and the rationalization of economic organization. It also has retained a major role in resource allocation decisions.

A number of lessons are specific to the agricultural sector:

1. There is no support from the Korean experience for the conventional view that agricultural development is a precondition for industrial development. "Agriculture has been a major beneficiary of Korean economic growth, but not a major cause of that growth" (Ban, Moon, and Perkins, 1980, p. 31). The role of agriculture in Korean development is consistent with the view that after the initial stages of industrial development, the emphasis in policy toward agriculture should shift from surplus extraction to surplus creation and to the generation of demand linkages with the rest of the economy (Adelman, 1984, p. 937).

From the late 1940s until the early 1970s the large U.S. food assistance program in Korea was effective in making food available to consumers on relatively favorable terms despite the South Korean government's failure to adopt policies capable of generating growth in agricultural production. A lesson we should have learned from this experience is that a food assistance program administered with the primary objective of restraining increases in food prices to consumers in an inflationary environment can have large disincentive effects on agricultural production. In the case of Korea, the effect of food assistance was to dampen farm commodity prices and thus probably to depress the rate of return to assistance efforts designed to support agricultural production.

2. Perhaps a most important lesson is that a small-scale, labor-intensive owner-operator system of agriculture can achieve both a high rate of growth in productivity and output and an equitable distribution of the gains from growth when it is supported by a prior land reform and by public investment in physical and institutional infrastructure.[6] The post–World War II land reform was an important element in creating a progressive rural structure. The support for land development and technical inputs was essential to achieving a reasonably rapid growth in agricultural production despite the regressive commodity pricing policies pursued by the South Korean government.

3. A commodity pricing policy that provides incentives to agricultural producers can play a critical role in inducing the rapid adoption of yield-increasing technology and in improving rural incomes. Pricing incentives became particularly important in Korea when advances in agricultural technology released the constraints on agricultural production and enabled farmers to respond to higher prices by using higher levels of purchased inputs. The large investments in education were important in enabling rural people to take advantage of the agricultural growth and nonagricultural employment opportunities that became available.

4. Higher incomes are not a sufficient condition for improvements in welfare or quality of life in rural areas. Incomes in rural areas rose during the 1970s as a result of rapid progress in agricultural technology and more favorable agricultural commodity prices. In this environment the Saemaul Movement played an important role in facilitating improvements in rural health, education, housing, and other aspects that contribute to the quality of life in rural areas.

14

Assistance to Turkey

**ANNE O. KRUEGER
AND VERNON W. RUTTAN**

Turkey, a member of NATO and an immediate neighbor of the Soviet Union, has been the object of important U.S. strategic and political interests as well as strong economic development concerns since World War II. The country has one of the longest histories of any nation as a U.S. aid recipient. The history of aid to Turkey is instructive for a variety of reasons. In this chapter we examine, if somewhat cursorily, Turkey's economic growth since the early 1950s and the interaction of the economic assistance with that growth. Following that we examine the interrelationship of trade and aid and then discuss assistance for agricultural development and for rural development.

Turkish Growth Performance

Turkey's postwar economic development shows three strikingly similar but characteristically different cycles of growth.[1] The pattern was as follows. Each cycle started with a period during which growth was fairly rapid, generally as a consequence of some external stimulus: the postwar reconstruction and commodity price boom of the late 1940s and early 1950s; the initiation of planning in the early 1960s; and then the large expansion in output following the initial success of the 1970 devaluation. Each cycle was also beset with difficulties: inflationary pressures, increasingly unrealistic exchange rates, various ad hoc measures by the government to patch up the situation, and finally, severe distortions in the economy. Little was done during the cycles to curb the sources of inflationary pressure, and when limited actions were taken, such as imposing price controls on state economic enterprises and financing their deficits through central bank credits, often the inflationary pressures were intensified.

As distortions mounted at the end of the cycles because of either a rising rate of inflation or increasingly scarce foreign exchange, the rate of economic growth declined. The decline in turn induced a new reform program. During the periods of reform growth was typically slow. In the first two cycles the reforms successfully stabilized the economy and reduced the degree of distortion. It is still too early to pass judgment on the success of the reforms of the 1980s to control inflation, reduce the balance of payments deficit, and stimulate economic growth.

This overly simplified pattern of the cycles makes the economic history of Turkey from 1950 to 1980 easier to understand (table 14.1). The first cycle started during the worldwide boom of the early 1950s and ended with a devaluation reform program in 1958. Turkey's economy had been dislocated during World War II; the postwar recovery was spurred by relatively high commodity prices for exports and by Point Four and Marshall Plan aid. Turkey even became a major exporter of wheat in the 1951–53 period (see below). The short-run expansion in real output was impressive; the rates of growth of real GNP are estimated to have been almost 10 percent annually from 1950 to 1953.

By 1953 difficulties arose, however. The increase in production associated with higher commodity prices, rising real volumes of exports, and foreign assistance could not be sustained, and inflationary pressures within the domestic economy mounted. Export earnings fell due to a worsening of the terms of trade, a poor harvest, and the decline in the real value of the Turkish lira.

The government's response was to levy surcharges on imports, to require import licensing, and to finance needed imports by permitting resort to suppliers' credits and bilateral arrangements. Nevertheless, the situation was desperate by 1958. Additional credits were virtually unavailable because of many arrears in debt service payments. Insufficient foreign exchange prevented importation of the petroleum needed to harvest crops and transport them to port. Finally, a devaluation-stabilization program was entered into with the International Monetary Fund (IMF) and donor countries (see below), and major domestic economic reforms were undertaken.

By 1960 the economy was responding to the reforms, and the ground was laid for the next cycle, which lasted throughout the decade of the 1960s and included the first Five Year Plan period (1963–67). Growth was rapid, averaging just under 7 percent annually in real terms. From the vantage point of the late 1960s Turks could justly point with pride to their cumulative growth rate since 1953 as one of the highest in the world. The retardation of the late 1950s appeared to have been a temporary aberration.

The 1960s also witnessed the initiation of major government investment programs and interventions in the economy to support development objectives. In particular, the development of a "modern" industrial sector was a major emphasis. Measures were taken to encourage the growth of domestic industry (see below); however, the expected support for this program from the Organization for Economic Cooperation and Development (OECD) aid consortium failed to materialize (Fry, 1971, p. 316). The combination of an

Table 14.1. Growth and Sectoral Composition of GNP in Turkey, 1950–1980
(TL millions in 1968 prices)

Year	Agriculture Amount	As % GNP	Industry Amount	As % GNP	Services[a] Amount	As % GNP	Import Taxes	GDP[b]	Net Factor Income from Abroad	GNP[b]	Index (1950= 100)	Population (millions, midyear)	GNP per Head (TL)
1950	15,867	41.2	5,054	13.1	15,761	40.9	1,915	38,598	–92	38,506	100.0	20.9	1,842
1955	21,483	37.9	8,382	14.8	24,097	42.5	2,950	56,912	–270	56,642	147.1	23.9	2,369
1960	26,836	37.9	11,254	15.9	30,276	42.7	3,025	71,391	–522	70,869	184.0	27.5	2,577
1965	28,101	31.0	17,761	19.6	40,155	44.4	4,061	90,078	+290	90,368	234.7	31.2	2,896
1970	32,870	26.2	28,032	22.3	58,692	46.8	4,355	123,949	+1,477	125,425	325.7	35.3	3,553
1975	40,889	22.5	44,268	24.4	86,953	47.9	5,651	177,761	+3,623	181,383	471.1	40.1	4,526
1980	46,766	22.7	49,549	24.0	103,968	50.5	3,613	203,896	+2,165	206,061	535.1	44.4	4,637
Average Annual Percentage Increase													
1950–60	5.4		8.3		6.7			6.3		6.3		2.8	3.4
1960–70	2.0		9.6		6.8			5.7		5.9		2.5	3.3
1970–80	3.6		5.9		5.9			5.1		5.1		2.3	2.7
1950–80	3.7		7.9		6.5			5.7		5.8		2.5	3.1

Sources: Turkish State Institute of Statistics, *National Income and Expenditures of Turkey, 1948–1972* (Ankara 1973), pp. 36–37, 143; idem, *Türkiye Milli Geliri, 1962–1977* (Ankara, n.d.), table 5; idem, *Statistical Yearbook, 1981* (Ankara, 1981), tables 20 and 398.

[a] Includes construction, wholesale and retail trade; transportation, storage, communications, banking, insurance and related financial activities; business, social, personal, and government services minus imputed bank service charges.

[b] Purchasers' prices.

ambitious plan with limited external support had several effects: (1) it placed heavy demands on imports for both investment goods and intermediate goods to permit the continued production of existing import-substitution activities; (2) it intensified inflationary pressures within the domestic economy; and (3) it increased incentives for production of import substitutes at the expense of the capacity to produce goods for export.

Unlike in the 1950s cycle, the cumulative effects of these strains in the 1960s developed gradually. The government acted to avoid the extreme dislocations of the 1950s; nevertheless, by the late 1960s, delays in obtaining foreign exchange and import licenses were again mounting. The black market exchange rate again soared well above the official rate, and dislocations were emerging in many economic activities. Although the rate of economic growth slowed somewhat, compensatory actions were taken before difficulties became severe. In August 1970 a devaluation-cum-stabilization program was announced again.

The response was immediate and pronounced. Partly because Turkish workers in Europe had been channeling funds through informal channels (or holding savings in Deutschmarks or other hard currencies) and partly for other reasons, export earnings and other foreign exchange receipts rose sharply. Turkey's international reserves—$221 million in 1969—rose in 1973 to a peak of $484 million. Meanwhile, imports also rose sharply: from $948 million in 1970 to $2,086 million in 1973. Again the economy responded markedly: real GNP rose 10.2 percent in 1971, 7.4 percent in 1972, and 5.4 percent in 1973.

The third cycle, which culminated in the reform program starting in January 1980, also contained the seeds of self-destruction. Unlike the second cycle, it was characterized by massive foreign deficit financing and rapid inflation. The initial contributing factor was the success of the devaluation-stabilization program itself. The sharp increase in workers' remittances and other foreign exchange was not effectively contained by the Central Bank of Turkey. As a consequence, inflationary pressures were released within the economy. The rate of inflation, which had fallen to an average of less than 8 percent in the 1960s, began rising again in 1973.

Although Turkey produces very little oil and thus was adversely affected by the oil price rise of 1973–74, the government's initial response was to borrow from abroad and to raid its foreign exchange reserves. This strategy was moderately successful in 1974 and 1975; in fact, real GNP rose 7.4 percent in 1974 and 8.0 percent in 1975. However, the rate of inflation rose even more—to 21 percent in 1975, 26 percent in 1977, and up to 96 percent in 1980. (Inflation declined subsequently—to 41 percent in 1981 and 26 percent in 1982.) By the end of the cycle in 1979 real GNP was declining despite several "programs" designed to rectify the situation. In 1980 real GNP stood at only 5.3 percent above its 1976 level—an average rate of increase of less than 2 percent annually and less than the rate of population growth over the same period.

Macroeconomic difficulties obviously have plagued the Turkish economy throughout the period during which foreign assistance has been a factor in the economy. Although satisfactory economic growth rates were achieved for part of the period, the rates proved unsustainable because of macroeconomic difficulties. The following section shows that much of aid policy toward Turkey (especially during the 1960s and late 1970s) has been strongly conditioned by those difficulties.

Macroeconomic Perspectives on Assistance

Despite the similarities of the cycles in Turkey's economic development, the role of foreign assistance in each was somewhat different. During the 1950s (until 1958) the United States was virtually the only donor country. Most aid was intended to be project assistance and was directed primarily at infrastructure and agricultural development.

During the second cycle U.S. funds were supplemented by assistance from several European donors and the World Bank. At that time assistance shifted to program rather than project support. In the third cycle U.S. assistance was greatly reduced in scope partly as a response to the apparent success of the 1970 devaluation. Assistance was resumed again, however, when the Turkish economy encountered difficulties in the late 1970s.

In the 1950s assistance centered primarily upon infrastructure, especially the construction of a nationwide road network that was deemed desirable for NATO-military purposes as well as economic development; it has been of major significance for regional and agricultural development. Infrastructure investment and additional development assistance activities were undertaken in a number of other sectors.[2]

Here, however, our focus is the interaction of U.S. assistance and the Turkish macroeconomic policy of the late 1950s. U.S. authorities were well aware of the problems inherent in the policy. As early as 1953, when a U.S. assistance–sponsored analysis of Turkish macroeconomic problems was conducted by Chenery, Brandow, and Cohn (1953), the Turkish reaction was to refuse permission for the authors to enter the country. However, because of U.S. political interests in Turkey, U.S. policy was torn between the desire to support the Menderes government politically and the desire for reform in Turkish macroeconomic policies. The consequence was a difficult and tense period in Turkish-American relations, but U.S. aid did not cease. Starting in 1956 the Menderes government several times requested continuation of U.S. project assistance and a U.S. program loan to provide financing for imports.[3]

American authorities refused those requests because they perceived the Turkish government's economic policies to be unsustainable. By the summer of 1958 the Menderes government was willing to accept the restrictions placed upon it under an IMF-led consortium. Whether the change came about because of the increased difficulties experienced by the Turkish economy (earlier a Turkish mission even had sought Soviet assistance) or because the U.S. position softened somewhat (the Iraqi revolution took place two months prior to the stabilization plan) is an open question. Still, the episode illustrates the dilemma of assistance in the context of strong political interests in a recipient country.

The 1960s cycle represents yet another type of experience. The focus of U.S. aid shifted largely toward program rather than project assistance at that time. Although Turkey received assistance from several donors, the United States was by far the largest funding source early in the decade. But the relative importance of the United States as a donor declined sharply in later years when associate membership in the European Economic Community led Turkey to stronger economic ties with European countries. The dilemma of U.S. program aid centered on how one donor could influence macroeconomic policy.

The solution was the formation of an aid consortium to meet with Turkish planners and other officials to discuss budget plans and associated import requirements (White, 1967). Donor agencies were concerned with allocation issues, such as the distortions caused by the trade regime and the sectoral allocation of resources. Bargaining, however, tended to focus on the level of investment and the rate of return in import substitution sectors rather than on development strategy. In the context of the 1960s, perhaps, the long-run consequences of such policies were appreciated less than they are today. Although the bargaining process implies some degree of give and take on both sides, it was understood by the members of the consortium that the fundamental premises of Turkish planning and the dominant role of state economic enterprises could not be challenged.

Two other lessons from the experience of the 1960s deserve mention. First, the program emphasized investment plans, foreign exchange allocations, and, to a certain extent, related macroeconomic issues. Inasmuch as the "foreign exchange shortage" associated with a given plan was what determined, at least in principle, the level of assistance from the consortium donors, the Turkish authorities were somewhat in conflict over the extent of their self-interest in minimizing the gap. Second, the consortium model itself was somewhat unwieldy. Multiple donors who differed concerning what should be emphasized probably limited their effectiveness in influencing Turkish policy. Delays were another problem. The Turkish plans had to be formulated before they could be discussed with donors. But the process of reaching a consensus of donors on assistance levels was difficult and complicated for donors and recipients alike.

The program approach to development assistance quite likely was a significant factor in limiting the distortions to which the Turkish economy previously had been subject. In the continuing dialogue between US/AID and the Turkish government officials (Krueger was occasionally a sideline observer) attempts were made to persuade the prime minister and his cabinet that a change in macroeconomic policies, especially in the exchange rate, was desirable long before a decision was reached. In principle it is impossible to know whether the devaluation of 1970 would have been delayed even longer if donor pressure had been absent. What is clear, however, is that remedial action was taken in 1970 at a far earlier stage of the cycle than in the 1950s.

The third cycle is in a way the most interesting. Except for the multilateral lending agencies, donors were far less involved in the process than they had been earlier. U.S. assistance resumed only with the re-emergence of severe balance of payments difficulties and other symptoms of extreme dislocation. Consequently, starting in 1978 repeated "programs" were announced to stem the difficulties. An IMF stabilization program of U.S. $450 million in 1978, combined with an OECD consortium debt rescheduling, provided Turkey with about $1.2 billion in balance of payments support over a two-year period. The conditions attached to the stabilization program were generally underachieved in 1978 and 1979. Despite changes in the exchange rate, the rate of inflation was sufficiently high that the real rate was increasingly overvalued and export earnings and workers' remittances faltered further. One Turkish economist characterized the period as one of export prevention rather than import substitution (Akat, 1983).

From hindsight, two major mistakes were made in the 1970s: (1) Turkish borrowing, primarily from commercial sources, postponed adjustment in the mid-1970s, thereby making it more difficult when it did come; and (2) the severity of the imbalances was underestimated when they finally became apparent in 1977. In 1978 and 1979 the loans did little to rectify the underlying difficulties, and they increased the debt-servicing burden when Turkey undertook a genuine reform of economic policies in January 1980.

Clearly, a major lesson for development assistance is that making loans to a country when the macroeconomic signals are massively out of line only makes the cost of adjustment higher unless sufficient remedial actions are undertaken. Unfortunately, there is no widely accepted technique for estimating when policy changes are sufficient to remedy underlying difficulties. At least until our knowledge improves, advice on policy reform must continue to contain a large element of judgment.

Trade and Aid in Turkey

In any country that maintains a fixed exchange rate when its rate of inflation exceeds the rate in the rest of the world, the first symptom of actual difficulty (other than the inflation itself) generally arises in its balance of payments and mounting debt service obligations. Inevitably, therefore, countries with expansionary policies and fixed exchange rates will seek support from donor countries and institutions. If the macroeconomic policies are appropriate, such support can be used productively to support economic development; otherwise the support may be largely dissipated by the policies that, in any event, must be remedied if growth is to resume or continue.

The Turkish experience amply demonstrates this conclusion. Many individual projects financed by the United States and other donors have had a high rate of return, yet on three occasions when the Turkish macroeconomic policy was unsustainable, all donors were caught in a weak bargaining position on economic reform because of their political interest. In the 1960s, corrective measures were taken relatively early in the cycle. In the 1950s and 1970s, however, donors were induced to provide support (1956–58 and 1977–79) despite the failure to change underlying programs sufficiently to promise great macroeconomic relief.

The fact that aid can be a substitute for trade means that supporting inappropriate macroeconomic policies can affect the trade sector of the domestic economy in fundamental ways. In the Turkish case the most vivid illustration of this lesson is the cycle of the 1960s. Even when broad macroeconomic policy was not highly out of line, the aid inflow helped to mask the underlying trade distortion between import substitutes and exports. Krueger (1974a) estimated that whereas most exports sold for only TL 9 per U.S. dollar, the implicit cost of many import-competing goods was TL 20 or more per dollar.

Had it not been for aid flows, this situation could not have persisted as long as it did. Aid officials correctly pointed to the distortions resulting from overvaluation, yet they persisted in supporting this major stumbling block to the expansion of export earnings. The difficulty was compounded by Turkish workers' remittances; they also were a major source of foreign exchange. Nonetheless, a major lesson from the Turkish experience is that the effectiveness of aid, particularly program aid, is greatly diminished unless it is administered in the context of a fairly realistic exchange rate and a liberal trade policy.

The relation between trade policies and aid does not end at the macroeconomic level. It also may distort the effectiveness of assistance at the individual project and sectoral level. Two cases in Turkey illustrate the link: the Eregli steel mill and the Turkish Industrial Development Bank.

In the early 1960s, when protection for new industrial activities was automatic, the U.S. government decided to provide the major financing for the Eregli steel mill. By Turkish standards at the time, the mill was a massive undertaking. For us, the important point is that the project used the anticipated domestic steel price in the feasibility study to evaluate the prospects. The Eregli plant had numerous technical problems. In addition, it substantially increased the Turkish domestic price of steel. Indeed, the price was so high that in a liter can of processed tomatoes the cost of the tinplate alone exceeded the retail price of a comparable can of processed tomatoes in Germany. Thus, during the late 1960s the development of food canning for export was unprofitable and hence was not undertaken. In sum, an inappropriate set of trade policies fostered an initially uneconomic steel mill that in turn prevented the development of an efficient food-processing industry.

The Turkish Industrial Development Bank (TSKB) was founded in the early 1950s to lend money to private sector industrial activities. It received loans, primarily from the World Bank, which also provided foreign exchange. Because the latter was scarce, TSKB loans were eagerly sought by the Turkish business community. Over the years the TSKB undoubtedly has made major contributions to the economic and technical efficiency of Turkish industry through its technical assistance, project appraisal, and other activities; it adopted shadow pricing and cost-benefit analysis early in its history. However, during its first ten years it based its project appraisals on market prices. Many projects that it funded were very profitable at market prices but uneconomical at international prices. When the TSKB finally began using international prices in project appraisals, it was able to weed out loan applications made by some high-cost industries. However, the policy did not encourage loan applications from those activities (especially for export) that would have been profitable at a realistic exchange rate but not at the actual exchange rate. The benefits accruing from assistance to the Turkish Industrial Development Bank were less than they might have been (even when the TSKB used appropriate appraisal criteria) had Turkish trade and exchange rate policies been more realistic.

Assistance for Agricultural Development

A review of U.S. assistance to agricultural development in Turkey is particularly enlightening for several reasons.[4] Turkey, along with Korea, was one of the first aid recipients. The experience proved valuable as assistance programs expanded. Although the United States made almost every false start and committed most of the development assistance errors possible, some successes were achieved. Indeed, U.S. development assistance has been an important contribution to the agricultural sector's expanded productive capacity and to the economic well-being of Turkey's rural areas.

We focus here on assistance to (*a*) agricultural inputs (tractors and fertilizer); (*b*) land and water development; (*c*) agricultural education, research, and extension; and (*d*) wheat production campaigns. The activities of other donors are discussed primarily as their programs interacted with U.S. development interests. The United Nations Food and Agriculture Organization (FAO) actively supported development of the forestry sector, fertilizer use, development of animal health and production programs, and crop introduction and research; and the World Bank actively supported soil and water conservation, irrigation development, and the development of the livestock industry.

AGRICULTURAL INPUTS: TRACTORS AND FERTILIZER

After World War II the use of tractors and fertilizer spread rapidly in Turkey. Fertilizer use started from very low levels in the early 1950s and expanded steadily until the mid-1960s. The largest increases in fertilizer use followed the introduction of the new higher-yield, fertilizer-responsive crop varieties in the mid-1960s. U.S. assistance played a very important role in the rapid postwar introduction of tractors but a smaller direct role in stimulating fertilizer use.

Tractors. During the Marshall Plan period (1948–52) and during the first several years under the Mutual Security Act, support for agricultural development represented a very large share of U.S. economic development assistance to Turkey (Wilson, 1971, pp. 2,3), most of it for agricultural mechanization (table 14.2). Nearly forty thousand tractors were imported during the Marshall Plan period alone. Although U.S. assistance for mechanization declined after the mid-1950s, mechanization, as indicated by the growth in tractor numbers, has continued. A major effect was to expand the land under cultivation.

Despite the mechanization program's initial impact on production, there are substantial questions concerning its longer-run viability. A 1951 World Bank mission criticized the number of tractors being imported; it estimated that tractor cultivation was economically viable for only about ten thousand farms (IBRD, 1951). Also, much of the land converted to cotton and grain production should have remained in pasture. In some areas the productive capacity of the newly cultivated lands deteriorated rapidly. Income distribution was also distorted. At the village level the ownership of resources became more concentrated, and large numbers of peasants were pushed into the migration stream (Robinson, 1952 and 1958; Mann, 1980).

In retrospect, it is hard to escape the conclusion that a slower pace of agricultural mechanization in Turkey would have been desirable. The negative effects of both the conversion of land use and the effects of income distribution would have been mitigated if tractors had been introduced more slowly and more selectively. Unquestionably, external assistance was partly at fault. Furthermore, the fault stemmed, not from a failure of analysis, but from the dearth of analysis. Both U.S. assistance personnel and the Turkish government identified mechanization with the modernization of agriculture (Chenery, Brandow, and Cohn, 1953; Aresvik, 1975, pp. 76–81; Mann, 1980).

Fertilizer. The expansion of fertilizer use was a major focus of several U.S. assistance projects. The U.S. assistance programs' extensive involve-

Table 14.2. Mechanization in Turkish Agriculture, 1950–1980

Year	Tractors		Draft Animals		Total Area Cultivated (million hectares)
	Number (thousands)	Area Cultivated (million hectares)	Number (thousand pairs)	Area Cultivated (million hectares)	
1950	17	1.2	2,495	13.3	14.5
1955	40	3.0	2,564	18.0	21.0
1960	42	3.2	2,648	20.1	23.3
1965	55	4.1	2,674	19.5	23.6
1970	116	8.7	2,099	15.8	24.5
1975	243	18.2	1,987	—	24.4
1980	436	32.7	1,988	—	27.0

Sources: Turkish State Institute of Statistics, *Summary of Agricultural Statistics,* various annual issues; Ministry of Agricultural, Forestry and Rural Affairs, General Directorate of Agricultural Affairs; OECD, *Agricultural Policy in Turkey* (Paris, 1974); World Bank, *Turkey: Industrialization and Trade Strategy: Methodological and Statistical Annex,* (Washington, D.C., 18 February 1982).

ment in fertilizer began with a US/AID-supported team of six fertilizer experts from the Tennessee Valley Authority. In early 1966 this team spent two months advising the Turkish State Planning Organization; the result was a detailed fertilizer study whose conclusions were incorporated into the second Five Year Plan. The Turkish government worked extensively with US/AID to develop a suitable fertilizer project but in the end did not seek US/AID financing for any fertilizer investment project. US/AID continued to work with the Turkish government on fertilizer-related questions, nevertheless. A US/AID fertilizer adviser spent about four years (1967–71) working with the State Planning Office, the Ministry of Agriculture, the Agricultural Supply Organization (TZDK), the Agricultural Bank, and Turkish industry to coordinate the development of a fertilizer industry (Hill, 1969). A major change occurred in Turkish agriculture in the late 1960s following the US/AID fertilizer adviser's recommendations: the Turkish government accepted the use of nitrogen fertilizer on wheat, and the results achieved on state farms from applying nitrogen on high-yield winter wheat varieties convinced research workers of the merit of using nitrogen fertilizers in addition to phosphates. As a result the first recommendations for applying nitrogen to winter wheat grown on the Anatolian Plateau were made in spring 1969. After the introduction of the high-yield winter and spring wheat varieties, the amount of fertilizer used for wheat in Turkey increased dramatically.

Fertilizer consumption increased very rapidly, in part because prices were heavily subsidized by the Turkish government. Excess demand conditions have prevailed, consequently, and a nonprice allocation mechanism has been used to distribute fertilizer to farmers and to specific crops. Unfortunately, available supplies are distributed unevenly. A World Bank simulation based on its agricultural sector model for Turkey indicated substantial malallocation of fertilizer use among crops and regions due to the pricing policies (World Bank, 1982b, vol. 2, p. 252). In retrospect it is doubtful that subsidies were needed to induce more intensive fertilizer use. Before the new wheat varieties were introduced there was little economic return to higher levels of fertilizer use on most crops; with the new fertilizer-responsive varieties the economic incentive for fertilizer use has been was very great. Thus, the primary effect of fertilizer subsidies was to distort use patterns.

LAND AND WATER DEVELOPMENT

Both US/AID (and its predecessor) and the World Bank have substantially assisted land and water development in Turkey. For over thirty years the Seyhan Irrigation Project, a large hydroelectric, flood control, and irrigation undertaking, was a major focus of funding by the two agencies.[5] The project illustrates all the difficulties inherent in such large-scale, multipurpose ventures. At Seyhan the problems stemmed from the coordination of the irrigation phase with the power and flood control phases.

Prior to requesting funds for a dam from the World Bank, the Turkish Ministry of Public Works authorized a two-year design study (1948–50). The Bank, however, made its own economic study. Despite serious reservations, the Bank agreed to help finance the construction, and work on phase 1 (power and flood control) began in 1952. Although at the very beginning of the project the attainment of all the objectives was deemed necessary for the undertaking to be economically viable, phase 2 (irrigation and drainage) was not begun until phase 1 was drawing to a close.

The irrigation and drainage studies estimated the cost of phase 2 to be several times that of phase 1; this estimate, however, did not include the even larger expense of on-farm land and water development, which was essential to realizing the irrigation benefits. In the early 1980s, when a large portion of the irrigation system was operational, it was apparent that the Seyhan Project had been more of a burden to the Turkish economy than a source of growth.

Because of the long delays attendant on completion of phase 2, the Bank insisted upon an intensive extension effort to ensure effective use of the irrigation facilities as they were completed. A "training and visit" (T&V) program was developed with the assistance of Daniel Benor, an Israeli extension specialist. Unlike existing programs, it offered more intensive assistance to farmers; coordinated the activities of the different agencies; instituted regular sessions to train village-level "contact" workers to make scheduled visits to farmers; and backed up the contact workers with a hierarchy of specialists. T&V was so successful that the Bank made it part of other projects (see chapter 10), and it has become a model for Bank-sponsored programs in many other countries (Benor and Harrison, 1977; chapter 9).

To strengthen Turkey's capacity to increase farmers' effective use of the land and water resources under development, the United States in 1960 helped to establish a Department of Land and Water Resource Development (Devlet Su Isleri, or DSI) in the Ministry of Public Works (modeled on the U.S. Bureau of Reclamation) and TOPRAKSU (modeled on the U.S. Soil Conservation Service) in the Ministry of Agriculture, Forestry and Rural Affairs. US/AID funding was extended to training DSI and TOPRAKSU staff and to financing investments in soil and water development by farmers. By the late 1960s the two new agencies had become highly professional and technologically proficient.

TOPRAKSU resources were concentrated in the Seyhan and Gediz project areas, where a state-managed (force account) approach to land and water development effectively generated on-farm development. Although both the World Bank and the European Investment Bank strongly supported the force account approach, US/AID was critical of it because it neglected the million-plus hectares of irrigated land outside the project areas (US/AID, 1969b; Mann, 1972). Indeed, by 1970 it was clear that Turkey still could not deliver irrigation water to farmers outside the state-managed project areas. Furthermore, DSI's capacity to design and construct irrigation facilities exceeded TOPRAKSU's capacity to manage the delivery of water and to provide technical assistance at the farm level.[6]

To increase TOPRAKSU's capacity for on-farm water development and to enlarge the private sector's capacity to serve farmers outside the project areas, US/AID assisted in the development of a new On-Farm Water Development Project.[7] The pilot demonstration in the Izmir region was regarded as highly successful (Mann, 1972; OECD, 1974, p. 26). Unfortunately, the limited credit available to farmers, contractors, and equipment suppliers and TOPRAKSU's less than adequate engineering and agronomic capacity hampered the diffusion of the so-called Izmir model.

Mann (1972) compared the advantages of the Seyhan and Izmir models and overall gave the latter higher marks, for the following reasons. First, despite rapid and intensive development, the effect of the older Seyhan model was constrained by government budget limitations. In contrast, the Izmir project, by drawing heavily on private funding, was able to spread public resources more broadly and to separate the pace of irrigation development from the size of the TOPRAKSU budget. Second, in the Izmir model most land development costs were borne privately; the government supported only T&V assistance. The returns to public investment were higher. Third, the Izmir model was more labor-intensive, made greater use of local resources, generated more employment, and provided greater opportunity for the development of local private entrepreneurship. Finally, the distributional effects of the Izmir strategy were more favorable because public resources were spread more broadly in Izmir-type projects. In the Seyhan Project large farmers tended to receive a relatively large share of the land development subsidies and technical assistance.

Turkey has institutionalized a substantial capacity to develop and manage land and water resource activities over the period of thirty years. The experience with the Seyhan and Izmir projects contributed to the experience that has led to better bureaucratic performance. Over the last decade Turkey seems finally to be realizing returns from its major investments in the multipurpose water resource projects and from its smaller investments in land and water development outside the major project areas.

AGRICULTURAL EDUCATION, RESEARCH, AND EXTENSION

Turkey established the Ministry of Agriculture in 1931 and the extension service in 1943 and first undertook agricultural research in 1950. In the early 1950s, however, these areas were exceptionally weak; research was highly fragmented, and the staff members were technicians rather than scientists.

Following assessments by U.S. technical assistance missions in the early 1950s, efforts were made to strengthen agricultural extension by focusing on training and technical assistance at the field level (Horton, 1964) and, later, on extension planning and administration.[8] In the mid-1960s the development of extension services still lagged, perhaps because of the different concepts held by the Turkish bureaucracy and the U.S. advisers. In the Turkish view extension agents were part of the Kaymakam ("county administration") staff and had regulatory and administrative functions, but in the American view extension services were supposed to reform the county system so that it would carry out educational and technology transfer functions for the Ministry of Agriculture.

In 1966 US/AID and the Turkish government initiated an Integrated Agricultural Services Project on a pilot basis in Denizli Province, in southwestern Turkey, to move agricultural planning to the provincial and county levels and to coordinate the various agencies for agricultural development at the local level (Wilson, 1971). The Project's three major activities were (a) coordinating a support system to integrate the supplies and services needed to increase agricultural production; (b) increasing supplies of fertilizer and credit and improving seed, breeding stock, and land and water management; and (c) testing and evaluating new technology locally. Despite increased production in many individual programs, the integrated approach to agricultural development was never achieved. US/AID terminated support in June 1970. US/AID's efforts to strengthen extension services by improving on-farm water management in the Izmir region continued (see above), but the national agricultural extension services showed little improvement.

In the early 1980s Turkey again confronted the problem of an effective agricultural extension system because of World Bank and US/AID concerns. The decision was made then to adopt nationally the T&V system that had been tested in the Seyhan area.

During the 1950s, research, like extension, was fragmented among several departments and agencies. Both the Turkish government and US/AID recognized the weakness of agricultural research, but the first assistance project in support of agricultural research, with the objective of reorganizing the Turkish agricultural research system, was not initiated until 1963 (US/AID, 1965). A second and complementary project was the strengthening of economic research and agricultural planning (US/AID, 1967). Bureaucratic opposition was strong, however, and both projects failed. Turkish agricultural research programs remain fragmented.

A more successful undertaking was US/AID's support for the establishment of Ataturk University in eastern Turkey. Beginning in 1955 US/AID provided support, through a contract with the University of Nebraska, for an extension training institute and an agricultural experiment station. An external review commissioned by US/AID in the early 1970s concluded that the new university appeared to be effectively institutionalized (Wilson, 1971).

WHEAT PRODUCTION CAMPAIGNS

In the late 1960s and early 1970s US/AID shifted its development assistance to the direct support of specific agricultural production objectives. (Some funds still were channeled to training, research, and extension, however.) This shift followed the demonstration in 1965 of the dramatic possibilities of new high-yield wheat varieties.[9] Seeds of two varieties developed in Mexico (Sonora 64 and Lera Rojo) had been tried out by a farmer on the Mediterranean coast; his yields of about 4.0 tons per hectare were roughly double the yields of the best local wheat. Large-scale demonstrations followed when US/AID provided economic and technical assistance (*a*) to import twenty-two thousand tons of the seed for planting in different regions and (*b*) to educate farmers in the necessary production practices for obtaining high yields: higher rates of fertilizer application, better seedbed preparation, and better weed control.

A study by the Agricultural Planning and Economic Research Department showed that net income from land and management per hectare increased about 150 percent in the first year (1967–68) with the new technology. The cost-benefit ratio of the seed import program probably was the highest of any US/AID program to Turkey (Aresvik, 1975, p. 164).

Many indirect benefits followed. A number of agencies (e.g., the Agricultural Bank, the Government Supply Agency, the Soils Products Office, and State Farms) learned that they could demonstrate program success by coordinating their support for the wheat production campaign. Furthermore, technical capacity and morale in the Turkish Extension Service improved, and the staff responded by changing their techniques, procedures, and education approach. Having something valuable to disseminate generated greater interest among farmers.

The widespread adoption of the Mexican wheats in coastal Turkey underscored the rapidity with which farmers can respond to new technology. However, the Anatolian Plateau, which comprises three-quarters of Turkey's wheat land, was unaffected. It requires cold-tolerant winter wheats. A program sponsored by the Turkish government, the Rockefeller Foundation, and US/AID—the High-Yielding Winter Wheat Project—developed some high-yield winter wheat in time to introduce it during the same season as the Mexican spring-type varieties (Johnson, 1971). By 1974 Turkish and Rockefeller Foundation scientists were able to recommend practices that would give farmers yields of at least 2,000 kilograms per hectare in all years except those with unusually low rainfall. The recommendations were demonstrated on ten locations in Ankara Province in 1974–75; the trials yielded 2,530 kilograms per hectare, as opposed to 1,810 kilograms per hectare in adjacent fields. Modest amounts of additional inputs combined with better crop management appeared to account for the yield increases. A subsequent analysis suggested that not all practices in the recommended package were profitable, however (Somel, 1979).

The High-Yielding Winter Wheat Project led to a major reorganization of wheat research in Turkey. Scientists with different specialties joined multi-disciplinary staffs; plant pathologists worked with breeders to select resistant strains; and a truly national wheat improvement program was created with eleven research stations: three breeding stations (two for winter wheat and one for spring wheat) and eight selection and testing sites.

In February 1982 a comprehensive review judged the wheat project to be highly successful (Mann and Wright, 1982).[10] It was the first important demonstration of the Green Revolution in rainfed agriculture. Turkish wheat production moved from approximately 10 million tons per year in 1970 to six consecutive years of over 16 million tons. About half of Turkey's present wheat area, both irrigated and rainfed, is planted with high-yield varieties, and as of the mid-1970s Turkey again became a wheat exporter (Nyrop, 1980, p. 154; World Bank, 1982b, pp. 244–93). The project also is a model for research organization and management for all of Turkey's agricultural research.

Assistance to Improve the Quality of Life in Rural Turkey

U.S. assistance for rural development has been directed primarily toward providing direct input for agricultural production and strengthening institutions that directly support agricultural production (agricultural research and extension). To the extent that these programs have raised rural incomes, they also have increased the quality of life in rural areas. In addition, U.S. assistance has been directed toward improving rural education and health, family planning, and nutrition. The resources for these activities have been smaller than those for support of agricultural production, and less attention has been given to evaluating the effects.

RURAL EDUCATION

During the late 1950s and 1960s U.S. assistance supported educational planning, school design and construction, and mass literacy programs. In the late 1960s attention shifted to supporting technical education and modernizing university-level education. Clearly, the low level of rural literacy in the early 1950s was a major obstacle to improvements in both the efficiency of agricultural production and the quality of rural life. Two projects—Literacy Training in the Armed Forces (1959–62) and Adult Education Resources Development (1960–65)—were reasonably successful. Rural education and literacy projects, however, apparently captured less interest or support from the Turkish educational bureaucracy than did the later programs to reform and develop higher education (Price, 1970).

RURAL HEALTH AND FAMILY PLANNING

Several US/AID-sponsored studies, beginning with the 1963 survey by the Population Council, indicated that a high percentage of the population (both urban and rural and representing all economic classes) had favorable attitudes toward family planning methods but lacked appropriate information and technology. Since the mid 1960s US/AID has made several loans to support integrated family planning and rural health programs, especially in the more disadvantaged areas of eastern Turkey. One interesting result was demonstrated by the reinforcement resulting from integrating health and family planning education with literacy improvement (US/AID, 1974).

NUTRITION

Early efforts to improve nutrition focused on home economics, education, and extension. From the mid-1950s to the early 1970s, food imports were supported through the PL 480 program. School feeding programs also were developed with PL 480 support. However, no strong integrated approach to nutrition planning or nutrition programs has been devised by US/AID or the Turkish government.

Some Conclusions

During much of its history, U.S. economic assistance to Turkey has been confronted with difficult tradeoffs between economic and political objectives. At several critical junctures political concerns clearly limited the pursuit of accurately diagnosed economic reforms by assistance programs. In retrospect, the failure to carry out needed monetary, fiscal, and trade reforms, particularly in the late 1950s and the late 1970s, seriously weakened the Turkish economy. If necessary reforms could have been carried out in a more appropriate and timely manner, the Turkish living standard would be higher and the Turkish economy would now be stronger.

Major attention has been given to program assistance in this review, even though project and technical assistance were dominant in the 1940s and 1950s. Infrastructure assistance during this period was important to later development. The Turkish experience suggests that even when project aid is the dominant form of assistance, a substantial program component is useful to induce effective policy dialogue between donors and recipients. The dialogue between donors and the Turkish government during the mid- and late 1960s helped to ensure that the reforms undertaken toward the end of the 1960s growth cycle were carried out both earlier and more effectively than the belated reactions to the cycles of the 1950s and 1970s.

A closely related lesson is that when macroeconomic policy results in several economic distortions, lending is both costly and unproductive unless effective remedial actions are taken at the same time. When macroeconomic policies are inappropriate, assistance resources are largely dissipated until the remedial policies are accepted and implemented. This conclusion must be tempered by a recognition that we have no widely accepted techniques for determining whether particular policy changes will be adequate. Until knowledge improves, advice on policy reforms must continue to be weighted heavily by judgment.

Other rather strong conclusions have emerged from our review of assistance to agricultural development in Turkey:

1. Allocation of development assistance funds for the purchase of material inputs (e.g., tractors and fertilizer) rarely is a productive use of development assistance. At best, material transfers are an indirect method of overcoming foreign exchange limitations. When appropriate economic incentives exist for the use of such inputs, they are rapidly adopted by farmers even in the absence of subsidies.

2. Both US/AID and the World Bank should have learned in Turkey that building the *physical* infrastructure for irrigation development is much simpler than building the *institutional* infrastructure. In retrospect, both the World Bank's commitment to physical infrastructure development and US/AID's commitment to institutional infrastructure development to support land and water development appear highly successful; but in both cases the economic returns would have been greater if attention had been given earlier to the institutional innovations that were needed to realize the production potential of the physical infrastructure development.[11]

3. Institution building is most effective when it is motivated by potential high economic returns. This is the lesson of the wheat programs. Generalized

efforts to reform and develop effective agricultural extension and agricultural research programs were largely ineffective until the new, high-yield wheat varieties offered the possibility of very large gains from institutional innovation.

The effect of development assistance often appears to be much more impressive a decade or more after completion. A major contribution of all development efforts is the building of human capital through learning by doing. Many young professionals who participated in policy development and project planning and management became, later in their careers, the architects of the reforms that currently are leading to more effective macroeconomic and sector development policies and to better program design and management.

15

Assistance to Ghana and
the Ivory Coast

J. DIRCK STRYKER
AND HASAN A. TULUY

The economic impact of development assistance has been very different in Ghana and the Ivory Coast. At independence in 1957 Ghana had a well-established export sector, which permitted the accumulation of substantial foreign exchange reserves. Its physical infrastructure and educational establishment were reasonably well developed, and its per capita income was the highest in Africa south of the Sahara. Two and one-half decades later the Ghanaian economy was in ruins, with cocoa exports cut in half, a black market exchange rate many times the official rate, an extensive and complex system of trade and exchange controls, and real per capita income substantially below the level at independence. Foreign aid by this time was almost totally ineffective in stimulating development.

The Ivory Coast at independence, on the other hand, was far behind Ghana in terms of roads, schools, agricultural production, per capita income, and practically every other indicator of development. By the early 1980s, however, the country had one of the best rural infrastructures in Africa, had made substantial progress in the education and health of its population, had a relatively well-developed and diversified agricultural sector, and had experienced an average annual growth of real per capita income of close to 3 percent. Concessional foreign aid had declined in importance as the Ivory Coast financed its development out of its own resources and by borrowing abroad on commercial terms.

By the mid-1980s the economic situation in the two countries had once again substantially changed. In 1983 Ghana began a major process of structural reform that drastically improved its potential for effectively utilizing foreign aid. The Ivory Coast, on the other hand, found itself saddled with a fixed exchange rate and resorted increasingly to import restrictions in order to correct its balance of payments and to protect its domestic industries. This biased incentives against exports and toward the production of nontradables and import-competing goods, both of which had limited potential for future growth.

The difference between the experiences of these two neighboring countries is the subject of this chapter. A major thesis is that the effectiveness of foreign aid was conditioned in each instance by the economic policy environment in which that aid was administered. This policy environment was the result of many factors. Initially it was strongly influenced by the opposing directions taken by the two leaders, Kwame Nkrumah and Felix Houphouet-Boigny. Whereas Ghana chose the path of socialism and state control, the Ivory Coast government saw the role of the state more as one of influencing rather than as one of controlling the private sector. A second factor until recently was the political turmoil that characterized Ghana in comparison with relative political stability in the Ivory Coast. Finally, the Ivory Coast was more open than Ghana to foreign trade, investment, and financial flows.

A second theme is that foreign aid can be very effective in promoting and enhancing the impact of policy reform. This is especially true if aid is given as program assistance in support of broad sectoral or macroeconomic policy changes, but project aid can also help to identify issues and to develop the mutual trust and confidence necessary for major reform.

Aid in a Historical Context

Foreign assistance to Ghana and the Ivory Coast within its historical context is the subject of this section. This is followed by an assessment of aid's macroeconomic contribution to growth through the transfer of resources for investment and improving the balance of payments. The role of foreign aid in facilitating the transfer of specific technical-organizational packages in the form of projects is then examined, with special emphasis on agriculture and rural development. Following this is an analysis of the economic policy environment in each country and of how foreign aid has been used to improve that environment. A final section summarizes the principal conclusions of the chapter.

THE PRE-WORLD WAR II COLONIAL PERIOD

Foreign aid in Ghana and the Ivory Coast must be seen within the historical context of development in these two countries. In Ghana much of this development occurred during the colonial period, though not all of it was due to the initiatives of the colonial government.[1] The rapid expansion of cocoa farming prior to World War I, for example, occurred spontaneously, without substantial government intervention. Furthermore, investment was financed largely out of local resources, since a basic policy of the British government was that colonies should be financially self-sufficient. Nevertheless, there was major investment in infrastructure, and an important beginning was made in the provision of education and health services, paid for largely out of export earnings from cocoa. With the depression and decline in world cocoa prices during the 1930s, however, most of this investment came to a halt.

Development in the Ivory Coast during this period was much less important than in Ghana. Cocoa was a relatively minor crop at this time, and coffee, which contributed most to exports until well after independence, was largely in the hands of European planters, many of whom did not survive the depression. Like the British, France also contributed little to its colonial empire during this period. Since Ivory Coast exports were not nearly as well developed as those of Ghana, few resources were available for investment in infrastructure and human services.

THE POST–WORLD WAR II COLONIAL PERIOD

World War II marked an important turning point for the Ivory Coast. France at last abandoned its policy of financial self-sufficiency in its colonies and in 1946 created an overseas development fund, the Fonds d'Investissement pour le Développement Economique et Social (FIDES). From 1946 to 1959 this fund provided grants worth close to 70 billion CFA francs. Of this about 9 percent went directly into agriculture, 29 percent was for bridges and roads, and 37 percent was used for construction of the port at Abidjan. FIDES was succeeded in 1959 by the Fonds d'Aide et de Coopération (FAC). FIDES and FAC grants were managed by the Caisse Centrale de Coopération Economique (CCCE), which also provided loans and advances and sometimes took an equity position for its own account (Ivory Coast, 1960, pp. 236–40).

This aid was instrumental in improving infrastructure in the Ivory Coast. Of greatest importance were the opening of the Vridi Canal and the construction of a protected, deep water port at Abidjan. Some progress was also made in road construction. There were only six hundred kilometers of paved roads by 1958, however, and many villages were not served by feeder roads of any kind (Ivory Coast, 1960, p. 118). Educational and health facilities and staff, especially of local origin, were also very meager. On the other hand, agricultural research was well established in a number of French research institutes.

Ghana also benefited from foreign assistance resulting from the Colonial Development and Welfare Act, passed during the interwar period. Ghana's first Ten Year Development Plan, published in 1946, called for the expenditure of about £1 million. These were booming years for cocoa, however, and the accumulation of reserves soon led to a series of plan reformulations that increased the level of investment. Despite this, at independence in 1957 the government held about £250 million in foreign exchange reserves (Hymer, 1971, pp. 166–67). Foreign aid thus offered relatively little in comparison with Ghana's own resources. This windfall for the colonial and postindependence governments was possible because of the decision not to transfer the profits from high cocoa prices back to the farmer. Instead the Cocoa Marketing Board and the government accumulated these earnings as sterling balances held abroad.

Overall the level of development in Ghana at the end of the colonial period was considerably more advanced than that in the Ivory Coast. At the time of independence, per capita GDP at market prices and official rates of exchange was $181 in Ghana, compared with $157 in the Ivory Coast. With only three-quarters of the Ivory Coast's area of land, Ghana had three times the length of roads, of which nearly four thousand kilometers were paved. The primary school enrollment rate in 1960 was 59 percent in Ghana, compared with 46 percent in the Ivory Coast (World Bank, 1976).

FROM INDEPENDENCE TO 1966

The years from independence to 1966 were critical for both Ghana and the Ivory Coast. During this period the leaders of both countries created the ideological and policy frameworks in which development was to take place. Strategies were formulated and the first steps toward implementation were undertaken. These proved so economically disastrous in Ghana that Nkrumah was deposed in 1966, leaving a legacy of debt and distortions from which the country has not yet fully recovered. In the Ivory Coast, on the other hand, 1966 marked the turning point from a period of strong, concentrated economic management to one in which decision making became more diffused and decentralized in keeping with the growing complexity of the economy.

Under Nkrumah, Ghana embarked on a radical structural transformation of the economy, giving priority to import-competing industrialization and capital-intensive, state-managed agricultural development. There was heavy emphasis on socialist ideology, decreased external dependence, Ghanaianization of the economy, and the importance of the public sector in promoting development. The Ivory Coast, in contrast, concentrated more on small-farm agriculture and exports, created an atmosphere conducive to private foreign investment in industry, and maintained close links to France, the European Economic Community, and neighboring Francophone countries. The state was active in influencing and promoting development, but as a partner rather than a replacement for the private sector (Berg, 1971).

From 1960 to 1964 Ghana received $68 million in net foreign aid from OECD countries and multilateral institutions, of which $18.53 million was in the form of grants, primarily from the United States and the United Kingdom. Official bilateral loans, mostly from the same sources, amounted to $29.82 million, and loan repayments equaled $1.38 million. Multilateral borrowing totaled $25.6 million, primarily from the World Bank, and repayments amounted to $4.74 million (OECD, 1966).

The Ivory Coast received $70.16 million in grants during the same period, of which $34.34 million was from France and the rest from the European Development Fund. Official bilateral loans during this period equaled $82.26 million, two-thirds of which were from France. Total aid to the Ivory Coast was therefore more than twice the amount received by Ghana.

These aid figures are only partial, however. In Ghana's case, they do not include the numerous bilateral arrangements made with Eastern bloc countries, some of which contained concessional elements. Nor do they include direct French budget subsidies to the Ivory Coast for agricultural research, mineral exploration, and technical assistance.

The contribution of this aid was heavily influenced by the course of development in each of the countries. Gross domestic product in the Ivory Coast, for example, increased in real terms during this period at an annual rate of 6–7 percent; in Ghana it increased at only 2–3 percent. Low rates of inflation and balance of payments surpluses in the Ivory Coast contrasted with rapid price increases and mounting current account deficits in Ghana.

With exports stagnant, imports rising, and foreign exchange reserves falling, the government of Ghana resorted to suppliers' credits and deficit financing. At the beginning of 1966, consumer prices in Ghana were 75 percent higher than in 1960, and imported goods were in very short supply owing to import quotas and exchange controls. As a result, industrial and other enterprises that were heavily dependent on imports of capital equipment and intermediate goods were forced to operate substantially below capacity (Berg, 1971, p. 188). In addition, large sums had been allocated to prestige projects with very low rates of return.

Most significant for the future, by 1966 Ghana had acquired an enormous medium- and long-term external debt of about $500 million, whereas its foreign exchange reserves had decreased to $50 million. About 80 percent of this debt comprised costly suppliers' credits. Debt service obligations rose to 25 percent of exports in 1966. In addition, the system of import quotas and exchange controls, introduced to reduce imports in the face of the overvalued exchange rate, was a bureaucratic nightmare and gave rise to severe distortions in domestic prices.

The development strategy of the Ivory Coast was conceived during the first six years after independence. A key man in this process was Raphael Saller, who served as the first minister of finance, economic affairs, and planning. This was an extremely powerful position that enabled him to put his "pragmatic, modern, liberal and disciplined" stamp on the economy with the full approval of the president (Woronoff, 1972, p. 201). The incentive code to encourage private foreign investment, which was adopted in 1959 and revised in 1962, provided tax holidays, guaranteed the transfer of capital, and allowed for repatriation of profits. Foreign trade and domestic marketing were left in private hands, and government investments in industry generally involved minority participation. Public enterprises were created primarily for infrastructure development, to expand housing and utilities, and to introduce new crops such as rubber and oil palm into agriculture (Woronoff, 1972, p. 204).

It was in the area of economic planning that the Ivory Coast was most innovative. Several development commissions, comprising public and private representatives, were created to determine production targets, desirable reforms, and the general orientation of the respective sectors. On the basis of this information, a Comité Interministériel du Développement examined the broad economic situation and established the general framework for development and the overall rate of growth. Frequent contacts between government and the private sector were also maintained through the Conseil Economique et Social and the Chambers of Commerce, Industry, and Agriculture. Using these networks, technical elaboration of the plan was carried out by the Ministry of Finance, Economic Affairs, and Planning with heavy input from French technical assistants. The plan was then incorporated into annual development budgets. Numerous studies provided a solid foundation for the planning process (Woronoff, 1972, pp. 206–8).

In 1966 the economic superministry was divided into separate ministries for finance and economic affairs and for planning. Substantial power was retained by the planning ministry, since it continued to have primary responsibility for managing the development budget—the Budget Spécial d'Investissement et d'Equipement, or BSIE—funded by earmarked receipts from taxes, customs duties, loans, and surpluses from the state's operating budget. The priorities laid down by Saller were retained, but a decentralization of authority began that has continued until this day.

FROM 1967 TO 1981

By the time the Nkrumah government was replaced and economic decision making in the Ivory Coast had become more decentralized, the basic pattern of economic development in these two countries was well established.

Ghana. Ghana after Nkrumah was characterized by succeeding phases of devaluation, austerity, import liberalization, inflation, tightened import and exchange controls, and political turmoil. The real value of exports (in 1975 prices) fell from N¢1,249 million in 1966 to N¢486 million cedis in 1983. Production of cocoa decreased from 538,000 metric tons in 1965 to 173,000 tons in 1983, primarily as a result of a 58 percent decline in the real value of the producer price over the same period (Stryker, 1988).

The National Liberation Council (NLC) government devalued the cedi by 43 percent in 1967 and rescheduled the country's short-term debt. An initial austerity program and a brief increase in world cocoa prices in 1967–68 permitted some relaxation of exchange controls, but as imports rose, lax macroeconomic policies and ambitious investment programs put pressure on aggregate demand and the balance of payments. The system collapsed, and Busia's civilian government, elected in 1969, moved toward a devaluation of 80 percent in late 1971. Before the devaluation could take effect, the government was overthrown by the National Redemption Council (NRC). The NRC proceeded to revalue the cedi, so that the final devaluation was only 40 percent. Debts were unilaterally rescheduled, and some supplier credits, purportedly incurred under irregular circumstances, were repudiated (Leith, 1974, pp. 5–8). This prompted the donors to begin negotiations on an overall settlement.

The NRC managed during its early years to curb the demand for imports through strict, less corrupt licensing. Inflation accelerated, however, and the cedi became increasingly overvalued. It was devalued in 1978 from 1.15 N¢/$ to 2.75 N¢/$ but continued to depreciate on the black market until by 1981 the rate was about 26 N¢/$. By this time the government's budget was almost totally out of control. This led to an annualized increase in the money supply of 261 percent and triple-digit inflation. In December 1981 the civilian government installed by Jerry Rawlings after his ousting of the NRC in 1979 was replaced by the military (Economist Intelligence Unit, 1982, no. 1, pp. 10–12).

The major form of foreign assistance that Ghana received following the Nkrumah period was debt relief. A series of early bilateral agreements culminated in March 1974 in a multilateral arrangement for rescheduling on concessionary terms. The grant element of this repayment scheme was estimated at 61 percent of the present value of the debt relief, though rising world inflation subsequently increased its relative importance.

Gross official disbursements to Ghana averaged about $48 million a year during 1967–69, but few new loan commitments were made until 1974 because of the outstanding debt dispute. Public transfers received by Ghana in the form of grants and technical assistance equaled about $30 million a year. By the end of the 1970s, on the other hand, Ghana was again receiving a substantial amount of foreign assistance (see table 15.1). Approximately 60 percent of this was bilateral in nature, mostly from West Germany, the United Kingdom, and the United States. Of the $581 million in investment grants and loans received during 1977–80, 18 percent was in the form of grants, and 62 percent was in the form of development loans, with a grant element of at least 25 percent. As a result of rescheduling, the debt service averaged only about 3–4 percent of the total value of exports.

Ivory Coast. The Ivory Coast economy became increasingly diversified after 1966. The share of primary production in total GDP declined from 34 percent in 1966 to 24 percent in 1977. Even within agriculture there was a marked increase in the production and export of a range of crops in addition to coffee and cocoa. These included palm oil and kernels, copra, rubber, bananas, pineapples, and cotton. Real annual growth of GDP remained high but decreased from 7.3 percent in 1965–70 to 4.9 percent in 1975–78. Prices accelerated from 4.2 percent per annum in 1965–70 to 17.7 percent in 1975–78, more because of world inflation than because of growth in the domestic money supply, which was constrained by the Ivory Coast's membership in the West African Monetary Union. Gross domestic investment rose from 20 percent of GDP in 1966 to 29 percent in 1978.

Table 15.1. Official Foreign Capital Flows for Ghana, 1977–1980
($ millions)

	1977	1978	1979	1980
Grants				
Investment	23.7	29.4	31.7	20.0
Technical assistance	29.2	37.5	35.4	44.9
Total	52.9	66.9	61.7	64.9
Loans				
Concessionary	47.3	55.7	114.6	140.9
Other	19.0	34.1	34.9	30.5
Total	66.3	89.8	149.5	171.4
Debt service	13.1	15.4	20.6	22.9
Net official flows	106.1	141.3	196.0	213.4

Source: OECD, *Geographical Distribution of Financial Flows to Developing Countries* (Paris, 1981), pp. 82, 83.

There were some disturbing trends nevertheless. The balance of trade, which had been in surplus in every year prior to 1971, moved into deficit during the 1970s. The Ivory Coast also appeared to be running out of its most profitable investments in agriculture and import-competing industry. Greater decentralization in decision making created problems of coordination and government control of foreign borrowing by parastatal enterprises. At the same time, the government undertook some very costly investments. This necessitated substantial foreign borrowing, much of it at relatively high commercial interest rates. As a result, the disbursed external debt of the Ivory Coast rose from $256 million in 1970 to $4,062 million in 1980, and the debt service ratio increased from 6.7 percent in 1970 to 23 percent in 1980. The capacity of the Ivory Coast to continue borrowing from abroad had reached its limit.

This was especially important because foreign assistance to the Ivory Coast increasingly took the form of hard loans rather than concessionary grants. This was a sign of the creditworthiness of the country as well as of the perception among international donors and lenders of its lack of need for concessionary aid. During 1960–66 grants constituted 49 percent of project-related official capital flows, and loans had a large concessionary element. From 1967 to 1973, however, grants amounted to only 11 percent of these flows (France, Ministère de la Coopération, 1976, p. 134). In 1977–80 out of $907 million in official flows related to investment, only 9 percent was in the form of grants, and 31 percent was in the form of development loans, with a grant element in excess of 25 percent (see table 15.2). One result was that

Table 15.2. Official Foreign Capital Flows for the Ivory Coast, 1977–1980
($ millions)

	1977	1978	1979	1980
Grants				
Investment	17.4	11.8	24.1	25.1
Technical assistance	57.3	61.6	83.7	101.4
Total	74.7	73.4	107.8	126.5
Loans				
Concessionary	42.4	73.3	67.8	100.0
Other	136.2	117.8	102.3	188.4
Total	178.6	191.1	170.1	288.4
Debt service	22.2	29.7	34.5	44.8
Net official flows	231.1	234.8	243.4	370.1

Source: OECD, *Geographical Distribution of Financial Flows to Developing Countries* (Paris, 1981), pp. 108, 109.

the Ivory Coast paid out $131 million in debt service during this period, reducing net capital inflows to $776 million, plus another $304 million in technical assistance.

The Ivory Coast also encountered problems in raising the level of domestic savings. During the early years following independence the export sector was a source of growing government revenues in the form of export taxes and the profits of the Caisse de Stabilisation et de Soutien des Prix des Produits Agricoles (CSSPPA), the Ivory Coast's export stabilization fund. In addition, a broadening tax base and direct financial participation in profitable enterprises enabled the government to benefit from the growth of the economy's formal sector. As the structure of exports evolved, however, and as new investments became less profitable, there was less room for expansion of public revenues. Taxes were already high in relation to income in comparison with other countries, so additional savings had to be generated by the private sector. This required, however, the development of appropriate financial institutions.

FROM 1982 TO THE PRESENT

In 1982 the Rawlings government faced massive budget deficits, spiraling inflation, very low export earnings, minimal foreign exchange reserves, and a huge foreign debt. Its immediate response was to cut back public spending, reduce the money supply, crack down on smuggling, and tighten foreign exchange controls. At first it appeared that the new government would regulate economic activity closely and pursue a strategy of self-sufficiency and autonomy rather than negotiate agreements with the IMF and the World Bank to undertake major reforms in return for substantial program lending. As pressures on the government tightened, however, it relented in August 1983 and signed IMF standby and compensatory financing facility arrangements totaling $382 million. Other donors quickly fell in line with offers of further grants and loans.

In return for this aid, Ghana agreed to a major package of reforms. In October 1983 the multiple exchange rate that had been established earlier was unified at 30 N¢/$, and thereafter the country pursued a policy of periodic adjustment, which in September 1986 was institutionalized into a biweekly foreign exchange auction. Prices, wages, and interest rates also were substantially raised and allowed to move more freely. Import restrictions were decreased, and tariff rates were simplified and lowered. The budget deficit was also drastically reduced, so that the rate of inflation fell from 123 percent in 1983 to 10 percent in 1985.

The result was a significant revival of economic activity as real GDP increased by 8.6 percent in 1984, 5.1 percent in 1985, and 5.3 percent in 1986. Government revenues as a proportion of GDP rose from 5.5 percent in 1983 to 10.4 percent in 1985. Export earnings expanded by 12 percent in 1985. Nevertheless, the process of structural adjustment had just begun, as much work was required to repair the damage inflicted on the economy over the previous two and one-half decades (Stryker, 1988).

By the mid-1980s it was becoming increasingly apparent that there were substantial structural imbalances in the Ivory Coast economy. One of the most important of these was the rigid exchange rate adhered to by the Ivory Coast, along with the other members of the West African Monetary Union. Domestic inflation and a deterioration in the terms of trade after 1972 led to appreciation of the real value of the official exchange rate in relation to the equilibrium rate vis-à-vis the Ivory Coast's major trading partners. This was especially harmful for industrial exports, to which the country was turning increasingly in order to sustain its economic growth (Michel and Noel, 1984, p. 88). Efforts to solve the problem through the use of an export subsidy proved to be administratively difficult and financially expensive.

Industrial exports suffered not only from overvaluation of the CFA franc, but also from the bias against exports introduced by the system of industrial incentives. Much of the industrial growth that occurred during the 1960s and 1970s was in import-competing activities that benefited from high rates of effective protection. In addition, just when the Ivory Coast was forced to turn to nonregional markets because those within West Africa were becoming saturated, the European and other industrial countries became increasingly protective of their own industries (Myfelka, 1984, p. 167). As a result, aid donors once again placed emphasis on agriculture and agroindustry even though the most profitable opportunities in the sector had already been exploited.

The Ivory Coast in the mid-1980s also remained highly dependent on foreign capital and expertise. Over fifty thousand French lived in the country, many of them for a number of years, where they occupied key positions in both the public and private sectors. In addition, the industrial sector was heavily dominated by foreign capital and decisional authority, rendering it vulnerable to any sign of political instability or to a change in the exchange rate or monetary regime.

A Macroeconomic Assessment

In the two-gap model, foreign aid supplies the resources that permit a country to attain higher levels of investment or to import the goods required for development (Chenery and Strout, 1966).[2] The ability of a country to use foreign aid is determined in this model by the capacity to absorb investment, the target rate of growth, the ratio of savings to income, the capital-output ratio, the marginal propensity to import, and the growth rate of exports. These parameters were estimated for Ghana and the Ivory Coast using data from the national accounts for 1960 through 1981 (World Bank, 1976, pp. 132–33, 1980b, pp. 112–13; and 1983, pp. 94–95; Stryker, 1988). The results of these regressions are given in table 15.3.[3] Most important among the conclusions of this analysis is the high degree of responsiveness of savings, and especially imports, to changes in income in the Ivory Coast compared with Ghana. This is shown by large positive and statistically highly significant slope coefficients for these parameters in the Ivory Coast compared with the same coefficients in Ghana. The Ghanaian savings coefficient is not significantly different from zero, and the import coefficient is negative, reflecting the major influence of trade restrictions and exchange controls. There was, in fact, a steady reduction of the ratio of imports to income from 0.34 in 1960 to 0.14 in 1981.

The growth rate of exports for Ghana, shown in equation (3) in table 15.3, is −2.5 percent, which is significantly different from zero. In contrast, the growth rate of exports for the Ivory Coast is +6.9 percent, which is also highly significant. The real value of Ivory Coast exports increased by almost four times from 1960 to 1981, generating large amounts of foreign exchange with which to finance the rapidly rising level of imports.

With labor held constant, the influence of investment on changes in output appears to have been negative in Ghana and nil in the Ivory Coast. The reasons for this are unclear. They may have to do with the lag structure used in the equations, or there may be other statistical anomalies; on the other hand, these results may occur because investment in both countries, and especially in Ghana, was unproductive.

Some insight into the relationship between income and investment in Ghana may be gained by looking at table 15.4, which shows average annual

Table 15.3. Regression Results for Key Macroeconomic Parameters—Ghana and the Ivory Coast

Equation[a]	Slope Coefficients[b]		R^{2c}	DW[d]
Ghana				
(1)	0.144		0.091	0.950
	(0.082)			
(2)	−0.343		0.508	1.912
	(0.072)			
(3)	−0.025		0.441	0.635
	(0.006)			
(4)	−7.012	−0.671	0.157	2.256
	(3.274)	(0.389)		
Ivory Coast				
(1)	0.250		0.795	0.703
	(0.028)			
(2)	0.425		0.979	0.963
	(0.014)			
(3)	0.069		0.947	1.021
	(0.004)			
(4)	0.273	−0.016	0.021	2.731
	(0.198)	(0.087)		

[a] The regression results apply to the parameters of the following equations:

$$S/P = a + b\,Y/P \tag{1}$$
$$M/P = c + d\,Y/P \tag{2}$$
$$\log(X/P) = \lg A + e\,T \tag{3}$$
$$(Y/P)_t - (Y/P)_{t-1} = f + g\,(L_t - L_{t-1}) + h\,(I/P)_{t-1} \tag{4}$$

where S = gross national savings (excluding net current transfers)
     P = the GDP deflator
     Y = gross domestic product at market prices
     M = imports of goods and nonfactor services
     X = exports of goods and nonfactor services
     T = time (year)
     I = gross domestic investment
     L = the agricultural labor force
     t = the year to which the relevant values of the variables refer. Where t does not appear, all variables in the equation refer to the current year.
     b = the marginal propensity to save
     d = the marginal propensity to import
     e = the growth rate of exports
     h = the incremental capital-output ratio holding labor constant.
[b] Figures in parentheses are standard errors of the coefficients.
[c] Coefficients of determination adjusted for the number of degrees of freedom.
[d] Durbin-Watson statistic.

Table 15.4. Average Annual Growth Rates of Gross Domestic Product (GDP) and Gross Domestic Investment (GDI) for Ghana, in Constant Prices (%)

	1950–60	1960–70	1970–81
GDP	4.1	2.2	−0.3
GDI	8.9	−3.1	−4.3

Source: World Bank, *World Tables: 1980* (Baltimore: Johns Hopkins University Press, 1980), p. 86.

rates of growth of the real value of output and investment over the past three decades. During this period the growth of output declined steadily and became negative during the 1970s. The growth of investment was quite rapid during the 1950s but became increasingly negative after independence. During the 1970s gross investment averaged only 5.7 percent of GDP, and net investment was probably negative, especially in the cocoa sector, where replanting ceased and trees were rapidly going out of production because of their advanced age. The decline in investment was associated more with restrictions on imports of capital goods and replacement parts than with the drop in domestic savings that occurred, since gross savings actually increased as a share of gross investment from 62 percent during the 1960s to 85 percent during the 1970s. The binding constraint on development in Ghana from a macroeconomic point of view, therefore, was foreign exchange rather than resources for investment. This was clearly related to stagnation in the export sector. It was also due to the failure of foreign aid and capital inflows to fill the foreign exchange gap.

The reasons for this were multiple. They had to do, first of all, with the overall constraints that existed on the total amount of foreign aid made available by donors and how that aid was distributed among countries. Second, Ghana's debt problem greatly complicated its access to loans, whether commercial or concessionary. Only after this debt was rescheduled in 1974 was it possible for Ghana once again to have access to foreign capital on a large scale. Finally, for donors there remained the critical question whether foreign aid would lead to increased investment and economic growth given the government's inflationary macroeconomic and restrictive trade policies, which contributed to an overvalued exchange rate and a sustained decline in exports.

The situation in the Ivory Coast was quite different. During the 1960s the real value of exports grew at an average annual rate of 5.5 percent, though this declined to 5.0 percent from 1970 to 1981. The real value of imports grew even more rapidly during these periods, at 6.8 percent and 9.8 percent per annum respectively, because of official borrowing and private capital inflows. As a result, the real value of domestic investment increased at 12.7

percent per year during the 1960s and 12.1 percent annually from 1970 to 1981 (World Bank, 1983, vol. 1, p. 95).

After the mid-1970s this picture changed. A two-gap model estimated by the World Bank for the Ivory Coast to analyze the effects of the 1976–80 plan during the 1980s suggested that the Ivory Coast economy would be constrained more by domestic savings than by exports (den Tuinder, 1978, pp. 160–86). The country was having to invest in projects that yielded a lower rate of return than in the past, and the Ivory Coast government was unable to generate the domestic resources in the public sector required to finance the investment required by its growth targets. In addition, increases in foreign borrowing could not be sustained because of rising debt service payments and their potential for lowering the Ivory Coast's credit rating abroad. Substantial policy changes were required, therefore, to encourage private savings and lessen dependence on foreign borrowing.

Project Aid: Agricultural and Rural Development

Most foreign assistance is offered in the form of specific projects embodying technical-organizational packages in the design of which donors usually play a very significant role. The resource transfer may be of less importance than the package itself, though the host government's acceptance of the project is generally conditional upon the donor's furnishing the bulk of the financing. In effect, the donor buys the right to influence how its resources are to be used to promote development. The effectiveness of this form of aid is measured by the degree to which project objectives are attained.

This section examines the effectiveness of project aid in promoting agricultural and rural development in Ghana and the Ivory Coast. It begins with a brief historical overview of rural development, followed by a description of foreign assistance programs and projects in the rural sector of the two countries. A discussion of the constraints on project design and implementation then precedes the concluding section, which assesses the usefulness of project assistance in an unfavorable policy environment.

THE HISTORY OF RURAL DEVELOPMENT

Ghana. Cocoa, the mainstay of the Ghanaian economy, was introduced in the latter part of the nineteenth century and quickly grew to become the principal export (Gordon, 1974, p. 71). In 1947 the Ghana Cocoa Marketing Board (GMB) was established to stabilize farmer incomes and real prices. This resulted initially in substantial public savings even though world prices were sufficiently high that strong incentives could also be offered to farmers. As world prices fluctuated, however, Ghana's export earnings also varied (see table 15.5). Until the mid-1960s, shortfalls were compensated by drawing

Table 15.5. Average World Price and Ghana's Production and Export Receipts of Cocoa, 1950–54 to 1980–84

Period	World Prices[a] ($/M.T.)	Production[b] (000 M.T.)	Export Receipts[c] ($ millions)
1950–54	3,011	230.1	693
1955–59	2,604	254.3	662
1960–64	1,770	444.6	785
1965–69	1,971	389.6	768
1970–74	2,041	418.0	853
1975–77	3,690	330.8	1,221
1980–84	2,236	218.4	488

[a] In constant U.S. dollars, from World Bank, *Commodity Trade and Price Trends* (Baltimore: Johns Hopkins University Press, 1986), p. 49.
[b] From J. Dirck Stryker, "A Comparative Study of the Political Economy of Agricultural Pricing Policies: Ghana—Final Draft Report" (Somerville, Mass.: Associates for International Resources and Development, 1988, Photocopy).
[c] Estimated by multiplying world price times production.

down the country's large reserves, but thereafter these fluctuations presented successive governments with formidable problems.

The Nkrumah government had little confidence in small-scale agriculture; it felt that agricultural output could only be increased through large motorized farms. By 1966 there were 135 state farms and about 35 Workers' Brigades employing a total of 21,000 salaried workers. The results of these projects were disappointing. The program cost $21 million in local capital expenditures, imported farm equipment, and current operating expenses, but output was valued at only $4 million (Woronoff, 1972, pp. 186–87).

Government policy on balance penalized smallholder agriculture. Activities of the extension service, which were critical for the cocoa subsector, were suspended in 1962 (McMurtry, 1974, p. 219). The GMB marketing monopoly was extended to other crops, and private licensed buying agents (LBA) were replaced by the United Ghana Farmers' Cooperative Council (UGFCC), which reduced the purchasing system's flexibility and increased its costs.

The government's ambitious development and industrialization plan coincided with a slump in world cocoa prices in the early 1960s. To maintain its revenue needed for growing capital expenditures, the government cut the cocoa producer price. By 1965–66 the nominal farmgate price of cocoa was only one-half of the 1951–52 price (Batemen, 1974, pp. 318–19). In real terms the decline was even more severe, as inflation accelerated from about

2 percent in 1960–63 to over 20 percent in 1965 (Leith, 1974, p. 93). Few additional cocoa plantings occurred thereafter, and plantations were progressively allowed to deteriorate.

Administrations after 1966 sought to redress the distortions of the early years of independence. All governments espoused the objective of self-sufficiency in food and industrial crops and the rehabilitation of the cocoa sector. Additional funds were allocated to agriculture, and the agricultural extension service was reestablished in 1967–68. Mechanized services were heavily subsidized, as were intermediate inputs such as seeds, fertilizers, and insecticides. Most of these inputs, however, went to large, mechanized farms for which yields remained low and economic costs were very high (Winch, 1976).

In the meantime, there was an acute scarcity of agricultural inputs for the small farmer. Furthermore, import restrictions on consumer goods resulted in few of these reaching the countryside, and those that did were very expensive. Cocoa farmers continued to suffer from low producer prices and were unwilling to maintain, and at times even to harvest, their farms even though cocoa would have been very profitable at undistorted prices (Stryker, 1975, p. 21). Production of cocoa declined by about 3–5 percent per annum from 1965–66 to 1983–84.

Ivory Coast. Export-oriented agriculture in the Ivory Coast dates back to the turn of the century. Rubber, palm products, and timber, the first export crops, were replaced in importance during the interwar period by cocoa and coffee. Timber exploitation expanded after World War II and independence in 1960, accounting with coffee and cocoa for 85 percent of the country's export earnings.

Three policies were key to the success of agriculture in the Ivory Coast. One was the construction of transportation infrastructure, opening up zones of unexploited potential. Equally important was the establishment of crop-specific agricultural research for the development, testing, seed multiplication, and dissemination of new varieties and technologies. Finally, coffee and cocoa production was supported through the operations of the stabilization funds established in 1956.

After independence the Ivorian government continued the colonial strategy of development based on agricultural exports. In addition, the government sought to broaden these exports by diversifying into other crops, such as palm products, pineapples, and cotton (see table 15.6). Research remained the domain of specialized agricultural research institutions, but extension of the new technologies was delegated to autonomous regional authorities and crop-specific development agencies.

Immigration and urbanization accelerated after independence, and national food requirements tripled in ten years. Even though food production increased more rapidly than population growth, urbanization and rising in-

Table 15.6. Production of Key Agricultural Products in the Ivory Coast, 1960–1974

Product	1960–63	1971–74	Percentage Increase per Annum
Palm clusters (mt)	290,188	705,737	10
Pineapples (mt)	23,142	192,790	24
Timber (000 m³)	3,470	4,669	4
Coffee (mt)	184,477	258,409[a]	3
Cocoa (mt)	91,965	199,829	8
Cotton (mt)	8,094[b]	55,933[b]	21

Source: Ivory Coast, Ministère du Plan, *La Côte d'Ivoire en Chiffres, Edition 76* (Abidjan, n.d.).
[a] 1972–75.
[b] 1959–60 to 1962–63 and 1971–72 to 1973–74.

comes placed large and increasing demands on the food sector. Food imports, perceived as threatening the positive trade balance, became a major concern for the Ivorian government.

The 1973 drought and the commodity price boom of 1973–74 strengthened this concern. Increasing food imports, especially of rice, and fluctuating export earnings resulted in greater importance being attached to the reduction of these imports as a central national objective. As rice imports rose to over one hundred thousand metric tons per year in the early 1970s and world prices quadrupled, the Ivorian government accelerated its investment in swamp and irrigated paddy production. As an added incentive to producers and to aid poorer farmers in the north, prices were increased sharply. Production rose significantly, but at a relatively high cost, and the subsidies on output, inputs, infrastructure, and services were a major fiscal burden. Questionable investments were also made in sugar production, which received the largest chunk of public investment funds between 1971 and 1980 (Hermann, 1981, p. 121). High production targets were established despite costs well in excess of world market prices, and the sugar industry became a major financial drain.

FOREIGN ASSISTANCE IN THE RURAL SECTOR

In the 1960s, foreign assistance stressed capital development projects such as irrigation, roads, ports, and power facilities. World Bank lending to the agricultural sector consisted mainly of irrigation projects. Bank policy shifted in the early 1970s toward maintaining the momentum of the Green Revolution to feed the developing countries and to increase the incomes of the poor (World Bank, 1972). Bilateral donors followed a similar transition. Whereas the United States Agency for International Development (US/AID) had been concerned in the 1960s primarily with infrastructural aid and balance of payments assistance, the "new directions" mandate and the "basic human needs" philosophy of the early 1970s shifted aid to small-scale projects that would help the poor (chapter 10).

Ghana. Until the 1970s most foreign assistance in Ghana was allocated to capital development projects and to assisting Nkrumah's industrialization policy. The World Bank had no projects in the rural sector, while US/AID, the largest donor, funded an Agricultural Extension and Production Project, which assisted Ghanaian production through price supports, subsidized input deliveries, and credit programs. Technical assistance and management training were also important components of this project.

The first World Bank rural development project was initiated in Ghana's cocoa sector in 1970. This was soon followed by a sugar rehabilitation project. About the same time, US/AID revamped the Agricultural Extension and Production Project to emphasize institutional areas such as extension and input delivery. Further resources were directed by US/AID to health and population programs, and significant amounts of PL 480 aid were made available.

The unilateral repudiation of part of Ghana's foreign debt by the NRC in 1972 resulted in a sharp drop in foreign assistance to Ghana. When Ghana's external debt was rescheduled in 1974 and long-term stabilization seemed a likely prospect, project assistance increased significantly. Four World Bank projects emphasizing agricultural and integrated rural development were approved. U.S. objectives sought to ensure that "the poor majority have more adequate income and greater access to health care services of sufficient quality" (US/AID, 1975, vol. 1, pp. 21–22). The basic approach of improved delivery of inputs and services, stronger planning and management, and development of local institutions was maintained for all three sectors of US/AID involvement—agriculture, health, and family planning. The Managed Input Delivery and Agricultural Services (MIDAS) Project, for example, comprised the importation and distribution of fertilizers, seed multiplication and distribution, extension services, rural credit, management training, studies of the marketing structure, and a number of other related components.

By 1977, however, economic mismanagement had created a highly distorted incentive structure with abundant opportunities for corruption and smuggling. Donor assistance programs were scaled down as existing projects came to completion. Only after Ghana and the IMF reached agreement in 1983 was this trend reversed, as donors sought to develop the projects necessary to relieve infrastructure and institutional bottlenecks.

Ivory Coast. Donor programs supported the Ivory Coast government's policy of rapid, export-oriented growth. In the early 1960s, infrastructure projects, training, studies, resource surveys, and research projects were important. French technical and managerial personnel assisted the Ivorian government in its development program. This, together with its financial support, accorded France an important influence on policy decisions and helped to establish a stable and conservative economic policy environment.

By 1968 the Ivory Coast had built up an impressive infrastructure of ports, roads, and electrical power networks. The government's emphasis on agriculture as the principal source of growth was lent support by increasing levels of project aid. A number of donors assisted the expansion and diversification of export crops. The World Bank group, for example, funded the first of over fifteen agricultural projects in 1969. During 1968–81, of the $710 million in aid extended by the World Bank one-quarter was for agriculture. This included cocoa, rubber, oil palm, coconut, and cotton production projects.

American assistance in the post-1967 period declined to $23.3 million in project and other economic assistance and $7 million in PL 480 aid from 1968 to 1981. This is not surprising, since with sound international creditworthiness and a per capita GNP of $1,200 in 1980, the Ivory Coast no longer met the requirements of the congressional mandate. On the other hand, the Export-Import Bank extended $225 million in loans during 1968–81.

Project aid proceeded satisfactorily until the late 1970s, when the government began to emphasize regional development and foodcrop production, thus moving away from the Ivory Coast's areas of comparative advantage. Foreign aid devoted to rice production, the sugar complexes in the north, development of the southwest, and the region surrounding the Kossou Dam in the center yielded much lower returns than had earlier investments in coffee, cocoa, timber, and other export crops.

CONSTRAINTS ON PROJECT DESIGN AND IMPLEMENTATION

Ghana. Two broad types of projects have been financed in Ghana's rural sector. Directly productive investments include cocoa, oil palm, rice, and livestock projects. At the other extreme are projects with only an indirect impact on production, such as those involving health, education, and training. Integrated rural development projects, such as the World Bank's Upper Region Project and US/AID's MIDAS Project, have sought to incorporate elements from both ends of the spectrum.

Few, if any, projects in the rural sector of Ghana have succeeded in attaining their targets. This is particularly true of the directly productive projects. The World Bank's Eastern Region Cocoa Project, for example, set as its goal the replanting of fifteen thousand hectares and the rehabilitation of an additional twenty thousand hectares. By the end of 1973–74, one year before foreign financing ended, only one-half of the acreage had been planted, while only 29 percent of the targeted twenty thousand hectares had been rehabilitated. The MIDAS Project, designed to increase agricultural production on small holdings through better input distribution, experienced similar results.

A common constraint on the design and implementation of projects was the lack of a clear overall rural development plan to guide donor participation (US/AID, 1973a, p. 1). In addition, rapid staff turnovers of upper- and middle-level Ghanaian management hindered constructive dialogue. These problems were relatively minor, however, compared with those created by the rapid rate of inflation and overvaluation of the cedi, which made it extremely difficult to maintain the real value of the producer price for cocoa given rising marketing costs and claims by the government on public revenue. Imported inputs were also underpriced in relation to the cost of nontradables such as labor, and local operating expenses of projects, when converted to dollars at official exchange rates, were prohibitive (North, 1982).[4] Price distortions encouraged people to take advantage of these differentials in order to supplement their meager incomes. Managerial inefficiency and corruption became entrenched.

Distorted prices and limited availability of inputs biased project techniques away from the directions originally intended. Ghanaian exchange rate policy, for example, favored capital-intensive, mechanized production techniques, since with the overvalued cedi imported equipment appeared to be less expensive than locally procured labor services. This bias was compounded by the government's decision to apply no duty on imports of mechanized equipment. Mechanical services were also highly subsidized by the government, with direct subsidies ranging from 70 percent to 90 percent of costs. These capital-intensive techniques, while financially attractive, were the least profitable economically (Winch, 1976, p. 92).

The Ghanaian government also heavily subsidized other agricultural inputs that frequently were obtained with foreign aid. The direct subsidy on fertilizer at the official exchange rate was 77 percent in 1974 and 56 percent in 1981, while the subsidy on sprayers and insecticides in 1975 was 80–90 percent. When overvaluation of the exchange rate is also taken into account, these subsidies were much higher. At these subsidized prices, insufficient inputs could be supplied to satisfy demand (Gilbert, 1972, p. 7; Christian, 1974, pp. 11–12).

The foreign exchange constraint was especially important in limiting the quantity of inputs that could be imported. Agricultural inputs did not receive priority in foreign exchange allocation. When funds were allocated, the licensing procedure was cumbersome, susceptible to corruption, and subject to long delays. Owing to the lack of fuel and spare parts, transport of inputs to project areas was delayed.

Relative scarcity induced by subsidized prices necessitated elaborate controls to ensure input use by target groups. But since, for example, sprayers in 1975 cost N¢30 in Ghana and the equivalent of N¢700 in the Ivory Coast, smuggling was widespread. Credit, too, was subsidized. Rural credit was made available through US/AID's MIDAS Project, for example, at 8–12 percent rate of interest. But with rapid inflation, the real rate of interest was highly negative. That the credit was used for its intended productive ends is very doubtful.

Finally, institutional weaknesses, often accentuated by macroeconomic mismanagement, hindered project success. Government agencies involved in agriculture were overstaffed, poorly trained and motivated, and under-equipped. Recurrent administrative expenditures were high. In 1982 the Cocoa Marketing Board, with a total staff of over one hundred thousand employees, spent an estimated N¢11,000 per ton of cocoa for marketing and administration, compared with the producer price of only N¢12,000 per ton.

Given these obstacles, it was extremely difficult to design and implement productive projects successfully. US/AID concentrated instead on training projects intended to improve the human resources base upon which future development would depend. Up to one-half of the training participants sub-sequently emigrated from Ghana, however, in search of more remunerative employment elsewhere. Furthermore, training and education projects had difficulty in covering recurrent costs, and US/AID ultimately had to pay about 90 percent of these costs.

After the Economic Recovery Programme was launched in 1983, conditions for successful project implementation improved considerably. By 1986, for example, the exchange rate was no longer a major problem. Nevertheless, there remained a serious shortage of trained and experienced managers, and the institutional structures necessary for successful development were not yet in place.

Ivory Coast. The economic performance of Ivory Coast agriculture was for many years one of the few successes of Sub-Saharan Africa. Not surprisingly, many rural development projects attained or surpassed their objectives. Most commercial crops grown in the forest zone, for example, reached or exceeded their production targets during the 1971–75 plan period. Nevertheless, large investments in ill-planned projects, financed chiefly by external borrowing, later led to difficulties in implementation.

One constraint in particular stands out. In its desire to develop the relatively poor northern savannah region, the Ivory Coast in the 1970s moved away from its comparative advantage in crops that were mostly produced in the higher rainfall areas of the south. The Ivorian government planned, for example, to construct twelve irrigated sugar complexes in the north capable of producing 600,000 metric tons of sugar. Since Ivorian demand was estimated at 100,000 metric tons, one-half million tons of sugar would have had to be exported. Yet total production costs were estimated at twenty three cents per pound, while 1980–85 world prices were projected at ten cents per pound. It was never clear, even at the later reduced capacity of 470,000 metric tons, where the surplus of sugar could be exported and how the difference between the world price and the domestic cost of production would be financed.

The objectives of the rice program were to achieve self-sufficiency, to transfer income to the north, and to diversify production. Both price and investment policy were used to achieve these objectives. Whereas program targets were attained—producing large quantities of rice—the costs were very high, involving irrigated and mechanized schemes with a large share of imported inputs (Humphreys, 1981, p. 102). To be privately profitable, these schemes required protection against lower-cost rice imports. This was accomplished primarily by raising the producer price and incurring public marketing losses. This was economically as well as financially unprofitable, since the rice program was an inefficient means of saving foreign exchange. Unsound projects could not be sustained over the longer run through public subsidies, and the rice development agency was disbanded.

The second major constraint on projects was the absorptive capacity of the Ivory Coast. Successful planning, design, and implementation of projects requires flexible and skilled administration. As the Ivorian economy grew in complexity, centralized programs operated or supported by the state became increasingly difficult to manage. A government reorganization occurred in the 1970s to allow for greater decentralization of decision making and to render ministries more responsive and effective in implementing policy, but skilled Ivorian managers, though growing in number, remained in short supply.

Donors were faced with similar constraints in realizing the objectives of their programs. As project selection became less obvious and the Ivorian government's objectives increased in complexity, the importance of planning become evident. Without effective planning of sector and intersector resource allocation, bad investment choices, such as the sugar complexes, diverted scarce human and financial resources into inefficient activities.

Finally, public enterprises played a crucial role in project design and implementation. The Ivory Coast used these enterprises in relatively high-risk agricultural programs and to further its efforts to promote Ivorianization. But over time these enterprises became overstaffed and bureaucratic. At the same time, many of them lacked the flexibility and autonomy to increase their operating efficiency. Thus donors participating in sectors where public development agencies were involved were increasingly confronted with high administrative costs and inefficiency.

PROJECT AID IN AN UNFAVORABLE POLICY ENVIRONMENT

As the previous discussion suggests, the impact that project aid is likely to have depends critically on the economic policy environment of the recipient country. Foreign assistance to the rural sector of a severely distorted economy such as Ghana's is generally ineffective as a means of achieving either donor or host country goals. In many instances it is simply a transfer of resources to the government and to that segment of the population benefiting from the officially sanctioned economy.

Donors have attempted to design projects that are impervious to the distortions and inefficiencies introduced by government policy. Local expenditures are minimized, since these are much more expensive at the overvalued exchange rate than purchases in foreign currency. The Volta River aluminum project, for example, imported capital and intermediate inputs directly from overseas, bypassing the government's system of procurement. These projects may work, but they replace projects with greater linkages to the local economy and beneficial distributive effects.

At the other extreme are the integrated development projects designed with the view that a single component is more likely to fail than a comprehensive package that maintains a critical momentum. Despite its size, however, the MIDAS Project could not overcome the constraints facing isolated projects with more limited objectives. Administrative and managerial capacity proved insufficient to coordinate elements of the project. Even though the project was exonerated, the import licensing mechanism delayed imports of goods and inputs. Lack of transport equipment slowed shipments upcountry. Costs increased owing to the fact that local currency prices were rising at an annual rate of over 100 percent.

Infrastructure projects, such as the construction or rebuilding of roads, have the advantage that their success does not depend on government incentives to producers. In many instances they can benefit the market economy outside the public sector. But they suffer from the same problems as other projects with respect to implementation, and they are particularly susceptible to cost overruns to the extent that they require large expenditures in local currency.

Most successful are the human resource projects (health, training, and education). The objective of these projects is to reach the people as directly as possible while minimizing dependence on government decisions. Although delays, cost overruns, and partial completions were encountered in Ghana, these projects were regarded by US/AID as a comparative success. Nevertheless, cost recovery was low, and many trainees left Ghana to work elsewhere. Some of them may return, however, now that economic conditions have improved. In addition, their remittances have for years been an important source of foreign exchange to the private sector, if not always to the Ghanaian government.

The Economic Policy Environment and Foreign Aid

The analysis thus far stresses the remarkable difference in the experience since independence of Ghana and the Ivory Coast. Despite a substantial inflow of foreign aid, Ghana for many years witnessed a steady deterioration in nearly all of its macroeconomic indicators, in large part associated with a severe shortage of foreign exchange. The Ivory Coast, on the other hand, until recently experienced high rates of growth, low rates of inflation, a strong currency with little or no overvaluation, and the ability to borrow on international capital markets as a substitute for concessionary aid.

At the project level Ghana had any number of problems, including poorly managed state farms, low prices to private producers, inefficient public trading agencies, and costly input subsidies. At the same time, inflation and the increasingly overvalued exchange rate raised the cost of project expenditures in local currency to prohibitive levels. While projects in the Ivory Coast also had problems, most of these were relatively isolated and were at no time as important as those in Ghana.

Over the past few years the situation in the two countries has changed rather markedly. The most fundamental changes have taken place in Ghana, where there have been substantial reforms in price and exchange rate policy. The need still remains to rebuild the infrastructure and institutions damaged by years of waste and neglect, but the current policy environment is the most propitious since independence for encouraging a resurgence of economic growth and development. Within the Ivory Coast, on the other hand, the magnitude of the structural disequilibrium has become increasingly clear, and though this does not begin to match that which characterized Ghana prior to 1982, it threatens to slow Ivorian growth in the future.

A major thesis of this chapter is that the experiences of Ghana and the Ivory Coast with respect to their ability to mobilize and make effective use of foreign aid is explained primarily by differences in their economic policy environments. The next section summarizes these environments and how they have influenced the effectiveness of foreign assistance. This is followed by a discussion of the role of foreign aid in improving the policy environment.

THE IMPACT OF THE ECONOMIC POLICY ENVIRONMENT
ON THE EFFECTIVENESS OF FOREIGN AID

The economic policy environment is the set of laws, decrees, regulations, and other legal or administrative devices that establishes the economic framework in which producers, processors, traders, and consumers, whether public or private, operate. This framework comprises taxes, subsidies, investment regulations, import quotas, exchange controls, regulated prices, and a host of other policy variables. All of these alter the profitability, from a private point of view, of economic activities. While some policies are linked with specific projects, most need to be understood at the sector or macroeconomic level.

Of major importance in this respect are the policies a country establishes that govern its economic relations with other nations. These influence domestic prices relative to those on world markets, create differences between private market and official exchange rates, determine the availability of imported goods and services, affect flows of labor and capital across international frontiers, and act in numerous other ways to relate one country's economy to that of the rest of the world.

Ghana. Ghana's economic policy environment for many years was characterized above all by shortages of foreign exchange and a system of import and exchange controls, which as a result of mounting inflation fed by government deficit spending led to an increasingly overvalued currency despite several devaluations and attempts at liberalization.[5] One result was artificially low official prices for tradable agricultural products, especially export crops such as cocoa. In addition, the government was heavily dependent upon cocoa exports as a source of tax revenue, further depressing the official price to producers. The combined effect of the overvalued exchange rate and the direct taxation of cocoa exports was producer prices that were below world market prices at the free trade, equilibrium exchange rate in every year but two over the period 1958–84. In many years the producer price was less than 50 percent of the equivalent world price, especially after 1975, as distortions in the incentive system were accentuated (Stryker, 1988).

Equally important was the effect of import and exchange controls on the prices and availability of consumer goods purchased by farmers in rural areas. The supply of these goods was severely restricted, with priority being given instead to imports of capital and intermediate goods and to basic foodstuffs consumed in the cities. As a result, there was a severe shortage of consumer goods in the countryside, and those that were available were sold at very high prices.

Beginning in the late 1960s the Ghanaian government tried to offset this disincentive by offering subsidies on credit and the purchase of agricultural inputs, such as seeds, fertilizers, insecticides, and machinery services. These subsidies were in addition to those created by the overvalued exchange rate at which the external prices of imported inputs were converted to domestic currency. The subsidies were a financial burden on public supplying agencies, encouraged inappropriate techniques and crops in which Ghana does not have a comparative advantage, and discouraged the distribution of agricultural inputs by private traders. Furthermore, severe shortages of the inputs, resulting from import restrictions and management problems, biased their distribution toward larger, more prosperous farmers and created uncertainty as to their availability.

Projects succeeded only where they were insulated from these problems by operating as enclaves with minimum linkages to the rest of the formal economy. Even where projects in the agricultural sector were able to procure inputs without difficulty, however, these were often diverted from the project area and smuggled outside of Ghana.

In the face of stagnant export earnings and rising agricultural imports, the government tried to promote the production of food and other import substitution crops through trade policy. Distribution of imported rice through established wholesale and retail traders, for example, was ostensibly made at officially regulated prices, but restrictions on imports and lack of enforcement of official prices resulted in large quantities' being sold at higher prices. The free market price of rice in Accra in 1972 was 77 percent higher than the c.i.f. price; by 1983 it was over 20 times higher (Stryker, 1988).

Although trade policy tended to protect domestic production of importable crops, exchange rate policy worked in the opposite direction, since overvaluation reduced the prices of these products relative to those of nontradables. The combined effect of trade and exchange rate policy was mixed, but on balance it tended to favor domestic production of rice, especially after 1970, as the economy became increasingly distorted. The incentives for local farmers to produce rice thus were strong as long as it could be sold to private traders.

The government was also concerned, however, about supplying urban areas with food at low prices. For this purpose, Nkrumah created the Food Marketing Corporation, which later became the Food Distribution Corporation (FDC). Ostensibly this agency was responsible for implementing guaranteed minimum prices designed to cover production costs, especially for rice and maize. In fact it was often obliged to sell at prices that were insufficient to cover its operating costs in order to keep retail prices to consumers at low levels. As a result, the FDC incurred heavy financial losses. In most years, moreover, market prices were higher than the minimum prices offered by the FDC, so that buying was difficult. Even when the minimum price was above the market price, buying operations were limited by lack of funds and storage space. Thus the influence of this agency on·domestic marketing of food was of little importance at best and detrimental at worst, since large producers and Agricultural Development Bank borrowers were at times required to sell at low official minimum prices.

At the same time that government policy in Ghana strongly discouraged cocoa exports but at times encouraged domestic food cultivation through restrictions on imports, it offered positive incentives to industry through import quotas and high tariffs. In addition, the Capital Investment Board provided tax holidays and exemptions from duties and other taxes on inputs.

A useful way of comparing the incentives offered in different agricultural and industrial activities is to examine effective rates of protection (ERPs). ERPs measure the incentives applicable to both outputs and inputs and indicate the extent to which policy permits domestic value added to diverge from its level in the absence of protection. Table 15.7 shows the ERPs for 1972, a year in which overvaluation of the cedi was not very great following its devaluation in late 1971.

The ERP values are essentially as expected. That of cocoa, Ghana's major export crop, is negative, showing the system's bias against this sector. The

Table 15.7. Effective Rates of Protection for Selected Agricultural and Industrial Activities in Ghana, 1972

Activity	ERP	Activity	ERP
Cocoa	−0.5	Wood and wood products	2.9
Maize	0.7	Fiber and paper products	1.3
Rice	0.7	Chemicals	0.7
Cotton	1.8	Nonmetallic mineral products	−2.4
Processed food	1.4	Basic metal products	0.6
Textiles and clothing	15.5	Fabricated metal products,	
Footwear	1.1	machinery, and equipment	7.4

Source: Scott R. Pearson, Gerald Nelson, and J. Dirck Stryker, "Incentives and Comparative Advantage in Ghanaian Industry and Agriculture" (N.p., 1979, Photocopy), pp. 38–40.

ERPs for maize, rice, and cotton are positive at fairly low levels, reflecting restrictions on agricultural imports, which led to high prices on the private market. Effective protection of industry was much greater, however, partly because there was less political resistance to restrictions on imports of manufactured goods compared with foodstuffs. The ERP for nonmetallic mineral products is negative, not because protection was negative, as was true for cocoa, but because it was so strongly positive that resources were misallocated to the extent that value added measured at world prices was negative.[6]

Although comprehensive data are not available, it is clear that the policy distortions shown in table 15.7 were accentuated after 1972. The producer price for cocoa divided by the rural consumer price index, for example, decreased by 66 percent from 1972 to 1983 (Stryker, 1988). Consumer goods in rural areas in many instances became unavailable at any price. With accelerating inflation, the cedi became increasingly overvalued, raising subsidies on inputs to the few who gained access to them and increasing local currency project costs. At the same time, restrictions on food and other imports increased their domestic prices on the free market, further biasing the structure of incentives against the export sector. By the beginning of the 1980s the result was a highly distorted economy in which incentives for black market operations, smuggling, and corruption were so great that any foreign aid project channeled through the formal public sector was unlikely to succeed.

Ivory Coast. In contrast to the economic policy environment of Ghana, the Ivory Coast's was one in which these kinds of distortions were minimal. First, the CFA franc was rigidly linked with the French franc and remained a convertible currency without exchange controls on current account. Second, until the late 1970s the use of quantitative import restrictions was unimportant, implying that the relation between domestic and world prices of tradable

Table 15.8. Effective Rates of Protection for Selected Agricultural and Industrial Activities in the Ivory Coast, 1972

Activity	ERP	Activity	ERP
Coffee	−0.4	Edible oils, soap	1.5
Cocoa	−0.4	Milk products	0.0
Palm products	−0.1	Tobacco	0.2
Copra	−0.1	Textiles and clothing	1.5
Pineapples	−0.3	Footwear	1.8
Bananas	−0.3	Lubricants	1.2
Cotton	−0.4	Chemical products	0.8
Rice	0.3	Rubber products	0.0
Maize	0.4	Cement	0.0
Grain milling	2.7	Transport equipment	0.2
Processed foods	0.1	Metal transformation, machinery	0.8
Beverages	−0.4	Paper products	−0.2

Sources: J. Dirck Stryker, Garry Pursell, and Terry Munson, "Incitations et coûts réels en Côte d'Ivoire" (N.p., 1975, Photocopy), table A; J. Dirck Stryker, "Western Africa Regional Project—Ivory Coast" chap. 2, "Economic Incentives and Costs in Agriculture" (Somerville, Mass.: Associates for International Resources and Development, 1977, Mimeo), tables 5, 7.

goods was determined primarily by tariffs, and of agricultural products, by the operations of the CSSPPA and the Caisse de Péréquation. Third, the bias toward industry was less than in Ghana. Coffee and cocoa were taxed, but the priority given by the government to agricultural development kept that sector from being squeezed too hard. Fourth, import tariffs were generally moderate, although effective rates of protection were higher than nominal rates because of low duties on intermediate inputs and because of benefits from the Ivory Coast's investment code. Finally, although input subsidies were hardly absent from Ivorian agricultural policy, they were much less important than in Ghana.

The lesser degree of distortions in the Ivory Coast economy compared with that of Ghana can be seen by looking at table 15.8. Although cash crops in the Ivory Coast were taxed and food grains were protected, these distortions were less severe than in Ghana. Furthermore, industry in the Ivory Coast received substantially less protection than in Ghana. The net impact of these distortions was that the exchange rate was overvalued by an estimated 15 percent in 1972. This degree of overvaluation did not increase significantly until the mid-1980s.

From time to time, nevertheless, particular policy distortions had an adverse impact on the effectiveness of foreign aid. One of the most notable of these, discussed earlier, was the sharp increase in 1974 of the official price offered to rice producers. This diverted large quantities of paddy from on-farm consumption and the private market to publicly operated mills that were required to sell to wholesalers at a price that did not cover their costs. The result was financial disaster for the public agency concerned.

More generally, during the last half of the 1970s there was a sharp decline in the productivity of public investment resulting from high-cost projects, not only the sugar complexes and the Kossou Dam, described earlier, but also several higher education projects and some excessive investment in highways. Much of this investment was financed by foreign borrowing on fairly hard terms. As a result, debt service obligations rose sharply just as coffee and cocoa earnings were declining. The resulting balance of payments crisis contributed to the growth of import licensing and quantitative restrictions, which in turn resulted in an overvalued exchange rate and an increase in the bias against exports.

THE ROLE OF FOREIGN AID IN POLICY REFORM

The role that foreign aid can play in promoting and enhancing policy reform has become increasingly recognized (chapter 6). To some extent this can be accomplished at the project level, but more often it requires structural adjustments that are sectoral, if not macroeconomic, in nature. The history of foreign aid in Ghana and the Ivory Coast offers illuminating examples.

Aid donors generally establish with host country governments certain understandings and preconditions considered necessary for the success of a particular project. These may involve institutional changes, better accounting practices, reduced input subsidies, higher producer prices, and any number of other reforms. Frequently compliance with these conditions has an influence not only on the project concerned but also on other projects in the same sector. This, plus political factors, may make agreement difficult and require extended discussions over a relatively long period of time, during which mutual confidence needs to be established.

As an example, the World Bank and the government of the Ivory Coast continued to discuss the issue of the producer price of rice for several years after the original project was first rejected. The government agreed in principle that a new policy was needed in order to eliminate the producer subsidies but argued that this would have to come about through inflation, since a reduction in the producer price was politically unacceptable. The Bank financed further studies but would not go ahead with a production project as long as its implementation was thought to worsen, rather than to improve, problems in the rice subsector. Nonetheless, the Bank's continuing involvement was thought to be useful if it could help to improve policies and institutions or to identify projects that would meet the needs of the subsector. A dialogue was thus maintained, though it became increasingly apparent that the agricultural policy problems were not limited simply to rice but extended across the sector. The rice issue was finally dealt with, therefore, as part of an overall approach to policy reform.

The US/AID-financed MIDAS Project in Ghana also offers some useful lessons. At the time the project was prepared in 1973–74 agricultural inputs and services were being supplied to farmers by the Ministry of Agriculture, with credit being handled primarily by the Agricultural Development Bank. These inputs and services were offered either free or at highly subsidized prices, but they were in very short supply because of foreign exchange shortages and because the ministry's capacity to manage a complex input distribution system was very limited. The MIDAS Project was designed to overcome these constraints by financing the foreign exchange costs of the project and by establishing autonomous agencies to handle distribution. The government agreed, in turn, to reduce or eliminate input subsidies.

Success with the MIDAS Project was highly uneven. The Ghana Fertilizer Company was established to import, blend, bag, and distribute fertilizers, but complications developed, partly because of deep vested interests, and the ministry continued to supply fertilizers at subsidized prices, primarily to influential larger farmers. On the other hand, the Ghana Seed Company was successfully established, and the seed subsidy was eliminated. The project was reduced in scope, however, from the national level to a single region, which decreased the impact it might have had on national policy.

These are two examples, but they suggest some important lessons. First, changes in economic policy are often very difficult because of vested interests and political pressures. The leverage offered by donor financing of projects is seldom great enough to overcome these obstacles. Second, policy changes do not come quickly and often involve a long period of dialogue and building of mutual trust. Finally, economic policy issues extend beyond the domain of a particular project and require a sectoral or macroeconomic perspective on foreign aid.

Ghana. The experience of both Ghana and the Ivory Coast suggests the importance of taking a comprehensive approach to policy reform and of designing foreign aid programs that can reinforce this approach. At the end of the Nkrumah period, for example, Ghana had serious macroeconomic difficulties because of mounting inflation, growing budget deficits, a deteriorating balance of payments, and rising debt service obligations. With assistance from the IMF, a stabilization program was undertaken by the NLC government, which used external aid and short-term debt relief to maintain Ghana's capacity to import at the same time that aggregate demand was reduced through credit and budgetary restraint. Although the exchange rate was devalued in 1967 from 0.714 to 1.02 N¢/$, relatively little attention was otherwise paid to removing the distortions resulting from overvaluation of the exchange rate, import and exchange controls, the tariff structure, the credit system, and the government's monopoly on the distribution of agricultural inputs (Gilbert, 1976, pp. 290–94). By 1969, when the Busia government took over, the economy was more stable and functioned more smoothly than three years earlier, but inflation had increased the distortions in relative prices, and long-term prospects for Ghana's economy were little improved.

In retrospect, it appears that the stabilization program of the post-Nkrumah era was too short-term in nature, partly because economists at that time were not fully aware of the serious effects that distortions could have on the allocation of resources and long-term development. In addition, the political situation may not have permitted more fundamental reforms without increased program aid to soften the blow to Ghana's urban population. Yet donors were unwilling to commit this level of aid, and the administrative machinery in Ghana was hard pressed to utilize the aid that was made available without a significant liberalization of procurement-tying provisions. Untied drawings on the IMF were made but were inadequate by themselves. World Bank loans were also available, but only for projects, which meant a slow process of identification and preparation. Finally, the contribution of debt rescheduling was limited because this was predominantly the responsibility of government export and investment credit guarantee agencies in the donor countries, and these were unsympathetic to broader foreign policy and development concerns (Gilbert, 1976, pp. 333–37).

By late 1971, however, this situation had changed. The Ghanaian government and the Consultative Group of donors, under the chairmanship of the IMF and the World Bank, had decided to shift away from the IMF-led stabilization program of 1966–69 and to combine broad-based economic reform and liberalization of the economy with large-scale balance of payments support and a generous rescheduling of the medium-term debt. The total package of external assistance required for commitment in 1972 was estimated at $150 million. The U.S. contribution was envisioned at $30 million in program loans, with direct U.S. involvement in policy questions being replaced by the establishment of the World Bank as the principal external economic policy advisory agent (US/AID, 1975, vol. 1, pp. 34–35).

The cedi was devalued in late 1971, but the rest of the reform program was cut short by the military coup in January 1972. The NRC, which came to power at that time, partially reversed the devaluation, repudiated much of the debt, imposed restrictions on private foreign investors, provided large subsidies for "essential" commodities, and otherwise undermined the reform. Donors and creditors, awaiting resolution of the debt issue, held up on their assistance plans.

There was another opportunity to deal comprehensively with policy reform in Ghana following the settlement of the debt situation in 1974. The donors appeared ready to commit over $100 million, and professional members of the World Bank staff were assisting Ghanaian economic policy and planning ministries. On the other hand, after the experience of the early 1970s, the government was more interested in concrete projects than in macroeconomic policy issues. Furthermore, the interests of the donors were shifting away from program loans toward projects that were particularly likely to aid the poor, especially in rural areas. These projects, however, took an especially long time to prepare in relation to the quantities of resources being transferred. Finally, there was a serious lack of coordination among donors, who frequently competed for projects rather than worried about structural reform. The opportunity for a change in economic policy was thus missed, and the situation in Ghana continued to deteriorate.

Another stabilization program was attempted in September 1978 with a 58 percent devaluation, an austerity budget, and a standby agreement with the IMF, but this program was abandoned following the coup d'état of June 1979. By this time, the correlation between devaluation and coup d'état was deeply embedded in Ghanaian minds, and attempts at austerity measures alone proved useless in the face of massive price distortions (Morrison and Wolgin, 1980).

Successful reform was instituted in Ghana only with the return to power of Jerry Rawlings in 1982. Yet movement toward reform was anything but clear during the first one and one-half years, as the new regime toyed with the possibility of going it alone. Throughout this period, however, discussions with the IMF and the World Bank continued, leaving the door open for the possibility of major structural adjustment. It was clear that substantial program and project lending would be forthcoming if agreement with these institutions was to be reached, but the specter of devaluation and its political consequences still held sway. Finally, political and economic pressures on the Rawlings government tightened to such an extent that it agreed to a program of reform. Once underway, these reforms were monumental in relation to past efforts, and within two or three years they had eliminated most of the serious distortions in the economy.

Ivory Coast. The use of foreign aid to support policy reform in the Ivory Coast was at first in sharp contrast to the experience in Ghana. The World Bank began project lending in the late 1960s and by 1981 had made forty-one loans and credits, mostly in agriculture and complementary infrastructure. Although the economic policy environment in the Ivory Coast was far superior to that in Ghana, a number of problems, discussed earlier, began to appear by the mid-1970s. Many of these were identified in the Bank's 1977 basic economic report and in its reviews of external borrowing and investment policies and programs between 1978 and 1980. The government responded well to the Bank's advice during this period, reducing the size of the public investment program and the external borrowing with which to finance it. In addition, the government began to seek the Bank's advice in devising a longer-term approach to the restructuring of the economy and to the institutional framework with which to manage the process. This was a natural consequence of the years of dialogue that had taken place at the project level related to various aspects of economic policy.

The result was a World Bank Structural Adjustment Loan (SAL) that responded to the government's programs for wide-scale reform, including improved economic management of agriculture and industry, as well as a revised role for public enterprises. This loan of $150 million complemented an IMF Extended Fund Facility (EFF) program and paved the way for further lending by private banks and bilateral donor agencies to cover the expected external payments gap over a period of several years. Prior to approval of the loan, the Ivorian government undertook a number of specific policy reforms, including eliminating cash subsidies on cocoa planting and lowering the producer price of rice. Under the terms of the EFF agreement, the government also agreed to limit its borrowings of less than twelve years' maturity. Further reforms included increasing budgetary discipline, centralizing public finances, strengthening the Ministry of Agriculture's capacity for sectoral planning and for project preparation and implementation, reforming the public enterprise sector, and improving the industrial incentives system.

Although the distortions in the Ivory Coast's policy environment were not nearly as great as those in Ghana prior to 1983, the reforms involved in restructuring the economy were also much less fundamental. Most important, the CFA franc remained rigidly linked with the French franc, and import policy continued to be quite restrictive. This maintained the bias of the incentive structure against exports.

Principal Conclusions

The major conclusion of this comparative analysis of the impact of development assistance in Ghana and the Ivory Coast is that foreign aid is unlikely to be effective in achieving either donor or host country goals in the absence of an economic policy environment that is conducive to long-term development. This is true regardless of whether aid is seen as a transfer of resources or as a means of implementing project packages involving a combination of capital, technology, and managerial know-how. When the policy environment is severely distorted, as it was in Ghana, it is difficult to find any type of foreign assistance that can be successfully implemented, except possibly some training and investment in human capital that may prove valuable in the future.

These two case studies also suggest that macroeconomic, trade, and exchange rate policies are especially critical in establishing an environment conducive to development. The distortions in Ghana associated with inflation and an overvalued cedi severely impeded the rational allocation of resources and prevented projects from achieving their objectives. The Ivory Coast economy, which was constrained more by domestic savings than by foreign exchange, performed much better over most of the period because domestic prices were not severely distorted in relation to those in the world market. Nevertheless, the magnitude of these distortions increased in the Ivory Coast toward the end of the 1970s. By the mid-1980s, in fact, there was greater flexibility in the Ghanaian than in the Ivorian economy because of the different exchange rate policies pursued by the two countries.

The historical experience in the two counties also demonstrates that the donors cannot be absolved of responsibility simply because the existing policy environment is inappropriate, since foreign aid can play an effective role in altering that environment. There were several occasions over the past two decades when that might have been the case in Ghana, but until 1983 the opportunity was always lost. At first there was excessive focus on short-term stabilization through control of demand without enough attention to eliminating the fundamental distortions that were restricting supply. Later, after the debt settlement, donors concentrated on designing projects to aid the poor, oblivious to the fact that the poor could never benefit if the entire economy was running downhill. Only by 1983 was there sufficient awareness of the need to link fundamental reform of the price and incentives structure with substantial amounts of program aid. This, coupled with the absence of viable alternatives for the Rawlings regime, plus the ongoing dialogue with the IMF and the World Bank, finally permitted the reform package to be put into place.

Even in the Ivory Coast, where both project and program aid were highly effective during the 1960s and early 1970s, it was project aid that was first seen as the means to improve the policy environment that threatened to stall growth in the latter half of the 1970s. It soon became apparent, however, that the problems were sectoral or macroeconomic in nature and that it was inappropriate to deal with them at the project level—even though experience with projects had helped to identify these problems and to build the mutual trust and confidence necessary to overcome them. Ultimately, it was medium-term program assistance from both the IMF and the World Bank that was most useful in supporting structural reform. Whether that reform will be sufficient in view of the distortions in the Ivory Coast economy that still persist is a question for the future.

Part Five

LESSONS

16

Some Lessons from Development Assistance

ANNE O. KRUEGER,
CONSTANTINE MICHALOPOULOS,
AND VERNON W. RUTTAN

In 1975 World Bank president Robert McNamara noted that there had been twenty-five years of development effort and decided to commission a study of how the experience contrasted with expectations of the 1950s. To almost everyone's surprise, when David Morawetz reviewed the record he found that success with economic development had been far greater than even the most optimistic forecasts in the 1950s (Morawetz, 1977). Although forecasters had been very wrong in their forecasts of which countries would succeed or fail, they had generally underestimated the rate of economic progress that was actually achieved by the developing countries as a group. A decade later a second study, commissioned by the Task Force on Concessional Flows, established by the governors of the World Bank and the International Monetary Fund, again addressed the question, does aid work? and concluded, most of it, yes! (Cassen, 1986, p. 13).

Despite this, there has been aid fatigue. Whether such fatigue is warranted is clearly questionable, especially in light of the fact that official development assistance has typically represented less than 2 percent of the GNP of the developing countries. Moreover, successful aid recipients (such as Korea) stopped receiving aid, while countries that experienced slower rates of growth became larger aid recipients. Indeed, the recent switch in emphasis from aid to South Asia to more aid to Africa once again underscores the point that aid is usually destined for countries and regions experiencing the greatest economic difficulties.

That much said, it remains true that much has been learned about the development process in the forty years of aid experience. In some instances it was experience with aid that led to the learning; in other cases experience with development taught lessons useful for aid. And both aid experience and development experience have interacted with the development of thought about aid and development in the academic community. Clearly, a great deal more remains to be learned. In this final chapter we attempt to assess the lessons from the evolution of thought about aid that appear to be the most

important, as well as to pinpoint those areas in which it seems likely that the
next major lessons will be learned.

Lessons from Macroeconomic Assistance Policy

The most important lesson learned about economic development, and
therefore about the role of assistance, is the significance of the overall macroeconomic environment for economic growth. Over the past thirty years appreciation of the importance of the appropriate trade and exchange rate policies, of fiscal and monetary policies, and of the overall incentive structure
provided by government policies has increased continuously. Even the experience of the 1980s has caused a further appreciation of the importance of
macroeconomic policy.

Experience indicates that the macroeconomic setting is an important determinant of the success of sectoral and project assistance. In countries where
the macroeconomic framework is appropriate, real rates of return to investment projects tend to be high; in countries where the framework is inappropriate, they tend to be low. When assistance is in the form of input subsidization, which implicitly offsets currency overvaluation, much of the impact
is simply to offset other policies. Although we focus here on macroeconomic
issues, it should be recalled that microeconomic issues are exceedingly important for the effectiveness of individual development projects and sectoral
assistance.

DOMESTIC ECONOMIC POLICY AND THE EFFECTIVENESS OF DONOR ASSISTANCE

The effectiveness of economic assistance has been strongly conditioned
by the economic policy environment of the host country. It is now generally
conceded that economic assistance to Korea and Taiwan was much less effective in generating income growth during the 1950s and early 1960s, when
these countries were pursuing import substitution policies, than after they
made the transition to outward-oriented industrial policies (chapter 13). The
contrasting role of domestic economic policy on the effective use of development assistance is illustrated in a particularly striking way in the case of
Ghana and the Ivory Coast (chapter 15). Following independence, Ghana introduced extensive government regulations and controls. The Ivory Coast
adopted a more modest role for the state, viewing its role as influencing and
guiding rather than replacing private sector decision making.

It would be a mistake to view the contrast between Ghana and the Ivory
Coast as simply too much or too little planning or too much or too little direct
public participation in economic affairs. The intervention of the Ivory Coast
in its sugar industry was almost as damaging as the intervention of Ghana in
its oil palm industry. The contrast is between (a) a misguided attempt to

determine and control the supply and demand of private goods across a wide spectrum of economic activity in Ghana and (*b*) a program that provided reasonable incentives for private economic activity along with investment in physical infrastructure and services directed toward enhancing the productivity of the private sector in the Ivory Coast. In addition, Ghana's successive delays in correcting overvalued exchange rates, its repression of the prices of agricultural commodities, and its establishment of parastatal enterprises in industry distorted its domestic infrastructure investments and led to excessively high capital output ratios in infrastructure, agricultural, and industrial development projects (chapter 15). It was only when significant reforms were introduced in the 1980s that Ghana's economic progress resumed.

Our reviews of country experience, and other analyses that we have cited, demonstrate in particular the close linkages between trade policies and the effectiveness of development assistance. There is firm evidence that an outward-oriented strategy and rapid growth of exports have been integrally associated with rapid economic growth. There are three reasons for the positive impact of an outward-oriented strategy. First, it permits countries to take advantage of comparative advantage, whether based on resource endowments or on technology development. Second, it prevents some of the costly mistakes often associated with heavy protection or related factor and product market distortions. Third, it forces governments to adopt policies that lead to better economic performance by the private sector (Krueger, 1984b, p. 264).

External development assistance has been very important at times in providing the economic and technical assistance needed to facilitate the transition to outward-oriented policies. Aid-financed infrastructure has also been important in permitting economies such as those of Korea, Brazil, Taiwan, and Turkey to respond to the incentives that were designed to encourage the transition to an export-oriented economy. Nonproject aid has been helpful in supporting developing countries' efforts to restructure their economies and pursue more liberal trade policies. Economists associated with both bilateral and multilateral development assistance agencies were also influential at times in the policy analysis and discussions that led to the policy reforms.

While foreign assistance has therefore been very positive in setting the stage for effective growth when policies are conducive to it, it has also provided some countries with the resources needed to perpetuate inefficient economic policies. This has been especially true when aid has been motivated by noneconomic policies. Certainly, for Korea in the 1950s, aid permitted the perpetuation of an inefficient set of economic policies. The relatively poor performance of the Korean economy was in large part a result of inappropriate trade, exchange rate, and other domestic policies. When these policies were altered in the 1960s, growth accelerated despite lower levels of assistance. American experts financed by the U.S. aid agency played an important role in the discussions that led to the monetary and fiscal reforms of the mid-1960s.

The conclusion that the effectiveness of assistance in generating economic growth is severely weakened in the absence of appropriate economic policy on the part of the recipient country poses severe policy problems for donors. A variety of assistance activities can be effective in an environment characterized by a favorable policy regime and substantial administrative capacity. The absence of these conditions severely limits the range of effective assistance activities, as illustrated by the Egyptian experience in the 1970s and 1980s. These deficiencies are often more pronounced, however, in the poorest countries where there may be strong equity arguments for providing development assistance even if it is less than fully effective. In such situations assistance can be more productive if focused on selected project development activities that will establish the foundations for growth if a time comes when it is politically and economically feasible for the recipient country to adopt more effective development policies.

POLICY DIALOGUE AND AID EFFECTIVENESS

In addition to the overall macroeconomic environment, two other factors influence the effectiveness of economic assistance: (*a*) the degree of convergence in the views of aid donor and recipient countries concerning the latter's economic policies; and (*b*) the importance of economic development objectives relative to other donor and recipient motivations in decisions concerning the nature and allocation of economic assistance. A convergence of views on the recipient's economic policy can occur only in the context of a donor-recipient aid dialogue.

How much impact policy dialogue associated with development assistance negotiations actually has on host country development policy is extremely difficult to determine. The impact may be quite large during a period when the host country is experiencing economic or political stress, as in Bangladesh immediately after independence, or during a period when both the donor and host governments share common political and economic objectives.

Policy dialogue between assistance agencies and the government of Turkey during the late 1960s appeared to be very influential in bringing about policy reforms that avoided an extreme crisis (chapter 14). In the 1970s French technical assistance personnel played an important role in guiding both macroeconomic and sector economic policy in the Ivory Coast along relatively efficient lines (chapter 15). At times inept or excessive donor pressure for reform has been counterproductive; India's 1966 devaluation (chapter 12) and Ghana's 1971 devaluation (chapter 15) are such examples.

With the events of the 1980s, emphasis on policy reform has come increasingly to be a focal point of concern for countries caught in heavy debt-servicing obligations and also for the development assistance community. It is far too early to assess the effectiveness of structural adjustment lending by the World Bank and of the International Monetary Fund's support of the heavily indebted countries. It is clear that some countries have been more receptive to the multilateral institutions' advice than have others. Even when recipients have been receptive, there have been difficult issues as to the extent and timing of needed reforms. Additional problems have arisen when a recipient country's progress has been much slower than was thought feasible when the reforms were initiated. It will be some years before the lessons associated with the approach of the 1980s can be definitively assessed.

A number of factors appear to influence the effectiveness of donor agencies' efforts to engage in constructive dialogue concerning a recipient country's macroeconomic policies. One is the recipient's commitment to policy reform; in the absence of such commitment it is exceedingly difficult to engage in meaningful dialogue. A second is the ability of both donor and recipient to bring substantial professional capacity and experience to the policy dialogue. A third is whether the donor agency is in a position to provide adequate nonproject aid during the period of transition to support the policy objectives agreed on by donors and recipient. Finally, no amount of policy dialogue or conditionality will be effective unless there is broad agreement within the recipient country on the reform objectives. When a large number of bilateral and multilateral donor agencies are involved in nonproject lending, policy coordination to achieve consistency among the several donor and recipient policy objectives often becomes exceedingly difficult (Cassen, 1986, p. 313).

When donor interests strongly influence the flow of aid resources, the effectiveness of policy dialogue is reduced. Donors find it extremely difficult to utilize policy dialogue to promote better policy in the recipient country when the representatives of that government are aware that the security or trade interests of constituencies in the donor country carry more weight than the policy reform objective.

The competing pressures between politically dictated support of particular countries and the desirability of policy reform to achieve development goals create a very difficult environment for development assistance. The public constituencies for assistance within donor countries often demand evidence that the assistance is effective in meeting aid objectives. At the same time, the more narrowly based constituencies concerned with security and trade objectives, both within and outside the donor governments, bring pressure on the assistance agency to direct resources to achieve the noneconomic objective favored by their particular interest groups.

Policy dialogue in the 1980s has been carried out in a somewhat more constructive environment than in the past. Both donor and host country political leaders and constituencies seem to be aware that policy dialogue and influence are inherent in the donor-recipient relationship and that the policy framework is a critical determinant of success in achieving development objectives. It is also possible that some bilateral donors have acquired a more sophisticated understanding of the limitations of leverage in pursuing ideological or political objectives in the recipient country. Nonetheless, noneconomic factors still are an important element of bilateral programs. As a consequence, there is a stronger presumption that multilateral aid, which is not as burdened with these constraints, is likely to be a more effective vehicle for a policy dialogue and for supporting economic development.

THE INFLUENCE OF ASSISTANCE ON NATIONAL ECONOMIC GROWTH

Measurement of the macroeconomic impact of development assistance represents a continuing theoretical and empirical puzzle. It seems clear that in relatively few instances has the flow of development assistance been large enough to significantly influence aggregate growth rates. This conclusion holds even if rates of return to the resources transferred in the form of development assistance are several multiples of the rates of return that the same investments would earn in the country providing the assistance. It is possible that the literature we have reviewed underestimates the impact of development assistance on growth; however, the evidence available supports a conclusion that development assistance has made a positive contribution to growth.

Generalizations regarding the effects of economic assistance on national economic growth are, however, complicated by the complex economic and political objectives of both the donor and the host country (chapters 4–6 and 12). Where donor country political objectives have dominated economic development objectives, as in the case of U.S. assistance to Korea in the early 1950s and recent U.S. assistance to Egypt, expectations regarding the impact of assistance on economic growth should be relatively modest. It seems apparent that this conflict in objectives is a major source of the difficulty in drawing generalizations regarding the impact of development assistance on growth rates.

A second reason why it has been so difficult to develop empirical evidence on the impact of development assistance on national growth is that except for short periods, the flow of official development assistance has generally been small compared with the sum of national and commercial resource flows available to sustain development. Aid flows have contributed importantly to initiating or sustaining the momentum of growth at critical periods, such as in India between 1957 and 1967 and Korea in the late 1950s and early 1960s. Turkey in the late 1970s and Chile in the early 1980s are more recent examples. But there have also been failures, such as Ghana in the 1960s and Tanzania in the 1970s.

A third reason why it is so difficult to estimate the impact of aid is that bilateral donors often provide support for those countries faring least well economically. Poor economic performance can and has caused political problems in poor countries, and official economic assistance has often been extended because of the political and strategic interests of the donor. There is, therefore, often an identification problem. If countries faring poorly are more likely to receive aid, any effort to assess the impact of aid must sort out performance as a cause of aid from performance as a result of aid. This is an extremely difficult task.

For those countries whose economic policies appear inimical to growth, there is evidence from specific country cases and from sector studies that development assistance has been most effective in generating growth when it has been focused on those investments that enhance productivity growth. Investment in agricultural research has been one such investment (chapters 9 and 13). Development of the professional capacity for investment planning and for economic policy is another (chapter 14). (The implications of development assistance for sector economic policy are discussed in greater detail in the following section.)

Thus, while it is not possible to document fully the positive contributions of aid to growth, it is also exceedingly difficult to find well-documented instances of aid having a negative impact on overall growth—though surely there have been many cases of specific inefficiencies and counterproductive interventions. Our analysis supports the conclusion of the Cassen Commission report (Cassen, 1986, pp. 294–326) that the focus of discussion on aid should be, not on its provision in principle, but on ways of improving its effectiveness.

Lessons from Assistance for Sector Development

We have already stated the overriding lesson for sector assistance: if overall macroeconomic policy is severely distorted, the effectiveness of sector and project aid will be greatly diminished. If, for example, exchange rate overvaluation greatly reduces the real return to agricultural producers, assistance to subsidize fertilizers and other inputs can at best offset part of the harm, but this will surely be a less desirable way of assisting agriculture than policies to restore producer prices to more realistic levels.

In this section, we draw some lessons from sector assistance experience. We draw from our reviews of major assistance program areas (chapters 8–11) and from the country studies (chapters 12–15).

PHYSICAL INFRASTRUCTURE DEVELOPMENT

During the 1950s and 1960s large-scale investment in transport facilities (roads, railroads, ports, and airports) and multipurpose resource development projects (power, flood control, irrigation) occupied a very prominent place in both bilateral and multilateral development assistance portfolios (chapter 8).

Many of these activities made substantive contributions to the development of the recipient countries; some, however, became a burden on the development process. We have presented examples of such projects in the case studies on India, Turkey, and Ghana (chapters 12, 14, and 15). A number of factors contributed to the low returns realized from such projects. Project cost overruns were often substantial; the time required to complete the projects was often much greater than projected in the planning studies; the technology and scale of such projects were often incompatible with the level of technological development in the rest of the economy; failure to consider the implications of exchange rate distortions led to investments that were excessively capital-intensive or entirely inappropriate; returns to infrastructure investment were delayed and reduced by inappropriate policy regimes.

Disappointment with the flow of benefits led to severe criticism of large infrastructure projects. In the Seyhan Project in Turkey, for example, the land and water development programs of the 1950s and 1960s did not exert a major impact on production until the 1970s (chapter 14). In Pakistan the Indus Basin Project placed such a large burden on both donor and recipient resources that many other public and private investments that could have generated higher returns were precluded (chapter 3). In Korea the payoff to transportation investments made during the 1950s was relatively low until the period of rapid growth in the late 1960s and 1970s (chapter 13). In India returns on large infrastructure and industrial projects were dampened by failure to invest in appropriate technical education (chapter 12).

Over the last several decades both technical and economic aspects of project planning and evaluation have become more sophisticated. Much has been learned, and the methodology and practice of benefit-cost estimation have been developed and applied more widely. Planning and implementation capacity in the aid-recipient countries has improved. The large errors of the 1950s and 1960s are being made much less frequently. And in many countries a broader, more balanced portfolio of projects embracing technical and professional training, research and development, and other complementary inputs has been able to overcome the constraints that have dampened the returns to infrastructure project investment in the past.

It now appears possible to take a positive view of lending for infrastructure investment, especially in connection with agricultural development. Furthermore, it appears that in a number of countries the enhanced capacity for infrastructure planning and development means that the assistance agencies can reduce the attention and resources devoted to the detail of project planning and implementation. This should free their staffs to give greater attention to the considerations of macro and sector policy that will influence the economic viability of infrastructure project investment.

DEVELOPMENT OF FINANCIAL INSTITUTIONS

We do not have a chapter devoted to the development of financial institutions. However, our chapter on development assistance to India (chapter 12) and the chapter on assistance to agricultural production (chapter 9) are useful in interpreting the results of assistance for the development of financial institutions.

In India, as in a number of other countries, both US/AID and the World Bank contributed to the establishment of several public and private development financial institutions. These institutions have become important sources of development finance. They have not, however, developed into effective institutions for mobilizing private domestic savings. Their resources continue to come primarily from external assistance or from government sources. The lending policies pursued by such institutions, particularly lending at below market rates of interest, have been a barrier to effective mobilization of private savings.

Efforts to assist in the development of agricultural credit institutions parallel the experience of industrial development credit institutions (chapter 9). Such institutions have been effective in making credit supplied by donor agencies and national governments available to farmers. They have made important contributions to the support of commodity production campaigns. Studies of the experience of such programs also indicate that their development as effective credit institutions has been limited by an almost universal tendency to make credit available at below market rates of interest. The effects of such policies have been widely documented (chapter 9): (*a*) subsidized credit is frequently diverted from production to consumption uses and from agricultural to nonagricultural investments; (*b*) when credit is available at below market rates of interest, it must be rationed, and when rationed, it tends to flow to the larger borrowers; (*c*) the wedge between market and institutional interest rates has made it difficult for rural credit institutions to become effective in mobilizing rural savings for development.

In view of the substantial body of evidence accumulated over several decades on the deficiencies of subsidized credit programs, one of the clear lessons of aid is the ineffectiveness of subsidized credit for assisting the poor or enhancing agricultural productivity. In light of this experience it is puzzling why subsidized credit programs continue to occupy a prominent role in the portfolios of many bilateral and multilateral donor agencies. Perhaps the most important lesson from assistance for the development of financial institutions is that the development community has refused to learn from experience.

RETURNS TO AGRICULTURAL RESEARCH

Agricultural research has consistently achieved rates of return among the highest available to either national governments or development assistance agencies (chapter 9). These high social rates of return reflect substantial underinvestment in agricultural research. Underinvestment by both the private and the public sector reflects the large spillovers that transfer the gains from the public and private suppliers of technology to producers, and from producers to consumers.

Sustained growth in agricultural production capacity requires a careful articulation of public and private sector support for technology research and development. The development of public sector institutions capable of training agricultural scientists and technicians is essential. Countries that have been successful in sustaining rapid technical change in agriculture have found it necessary to develop sufficient public sector capacity in agricultural research to enable them to develop and adapt agricultural technology suited to their own resources and institutional environments. India's relatively sophisticated agricultural research system has been an important factor enabling India to confound much of expert opinion and achieve self-sufficiency in food grain production in the late 1970s and early 1980s. Assistance by the U.S. aid agencies and by private foundations played an important role in strengthening India's capacity in agricultural education and research (chapter 12).

Those countries that have attempted to rely primarily on borrowed technology have rarely developed the capacity to adapt and manage it in a manner capable of sustaining agricultural development. The public sector generally has been most effective in the development of biological technology for crop and animal production. In contrast, the private sector has been relatively efficient in most countries in embodying new knowledge in technical inputs (machines, fertilizer, pesticides, seeds) and in marketing agricultural supplies in comparison with the public sector or parastatal organizations.

RURAL DEVELOPMENT PROGRAMS

The implementation of community and integrated rural development programs has been a continuing challenge and a source of frustration to development assistance agencies (chapter 10). The development of rural communities represented an important program thrust of both private and official development assistance in the 1950s. The integrated rural development thrust of the 1970s represented a renewed commitment to these same objectives. Yet the gap between the hopes for such programs and program accomplishments has remained large.

A review of the literature suggests that one of the major sources of disillusionment with the results of assistance to community development on the part of donors is a lack of consistency between the dynamics of community development processes and the imperatives of donor assistance. Successful rural development programs tend to be (a) small in geographic scope and slow to implement; (b) intensive in demands on professional and administrative capacity; (c) difficult to assess within the framework of conventional cost-benefit analysis; and (d) difficult to monitor and inspect. Donors, on the other hand, are under pressure to undertake large projects with measurable short-run accomplishments. They are more comfortable in dealing with projects that are (*a*) capital- and import-intensive; (*b*) amenable to cost-benefit or cost-effective project analysis; and (*c*) easy to monitor and evaluate.

A second source of disillusionment has been the difficulty of achieving consistency between the local self-help and resource mobilization philosophy of rural development programs and the objectives of donors to achieve measurable improvements in basic human needs indicators. This difficulty led to a program drift toward delivery of services to local communities and a neglect of the economic and political reforms necessary to achieve effective mobilization of community resources. It also tended to result in a decline in program performance when donor resources were phased out. Improvements in the level of services often have not been complemented by growth in the community resources necessary to sustain the services. There is now relatively good documentation, much of it from US/AID program evaluation studies, that success in local resource mobilization is an exceedingly important factor in accounting for continued program viability following the phasing out of donor support.

Although development assistance agencies have found it difficult to achieve success in programs designed to enhance the quality of life in rural areas, one cannot conclude that there is an inherent conflict between growth and equity objectives in rural development. Indeed, the literature suggests that these objectives are potentially highly complementary (Cassen, 1986, pp. 45–68). The constraint on the effectiveness of development programs has been due to the complex interaction between political and economic development at the local level that is required to generate effective demand and to sustain that demand.

FOOD AID

The issue of food aid is discussed in chapter 5 and in several of the country studies (chapters 12 and 13). During the 1970s and into the early 1980s, food aid declined both absolutely and as a share of development assistance. U.S. food aid declined from almost 90 percent of total food aid by members of the OECD/DAC in 1965 to little more than half in 1980. Yet because of the diverse motives that sustain its use (surplus disposal and humanitarian assistance) and its ambiguous impact on recipient countries, it has remained a source of controversy in the countries that both supply and receive food aid. While it provides a net transfer of resources, it may easily result in a disincentive to agricultural development unless recipients pursue appropriate policies.

Food aid has been widely criticized and defended (Isenman and Singer, 1977; Clay and Singer, 1985). During the 1950s large shipments of food aid enabled the Korean government to set rice prices below market levels. The effect was to severely depress incentives to Korean farmers (chapter 13). In India food aid played an important role in meeting food needs between the mid-1950s and the late 1960s. It provided resources equivalent to 10 percent of gross investments in the Indian economy and appears to have had few negative effects on food grain production (chapter 12).

There is very little disagreement that as an in-kind income transfer food aid tends to be less valuable to the recipient country than a financial transfer. How much less valuable depends on its fungibility; and this in turn depends on the institutional arrangements and policy framework within which it is handled in the recipient country. There is also general agreement that in the past the disincentive effects of food aid have been greater and the development assistance impact has been smaller than they might have been if food aid programs had been designed more carefully to achieve development objectives. The continued availability of food aid does raise the question whether policies and programs can be designed to use it more effectively for development assistance in the future.

ASSISTANCE TO HEALTH AND FAMILY PLANNING

There has also been growing recognition among development assistance agencies of the potential for high rates of return in other areas of human capital investment. In this volume we do not attempt to review the history or effectiveness of development assistance in the area of health services; however, we do review assistance to family planning (chapter 11).

Substantial assistance for family planning began only in the mid-1960s. While it is premature to draw many lessons from this experience, it does appear that assistance for family planning has had a major impact on the development of national capacity for population planning in a number of developing countries. Assistance in this sector has had a major impact on the development of family planning programs, particularly in a number of Asian countries. Since the late 1970s, assistance for family planning has also begun to have a significant impact on fertility rates.

A review of development assistance to Turkey also suggests that besides the well-known fact that integrating health with family planning programs helps the attainment of objectives in both areas, the integration of population and health with literacy programs resulted in increased effectiveness of all three programs (chapter 14).

Support for family planning programs has been controversial in both donor and recipient countries. This has caused external support by donors such as the United States and Sweden to waver and has resulted in the erosion of commitment in recipient countries such as the Philippines. The evidence seems clear that foreign assistance to population programs can have only *limited* success in the absence of strong political and administrative commitment in recipient countries. It has been effective in providing technical and material support where there has been a strong commitment on the part of the host government.

HUMAN RESOURCE DEVELOPMENT

Both development theorists and the development assistance agencies were slow to recognize the importance of investment in education and in other forms of human capital for economic growth (chapters 2 and 3). In the early literature the dominant view was that education and health programs should be considered primarily as enhancing consumption rather than as productive investments. It was generally held that such programs should be subordinated to the goal of expanding production until the country had achieved a substantial increase in the level of per capita income.

As evidence indicating high rates of return to education began to accumulate, perspectives began to change. The U.S. development assistance agency made major investments in university development in the 1960s. The World Bank made its first educational loan in 1963; by 1980 it had financed over two hundred educational development projects. Initial emphasis was placed primarily on scientific and technical education because of its obvious complementarity with infrastructure, industrial, and agricultural development projects. Continuing research has indicated, however, that the highest rates of return often are at the primary level and decline as the level of educational attainment increases. Evidence from a large number of studies suggests that returns at all levels of education are substantially higher than the rate of return levels that development assistance agencies use to justify investment in many other project areas (Psacharopoulos, 1984).

In light of the growing recognition of the importance of education, it is unfortunate that there has not been enough experience with the evaluation of assistance to education to warrant a full-scale review in this volume. A preliminary review of the literature indicated that studies of the economic return to education have given little attention to the role of aid. Studies of aid to education have given little attention to economic impact.

There are a number of important unanswered questions. Some relate to the relative importance and efficiency of formal primary and secondary education in developing countries. There is as yet little evidence that the development assistance agencies have been especially effective in attempts to improve the efficiency of primary and secondary education programs. This stands in sharp contrast to the contributions that both private and official assistance have made to the modernization and reform of higher education in a number of countries. One of the more important deficiencies, for example, is that we have not been able to document the impact on individual developing countries of the very large numbers of professionals and scientists who have been trained with aid support in the developing countries. Yet we are aware, when we visit the countries that have made substantial progress, that many leaders in the private sector, in higher education, and in government service have received support for their training through development assistance.

AID INSTRUMENTS

Most governments are open to a policy dialogue that can take place at different levels and through the use of various aid instruments. After vigorous debates about the merits of project and program aid, the evidence suggests that there is an appropriate role for each (Singer, 1965; Mason and Asher, 1973, pp. 229–94). A careful reading of the literature leads to the conclusion that an effective assistance program will include in its portfolio both program and project assistance.

At one extreme, nonproject aid can play an important role in legitimizing a donor-recipient dialogue concerning the elements of the macroeconomic reform package. A level of professional capacity on the part of both the donor agency and the recipient government that commands the respect of both sets of participants in the policy dialogue is an essential element. There have been situations in which donors have forced inappropriate or inadequate policy reforms on reluctant recipients, not because of the weight of the donor policy analysis, but because of the need for assistance on the part of the recipient. And there have also been situations in which the recipient countries have accepted, in principle, highly appropriate donor policy recommendations but have failed to articulate the rationale for the policies within their own political and bureaucratic environment, with consequent program failure.

At the other extreme, project assistance is most appropriate when directed toward fairly specific physical, human, and infrastructure development projects. Transportation, communication, and sanitary and irrigation facilities are prerequisites for both rural and urban development. Primary education and health facilities and agricultural research and technology transfer capacity are essential. The capacity to construct and maintain the physical infrastructure and to staff and manage the institutional infrastructure is basic to the development process. These capacities are acquired slowly, over a generation or more rather than during a single plan period. Project assistance can contribute to the development of the basic physical and institutional infrastructure even in environments in which governments have limited political or economic capacity to implement appropriate macroeconomics in sector policies. But donor assistance can also be overdone. There are situations in which donor project assistance has exceeded recipient capacity for project management. In a number of countries it appears that project assistance has contributed to the fragmentation and even the disintegration of the capacity for local governance.

The difficulty of providing effective sustained support for institutional development within the traditional development assistance project mechanism can be illustrated in the case of agricultural research. In a number of countries assistance for the development of national agricultural research systems has contributed to the rapid development of professional capacity and facilities. But too often the period of rapid development has been followed by the erosion or collapse of the research system's capacity when external project support has declined (chapter 9). Similar examples could be drawn from other areas.

There is now a substantial body of literature suggesting that the project approach has, under a variety of circumstances, contributed to a cycle characterized by the development and subsequent erosion of institutional capacity. The reason is that external project assistance often provides an alternative to the development of internal political support. National program directors have frequently found that the generation of external support requires less intensive entrepreneurial effort than does the cultivation of domestic political support. Development assistance agencies have given too little attention to how to provide development assistance in a manner that will strengthen rather than weaken the domestic political support for programs that donors place high priority on in their assistance efforts.

Many assistance activities incorporate features of both program and project assistance. The World Bank, in particular, is now undertaking a significant number of such "hybrid" activities. The key issue is not which type of assistance in principle is superior but rather which combinations of assistance forms can best promote development objectives in specific country settings. As a result, specific rules limiting or setting target allocations of different types of assistance in bilateral or multilateral institutions are distinctly inappropriate. The same is true for overall targets on local cost financing or general rules on financing solely foreign exchange components of projects.

ASSISTANCE IN AN UNSTABLE ENVIRONMENT

One of the most difficult problems of development assistance policy is how to provide effective assistance in an unfavorable political environment. Should the development assistance community simply conclude that where the environment for development assistance is so adverse, assistance should be discontinued until a political and administrative environment emerges that is more conducive for efficient use of development assistance?

There are at least some tentative indications from the experience of the countries studied in this review and in other literature (Brokensha, Warren, and Werner, 1980) that there are a number of areas where it is possible for development assistance to be at least moderately "policy proof"—where assistance can be designed to make an effective contribution in spite of (a) the limited effectiveness or even perversity of the policies pursued by national governments and (b) the absence of a realistic chance that government will improve the policy setting in the foreseeable future. These activities fall under the broad headings of investment in human capital and community infrastructure.

One finding that comes across strongly is the high rates of return to investments in human capital, particularly education and health, under a wide range of circumstances. It is quite clear that education represents a high-priority investment. There are few development success stories, either in agricultural or industrial development, in societies in which a large share of the population is neither numerate nor literate. There is also evidence, though perhaps less strong, that the loss of productivity caused by poor health can be very large even in poor societies. Among the major costs of poor health are the high birth rates needed to offset high death rates under conditions of high infant mortality and the high dependency rates associated with chronic illness.

A second area of investment that is essential for both rural and urban development is the development of communal institutional and physical infrastructure. A network of farm-to-market roads is essential if even the least developed area is to move very far beyond local self-sufficiency in commodity production. An adequate water supply and adequate waste disposal are essential to the achievement of even minimal improvements in health. The development of institutions of local government that enable communities to mobilize their own resources for development and that can induce efficient delivery of bureaucratic services is essential.

Programs to achieve the minimum levels of investment in human capital and in community infrastructure do not need to draw heavily on external resources. Institutional innovations that provide incentives for local units of government to mobilize indigenous labor and material resources should be encouraged. Most of the resources needed to support institutional development or reform can be mobilized at the local or regional level. Such programs are usually regarded as desirable even by national governments that do not have the bureaucratic capacity, or that are too corrupt, to effectively implement larger-scale agricultural or industrial development projects. In many cases such programs may be more effectively carried out through either expatriate or indigenous private voluntary organizations rather than through direct administration by bilateral or multilateral assistance agencies.

In addition to the immediate benefits, there are substantial longer-term benefits from strengthening the capacity of provincial and local institutions to manage and sustain investments in human capital and community infrastructures. Development of local institutional capacity can also contribute to the development of political, bureaucratic, and technical skills necessary for more efficient and responsive national political regimes. When a more effective national regime does emerge, the local institutional infrastructure needed to sustain rapid development is in place—as in Korea after the fall of the Rhee government. Finally, considerable experimentation is often necessary to create viable institutions capable of sustaining the necessary investment in human capital and community infrastructure. A period of trial and error is often necessary to develop systems that are sustainable in terms of community economic resources and compatible with local cultural endowments.

ECONOMIC ASSISTANCE AND POLITICAL DEVELOPMENT

The view that development assistance is a useful complement to other elements of donor political strategy—that its primary rationale is to strengthen the political commitment of the aid recipient to the donor country or to the West—has been a consistent and at times dominant theme in the motivation for development assistance (Ruttan, 1989). The strengthening of the capacity of Western Europe to resist external aggression and the enhancement of the political appeal of centrist political forces were major motivations for the Marshall Plan. Strategic concerns were a prominent feature of the Kennedy administration's Alliance for Progress in the early 1960s. The Carlucci report (Carlucci Commission, 1983), commissioned by the Reagan administration, insisted that the foreign security and economic cooperation programs of the United States are mutually supportive and interrelated and together constitute an integral part of the foreign policy of the United States. The commission urged that efforts be made to enhance the complementarity between the achievement of political or strategic objectives and the economic development in the recipient country. A common assumption in the earlier literature was that Western-style democratization and bureaucratization would be in the interest of both the donor and the recipient. But the study of political development has provided few guidelines for policymakers or practitioners who would guide political development along mutually advantageous lines.

There is an interesting dichotomy in the research literature about the use of foreign assistance in the pursuit of domestic economic and strategic interests. There have been many attempts—and this book is an example—to evaluate the economic and social impacts of economic assistance in developing countries. The security rationale has not, however, been subject to nearly as rigorous theoretical or empirical analysis. The single background paper on the effectiveness of military assistance prepared for the Carlucci Commission asserted a positive linkage between U.S. security assistance expenditures and security interests while admitting that the evidence to support the assertion is "elusive." This is not to suggest that empirical support cannot be provided to support the political and strategic self-interest arguments. It is simply to argue that in spite of assertions to the effect that the results of security assistance have been at least as successful as efforts to promote economic development (Huntington, 1970/71, p. 170), little convincing evidence has appeared in the professional literature on development assistance.

Changes in Assistance Policy

The lessons we have been able to draw from the past are likely to be of considerable relevance for the future. In the early 1980s two trends emerged in donor assistance, with potentially conflicting impacts on aid effectiveness. The first is that in the case of the United States an increasing share of assistance has been provided through instruments such as US/AID's Economic Support Fund, which by their very nature tend to emphasize strategic and foreign policy objectives rather than economic development. The second is the rise in the role of policy-based assistance in the form of sector and structural adjustment lending in both the multilateral and bilateral aid programs. This aid is designed to induce and support reforms in sector policy— agricultural price policy, for example—and in macroeconomic policy.

The increasing share of U.S. bilateral assistance provided with explicit strategic and foreign policy objectives undermines broader U.S. efforts to raise the effectiveness of all aid provided by the international community in support of development. The U.S. government has been at the forefront of such efforts at the international level (such as, for example, the Development Committee's Task Force on Concessional Assistance). Part of this U.S. concern has been motivated by a genuine interest to raise aid effectiveness; part of it has been a tactical response to deflect international criticism that the volume of U.S. aid relative to its GNP has been quite low by comparison with other donors. Whatever the motivation, the capacity of the United States in providing leadership in international efforts to raise aid effectiveness is undermined by current trends in U.S. aid that emphasize the use of aid instruments stressing U.S. strategic objectives.

Aid support for macroeconomic policy reform is not new. During the 1960s US/AID participated in dialogue about macroeconomic policy with recipient governments such as Brazil, India, and Turkey and experimented with allocating performance conditions to assistance agreements. During the 1970s, however, US/AID narrowed its focus and concentrated more of its resources on sector development in areas such as agriculture, health, and education (Nelson, 1986). From the outset the World Bank funded projects almost exclusively. The effect of the global recession of the early eighties and the debt crisis that has faced a large number of developing countries has been to propel the Bank to rapidly increase the share of its lending in the form of sector and structural adjustment loans. US/AID has also expanded its sector and structural adjustment lending under the Economic Support Funds, but the effectiveness of such lending in promoting policy reform has been undermined in countries where U.S. strategic interests dominate the aid programs.

This change interjects an entirely new set of criteria into the evaluation of assistance programs. Joan Nelson has emphasized that "the core task of policy-based lending in support of adjustment is to create and sustain commitment (to reform) rather than to press for specific measures at a particular moment" (Nelson, 1986, p. 72). This involves efforts to bring about sustained institutional change in recipient countries rather than change in physical facilities, technology, or even human capital. This is a challenging task. Neither the recipient countries nor the donors have as much experience in moving from the existing policy distortions to a sound macroeconomic regime characterized by an appropriate real exchange rate, appropriate incentive structures, adequate rates of domestic savings and investment, and responsible fiscal and monetary policies as they have in designing specific projects. The political and economic costs associated with such a transition also are often substantial and could bear unequally on different economic sectors and social classes.

There is little doubt that a policy reform effort is needed. There is simply no alternative. Without such an effort, supported by international aid resources, the developing countries' economic prospects will be very gloomy indeed. The recognition of the importance of policy reform in improving aid effectiveness is the necessary first step. What needs to follow is a concerted effort by donors and recipients to design effective reform programs that also take into account the social and economic costs of transition. Experience suggests that this will not be easy; it will require a willingness to experiment, as well as patience in getting results. The latter may be difficult for donors, especially those that suffer from significant aid fatigue. But the difficulties that the donors face in bringing about needed reforms and structural change in their own economies should serve as a useful reminder not to be excessively critical of developing countries that are attempting similar reforms within a weaker institutional structure and a more fragile political environment.

Notes

1. Introduction

1. Assistance for economic development was provided by the United States to a number of developing countries as part of the postwar reconstruction effort. From the end of World War II until 1950, economic assistance was provided to Japan and Korea under the Army program for Government and Relief in Occupied Areas (GARIOA) and to the Philippines under the Philippine Rehabilitation Act and the Philippine Military Assistance Act, both 1946. Economic and military assistance for Greece and Turkey was initiated according to the Truman Doctrine, which stressed the containment of Soviet expansionism, and the Greek-Turkish Aid Act of 1947. Aid to China was included in the Foreign Aid Act of 1947, which authorized the Marshall Plan, and the China Aid Act of 1948. When the Chinese Nationalist government fell in 1949, the funds initially intended for China were redirected to South and Southeast Asia (Wolf, 1960, pp. 11–72). We identify Truman's 1949 inaugural address and the 1950 Act for International Development as the beginning of the official long-term commitment to economic assistance to poor countries because the earlier commitments were short-term responses to particular concerns. For a useful survey of the political aspects of U.S. foreign assistance policy see Pastor, 1980, pp. 251–84. For examples of early post–World War II assistance to French and British colonies see chapter 15.

2. The international donor consortia authorized earlier studies by the Commission on International Development (hereafter Pearson Commission, 1969) and the Independent Commission on International Development Issues (hereafter Brandt Commission, 1983). National assistance agencies responded similarly to challenges in assistance policy. In the early 1980s the Reagan administration also commissioned several internal and external studies (Commission on Security and Economic Assistance [hereafter Carlucci Commission], 1983; Krueger and Ruttan, 1983; Mikesell, Kilmarx, and Kramish, 1983).

2. Development Thought and Development Assistance

The authors are indebted to T. N. Srinivasan and Ramon Marimon for comments and suggestions on an earlier draft of this chapter.

1. One notable exception was Turkey, where economic development became a major objective of government policy in the 1930s. During the interwar period, the

Soviet Union was the most dramatic example of a nation attempting to mobilize its economic and political resources to generate economic growth. Other developing countries, in Latin America and Thailand, for example, were not colonies, but the conscious pursuit of development there was not a primary objective of government until after World War II.

2. Two very useful sources of development thought in the 1940s and 1950s are Williamson and Buttrick, 1954; and Agarwala and Singh, 1958. The origins of academic interest in foreign economic development have been reviewed by Simpson (1976) and Arndt (1981 and 1987).

3. For a review of development planning theory and practice as viewed from the early 1960s see Waterston, 1965. His book was commissioned by the World Bank to evaluate the methodology and experience of plan formation and implementation at a time when the "planning ideology" still dominated much of development practice. However, Waterston warned that "even a casual examination of the results achieved from development planning in most less developed countries indicates that they are falling short of what is reasonable to expect. The record is so poor—it has been worsening in fact—that it has sometimes led to disillusionment with planning and the abandonment of plans" (p. 4).

4. For a fuller account of Indian planning experience see chapter 12. See also Bhagwati and Desai, 1970; and Bhagwati and Srinivasan, 1975.

5. The MIT perspective was first articulated by Millikan and Rostow in a paper prepared for a small foreign policy conference of thinkers associated with the Eisenhower administration in 1954. That draft was subsequently enlarged and published in 1957 (Millikan and Rostow, 1957).

6. For the published results see the monographs by Maddox (1956), Schultz (1956b), Glick (1957), Maddox and Tolley (1957), Mosher (1957), Rottenberg (1957), and Samper (1957).

7. The generalized human capital approach reflects, in part, a dissatisfaction with the treatment of technical change in the growth-accounting approach of the mid-1950s. Schmookler (1952), Ruttan (1956), Solow (1957), and Denison (1962) had demonstrated that a very large part of output growth in the developed market economies could be accounted for, not by the growth of labor and capital inputs, but by productivity growth, growth in output per unit of total input, termed "total factor productivity."

8. For an earlier attempt to incorporate human capital investment into growth theory see Uzawa, 1965. Uzawa's was a two-sector model in which one sector produced capital goods, including human capital, and a second sector produced consumption goods. He assumed a linear technology in the education sector and constant returns to scale in the consumer goods sector. The model has no tendency for growth rates to converge. The Lucas model, in contrast, incorporates a positive externality in the education sector and increasing returns to education in the production of consumer goods. We are indebted to Stephen L. Parente for the comparison of Uzawa and Lucas.

9. Numerous studies were conducted during this period of the ethnic and religious origins and psychological and educational characteristics of entrepreneurs. Schumpeter placed entrepreneurship, along with technical change, at the center of the development process. Influenced largely by the literature from psychology, sociology, and anthropology, many development economists during the 1950s viewed lack of entrepreneurship as a major constraint on the development process (Brozen, 1954).

The most ambitious attempt to incorporate the factors contributing to the development of entrepreneurship in development theory was by Hagen (1962). He did not, however, contribute much more than a checklist of social and psychological attributes characterizing entrepreneurs in different societies at different times. Subsequently, he implied that little can be said beyond the fact that a disproportional number of entrepreneurs emerged from cultural minorities that were excluded from elite roles in traditional societies (Hagen, 1980, pp. 215–31).

10. Yujiro Hayami and Vernon W. Ruttan identified three levels of technology transfer: (*a*) *material transfer*, the simple transfer of new materials such as seeds, machines, and techniques; (*b*) *design transfer*, the transfer of designs, blueprints, and formulae; and (*c*) *capacity transfer*, the transfer of scientific and technical knowledge and personnel and the development of domestic research and development capacity. A country finds it difficult to capture more than a small share of the gains from technical change until it has achieved substantial capacity to adapt, redesign, and design technology suited to its own factor endowments and socioeconomic environment (Hayami and Ruttan, 1985, pp. 260–62).

11. See Stiglitz, 1986, for an excellent survey of the current state of the economics of information literature as it applies to development.

12. This view is a direct extension of the welfare economics approach to the reform of public policy in the 1940s and 1950s. It is illustrated by Abba P. Lerner in his classic, *The Economics of Control* (1944, p. 6), and reinforced by Samuelson (1948).

13. For a fuller discussion of the changing perception of the role of government see Lal, 1983, and Srinivasan, 1985.

14. Within welfare economics itself an "institutional design" perspective began to emerge in the work of economists such as Hurwicz (1972) and Reiter (1977). Initial contributions to the new political economy literature included work by Downs (1957), Buchanan and Tullock (1962), Olson (1965), and Niskanen (1971).

15. In the 1960s US/AID funded several major research projects designed to provide insight into the process of institution building and political development (e.g., land tenure, agricultural credit markets, international trade regimes, and rural development). The two major institution building research projects were centered at (*a*) the Universities of Pittsburgh and Indiana and (*b*) Purdue University, North Carolina State University, and the University of Missouri. For an early conceptual paper see Esman, 1962; and the papers in Thomas et al., 1972. A major weakness of the institution building approach is that it focuses on bringing about institutional innovations with the guidance of technicians and planners. According to Esman, it is "an elitist theory with an implicit social engineering bias" (1962, p. 27). The literature on political development gave greater attention to endogenous development in politics and administration; by the late 1960s, however, much of the intellectual excitement and scholarly commitment of the field had evaporated. Much of the political development literature of the 1960s is brought together in Braibanti, 1969.

3. Toward a Theory of Development Assistance

The authors have benefited from comments by Henry Bruton, Hollis Chenery, Nathaniel H. Leff, Ramon Marimon, Constantine Michalopoulos, and Jo Ann Paulson on an earlier draft of material in this chapter. Keith Jay provided the information on aid flows.

1. This chapter draws very heavily on an earlier paper by Anne O. Krueger (1986). We have also benefited from Riddell, 1987, pp. 85–101.

2. Private donors, usually motivated by humanitarian concerns, contribute to private voluntary organizations, which in turn undertake humanitarian or development assistance programs. Some nongovernment organizations (NGOs) also receive cash, services, and commodities from official sources. In the early 1980s NGOs were providing about $2.3 billion a year in aid, compared with about $32 billion of official concessional flows. For more detail see Bolling and Smith, 1982; and Gorman, 1984.

3. See the series of articles by Chenery and Bruno (1962); Adelman and Chenery (1966); Chenery and MacEwan (1966); and Chenery and Strout (1966); and clarifications of the model by Chenery and Strout (1968); Fei and Ranis (1968); Bruton (1969); and Chenery (1969). The key papers by Chenery and his collaborators and subsequent reflections on the two-gap approach have been reprinted in Chenery, 1979. See also the review by Mikesell, Kilmarx, and Kramish (1983).

4. Much of the professional criticism of the two-gap approach in the 1960s was based on either the presumption or evidence that the world—even the developing world—could be more adequately understood through a neoclassical perspective than through a structural disequilibrium perspective (Fei and Ranis, 1968; Bruton, 1969). In his critique of the two-gap approach, Bruton insisted that the emergence of either a savings or a trade gap could be voided with policies that included appropriate pricing of home goods and imports, encouragement of investment in human capital, and capacity for technology development. He did not question, however, the propriety of either financial or technical assistance during the initial phases of development.

5. A substantial body of literature documents the incomplete integration among national financial markets. Recent debate on this issue was stimulated by Feldstein and Horioka (1980). However, debate continues over the relative importance of lack of integration in financial and goods markets. For a recent review see Frankel, Dooley, and Mathieson, 1986.

6. Evidence that rates of return to capital are, in fact, higher in the less developed than in the developed countries has been the subject of substantial disagreement. Lower than anticipated returns have been attributed to inadequate investment in physical and institutional infrastructure and/in human capital. For a review see Leff, 1975.

7. A World Bank staff report noted that the Bank engages in two types of project-related technical assistance. "Engineering TA . . . receives more financial support and is the more successful of the two types" (Lethem and Cooper, 1983, p. 15). This view is not shared by all observers (Annis, 1986).

4. Recipient Policies, National Development, and Aid Effectiveness

1. For a summary of estimates of protection in developing countries see World Bank, 1987, box 5.3, and sources cited therein.

2. Even in such instances a certain amount of assistance motivated by humanitarian considerations and extended usually through private voluntary organizations (PVOs) has frequently continued (e.g., the economic assistance provided by the United States to Ethiopia during the 1983 famine).

3. In other cases, for example, in Kenya and Malawi, the fundamental problems were related to land policy. Donors that devoted significant resources to agricultural development found that without reform in this politically sensitive area, the payoff in terms of increased agricultural production was generally quite meager (Lele and Meyers, 1987).

4. It should also be noted that use of economic assistance for this objective would usually require that it be in the form of program rather than project aid (see chapter 6).

5. Donor Policies, Donor Interests, and Aid Effectiveness

1. The value of food aid to developing countries was challenged in an early article by Theodore W. Schultz (1960). Schultz's critique generated a large body of academic literature but had only a marginal impact on development assistance policy. For a somewhat more favorable review of the literature on food assistance and in-depth analysis of this issue see Isenman and Singer, 1977. One point made in the article is that where food aid represents for the donor a method of surplus disposal, this assistance may to a significant extent be additional to the donor's other aid budget resources. For a discussion of the administrative problems in using food aid as a tool of development see Garzon, 1984. Some of the same type of distortions can result from non-food commodity aid. Hendra (1987) cites an example of Canada supplying to Bangladesh potash instead of desperately needed untied fertilizer grants (p. 267).

2. For example, in describing the U.S. Trade and Development Program (a component of the U.S. assistance program), the Chairman of the Development Coordination Committee states in his 1984 annual report (International Development Cooperation Agency, 1984, p. 207) that the "TDP provides grants to developing countries for project planning services conducted by American firms for major development projects which represent significant markets for the exportation of U.S. goods and services. When feasibility studies are carried out by U.S. entities, U.S. contractors are more likely to be selected to undertake the downstream projects."

3. A 1975 policy statement by the German cabinet also indicated that "the Federal Government will endeavor to harmonize the German interest in ensuring supply of raw materials for the German economy with the interest of the developing countries in increasing their exports and expanding their raw material processing industry" (Arnold, 1982, p. 24).

4. "Associated financing" is the term used by the DAC for the combination in law or in fact of concessional flows with nonconcessional flows in a single trade transaction where either or both are effectively tied to procurement in the donor country. The majority of these are credits that associate ODA flows with export credits, that is, mixed credits (OECD, *Development Cooperation*, 1984).

5. In the early 1980s mixed credits involved only 1 percent of overall developed country trade with the developing world and 3 percent of total export credits to the developing countries. Their small amount relative to total trade does not, however, mean that their impact is necessarily negligible: in specific country circumstances and in specific sectors, mixed credits can significantly affect trade flows.

6. This is most likely to occur in recipient countries where there are significant domestic policy and price distortions and where there is a lack of an internal mecha-

nism to adequately monitor the use of external resources and assure that they are utilized in support of the country's investment priorities. These conditions are most likely to be present in the lower-income countries, many of which do not yet have a central control mechanism over the use of aid flows, with line agencies often negotiating directly with donors.

7. The additional costs involved can be considerable. The U.S. shipowners are known to have charged freight rates up to three times the open-market rates quoted by other companies for aid-financed shipments. The excess freight on PL 480 shipments, however, is covered by the United States, rather than by the recipients, in the budget (Bhagwati, 1970b).

8. By comparison, the report estimates that the U.S. share of exports procured through untied U.S. aid would have been 25–27 percent, assuming the same geographical distribution of aid (Cooper, 1972, p. v).

9. The practice has also been pursued by multilateral donors, even though they do not share the motivation of bilateral donors to promote exports.

10. In these guidelines donors agreed (1) not to provide an associated financing package with a grant element of less than 20 percent; (2) to confine their use to priority projects and programs that are carefully appraised against development standards and criteria; and (3) to tailor the terms of associated financing to the economic situation, stage of development, and debt-servicing capacity of the recipient country. The objective of setting a minimum permissible grant element was to eliminate low-cost (in terms of the volume of concessional funds needed to support the credit) mixed credits. It was hoped that if the minimum cost of promoting a commercial transaction through a mixed credit were high enough, it might act as a deterrent to their use.

11. In 1985 the minimum grant element was raised to 25 percent, and a twenty-day prior notification requirement for credits with a grant element of 25–50 percent was established. In 1987 agreement was reached to raise the minimum grant element to 35 percent.

6. Interaction between Donors and Recipients

1. This section draws on the concepts discussed in US/AID, 1982a.

2. Past military occupation can also influence the willingness to engage in policy dialogue. For example, until recently Japan has been viewed as being generally reluctant to be involved in policy dialogue because of its perception that Asian countries, where most of its aid has traditionally gone, would object because of memories of World War II.

3. Initially referred to as the Meeting on India's Foreign Exchange Needs, by 1960 it had become known as the Aid-India Consortium. This early history of the aid consortia is discussed in detail by John White (1967).

4. These country-specific aid coordination mechanisms between donors and recipients go by a variety of labels, including "aid groups," "donor meetings," "consortia," and "consultative groups." The terms "aid group" and "consultative groups" are used here to refer to these country-level aid coordination efforts. While most of these aid coordination groups are sponsored or supported by the World Bank, several have been sponsored by others, for example, Indonesia by the Netherlands, Turkey by the OECD, and country-chaired donor conferences in Zimbabwe and Malawi. In a few

cases the IMF has taken the lead in organizing a meeting of donors as part of an effort to develop a stabilization program.

5. In response to some of the identified shortcomings of the early roundtable meetings, changes in format have been made. According to the United Nations, these format changes seek to increase the emphasis on policy reforms, exercise more selectivity in the choice of countries and participants, improve the analysis and in-country follow-ups, provide better preparation and organization, and achieve better coordination with the World Bank (United Nations, 1986).

6. Kjellstron and d'Almeida, 1986, contains an overview of the increased level of donor and recipient aid coordination in recent years in the small African country Togo.

7. The Impact of Development Assistance

1. It is not clear what precise methodology was used in reaching these conclusions. Sometimes rates of return analyses were used; at other times more qualitative measures were employed.

2. See also Leff, 1968; and Stewart, 1971.

3. For a discussion of the limitations of the two-gap model see chapter 3.

4. For the sake of completeness, one should also add a third line of inquiry, studies on the links between aid and self-reliance (Dacy, 1975; Grinols and Bhagwati, 1976). These studies are partially based on earlier aid-savings studies and consequently suffer from the same kinds of methodological problems. Some of their empirical simulations yield results that with hindsight appear peculiar. For example, Grinols and Bhagwati estimate that Korea's level of savings could take over two hundred years to recover from the declines it is supposed to have sustained as a consequence of the large influx of assistance Korea received in the 1950s and 1960s.

5. See Heller, 1975, table 4, p. 440.

6. Another recent investigation of aid also reached the same conclusion (Landau, 1986). However, this study is plagued by some of the same serious data shortcomings present in earlier efforts. Landau concluded that foreign aid, which he defines as official unrequited transfers from the IMF's *International Financial Statistics*, was not related to the economic growth of developing countries; moreover, private transfers (using data from the same source) were. However, the statistics used included only official grants, which account for a very small proportion of total economic aid, roughly 15 percent. Similarly, private transfers include emigrant remittances plus transfers from PVOs, which also represent a very small portion of private capital flows to developing countries. It would be hard to postulate any relationship between the variables thus estimated and GNP growth in developing countries. The results certainly show nothing about the relationship or contribution of official or private capital flows to developing countries' growth.

7. Onchocerciasis, or river blindness, is a parasitic disease prevalent in West Africa and is transmitted to humans by the bite of the female blackfly. The Onchocerciasis Control Program (OCP) is a multidonor, twenty-year, single-disease control program initiated in 1974. An epidemiological evaluation prepared in 1984 showed that in 90 percent of the control area there was no significant infection of children born since the program began. By opening up 15 million hectares of tillable land in the

former onchocerciasis-endemic areas, OCP has improved opportunities for increased agricultural productivity.

8. Assistance for Infrastructure Development

1. Indeed some institution building in donor countries may also be needed. Some years back US/AID set up a pioneering, but unsuccessful, program in a U.S. engineering school to develop curricula based on labor-intensive techniques appropriate for road construction in developing countries.

9. Assistance to Expand Agricultural Production

Mary Forsberg and Kent Miller assisted in the preparation of this chapter. The section on agricultural credit markets was reviewed by Dale Adams.

1. This chapter draws very heavily on two earlier reviews: Hayami and Ruttan, 1985, pp. 416–33; and Ruttan, 1986a.

2. For a more complete treatment of the history of the Indus Basin Project see Falcon and Gotsch, 1968; Nulty, 1972; Gotsch and Brown, 1980; Johnson, 1980; Painter et al., 1982; US/AID, 1982c; and Traxler and Ruttan, 1986.

3. This section summarizes material treated in considerably more detail in two previous reviews: Arndt, Dalrymple, and Ruttan, 1977; and Ruttan, 1982. Other useful studies include Moseman, 1970; Piñeiro and Trigo, 1983; Judd, Boyce, and Evenson, 1986; and Baum, 1987.

4. During the 1970s a large body of critical literature viewed the international agricultural research system and the Green Revolution seed-fertilizer technology, which was developed at the international agricultural research institutes and cooperating national research centers, as a source of unequal income distribution in rural areas. For a review of this literature and an assessment of the income distribution consequences of the new biological technology see Hayami and Ruttan, 1985, pp. 336–62. The conclusion of this assessment is that the development and diffusion of biological technology that generates increased output per hectare has been an important factor in offsetting the tendency toward worsening income distribution arising from the growing population pressure on the land.

5. The contribution of research to increased agricultural productivity has been studied primarily by two methods. The estimates listed under the "index number" subheading in table 9.2 were computed directly from the costs and benefits of research on, for example, hybrid corn. The calculated returns represent the average rate of return per dollar invested over the period studied, with the benefits of past research assumed to continue indefinitely. Benefits include those retained in the form of higher incomes to producers or those passed on to consumers in the form of lower food prices. The studies listed under the "regression analysis" subheading use a methodology that permits estimation of the incremental return from increased investment rather than of the average return from all investment. Because regression methods are used, the significance of the estimated returns from research can be tested statistically. The objective of the regression procedure is to estimate that component of the change in productivity that can be attributed to research.

6. Albert H. Moseman (1970, pp. 69, 71) argued that the "extension bias" was based partially on the successful transfer of hybrid corn technology from the United States to Western Europe under the Marshall Plan. This transfer was successful because the climate in Western Europe is reasonably close to that in the corn-producing areas of the United States, and there was indigenous human capital in the form of agricultural scientists and technicians in Europe to conduct adaptive research.

7. Despite the deemphasis on extension, in the mid-1970s US/AID was continuing to allocate close to $100 million per year for the support of agricultural extension activities (Stavis, 1979, p. 12). For a discussion of the concerns that led to the new emphasis on extension see Feder, Just, and Zilberman, 1985.

8. For a description of the T&V system and obstacles to its effectiveness see Benor and Harrison, 1977; and subsequent reviews by Stavis (1979); Lowdermilk (1981); Cernea, Coulter, and Russell (1983); and Feder, Lau, and Slade (1987).

9. Benor suggests selection by the extension worker in consultation with local officials. This may be the best way of choosing contact farmers who are most in line with the T&V system's criteria for socioeconomic status, credibility, influence, and role in the community. However, Anne Van de Ban, of the Agricultural University, Netherlands, expressed her concern that "too often the contact farmers are those farmers who are interested to cooperate with the extension service. This means that these are farmers with a better education and more resources than the average farmer. In such a situation it is not sure that the other farmers will follow their example" (quoted in Lowdermilk, 1981, annex 3). For case studies of the operation and impact of T&V programs in several Asian countries see Cernea, Coulter, and Russell, 1983.

10. Much of the history of U.S. support for land reform in East Asia can be written around the remarkable career of Wolf Ladejinsky (Walinsky, 1977). For reviews of the land reform efforts and accomplishments of the 1950s and 1960s see Feder, 1965; Raup, 1967; Ruttan, 1969; Warriner, 1969; Montgomery, 1972; and de Janvry, 1981.

11. For reviews of the new land tenure literature see Binswanger and Rosenzweig, 1984; and Jaynes, 1984. For important contributions to the reevaluation of the literature see, e.g., Bardhan and Srinivasan, 1971; Stiglitz, 1974; Newbery, 1975; Bell and Zusman, 1976; Reid, 1976; Rosenzweig, 1978; Bell and Zusman, 1980; and Newbery and Stiglitz, 1979.

12. A remarkable feature of the Latin American literature is the almost complete failure to confront the arguments of the new land tenure economics. See, e.g., the literature reviewed by Feder (1965), Dovring (1970), Eckstein et al. (1978), and de Janvry (1981). There has been almost a complete lack of reference to African experience in the theoretical and empirical debates about land tenure economics and policy (Robertson, 1987).

13. This section draws very heavily on the major review of agricultural credit programs conducted by US/AID in 1972 and 1973 (US/AID, 1973b); the review of the materials prepared for the US/AID agricultural credit review by Donald (1976); and the discussion of agricultural credit programs by Hayami and Ruttan (1985).

14. Information on ACAR is drawn from Mosher, 1957; Wharton, 1960; and Ribeiro and Wharton, 1969.

10. Improving the Quality of Life in Rural Areas

This chapter was prepared with the assistance of Charles Adelberg. The author is indebted to Michael Cernea, Brady Deaton, David Korten, Michael Patton, and Norman Uphoff for comments on an earlier draft.

1. This chapter draws on two earlier reviews: Ruttan, 1975 and 1984. The voluminous literature on rural development and basic needs programs almost defies any attempt at a comprehensive review or evaluation. For example, Holdcraft (1978, pp. 61, 62) listed eighteen community development bibliographies; the Moris (1981) review of rural development literature contains over thirteen hundred references; and the Cornell University Rural Development Committee catalogued over seventy research monographs and papers. Much less attention has been given by development assistance agencies to programs to enhance the quality of life in urban areas; see, however, Tolley, 1987. For a discussion of the similarities and differences in the implementation of poverty-oriented rural and urban development projects see Tendler, 1982.

2. For a history of the Etawah Project see Mayer, 1958; and Sussman, 1982. Neale (1985) reviewed the history of community development in India. The community development movement was strongly influenced by American domestic and British colonial experience. For a comparison with the "animation rural" strategy for promoting rural modernization in French Africa see Uphoff, Cohen, and Goldsmith, 1979, pp. 13–31.

3. See Mosher, 1976; Lele, 1979; Montgomery, 1988; and Cohen, 1980 and 1987, pp. 13–38. Other projects that have received widespread attention and analyses include the Chilalo project (CADU/ARDU) in Ethiopia and the Puebla project in Mexico. The Chilalo project has been carefully reviewed by Cohen (1987). For a critical review of the Puebla project see Redcliff, 1983; for a more positive view see Swanberg, 1982. For a history of the evolution of poverty-oriented rural development programs at the World Bank see Ayres, 1983, pp. 409–36. The integrated approach to rural development programming had been developed and tested by the Bank in a number of locations prior to 1973 (Lacroix, 1985).

4. See Raper, 1970; Haq, 1973; Khan, 1974; Stevens, 1974; and Khan, 1979. It is somewhat surprising that the very successful Saemaul (New Village) Movement in Korea received so little international attention (see Park, 1981; Douglass, 1984; Wang, 1984; and chapter 13).

5. See Chenery et al., 1974; Ghai et al., 1977; Crosswell, 1978; Streeten and Burki, 1978; and Streeten, 1979. Within the World Bank there were two major doctrines on the approach to poverty alleviation: the redistribution with growth school, associated with Hollis Chenery; and the basic needs school, associated with Mahbub ul Haq and Paul Streeten (see Ayres, 1983, pp. 76–91).

6. Bruce Johnston reported that "as late as 1979 the AID Mission Director in Tanzania responded to a request from the Minister of Agriculture for more advanced degree training by asserting that AID/Washington preferred projects that benefit the poor in the shortest amount of time possible" (Johnston et al., 1987, p. 190).

7. Judith Tendler argued that this problem is particularly difficult in rural areas, where the projects "focus on the production activities of the rural poor in agriculture—credit, inputs, planting practices. Rural projects therefore involve the domain

of the elite as landlords and employers of the rural poor—whereas urban projects do not" (Tendler, 1982, p. iii).

8. For a more detailed analysis of the initial set of US/AID project impact evaluations see Wunsch, 1986.

9. The evaluation literature can be classified under two broad headings. One body of literature focuses primarily on process evaluation; it emphasizes planning, monitoring, and impact and is largely the product of research in psychology and sociology. Its greatest use has been in the field of education. The second body of literature emphasizes the relationship between program inputs and outputs; it emphasizes the use of cost-benefit and cost-effectiveness methodologies and is largely the product of research in economics. For useful reviews see Little and Mirrlees, 1969; and Freeman, Rossi, and Wright, 1980. The effective integration of these two bodies of evaluation methodology remains underdeveloped (see Dunlop, 1982).

10. In this section I draw very heavily on Esman and Uphoff, 1984; and Korten, 1987. In their work, Esman and Uphoff emphasize the role of local membership organizations. For a discussion of local governance see Mawhood, 1983; for a discussion of the problems of financing regional and local governance see Davey, 1983.

11. See, e.g., the *New York Times* article by US/AID director Peter McPherson (1986).

12. Lele and Meyers (1987), in their review of rural development programs in East Africa, note that a common source of poor performance in World Bank–sponsored rural development projects has been the "expansion of projects to additional areas without clear evidence of technologies appropriate to these areas" (p. 13).

11. The Impact of International Population Assistance

1. The basic figures on population assistance are taken from OECD annual reviews and the United Nations Fund for Population Assistance (UNFPA). The *World Development Report, 1984* (World Bank, 1984b) includes a lengthy discussion of population issues, with data on amounts, sources, and policies on international assistance; see also Herz, 1984, for the background paper used in the Development report. Total development assistance figures are taken from OECD annual reports and the World Bank development reports. Because all figures are in current dollars, they overstate considerably the magnitude of real international assistance; however, the ratio of population assistance to total economic aid is not affected.

2. For a fuller analysis of these regional differences see Ness and Ando, 1984, chap. 2.

3. Ethno-political tensions relevant to population policies are reported, for example, in India (Frankel, 1977), Sri Lanka (UN/ESCAP, 1976), and Malaysia (Ness, 1976), where the antinatalist policy was reversed in 1982 with the unspoken aim of increasing the Malay population. The list easily could be expanded.

4. Various development assistance programs affect fertility, for example, through raising levels of socioeconomic development (Rosenzweig, 1981). They also affect mortality, but these effects generally are considered to be results of *health* programs. Few development programs attempt to affect migration or population distribution, but many are concerned with problems of urbanization (Kuroda, 1987).

5. It is important to recognize the profound policy revolution that such adoption represents. Throughout human history virtually all governments have been pronatalist. Thus the recent shift to antinatalism as official policy is a revolutionary change. There is also something of a revolutionary character in the focus on reducing *marital fertility*. In the past, whenever a community or government attempted to regulate population growth, it was usually either by encouraging outmigration or restricting marriage, almost never by direct intervention (Ness and Ando, 1984, chap. 2). Yet today the majority of international funds for population assistance go to national family planning programs and are direct attempts by government to reduce marital fertility.

6. In a number of countries the use of such traditional methods as withdrawal or abstinence constitutes a substantial proportion of the contraceptive behavior practiced by couples. See, for example, Laing, 1987, for recent evidence on the Philippines; Viaria and Jain, 1976, on India; and Population Information Program, 1985, for World Fertility Survey collections of data on this issue.

7. For evidence of program effects see, for example, Freedman and Berelson, 1976; Srikantan, 1977; Berelson and Mauldin, 1978; Rosenzweig, 1981; and Ness and Ando, 1984. For dissenting opinions see McNicoll and Singarimbun, 1982; and Hernandez, 1984.

8. Evaluations of programs in Indonesia (Heiby, Ness, and Pillsbury, 1979), Thailand (US/AID, 1980b), and even the Philippines (Laing, 1981) show clearly that moving family planning outlets to the villages and directly reducing the costs of contraceptives was in large part responsible for the increase in acceptors and prevalence rates. The measure of political-administrative system strength used an expert-completed grounded coding device combining three different dimensions that had been identified in prior theoretical and empirical work: the strength of the central government; the commitment to national economic development; and the capacity for monitoring social and economic change. The intercoder reliability of this instrument was found to be high.

9. The level of socioeconomic development used an index of three conditions in combination: infant mortality, per capita GDP, and female school enrollment. The strength of the family planning program was taken from a measurement developed by Lapham and Mauldin (1972) and updated by Freedman and Berelson (1976).

10. Note that in these studies there was no attempt to assess the source, character, or quality of the assistance. Foreign assistance was measured by volume alone. More rigorous and systematic studies should assess character and quality to identify the dynamics of effect.

11. According to our most recent estimates, the Philippines have received a total of about $135 million in external assistance since 1962. From 1977 to 1980, when the outreach program was in operation, foreign assistance averaged more than $15 million per year, compared with an annual average of just over $10 million in the six preceding years.

12. Robert Hackenberg, personal communication to the author. Accounts of various changes and the disruption in Population Commission leadership appear in various issues of the *Far Eastern Economic Review* and in local Philippine underground newspapers.

13. This is not to argue that such effects do not exist. On the contrary, there are strong arguments favoring such effects. My point is that systematic studies do not now

exist to show them. Further, given the highly complex nature of the relationship, a conclusive demonstration of the independent influence of foreign assistance on fertility *through* other development programs may be impossible to find.

12. Assistance to India

The author is indebted to Anne Krueger, Constantine Michalopoulos, Vernon Ruttan, and T. N. Srinivasan for detailed and helpful comments on earlier drafts of this chapter.

1. Government of India sources and documents on the inflow of external assistance report data on "authorizations" and "utilizations" of external assistance. Donor agencies report data on "commitments" and "disbursements." Aid authorizations represent aid commitments, whereas aid utilizations reflect actual transfer of resources. In the following discussion and in the data reported in table 12.1, the Government of India's *Economic Survey* was the primary source, and the discussion is in terms of aid utilizations.

2. The India Consortium came into being in response to India's 1958 foreign exchange crises. By the early 1960s the term *consortium* was being used for annual meetings devoted to the coordination and "pledging" of assistance in support of India's development program. A Pakistan consortium was framed in 1960. By the early 1970s there were donor consortia for approximately twenty developing countries, supported by over thirty bilateral and multilateral donors (Mason and Asher, 1973, pp. 510–28).

3. The data in table 12.1 are not strictly comparable with those reported in either Mellor, 1976 (p. 219), or Bhagwati and Srinivasan, 1975 (p. 11), but they are consistent with them in highlighting the "era" of aid until the late-1960s.

4. Bhagwati and Srinivasan, 1975, is the standard reference on the foreign trade regime in India for the period 1950–70.

13. Assistance to Korea

The authors indebted to David C. Cole, Young-Jin Kim, Paul W. Kuznets, and David I. Steinberg for comments on an earlier version and to Mary Forsberg and Kent Miller for assistance in preparing the first draft of this chapter. They also are indebted to the Korea Rural Economics Institute for permission to reprint material from the earlier version (Ruttan and Krueger, 1986).

1. The contribution of economic assistance to economic growth in the Republic of Korea has become the subject of a massive literature. A seminal early work was the assessment of the interplay between development assistance and Korean economic and political development by Cole and Lyman (1971). It was followed by a series of studies on the economic and social modernization of Korea, undertaken with support from US/AID, the Harvard Institute for International Development, and the Korea Development Institute. The individual studies were by Kim and Roemer (1979); Krueger (1979); Mills and Song (1979); Ban, Moon, and Perkins (1980); Cole (1980); Jones and SaKong (1980); McGinn et al. (1980); Mason et al. (1980); Repetto et al. (1981); and Cole and Park (1983). The University of Hawaii Press published a series of specialized studies by staff members of the Korea Development Institute, edited by Chuk

Kyo Kim (1977a, 1977b, 1980a, 1980b). Other important studies focused on income distribution (Adelman and Robinson, 1978), local institutions and rural development (Aqua, 1974), price policy (Brown, 1973), and growth and structure (Kuznets, 1977). The US/AID Office of Evaluation conducted a number of internal studies, including a review of the Harvard–Korea Development Institute studies (Steinberg, 1982 and 1985) and specialized studies of development assistance in the areas of irrigation (Steinberg et al., 1980), agricultural research (Steinberg et al., 1982), health (Dunlop et al., 1982), and rural services (Steinberg et al., 1984). For a review of more recent economic growth see Dornbusch and Park, 1987.

2. Data cited in this and the subsequent two paragraphs are from table 13.1 and from Mason et al., 1980, chap. 4. This section also draws heavily on Krueger, 1979. For a detailed study of the sources of economic growth in Korea for the 1963–82 period see Kim and Park, 1985.

3. Even during the very rapid growth years, 1960 to 1978, South Korea never achieved full control over domestic inflation. During most of that period, however, the rate of inflation was fairly stable and significantly below the rates of earlier years. The inflation rate rose in the 1970s, as did rates in the rest of the world, but overall the South Korean inflation experience in the 1970s must be judged as no worse than that of many other countries.

4. Interest rate subsidies were continued for exporters and farmers. The nominal interest rate was not permitted to rise as much as the domestic inflation rate in the 1970s. By the late 1970s, however, the negative real interest rate once again was an identifiable source of major distortion within the system.

5. For a more detailed discussion of Korean rice price policy from the Japanese period to the early 1970s see Moon, 1977.

6. Korean data showing comparable incomes for urban and rural households must be interpreted with caution. Urban households are smaller than rural households; in addition, the published series on urban and rural incomes omit higher-income salaried professional and government workers. The data are most appropriately interpreted as indicating that farm household incomes were approximately equal to the incomes of urban wage earner households (Steinberg et al., 1984, p. 2). This in itself is a remarkable achievement. In most developing countries growth of nonfarm employment is restrained by wage rates in manufacturing that are about double those in agriculture (Fields, 1985, p. 368). During the 1960s the incomes of the lowest 40 percent of both urban and rural households increased as a result of the labor-intensive industrial development policy, productivity gains, and more favorable agricultural commodity policies; a slight decline occurred during the 1970s, however. Suh (1986, pp. 24–27) attributed the worsening of income distribution in the 1970s in part to the greater emphasis on capital-intensive industrial growth.

14. Assistance to Turkey

The initial draft of this chapter was prepared with the assistance of Susanna Fishel and Arnold Sheetz. It has benefited from critical reviews by Charles K. Mann, Kutlu Somel, and Erinc Yeldan.

1. For a fuller account of Turkey's economic history following World War II see

White, 1967; Hershlag, 1968; Krueger, 1974a; and Hale, 1981. The analysis of the effects of development assistance presented in this chapter extends through 1980, to the time when Turkey embarked on a major stabilization program and simultaneously began reforming its domestic incentive structure. As of 1985 the reforms were continuing. The period 1980–84 was characterized by relatively rapid economic growth.

2. The Turkish construction activities now going on in the Middle East owe their origin at least in part to U.S.-supported construction activities of earlier years, which led to the development of Turkish entrepreneurs. See below for an analysis of assistance to the agricultural sector. In the early 1950s not only agricultural mechanization but roads were emphasized. Many worthwhile projects in individual sectors (e.g., U.S. assistance to Turkish economics education, which has had numerous intangible payoffs) cannot be covered here; for greater detail see Sheetz, 1982.

3. Project aid continued, but the U.S. government simply refused an additional program loan. From 1948 to 1958, U.S. economic aid to Turkey totaled $764.6 million, of which $172 million was PL 480 commodity aid (Burke, 1977).

4. A much more complete set of notes and bibliographical references were prepared for this project by Sheetz (1982). We also have benefited from the very complete bibliography by Gorun and Somel (1979).

5. This review of the development of the Seyhan Project is based very largely on IBRD, 1951; and Wilson, 1971.

6. It is much easier to develop the engineering capacity for the design and construction of irrigation systems than the institutional infrastructure needed to deliver and use water and to maintain the system (see chapter 10).

7. During the 1970s US/AID gave increased attention to on-farm water development and use in a number of countries (Easter, 1986, p. 2). US/AID supported the On-Farm Water Development Project from 1969 to 1975 only. Turkish government support declined in the late 1970s but was reversed in the 1980s (World Bank, 1981, vol. 2, pp. 291–93).

8. U.S. agricultural assistance programming showed a strong extension bias during the 1950s and 1960s. The assumption was that peasant resistance to innovation was a more important barrier to productivity growth than the lack of productive agricultural technology (see chapter 2; see also Moseman, 1970, pp. 66–67).

9. A similar refocusing of research and extension efforts occurred in a number of countries (Wortman and Cummings, 1978, pp. 186–226).

10. The review also identified some continuing problems: (*a*) an inadequate pipeline of well-trained young scientists; (*b*) no effective research teams in several important wheat producing areas; (*c*) the difficulty of maintaining effective working relationships between the extension service and the wheat research group; (*d*) failure to hold economists in the research team; and (*e*) little structured planning of national policies to address the problems and opportunities created by becoming a surplus producer.

11. This comment should not be interpreted as excessively critical of development assistance practice. We noted in chapters 2 and 3 that development thought did not begin to adequately consider the role of human capital investment and institutional innovation until well into the 1960s.

15. Assistance to Ghana and the Ivory Coast

1. Stephen H. Hymer has argued that the colonial government's investments and policies in Ghana were largely unproductive and may even have retarded growth of the economy (Hymer, 1971, p. 129).

2. For the several criticisms of the two-gap model see chapter 3.

3. The major econometric problem posed by the regression results is positive serial correlation in several instances, shown by relatively low values of the Durbin-Watson statistic. This implies that some of the estimates are biased given the small sample of observations. The bias is not particularly disturbing, however, because the conclusions drawn from the analysis are very rough and insensitive to large errors in the estimates.

4. U.S. government per diem in Ghana ranged in the fall of 1982 from $130, when local staff housing was provided, up to $283 with hotel accommodations, compared with $88 in Abidjan, Ivory Coast (U.S. Department of State, 1982, pp. 3–4).

5. Part of this section is drawn from Pearson, Nelson, and Stryker, 1979, which summarizes the literature available on the Ghanaian incentive system in the mid-1970s and analyzes a substantial body of new data. For a discussion of the origins of this system and the changes in it that took place over time see Stryker, 1988.

6. The effective rate of protection can be written as

$$\frac{\text{Value Added in Domestic Prices}}{\text{Value Added in World Prices}} - 1.$$

If value added in world prices is negative but value added in domestic prices is positive, the ERP is less than -1.

References

Abbott, Philip C. and F. Desmond McCarthy (1982). "Welfare Effects of Tied Food Aid," in *Journal of Development Economics* 11 (August),63–79.

Adams, Dale W. (1971). "Agricultural Credit in Latin America: A Critical Review of External Funding Policy." *American Journal of Agricultural Economics* 53 (May): 163–72.

———— (1978)."Mobilizing Household Savings through Rural Financial Markets.' *Economic Development and Cultural Change* 26 (April): 547–60.

Adams, Dale W. and Douglas H. Graham (1981). "A Critique of Traditional Agricultural Credit Projects and Policies." *Journal of Development Economics* 8, (June): 347–66.

Adelman, Irma (1984). "Beyond Export Led Growth." *World Development* 12 (September): 937–49.

Adelman, Irma and Hollis B. Chenery (1966). "Foreign Aid and Economic Development: The Case of Greece." *Review of Economics and Statistics* 48 (February): 1–19.

Adelman, Irma, Michael Hopkins, Sherman Robinson, Gerry Rodgers, and R. Wery (1979). "A Comparison of Two Models for Income Distribution Planning." *Journal of Policy Modeling* 1 (January): 37–82.

Adelman, Irma and Sherman Robinson (1978). *Income Distribution Policy in Developing Countries: A Case Study of Korea.* Stanford: Stanford University Press.

Agarwala, A. N. and S. P. Singh (1958). *The Economics of Underdevelopment.* New York: Oxford University Press.

Ahluwalia, Isher (1985). *Industrial Growth in India.* New York and New Delhi: Oxford University Press.

Ahmed, Rais Uddin (1988). *Employment and Income Growth in Asia: Some Strategic Issues.* Washington, D.C.: International Food Policy Research Institute.

Akat, A. S. (1983). *Alternatif Buyume Stratejisi.* Istanbul: Iletisim.

Anderson, G. William and Charles G. Vandervoort (1982). *Rural Roads Evaluation Summary Report.* US/AID Program Evaluation Discussion Paper No. 5. Washington, D.C.

Anderson, Kym and Yujiro Hayami (1986). *The Political Economy of Agricultural Protection.* Boston and Sydney: Allen and Unwin.

Ankara University, Faculty of Political Science (1953). *Economic and Social Effects of Farm Mechanization.* Ankara.

Annis, Sheldon (1986). "The Shifting Grounds of Poverty Lending at the World Bank." In *Between Two Worlds*, pp. 87–109. *See* Feinberg (1986).

Aqua, Ronald (1974). *Local Institutions and Rural Development in South Korea*. Cornell University Special Series on Rural Local Government, Center for International Studies. Ithaca: Cornell University Press.

Areskoug, Kaj (1969). *External Borrowing: Its Role in Economic Development*. New York: Praeger.

Aresvik, Oddvar (1975). *The Agricultural Development of Turkey*. New York: Praeger.

Arndt, Hans W. (1979). "Problems of the Aid Recipient Country." In *International Aid: Some Political, Administrative and Technical Realities*, ed. R.T. Shand and H.V. Richter, pp. 34–45. Canberra: Australian National University.

——— (1981). "Economic Development: A Semantic History." *Economic Development and Cultural Change* 29 (April): 457–66.

——— (1987). *Economic Development: The History of an Idea*. Chicago: University of Chicago Press.

Arndt, Thomas M., Dana G. Dalrymple, and Vernon W. Ruttan, eds. (1977). *Resource Allocation and Productivity in National and International Agricultural Research*. Minneapolis: University of Minnesota Press.

Arnold, Steven (1982). *A Comparative Study of Five European Development Assistance Programs*. Occasional Paper in Development Assistance No. 4. Washington, D.C.: US/AID.

Arrow, Kenneth J. (1983). *Social Choice and Justice*. Cambridge: Harvard University Press.

Asian Development Bank (1984). *Annual Report*. Manila.

Askari, Hossein and John T. Cummings (1976). *Agricultural Supply Response: A Survey of the Econometric Evidence*. New York: Praeger.

Ayres, Robert C. (1983). *Banking on the Poor: The World Bank and Rural Poverty*. Cambridge: MIT Press.

Balassa, Bela (1978). "Exports and Economic Growth: Further Evidence," *Journal of Development Economics* 5 (June): 181–89.

——— (1984). "Adjustment Policies in Developing Countries: A Reassessment." *World Development* 12 (September): 955–72.

——— (1985). "The Role of Foreign Trade in the Economic Development of Korea." In *Foreign Trade and Investment: Economic Development in the Newly Industrializing Asian Countries*, ed. Walter Galenson, pp. 141–75. Madison: University of Wisconsin Press.

Balasubramanyam, V. N. (1984). *The Economy of India*. Boulder, Colo: Westview Press.

Baldwin, Robert E. (1969). "The Case against Infant-Industry Tariff Protection." *Journal of Political Economy* 77 (May): 295–305.

Ball, J. (1985). "Mixed Credits: Winners, Losers and Users." *Euromoney Trade Finance Report* [London] 30 (October): 18–22.

Ban, Sung Hwan, Pal Yong Moon and Dwight H. Perkins (1980). *Rural Development*. Cambridge: Harvard University Press.

Bardhan, Pranab (1984). *The Political Economy of Development in India* Oxford: Basil Blackwell.

Bardhan, Pranab and T. N. Srinivasan (1971). "Cropsharing Tenancy in Agriculture: A Theoretical and Empirical Analysis." *American Economic Review* 61 (March): 48–64.

Bateman, Merrill J. (1974). "An Econometric Analysis of Ghanaian Cocoa Supply." In *The Economics of Cocoa Production and Marketing*, ed. R. A. Kotey, C. Okali, and B. E. Rourke, pp. 286–326. Legon: Institute of Statistical, Social and Economic Research, University of Ghana.

Bates, Robert H. (1981). *Markets and States in Tropical Africa: The Political Basis of Agricultural Policies*. Berkeley: University of California Press.

Bauer, Peter T. (1961). *Indian Economic Policy and Development*. Bombay: Popular Prakashan Press.

——— (1968). "International Development Policy: Two Recent Studies." *Quarterly Journal of Development Economics*, 5 (June) 181–89.

——— (1972). *Dissent on Development*. Cambridge: Harvard University Press.

——— (1981). *Equality, the Third World and Economic Delusion*. London: Weidenfeld and Nicholson.

——— (1984). *Reality and Rhetoric: Studies in the Economics of Development*. Cambridge: Harvard University Press.

Baum, Warren C. (1987). *Partners Against Hunger*. Washington, D.C.: World Bank.

Bautista, Romeo M. (1987). *Production Incentives in Philippine Agriculture: Effects of Trade and Exchange Rate Policies*. Research Report 59. Washington, D.C.: International Food Policy Research Institute, May.

Becker, Gary S. (1964). *Human Capital*. Princeton: Princeton University Press.

Behrman, Jere R. (1968). *Supply Response in Underdeveloped Agriculture: A Case Study of Four Major Annual Crops in Thailand, 1937–1963*. Amsterdam: North-Holland.

Bell, Clive and Pinhas Zusman (1976). "A Bargaining Theoretic Approach to Cropsharing Contracts." *American Economic Review* 66 (September): 578–88.

——— (1980). "Toward a General Bargaining Theory of Equilibrium Sets of Contracts—The Case of Agricultural Rental Contracts." Paper presented at the World Congress of the Econometric Society, Aix-en-Province, France, 28 August–5 September 1980.

Benedict, Peter, Ahmed Humeida Ahmed, Rollo Ehrich, Stephen F. Lintner, Jack Morgan, and Mohamed Abdulrahim Mohamed Salih (1982). *Sudan: The Rahad Irrigation Project*. US/AID Project Impact Evaluation Report No. 31. Washington, D.C.

Benor, Daniel and James Q. Harrison (1977). *Agricultural Extension: The Training and Visit System*. Washington, D.C.: World Bank, May.

Berelson, Bernard and W. Parker Mauldin (1978). "Conditions of Fertility Decline in Developing Countries, 1965–1975." *Studies in Family Planning* 9 (May): 90–147.

Berg, Elliot J. (1971). "Structural Transformation versus Gradualism: Recent Economic Development in Ghana and the Ivory Coast." In *Ghana and the Ivory Coast*, ed. Philip Foster and Aristide R. Zolberg, pp. 187–230. Chicago: University of Chicago Press.

Berry, Leonard, Richard Ford, and Richard Hosier (1980). *The Impact of Irrigation on Development: Issues for a Comprehensive Evaluation Study*. US/AID Program Evaluation Discussion Paper No. 9. Washington, D.C.

Bhagwati, Jagdish (1970a). *Amount and Sharing of Aid.* Overseas Development Council Monograph Series. Washington, D.C.

———— (1970b). "The Tying of Aid." In *Foreign Aid: Selected Readings*, ed. Jagdish Bhagwati and Richard Eckaus, chap. 10. New Brunswick: Transaction Books for Overseas Development Council.

———— (1971). "The Generalized Theory of Distortions and Welfare." In *Trade, Balance of Payments and Growth*, ed. Jagdish N. Bhagwati, Ronald W. Jones, Robert A. Mundell, and Jaroslav Vanek. Amsterdam: North-Holland.

———— (1986). "Rethinking Trade Strategy." In *Development Strategies Reconsidered*, pp. 91–104. *See* Lewis and Kallab (1986).

Bhagwati, Jagdish and Padma Desai (1970). *Planning for Industrialization: India.* London: Oxford University Press for OECD.

Bhagwati, Jagdish and Bert Hansen (1973). "A Theoretical Analysis of Smuggling." *Quarterly Journal of Economics* 87 (May): 172–87.

Bhagwati, Jagdish and T. N. Srinivasan (1975). *Foreign Trade Regimes and Economic Development: India.* New York: Columbia University Press for National Bureau of Economic Research.

Binswanger, Hans P. and Mark R. Rosenzweig (1984). "Contractual Arrangements, Employment and Wages in Rural Labor Markets: A Critical Review." In *Contractual Arrangements, Employment and Rural Labor Markets in Asia*, ed. Hans. P. Binswanger and Mark R. Rosenzweig, pp. 1–40. New Haven: Yale University Press.

Blitz, Rudolph C. and Millard F. Long (1965). "The Economics of Usury Regulation." *Journal of Political Economy* 73 (December): 608–19.

Bolling, Landrom R., with Craig Smith (1982). *Private Foreign Aid: United States Philanthropy for Relief and Development.* Boulder, Colo.: Westview Press.

Bondestam, Lars and Staff Bergstrom, eds. (1980). *Poverty and Population Control.* New York: Academic Press.

Bottomley, Anthony (1963). "The Cost of Administering Private Loans in Underdeveloped Rural Areas." *Oxford Economic Papers*, n.s., 15 (July): 154–63.

———— (1975). "Interest Rate Determination in Underdeveloped Rural Areas." *American Journal of Agricultural Economics* 57 (May): 279–91.

Bourne, Campton and Douglas H. Graham (1984). "Problems with Specialized Agricultural Lenders." In *Undermining Rural Development with Cheap Credit*, ed. Dale W. Adams, Douglas H. Graham, and J. D. Von Pischke, pp. 36–48. Boulder, Colo.: Westview Press.

Boutros-Ghali, Youssef and Lance Taylor (1980). "Basic Needs Macroeconomics: Is It Manageable in the Case of Egypt?" *Journal of Policy Modeling* 2 (September): 409–36.

Bowen, Richard L. and Robert A. Young (1986). "Appraising Alternatives for Allocating and Cost Recovery for Irrigation Water in Egypt." *Agricultural Economics* 1 (December): 35–52.

Braibanti, Ralph (1969). *Political and Administrative Development.* Durham: Duke University Press.

Brandt Commission. *See* Independent Commission on International Development Issues.

Brokensha, David W., D. M. Warren, and Oswald Werner (1980). *Indigenous Knowledge Systems and Development*. Lanham, Md.: University Press of America.

Brown, Dorris (1971). *Agricultural Development in India's Districts*. Cambridge: Harvard University Press.

Brown, Gilbert T. (1973). *Korean Pricing Policies and Economic Development in the 1960s*. Baltimore: Johns Hopkins Press.

Brozen, Yale (1954). "Entrepreneurship and Technological Change." In *Economic Development: Principles and Patterns*, pp. 196–241. *See* Williamson and Buttrick (1954).

Bruton, Henry J. (1969). "The Two Gap Approach to Aid and Development: Comment." *American Economic Review* 59 (June): 439–46.

Buchanan, James M. and Gordon Tullock (1962). *The Calculus of Consent*. Ann Arbor: University of Michigan Press.

Burke, Mary Patrice (1977). "United States Aid to Turkey: Foreign Aid and Foreign Policy." Ph.D. diss., University of Connecticut.

Burki, Shahid Javed and S. J. Voorhoeve (1977). "Global Estimates for Meeting Basic Needs." Basic Needs Paper No. 1. Washington, D.C.: IBRD.

Burmeister, Larry L. (1985). "State, Society and Agricultural Research Policy: The Case of South Korea." Ph.D. diss., Department of Rural Sociology, Cornell University.

Caiden, Naomi and Aaron B. Wildavsky (1974). *Planning and Budgeting in Poor Countries*. New York: John Wiley and Sons.

Cargill, I. P. M. (1973). "Efforts to Influence Recipient Performance: Case Study of India." In *The World Bank Group, Multilateral Aid, and the 1970s*, ed. John P. Lewis and Ishan Kapur, pp. 89–95. Lexington, Mass.: Lexington Books.

Carlucci Commission. *See* Commission on Security and Economic Assistance.

Cassen, Robert and Associates (1986). *Does Aid Work? Report to an Intergovernmental Task Force*. Oxford: Oxford University Press.

Cernea, Michael M. (1979). *Measuring Project Impact: Monitoring and Evaluation in the PIDER Rural Development Project, Mexico*. World Bank Staff Working Paper No. 332. Washington, D.C., June.

Cernea, Michael M., John K. Coulter, and John F. A. Russell, eds. (1983). *Agricultural Extension by Training and Visit: The Asian Experience*. Washington, D.C.: World Bank.

Cernea, Michael M. and Benjamin J. Tepping (1977). *A System for Monitoring and Evaluating Agricultural Extension Projects*. World Bank Staff Working Paper No. 272. Washington, D.C.

Chaudhuri, Pramit, (1978). *The Indian Economy: Poverty and Development*. New York: St. Martin's Press.

Chenery, Hollis B. (1969). "The Two Gap Approach to Aid and Development: A Reply to Bruton." *American Economic Review* 59 (June): 446–49.

——— (1979). *Structural Change and Development Policy*. New York: Oxford University Press.

Chenery, Hollis, M. S. Ahluwalia, C. L. G. Bell, J. H. Duloy, and Richard Jolly (1974). *Redistribution with Growth*. London: Oxford University Press.

Chenery, Hollis B., George Brandow, and Edwin Cohn (1953). *Turkish Investment and Economic Development*. Ankara: U.S. Foreign Operations Administration Special Mission to Turkey, December.

Chenery, Hollis B. and Michael Bruno (1962). "Development Alternatives in an Open Economy: The Case of Israel." *Economic Journal* 72 (March): 79–103.

Chenery, Hollis B. and Peter C. Eckstein (1970). "Development Alternatives for Latin America." *Journal of Political Economy* 78 (July–August suppl.): 966–1006.

Chenery, Hollis B. and Arthur MacEwan (1966). "Optimal Patterns of Growth and Aid: The Case of Pakistan." In *The Theory and Design of Economic Development*, ed. Irma Adelman and Erik Thorbecke, pp. 149–78. Baltimore: Johns Hopkins Press.

Chenery, Hollis B., Sherman Robinson, and Moshe Syrquin (1986). *Industrialization and Growth: A Comparative Study*. New York: Oxford University Press.

Chenery, Hollis B. and Alan M. Strout (1966). "Foreign Assistance and Economic Development." *American Economic Review* 56 (September): 679–733.

——— (1968). "Foreign Assistance and Economic Development: Reply." *American Economic Review* 58 (September): 912–16.

Cheung, Steven N. S. (1968). "Private Property Rights and Sharecropping." *Journal of Political Economy* 76 (November–December): 1107–22.

——— (1969). *The Theory of Share Tenancy*. Chicago: University of Chicago Press.

Choksi, Armeane M. (1986). *Adjustment with Growth in the Highly Indebted Middle-Income Countries*. World Bank Central Projects Department Discussion Paper No. 1986-36. Washington, D.C.

Christian, W. F. K. (1974). "Problems of Planning Cocoa Rehabilitation Schemes in Ghana." Mimeo.

Clark, Colin (1940). *The Conditions of Economic Progress*. London: Macmillan.

——— (1967). *The Economics of Irrigation*. Oxford: Pergamon Press.

Clay, Edward J. and Hans W. Singer (1982). *Food Aid and Development: The Impact and Effectiveness of Bilateral PL-480 Title I–Type Assistance*. US/AID Program Evaluation Discussion Paper No. 15. Washington, D.C.

——— (1985). *Food Aid and Development: Issues and Evidence*. World Food Program, Occasional Paper No. 3. Rome, September.

Cohen, John M. (1979). "Integrating Services for Rural Development." Harvard University, Lincoln Institute of Land Policy and Kennedy School of Government, September. Mimeo.

——— (1980). "Integrated Rural Development: Clearing Out the Underbrush." *Sociologia Ruralis* 20(3): 195–212.

——— (1987). *Integrated Rural Development: The Ethiopian Experience and Debate*. Uppsala: Scandinavian Institute of African Studies.

Colaco, Francis X (1973). *Economic and Political Considerations and the Flow of Official Resources to Developing Countries*. Paris: OECD/DAC.

Cole, David C. (1980). "Foreign Assistance and Korean Development." In *The Korean Economy—Issues of Development*, ed. David C. Cole, Youngil Lim, and Paul W. Kuznets, pp. 1–29. Berkeley: University of California Press.

Cole, David C. and Princeton N. Lyman (1971). *Korean Development: The Interplay of Politics and Economics*. Cambridge: Harvard University Press.

Cole, David C. and Yung Chul Park (1983). *Financial Development in Korea, 1945–1978*. Cambridge: Harvard University Press.

Commission on International Development (Pearson Commission) (1969). *Partners in Development. Report of the Commission on International Development*. New York: Praeger.

Commission on Security and Economic Assistance (Carlucci Commission) (1983). *A Report to the Secretary of State*. Washington, D.C.: GPO.

Cooper, Richard N. (1971). "Devaluation in Developing Countries." In *Government and Economic Development*, ed. Gustav Ranis. New Haven: Yale University Press.

Cooper, Richard V. L. (1972). *The Additionality Factor in Tied United States Development Assistance*. Santa Monica: Rand Corporation.

Crawford, John G. (1977). "Development of the International Agricultural Research System." In *Resource Allocation and Productivity in National and International Agricultural Research*, pp. 282–3. *See* Arndt, Dalrymple, and Ruttan.

Crosswell, Michael (1978). *Basic Human Needs: A Development Planning Approach*. US/AID Discussion Paper No. 38. Washington, D.C., October.

Cunningham, George (1974). *The Management of Aid Agencies*. London: Overseas Development Institute.

Currie, Lauchlin (1984). *Evaluación de la asesoría económica a los países a desarrollo*. Bogotá: CEREC.

Dacy, Douglas C. (1975). "Foreign Aid, Government Consumption, Saving and Growth in Less-Developed Countries." *Economic Journal* 56 (September): 548–61.

Davey, Kenneth J. (1983). *Financing Regional Government: International Practices and Their Relevance to the Third World*. New York: John Wiley and Sons.

David, Cristina C. and Richard L. Meyer (1980). "Measuring the Farm Level Impact of Agricultural Loans." In *Borrowers and Lenders: Rural Financial Markets and Institutions in Developing Countries*, ed. John Howell, pp. 201–34. London: Overseas Development Institute.

Davis, Lance E. and Robert A. Huttenback (1986). *Mamon and the Pursuit of Empire: The Political Economy of British Imperialism, 1860–1912*. Cambridge: Cambridge University Press.

de Guzman, Leonardo P. (1964). "The Effect of Productivity and Technological Change on Savings and Capital Accumulation in Philippine Agriculture." *Philippine Economic Journal* 3, 2d semester: 169–83.

de Janvry, Alain (1981). *The Agrarian Question and Reformism in Latin America*. Baltimore: Johns Hopkins University Press.

De Melo, Jaime A. P. (1987). "Effects of Foreign Aid: Issues and Evidence." World Bank Development Research Department Discussion Paper No. 300. Washington, D.C.

Demerath, Nicholas J. (1976). *Birth Control and Foreign Policy*. New York: Harper and Row.

Denison, Edward F. (1962). *The Sources of Economic Growth in the United States and the Alternatives Before Us*. Washington, D.C.: Committee for Economic Development.

den Tuinder, Basitiaan A. (1978). *Ivory Coast: The Challenge of Success*. Baltimore: Johns Hopkins University Press.

348   REFERENCES

Diaz-Alejandro, Carlos (1965). "On the Import Intensity of Import Substitution." *Kyklos* 18, fasc. 3: 495–511.
Donald, Gordon, ed. (1976). *Credit for Small Farmers in Developing Countries*. Prepared for US/AID by the National Planning Association. Boulder, Colo.: Westview Press.
Dornbusch, Rudiger and Yung Chul Park (1987). "Korean Growth Policy." *Brookings Papers on Economic Activity* 2: 389–444.
Douglass, Mike (1984). "The Korean *Saemaul Undong*: Accelerated Rural Development in an Open Economy." In *Rural Development and the State*, ed. David A. M. Lea and D. P. Chaudhri, pp. 186–214. New York: Methuen.
Dovring, Folke (1970). "Economic Results of Land Reforms." In *Spring Review of Land Reform*. Washington, D.C.: US/AID.
Downs, Anthony (1957). *An Economic Theory of Democracy*. New York: Harper and Row.
Drake, Louis S. (1952). "Comparative Productivity of Share- and Cash-Rent Systems of Tenure." *Journal of Farm Economics* 34 (November): 535–60.
Dunlop, David W. (1982). *Toward a Health Project Evaluation Framework*. US/AID Evaluation Special Study No. 8. Washington, D.C., June.
Dunlop, David W., B. Eilene Oldwine, Kyong-Kyun Chung and Bong-Young Kim (1982). *Korean Health Demonstration Project*. US/AID Project Impact Evaluation Report No. 36. Washington, D.C.
Easter, K. William (1986). *Irrigation Investment, Technology, and Management Strategies for Development*. Boulder, Colo: Westview Press.
Eckaus, Richard (1955). "The Factor Proportion Problem in Underdeveloped Areas." *American Economic Review* 45 (December): 539–65.
Eckstein, Shlomo, Gordon Donald, Douglas Horton and Thomas Carroll (1978). *Land Reform in Latin America: Bolivia, Chile, Mexico, Peru and Venezuela*. World Bank Staff Working Paper No. 275. Washington, D.C.
Economist Intelligence Unit (1982). *Quarterly Economic Review—Ghana*, no. 1. London: Economist.
Eicher, Carl, Thomas Zalla, James Kocher and Fred Winch (1970). *Employment Generation in African Agriculture*. Research Report No. 9, Institute of International Agriculture, College of Agriculture and Natural Resources, Michigan State University, East Lansing, July.
Ensor, Paul (1984). "South Korea." *Far Eastern Economic Review*, 27 September, pp. 94–106.
Esman, Milton J. (1962). "Institution Building in National Development." *International Development Review* 4 (December): 27–30.
Esman, Milton J. and Norman T. Uphoff (1984). *Local Organizations: Intermediaries in Rural Development*. Ithaca: Cornell University Press.
Evenson, Robert E. (1977). "Cycles in Research Productivity in Sugarcane, Wheat and Rice." In *Resource Allocation and Productivity in National and International Agricultural Research*, pp. 209–36. See Arndt, Dalrymple, and Ruttan (1977).
Evenson, Robert E. and Yoav Kislev (1975). *Agricultural Research and Productivity*. New Haven: Yale University Press.
Evenson, Robert E., Paul E. Waggoner, and Vernon W. Ruttan (1979). "Economic

Benefits from Research: An Example from Agriculture." *Science* 205 (September 14): 1101–17.

Faaland, Just (1981). *Aid and Influence: The Case of Bangladesh.* New York: St. Martin's Press.

Falcon, Walter P. and Carl H. Gotsch (1968). *Agricultural Policy and Performance in the Punjab: A Comparative Study of India and Pakistan.* Economic Development Report No. 96, Development Advisory Service and Project for Quantitative Research in Economic Development, Harvard University, Cambridge, May.

Family Health Care (1977). *A Review of the Philippines' Population Program: The Family Health Care Report.* Washington, D.C.

Feder, Ernest (1965). "Land Reform under the Alliance for Progress." *Journal of Farm Economics* 47 (August): 652–68.

Feder, Gershon, Richard Just, and David Zilberman (1985). "Adoption of Agricultural Innovations in Developing Countries: A Survey." *Economic Development and Cultural Change* 33 (January): 255–98.

Feder, Gershon, Lawrence Lau, and Roger H. Slade (1987). "Does Agricultural Extension Pay? The Training and Visit System in Northwest India." *American Journal of Agricultural Economics* 69 (August): 677–86.

Fei, John H.H. and Gustav Ranis (1968). "Foreign Assistance and Economic Development: Comment." *American Economic Review* 58 (September): 897–912.

Feinberg, Richard E., ed. (1986). *Between Two Worlds: The World Bank's Next Decade.* New Brunswick, N.J.: Transaction Books for Overseas Development Council.

Feldstein, Martin and Charles Horioka (1980). "Domestic Savings and International Capital Movements in the Long Run and the Short Run." *Economic Journal* 90 (June): 314–29.

Fields, Gary S. (1985). "Industrialization and Employment in Hong Kong, Korea, Singapore and Taiwan." In *Foreign Trade and Investment*, pp. 333–75. *See* Balassa (1985).

Finkle, Jason L. and Barbara Crane (1975). "The Politics of Bucharest: Population, Development and the New International Order." *Population and Development Review* (September): 2–44.

——— (1985). "Ideology and Politics at Mexico City: The United States at the 1984 International Conference on Population." *Population and Development Review* 11 (March): 1–28.

Finkle, Jason L. and Alison McIntosh (1980). "Policy Responses to Population Stagnation in Developed Societies." In *The Social, Economic and Health Aspects of Low Fertility*, ed. Arthur A. Campbell, pp. 279–96. Washington, D.C.: GPO.

Food and Agriculture Organization of the United Nations (FAO) (1952–72). *Production Yearbook.* Rome.

France, Ministère de la Coopération (1976). *Côte d'Ivoire: Données statistiques sur les activités économiques, culturelles, et sociales.* Paris.

Franke, Richard W. and Barbara H. Chasin (1980). *Seeds of Famine: Ecological Destruction and the Development Dilemma in the West African Sahel.* Montclair, N.J.: Allanheld, Osman.

Frankel, Francine (1977). *India's Political Economy, 1947–1977.* Princeton: Princeton University Press.

Frankel, Jeffrey A., Michael Dooley and Donald Mathieson (1986). *International Capital Mobility in Developing Countries vs. Industrial Countries: What Do Savings-Investment Correlations Tell Us?* National Bureau of Economic Research Working Paper No. 2043. Cambridge, Mass.

Freedman, Ronald and Bernard Berelson (1976). "The Record of Family Planning Programs." *Studies in Family Planning* 7 (January): 1–40.

Freeman, Howard E., Peter H. Rossi, and Sonia R. Wright (1980). *Evaluating Social Projects in Developing Countries.* Paris: OECD Development Centre.

Friedmann, Wolfgang G., George Kalmanoff, and Robert F. Meagher (1966). *International Financial Aid.* New York: Colombia University Press.

Fry, Maxwell J. (1971). "Turkey's First Five-Year Development Plan: An Assessment." *Economic Journal* 81 (June): 306–26.

——— (1988). *Money, Interest, and Banking in Economic Development.* Baltimore: Johns Hopkins University Press.

Garzon, Jose M. (1984). "Food Aid as a Tool of Development." *Food Policy* 9 (August): 32–44.

Georgescu-Roegen, Nicholas N. (1960). "Economic Theory and Agrarian Economics." *Oxford Economic Papers,* n.s., 12 (February): 1–40.

Ghai, D. P., A. R. Khan, E. L. H. Lee, and T. Alfthan (1977). *The Basic-Needs Approach to Development: Some Issues Regarding Concepts and Methodology.* Geneva: International Labour Office.

Gilbert, Elon. (1972). *Alternative Pricing Policies for Fertilizers.* Staff Study, Nigeria, Ministry of Agriculture, Planning and Coordination Unit.

Gilbert, Frederick E. (1976). "The Distributive Effects of Economic Policy during the Period of Stabilization and Reform in Ghana, 1966–69." Ph.D. Diss., Fletcher School of Law and Diplomacy, Tufts University.

Glick, Philip M. (1957). *The Administration of Technical Assistance.* Chicago: University of Chicago Press.

Gordon, Sara L. (1974). "The Role of Cocoa in Ghanaian Development." In *Commodity Exports and African Economic Development,* ed. Scott R. Pearson and John Cownie, pp. 67–89. Lexington, Mass: Lexington Books.

Gorman, Robert F., ed. (1984). *Private Voluntary Organizations as Agents of Development.* Boulder, Colo.: Westview Press.

Gorun, Guler and Kutlu Somel (1979). *Bibliography of Economics of Agriculture in Turkey, 1960–1975.* Middle East Technical University, Economic and Social Research Institute, Working Paper No. 1. Ankara, January.

Gotsch, Carl and Gilbert Brown (1980). *Prices, Taxes and Subsidies in Pakistan Agriculture, 1960–1976.* World Bank Staff Working Paper No. 387. Washington, D.C.

Government of India, 1976–85. *Economic Survey, 1975–76* to *1984–85.* New Delhi: Government of India Press.

——— (1985). *External Assistance 1984–85.* New Delhi: Government of India Press.

Grant, James P. (1978). *Disparity Reduction Rates in Social Indicators: A Proposal for Measuring and Targeting Progress in Meeting Basic Needs.* Overseas Development Council Monograph No. 11. Washington, D.C., September.

Greenaway, David (1987). "Characteristics of Industrialization and Economic Performance under Alternative Strategies." Background paper prepared for the World

Bank. *World Development Report, 1987*. Washington, D.C.

Griffin, Keith L. (1970). "Foreign Capital, Domestic Savings and Economic Development." *Bulletin of the Oxford University Institute of Economics and Statistics* 32 (May): 99–112.

Griffin, Keith L. and J. L. Enos (1970). "Foreign Assistance: Objectives and Consequences." *Economic Development and Cultural Change* 18 (April): 313–37.

Grinols, Earl L. and Jagdish N. Bhagwati (1976). "Foreign Capital, Savings and Dependence." *Review of Economics and Statistics* 58 (November): 416–24.

Gupta, Kanhaiya L. (1970). "Foreign Capital and Domestic Savings: A Test of Haavelmo's Hypothesis with Cross-Country Data: A Comment." *Review of Economics and Statistics* 52 (May): 214–16.

Guttentag, Jack M. and Richard J. Herring (1984). "Commercial Bank Lending to Less Developed Countries: From Overlending to Underlending to Structural Reform." *Brookings Papers in International Economics* 16 (June): 1–52.

Haaga, John (n.d.). "The Current State of Family Planning Program Evaluation: A Review of Two AID Projects." Palo Alto: Rand Graduate Institute. Mimeo.

Hagen, Everett E. (1962). *On the Theory of Social Change*. Homewood, Ill.: Dorsey Press.

——— (1980). *The Economics of Development*. 3d ed. Homewood, Ill.: Richard D. Irwin.

Hale, William (1981). *The Political and Economic Development of Modern Turkey*. New York: St. Martin's Press.

Halevi, N. (1976). "The Effects of Investment and Consumption of Import Surpluses of Developing Countries." *Economic Journal* 86 (December): 853–58.

Hankinson, Richard (1972). *Population Assistance to Asia 1960–1970*. Paris: OECD Development Centre.

Haq, M. Nural (1973). *Village Development in Bangladesh*. Comilla: Bangladesh Academy for Rural Development.

Haq, Mahbub ul (1967). "Tied Credits—A Quantitative Analysis." In *Capital Movements and Economic Development*, ed. John H. Adler, pp. 326–59. New York: St. Martin's Press.

Harberger, Arnold C. (1972). "Issues Concerning Capital Assistance to Less Developed Countries." *Economic Development and Cultural Change* 20 (July): 631–40.

——— (1987). "Reflections on Social Project Evaluation." In *Pioneers in Development*, 2d ser., ed. Gerald M. Meier, pp. 153–88. New York: Oxford University Press.

Hasan, Parvez (1976). *Korea: Problems and Issues in a Rapidly Growing Economy*. Baltimore: Johns Hopkins University Press.

Hayami, Yujiro and Vernon W. Ruttan (1985). *Agricultural Development: An International Perspective*. 2d ed. Baltimore: Johns Hopkins University Press.

Hayter, Teresa (1971). *Aid as Imperialism*. New York: Penguin Books.

Heiby, James, Gayl Ness, and Barbara Pillsbury (1979). *AID's Role in Indonesian Family Planning*. US/AID Program Evaluation Report No. 2. Washington, D.C.

Heller, Peter S. (1975). "A Model of Public Fiscal Behavior in Developing Countries: Aid, Investment and Taxation." *American Economic Review* 65 (June): 429–45.

Heller, Peter S. and Alan Tait (1983). *Government Employment and Pay: Some Inter-*

national Comparisons. IMF Occasional Paper No. 24. Washington, D.C.

Hendra, John (1987). "Only 'Fit to be Tied': A Comparison of the Canadian Tied Aid Policy with the Tied Aid Policies of Sweden, Norway, and Denmark." *Canadian Journal of Development Studies* 2: 261–81.

Hendrix, William E. and R. Giri (1970). *India's Agricultural Progress in the 1950s and 1960s.* New Delhi: Government of India, Directorate of Economics and Statistics.

Hermann, Eric R. (1981). *Analysis of Selected Agricultural Parastatals in the Ivory Coast.* Washington, D.C.: US/AID.

Hernandez, Donald (1984). *Success or Failure: Family Planning Programs in the Third World.* Westport, Conn.: Greenwood Press.

Herrin, Alejandro N. and Thomas W. Pullum (1981). "An Impact Assessment: Population Planning II." Prepared for the Commission on Population, Republic of the Philippines, and US/AID, Philippines. April. Mimeo.

Hershlag, Z. Y. (1968). *Turkey and the Challenge of Growth.* Leiden: E. J. Brill.

Hertford, Reed (1970a). "Mexico: Its Sources of Increased Agricultural Output." In *Economic Progress of Agriculture in Developing Nations, 1958–1968,* pp. 90–104. Washington, D.C.: Economic Research Service, U.S. Department of Agriculture, May.

——— (1970b). "Sources of Change in Mexican Agricultural Production, 1940–65." Ph.D. diss., Department of Economics, University of Chicago.

Herz, Barbara K. (1984). *Official Development Assistance for Population Activities: A Review.* World Bank Staff Working Paper No. 688. Washington, D.C.

Heyneman, S. P. (1985). *Investing in Education: A Quarter Century of World Bank Experience.* World Bank Economic Development Institute Seminar Paper No. 30. Washington, D.C., June.

Hill, John M. (1969). *Recommendations and Projections for the Turkish Fertilizer Industry.* Ankara: US/AID.

Hillman, Jimmye S. (1981). "The Role of Export Cropping in Less Developed Countries." *American Journal of Agricultural Economics* 63 (May): 375–83.

Hirschman, Albert O. (1982). "The Rise and Decline of Development Economics." In *The Theory and Experience of Economic Development: Essays in Honor of Sir Arthur W. Thor Lewis,* ed. Mark Gersovitz, Carlos F. Diaz-Alejandro, Gustav Ranis, and Mark R. Rosenzweig, pp. 372–90. London: Allen and Unwin.

Holdcraft, Lane E. (1978). *The Rise and Fall of Community Development in Developing Countries, 1950–65: A Critical Analysis and an Annotated Bibliography.* Rural Development Paper No. 2, Michigan State University, East Lansing.

Horton, C. R. (1964). *Project History and Analysis Report: Agricultural Extension.* TOAIDA-716. Ankara: US/AID, 27 October.

Huffman, Wallace E. (1978). "Assessing Returns to Agricultural Extension." *American Journal of Agricultural Economics* 60 (December): 969–75.

Humphreys, Charles P. (1981). "Rice Production in the Ivory Coast." In *Rice in West Africa: Policy and Economics,* ed. Scott R. Pearson, J. Dirck Stryker, and Charles P. Humphreys, pp. 61–105. Stanford: Stanford University Press.

Hunter, Guy (1970). *The Administration of Agricultural Development: Lessons from India.* London: Oxford University Press.

Huntington, Samuel P. (1970/71). "Foreign Aid for What and for Whom." *Foreign Policy* 2 (Winter): 161–89.

Hurwicz, Leonid (1972). "Organizational Structures for Joint Decision Making: A Designer's Point of View." In *Interorganizational Decision Making*, ed. Matthew Tuite, Roger Chisholm, and Michael Radnor, pp. 37–44. Chicago: Aldine.

Hymer, Stephen H. (1971). "The Political Economy of the Gold Coast and Ghana." In *Government and Economic Development*, pp. 129–78. See Cooper (1971).

Independent Commission on International Development Issues (Brandt Commission) (1983). *Common Crisis: North South Cooperation for World Recovery.* London: Pan.

Independent Group on British Aid (1982). *Real Aid: A Strategy for Britain.* Report of the Elliott Group. London.

Inter-American Development Bank (1982, 1983). *Annual Report on Operation Evaluation.* Washington, D.C.

International Bank for Reconstruction and Development (IBRD) (1951). *The Economy of Turkey: An Analysis and Recommendations for a Development Program.* Baltimore: Johns Hopkins Press.

International Development Cooperation Agency (1984). *1984 Annual Report of the Development Coordination Committee.* Washington, D.C.: GPO.

International Labour Office (1977). *Employment, Growth and Basic Needs: A One-World Problem.* New York: Praeger for Overseas Development Council.

Isaacs, Stephen L. (1981). *Population Law and Policy.* New York: Human Sciences Press.

Isenman, Paul and Hans W. Singer (1977). "Food Aid: Disincentive Effects and Their Policy Implications." *Economic Development and Cultural Change* 25 (January): 205–38.

Islam, Nurul (1972). "Foreign Assistance and Economic Development: The Case of Pakistan." *Economic Journal*, special issue, 82 (March): 502–28.

Ivory Coast (1960). *Inventaire économique et social de la Côte d'Ivoire—1958.* Ministère des Finances, des Affaires Economiques et du Plan, Service de la Statistique. Abidjan.

Jacoby, Neil, H. (1966). "An Evaluation of United States Economic Aid to Free China, 1951–1965." US/AID Discussion Paper No. 11. Washington, D.C.

Jaynes, Gerald D. (1984). "Economic Theory and Land Tenure." In *Contractual Arrangements, Employment and Wages*, pp. 43–62. See Binswanger and Rosenzweig (1984).

Jha, Lakshmi Kant K. (1973). "Comment: Leaning against Open Doors?" In *The World Bank Group, Multilateral Aid, and the 1970s*, pp. 97–101. See Cargill (1973).

Johnson, D. Gale (1950). "Resource Allocation under Share Contracts." *Journal of Political Economy* 58 (April): 111–23.

Johnson, Harry G. (1963). "Towards a Generalized Capital Accumulation Approach to Economic Development." In *The Canadian Quandary: Economic Problems and Policies*, pp. 227–52. Toronto: McGraw-Hill.

——— (1967). *Economic Policies toward Less Developed Countries.* Washington, D.C.: Brookings Institution.

Johnson, Harvey P. H. (1971). *High Yielding Winter Wheat for Turkey: A Progress Report*. Ankara: US/AID.

Johnson, Jeffalyn and Associates (1980). *A Review of United States Assistance to Pakistan, 1952–1980*. Washington, D.C.: US/AID.

Johnston, Bruce F. and William C. Clark (1982). *Redesigning Rural Development: A Strategic Perspective*. Baltimore: Johns Hopkins University Press.

Johnston, Bruce F., Allan Hoben, Dirk W. Dijkerman, and William K. Jaeger (1987). *An Assessment of AID Activities to Promote Agricultural and Rural Development in Sub-Saharan Africa*. MADIA Research Report No. 12. Washington, D.C.: World Bank, February.

Johnston, Bruce F. and Anthony J. Meyer (1977). "Nutrition, Health, and Population in Strategies for Rural Development." *Economic Development and Cultural Change* 26 (October): 1–23.

Jones, Gavin (1979). "Forms of AID: Population Control." In *International Aid*, pp. 212–34. *See* Arndt (1979).

Jones, Leroy P. and Il SaKong (1980). *Government, Business and Entrepreneurship in Economic Development: The Korean Case*. Cambridge: Harvard University Press.

Jorgenson, Dale (1961). "The Development of a Dual Economy." *Economic Journal* 71 (June): 309–31.

Judd, M. Ann, James K. Boyce, and Robert E. Evenson (1986). "Investing in Agricultural Supply: The Determinants of Agricultural Research and Extension Investment." *Economic Development and Cultural Change* 35 (October): 77–113.

Kane, Edward J. (1984). "Political Economy of Subsidizing Agricultural Credit in Developing Countries." In *Undermining Rural Development with Cheap Credit*, pp. 166–83. *See* Bourne and Graham (1984).

Karunaratne, Neil Dias (1986). "A Holistic Analysis of Trade versus Aid Issues: World and Australian Insights." *The Developing Economies* 24 (March): 44–55.

Kaufman, Burton I. (1968). *Trade and Aid: Eisenhower's Foreign Economic Policy, 1953–1961*. Baltimore: Johns Hopkins Press.

Kennedy, Joseph V. and Vernon W. Ruttan (1986). "A Reexamination of Professional and Popular Thought on Assistance for Economic Development: 1949–1952." *Journal of Developing Areas* 20 (April): 297–326.

Khan, Akhter Hameed (1974). "The Comilla Projects—A Personal Account." *International Development Review* 16 (September): 2–7.

Khan, Azizan Rahman (1979). "The Comilla Model and the Integrated Rural Development Program of Bangladesh: An Experiment in Co-operative Capitalism." In *Agrarian Systems in Rural Development*, ed. Dharam Ghai, Azizan Rahman Khan, Eddy Lee, and Samir Radwan, pp. 113–58. New York: Holmes and Meier.

Khan, Mohsen S., Peter Montiel and Nadeem U. Haque (1986). *Adjustment with Growth: Relating to Analytical Approaches of the World Bank and the IMF*. World Bank Development Policy Issues Discussion Paper Series, VPERS8. Washington, D.C.

Killick, Tony (1985). "Economic Environment and Agricultural Development." *Food Policy* 10 (February): 29–40.

Kim, Chuk Kyo, ed. (1977a). *Essays on the Korean Economy.* Vol. 1, *Planning Model and Macroeconomic Issues.* Seoul: Korea Development Institute; Honolulu: University Press of Hawaii.

——— (1977b). *Essays on the Korean Economy.* Vol. 2, *Industrial and Social Development Issues.* Seoul: Korea Development Institute; Honolulu: University Press of Hawaii.

——— (1980a). *Essays on the Korean Economy.* Vol. 3, *Macroeconomic and Industrial Development in Korea.* Seoul: Korea Development Institute; Honolulu: University Press of Hawaii.

——— (1980b). *Essays on the Korean Economy.* Vol 4, *Human Resources and Social Development in Korea.* Seoul: Korea Development Institute; Honolulu: University Press of Hawaii.

Kim, Kwang-suk and Joon-kyung Park (1985). *Sources of Economic Growth in Korea: 1963–1982.* Seoul: Korea Development Institute.

Kim, Kwang-suk and Michael Roemer (1979). *Growth and Structural Transformation Studies in the Modernization of the Republic of Korea: 1945–1975.* Harvard East Asian Monograph 86. Cambridge: Harvard University Press.

Kim, Sooyong (1988). "The Korean Construction Industry as an Exporter of Services." *The World Bank Economic Review* 2 (May): 225–38.

Kjellstron, Sven B. and A. d'Almeida (1986). "Aid Cooperation: A Recipient's Perspective." *Finance and Development* 23 (September): 37–40.

Knodel, John and Tony Bennett (1984). "Do Free Pills Make a Difference? Thailand's Experience." *International Family Planning Perspectives* 10 (September): 93–97.

Korea Development Institute (1984). *KDI Quarterly Economic Outlook.* Seoul, Fall.

Korten, David C. (1975). "Integrated Approaches to Family Planning Service Delivery." Development Discussion Paper No. 10. Cambridge: Harvard Institute for International Development.

——— (1980). "Community Organization and Rural Development: A Learning Process Approach." *Public Administration Review* 40 (September–October): 480–511. Reprinted as a Ford Foundation Reprint.

Korten, David C., ed. (1987). *Community Management: Asian Experience and Perspectives.* West Hartford, Conn.: Kumarian Press.

Korten, Francis F. (1982). "Building National Capacity to Develop Water Users Associations." World Bank Staff Working Paper No. 528. Washington, D.C., July.

Krauss, Melvyn B. (1983). *Development Without Aid: Growth, Poverty and Government.* New York: McGraw-Hill.

Krishna, Raj (1967). "Agricultural Price Policy and Economic Development." In *Agricultural Development and Economic Growth,* ed. Herman M. Southworth and Bruce F. Johnston, pp. 497–540. Ithaca: Cornell University Press.

——— (1980). "The Economic Development of India." In *Economic Development,* pp. 78–85. A Scientific American Book. San Francisco: W. H. Freeman and Co.

Krueger, Anne O. (1974a). *Foreign Trade Regimes and Economic Development: Turkey.* New York: National Bureau of Economic Research.

——— (1974b). "The Political Economy of the Rent Seeking Society." *American Economic Review* 64 (June): 291–303.

——— (1978). *Foreign Trade Regimes and Economic Development: Liberalization Attempts and Consequences.* Cambridge, Mass.: Ballinger for National Bureau of Economic Research.

——— (1979). *The Development Role of the Foreign Sector and Aid.* Cambridge: Harvard University Press.

——— (1983). *Trade and Employment in Developing Countries.* Vol. 3, *Synthesis and Conclusions.* Chicago: University of Chicago Press.

——— (1984a). "Comparative Advantage and Development Policy Twenty Years Later." In *Economic Structure and Performance,* ed. Moshe Syrquin, Lance Taylor, and Larry Westphal, pp. 135–56. New York: Academic Press.

——— (1984b). "The Newly Industrializing Countries: Experience and Lessons." In *Studies in United States–Asia Economic Relations,* ed. M. Dutta, pp. 253–74. Durham, N.C.: Acorn Press.

——— (1986). "Aid in the Development Process." *Research Observer* 1 (January): 57–78.

——— (1987a). "Debts, Capital Flows and Growth." *American Economic Review* 77 (May): 159–64.

——— (1987b). "Origins of the Developing Countries' Debt Crisis: 1970 to 1982." *Journal of Development Economics,* special issue, 27 (October): 165–87.

Krueger, Anne O. and Constantine Michalopoulos (1985). "Developing Country Trade Policies and the International Economic System." In *Hard Bargaining Ahead: United States Trade Policy and Developing Countries,* ed. E. Preeg, pp. 39–57. New Brunswick, N.J.: Transaction Books for Overseas Development Council.

Krueger, Anne O. and Vernon W. Ruttan (1983). *The Development Impact of Economic Assistance to LDC's.* St. Paul and Minneapolis: University of Minnesota Economic Development Center for US/AID and the Department of State, March. Mimeo. Vols. 1 and 2.

Kuroda, Toshio (1987). "Overview of Urbanization Trends and Development." In *Population and Development in Medium-Sized Cities.* Tokyo: Nihon University Population Research Institute.

Kuznets, Paul W. (1977). *Economic Growth and Structure in the Republic of Korea.* New Haven: Yale University Press.

Lacroix, Richard L. J. (1985). *Integrated Rural Development in Latin America.* World Bank Staff Working Paper No. 716. Washington, D.C.

Laing, John E. (1981). *Family Planning Outreach in the Philippines: Final Report on the Community Outreach Surveys.* Manila: University of the Philippines Population Institute.

——— (1987). "Periodic Abstinence in the Philippines: New Findings from a National Survey." *Studies in Family Planning* 18 (January–February): 2–8.

Lal, Deepak (1983). *The Poverty of Development Economics.* London: Institute of Economic Affairs, Hobart Paperback No. 16.

——— (1987). "Reflections on Social Project Analysis: Comment." In *Pioneers in Development,* pp. 193–202. See Harberger (1972).

Landau, Daniel (1986). "Government and Economic Growth in the Less Developed Countries: An Empirical Study for 1960–1980." *Economic Development and Cultural Change,* 35 (October): 35–75.

Lapham, Robert J. and W. Parker Mauldin (1972). "National Family Planning Programs: Review and Evaluation." *Studies in Family Planning* 3 (March): 29–52.

Lavy, V. (1985). "Anticipated Development Assistance, Temporary Relief Aid, and
Consumption Behaviour of Low-Income Countries." Washington, D.C.: World
Bank. Mimeo.

Leff, Nathaniel H. (1968). "Marginal Savings Rate in Development Process: The Brazilian Experience." *Economic Journal* 78 (September): 610–23.

——— (1975). "Rates of Return to Capital, Domestic Savings, and Investment in the
Developing Countries." *Kyklos* 28, fasc. 1: 827–51.

——— (1985). "The Use of Policy Science Tools in Public Sector Decision Making:
Social Benefit Cost Analysis in the World Bank." *Kyklos* 38, fasc. 1: 60–76.

Leith, J. Clark (1974). *Foreign Trade Regimes and Economic Development: Ghana.*
New York: Columbia University Press for National Bureau of Economic
Research.

Lele, Uma (1979). *The Design of Rural Development: Lessons from Africa.* 3d print-
ing with new postscript. Baltimore: Johns Hopkins University Press for the World
Bank.

Lele, Uma and Arthur A. Goldsmith (1989). "The Development of National Agricul-
tural Research Capacity: India's Experience with the Rockefeller Foundation and
Its Significance for Africa." *Economic Development and Cultural Change* 37
(January): 305–43.

——— (1984). "Tanzania: Phoenix or Icarus?" In *World Economic Growth*, ed.
Arnold C. Harberger, pp. 159–95. San Francisco: Institute for Contemporary
Studies.

——— (1988). "Agricultural Growth, Domestic Policy and External Assistance to
Africa: Lessons of a Quarter Century." Washington, D.C.: IBRD. Mimeo.

Lele, Uma and L. Richard Meyers (1987). *Growth and Structural Change in East
Africa: Domestic Policies, Agricultural Performance and World Bank Assis-
tance, 1963–1986, Part II.* MADIA Research Report No. 14. Washington, D.C.:
World Bank.

Lerner, Abba P. (1944). *The Economics of Control.* New York: Macmillan.

Lethem, Francis and Lauren Cooper (1983). *Managing Project Related Technical Assistance: The Lessons of Success.* Washington, D.C.: World Bank.

Lewis, John P. and Valeriana Kallab, eds. (1986). *Development Strategies Reconsidered.* New Brunswick, N.J.: Transaction Books for Overseas Development
Council.

Lewis, W. Arthur (1954). "Economic Development with Unlimited Supplies of Labor." *Manchester School of Economic and Social Studies* 22 (May): 139–91.

Lipton, Michael, John F. J. Toye, and Robert H. Cassen (1984). "Aid-Effectiveness:
India." Mimeo.

Little, Ian M. D. and J. M. Clifford (1965). *International Aid.* London: Allen and
Unwin.

Little, Ian M. D. and James A. Mirrlees (1969). *Manual of Industrial Project Analysis.* Vol. 2, *Social Cost Benefit Analysis.* Paris: OECD Development Centre.

Lockhead, Marlaine E., Dean T. Jamison, and Lawrence J. Lau (1980). "Farmer
Education and Farm Efficiency: A Survey." *Economic Development and Cultural
Change* 29 (October): 37–76.

Long, Millard F. (1968a). "Interest Rates and the Structure of Agricultural Credit Markets." *Oxford Economic Papers*, n.s., 20 (July): 275–88.

——— (1968b). "Why Peasant Farmers Borrow." *American Journal of Agricultural Economics* 50 (November): 991–1008.

Lowdermilk, Max K. (1981). *Promoting Increased Food Production in the 1980s: Approaches to Agricultural Extension in Different Production Systems*. Washington, D.C.: US/AID, May.

Lucas, Robert E., Jr. (1988). "On the Mechanics of Economic Development." *Journal of Monetary Economics* 22 (July): 3–42.

McGinn, Noel F., Donald R. Snodgrass, Yung Bong Kim, Shin-Bok Kim, and Quee-Young Kim (1980). *Education and Economic Development in Korea*. Cambridge: Harvard University Press.

McKinlay, Robert D. (1978). "The German Aid Relationship: A Test of the Recipient Need and the Donor-Interest Models of the Distribution of German Bilateral Aid, 1961–1970." *European Journal of Political Research* 6 (September): 235–57.

McKinlay, Robert D. and R. Little (1977). "A Foreign Policy Model of United States Bilateral Aid Allocation." *World Politics* 30 (October): 58–86.

——— (1978a). "The French Aid Relationship: A Foreign Policy Model of the Distribution of French Bilateral Aid, 1964–1970." *Development and Change* 9 (July): 457–78.

——— (1978b). "A Foreign Policy Model of the Distribution of British Bilateral Aid, 1960–1970." *British Journal of Political Science* 8 (July): 313–32.

——— (1979). "The United States Aid Relationship: A Test of the Recipient-Need and the Donor-Interest Model." *Political Studies* 27 (June): 236–50.

McKinnon, Ron (1986). "Comment." In *Economic Liberalization in Developing Countries*, ed. Armeane Choksi and Demetris Papageorgiou, pp. 219–23. Oxford and New York: Basil Blackwell.

McKitterick, Nathaniel and B. Jenkins Middleton (1972). *The Bankers of the Rich and the Bankers of the Poor: The Role of Export Credit in Development Finance*. Washington, D.C.: Overseas Development Council.

McMurtry, Virginia A. (1974). "Foreign Aid and Political Development: The American Experience in West Africa." Ph.D. diss., Department of Political Science, University of Wisconsin.

McNamara, Robert S. (1973). *Address to the Board of Governors*. Washington, D.C.: World Bank, September.

McNicoll, Geoffrey and Masri Singarimbun (1982). "Fertility Decline in Indonesia I: Background and Proximate Determinants," and "II: Analysis and Interpretation." *Working Papers* 92 (November): 1–52 and 93 (December): 1–49. New York: Population Council Center for Policy Studies.

McPherson, Peter (1986). "We Weren't Looking for a Quick Fix." *New York Times*, 23 November, Business section, p. 82.

Maddox, James G., (1956). *Technical Assistance by Religious Agencies in Latin America*. Chicago: University of Chicago Press.

Maddox, James G. and Howard R. Tolley (1957). *Case Studies of Training through Technical Cooperation*. Washington, D.C.: National Planning Association.

Maizels, Alfred and Machiko K. Nissanke (1984). "Motivations for Aid to Developing Countries." *World Development* 12 (September): 879–900.

Mandelbaum, Kurt (1947). *The Industrialization of Backward Areas*. Oxford University Institute of Statistics Monograph No. 2. Oxford.

Mann, Charles (1972). *Formulating a Consistent Strategy Toward On-Farm Land Development in Turkey*. US/AID Economic Staff Paper No. 8. Ankara.

—— (1980). "Effects of Government Policy on Income Distribution: A Case Study of Wheat Production in Turkey." In *Political Economy of Income Distribution*, ed. Ergun Ozbudun and Aydin Ulusan, pp. 197–245. New York: Holmes and Meier.

Mann, Charles and Bill C. Wright (1982). "Turkish Cereals Project Review." Ankara. Mimeo.

Mann, J. S. (1967). "The Impact of Public Law 480 Imports on Prices and Domestic Supply of Cereals in India." *Journal of Farm Economics* 49 (February): 131–46.

Mansfield, Edwin (1977). "Social and Private Rates of Return from Industrial Innovation." *Quarterly Journal of Economics* 91 (May): 221–40.

Masefield, G. B. (1972). *A History of the Colonial Agricultural Service*. London: Oxford University Press.

Mason, Edward S. and Robert E. Asher (1973). *The World Bank since Bretton Woods*. Washington, D.C.: The Brookings Institution.

Mason, Edward S., Mahn Je Kim, Dwight H. Perkins, Kwong-suk Kim, and David C. Cole (1980). *The Economic and Social Modernization of the Republic of Korea*. Cambridge: Harvard University Press.

Massell, Benton F., Scott R. Pearson, and James B. Fitch (1972). "Foreign Exchange and Economic Development: An Empirical Study of Selected Latin American Countries." *Review of Economics and Statistics* 54 (May): 208–12.

Mawhood, Philip, ed. (1983). *Local Government in the Third World: The Experience of Tropical Africa*. New York: John Wiley and Sons.

Mayer, Albert, and Associates, with McKim Marriott and Richard L. Park (1958). *Pilot Project, India*. Berkeley: University of California Press.

Measham, Anthony R. (1986). *Review of PHN Sector Work and Lending in Health, 1980–85*. World Bank Population, Health and Nutrition Department Technical Note 86-14. Washington, D.C., March.

Mellor, John S. (1976). *The New Economics of Growth*. Ithaca: Cornell University Press.

Michalopoulos, Constantine (1975). "Production and Substitution in Two-Gap Models." *Journal of Development Studies* 11 (July): 343–56.

—— (1987). "World Bank Programs for Adjustment and Growth." In *Growth-Oriented Adjustment Programs*, ed. Vittorio Corbo, Morris Goldstein, and Mohsin Khan, pp. 12–65. Washington, D.C.: IMF.

Michalopoulos, Constantine and Keith Jay (1973). "Growth of Exports and Income in the Developing World: A Neoclassical View." US/AID Discussion Paper No. 28. Washington, D.C.

Michel, Gilles and Michael Noel. (1984). "The Ivorian Economy and Alternative Trade Regimes." In *The Political Economy of Ivory Coast*, ed. I. William Zartman and Christopher Delgado, pp. 77–114. New York: Praeger.

Mikesell, Raymond F. (1968). *Economics of Foreign Aid*. Chicago: Aldine.

Mikesell, Raymond F., with Robert A. Kilmarx and Arvin M. Kramish (1983). *The*

Economics of Foreign Aid and Self-Sustaining Development. Boulder, Colo.: Westview Press.

Millikan, Max F. and David Hapgood (1967). *No Easy Harvest: The Dilemma of Agriculture in Underdeveloped Countries.* Boston: Little, Brown and Co.

Millikan, Max F. and W. E. Rostow (1957). *A Proposal: A Key to Effective Foreign Policy.* New York: Harper and Row.

Mills, Edwin S. and Byung-Nak Song (1979). *Urbanization and Urban Problems.* Cambridge: Harvard University Press.

Miyamoto, Ichizo (1974). "The Real Value of Tied Aid: The Case of Indonesia in 1967–69." *Economic Development and Cultural Change* 22 (April): 436–52.

Montgomery, John D. (1972). "Allocation of Authority in Land Reform Programs: A Cooperative Study of Administrative Processes and Outputs." *Administrative Science Quarterly* 17 (March): 62–75.

——— (1988). *Bureaucrats and People: Grassroots Participation in Third World Development.* Baltimore: Johns Hopkins University Press.

Moon, Pal Yong (1977). "The Evolution of Rice Policy in Korea." In *Essays on the Korean Economy*, 2:3–41. *See* Kim (1977b).

Morawetz, David (1977). *Twenty-Five Years of Economic Development.* Baltimore: Johns Hopkins University Press.

——— (1981). *Why the Emperor's New Clothes Are Not Made in Colombia: A Case Study in Latin American and East Asian Manufactured Exports.* London: Oxford University Press.

Moris, Jon R. (1981). *Managing Induced Rural Development.* Bloomington: International Development Institute, Indiana University.

Morrison, Thomas L. and Jerome M. Wolgin. (1980). "Prospects for Economic Stabilization in Ghana." Paper presented at the twenty-third annual meeting of the African Studies Association, Philadelphia, Pa., 15–18 October 1980.

Morss, Eliott (1984). "Institutional Destruction Resulting from Donor and Project Proliferation in Sub-Saharan African Countries." *World Development* 12 (April): 465–70.

Moseman, Albert H. (1970). *Building Agricultural Research Systems in Developing Nations.* New York: Agricultural Development Council.

Mosher, Arthur T. (1957). *Technical Cooperation in Latin-American Agriculture.* Chicago: University of Chicago Press.

——— (1976). *Thinking about Rural Development.* New York: Agricultural Development Council.

Mosley, Paul (1980). "Aid, Savings and Growth Revisited." *Bulletin of the Oxford University Institute of Economics and Statistics* 42 (May): 79–95.

——— (1985). "The Political Economy of Foreign Aid: A Model of the Market for a Public Good." *Economic Development and Cultural Change* 33 (January): 373–93.

Mosley, Paul, John Hudson, and Sara Horrell (1987). "Aid, The Public Sector and the Market in Less Developed Countries." *Economic Journal* 97 (September): 616–64.

Mukerjee, Tapan (1972). "Theory of Economic Drain: Impact of British Rule on the Indian Economy, 1840–1900." In *Economic Imperialism*, ed. Kenneth E.

Boulding and Tapan Mukerjee, pp. 195–212. Ann Arbor: University of Michigan Press.

Myfelka, Lynn Krieger (1984). "Foreign Business and Economic Development." In *The Political Economy of Ivory Coast*, pp. 149–73. *See* Michel and Noel (1984).

Nair, Kusum (1962). *Blossoms in the Dust*. New York: Praeger.

Narain, Dharm and V. K. R. V. Rao (1963). *Foreign Aid and India's Economic Development*. New York: Asia Publishing House.

Neale, Walter C. (1985). "Indian Community Development, Local Government, Local Planning and Rural Policy since 1950." *Economic Development and Cultural Change* 33 (July): 677–98.

Nelson, Joan M. (1986). "The Diplomacy of Policy-Based Lending." In *Between Two Worlds*, pp. 67–86. *See* Feinberg (1986).

Nelson, Michael (1973). *The Development of Tropical Lands*. Baltimore and London: Johns Hopkins Press.

Ness, Gayl D. (1976). "The Ethnic Numbers Game and Population Policy in Malaysia." Paper presented at the American Political Science Association meetings, Chicago, 2–5 September 1976.

—— (1979). "Organizational Issues in International Population Assistance." In *World Population and Development*, ed. Philip Hauser, pp. 615–49. Syracuse: Syracuse University Press.

—— (1984). "International Population Assistance to Asia." Paper presented at the annual meeting of the Population Association of America, Minneapolis, 3–5 May 1984.

Ness, Gayl D. and Hirofumi Ando (1984). *The Land Is Shrinking: Population Planning in Asia*. Baltimore: Johns Hopkins University Press.

Ness, Gayl D., J. Timothy Johnson, and Stan Bernstein (1983). *Program Performance: Assessment of Asian Family Planning Programs*. Technical Report to US/AID. Ann Arbor: University of Michigan Center for Population Planning.

Newbery, David M. G. (1975). "The Choice of Rental Contract in Peasant Agriculture." In *Agriculture in Development Theory*, ed. Lloyd G. Reynolds, pp. 109–37. New Haven: Yale University Press.

Newbery, David M. G. and Joseph E. Stiglitz (1979). "Sharecropping, Risk Sharing and the Importance of Imperfect Information." In *Risk, Uncertainty and Agricultural Development*, ed. James A. Roumasset, Jean-Marc Boussard, and Inderjit Singh, pp. 311–39. College, Laguna, Philippines: Southeast Asian Regional Center for Graduate Study and Research in Agriculture; New York: Agricultural Development Council.

Niskanen, William A., Jr. (1971). *Bureaucracy and Representative Government*. Chicago: Aldine-Alberton.

North, Douglass C. and Robert Paul Thomas (1970). "An Economic Theory of the Growth of the Western World." *Economic History Review* 23 (April): 1–17.

North, Haven (1982). Personal communication. North was the US/AID Mission director in Ghana from 1971 to 1976.

Nulty, Leslie (1972). *The Green Revolution in West Pakistan*. New York: Praeger.

Nyrop, Richard, ed. (1980). *Turkey: A Country Study*. Washington, D.C.: American University.

Oberai, A. S. (1988). *Land Settlement Policies and Population Redistribution in Developing Countries*. New York: Praeger.

Olson, Mancur, Jr. (1965). *The Logic of Collective Action: Public Goods and the Theory of Groups*. Cambridge: Harvard University Press.

Organization for Economic Cooperation and Development (OECD) (1966). *Geographical Distribution of Financial Flows to Developing Countries*. Paris.

——— (1968). *Population: International Assistance and Research*. Proceedings of the First Population Conference of the Development Centre. Paris.

——— (1974). *Agricultural Policy in Turkey*. Paris.

——— (1981). *Geographical Distribution of Financial Flows to Developing Countries*. Paris.

———. (1985). *Twenty-five Years of Development Cooperation: A Review—1985 Report*. Paris.

——— (1988). *Financing and External Debt of Developing Countries*, 1987 Survey. Paris.

Otten, A. and S. Reutlinger (1969). "Performance Evaluation of Eight Ongoing Irrigation Projects." IBRD Economics Department Working Paper No. 40. Washington, D.C.

Over, A. Mead, Jr. (1975). "An Example of the Simultaneous-Equation Problem: A Note on Foreign Assistance; Objective and Consequences." *Economic Development and Cultural Change* 23 (July): 751–56.

Painter, James E., Emily Baldwin, Sandra Malone, Ernest T. Smerdon, Akbar S. Ahmed, Masud A. Siddiqui, and Mahmood H. Kahn (1982). *The On-Farm Water Management Project in Pakistan*. US/AID Project Impact Evaluation Report No. 35. Washington, D.C.

Papageorgiou, Demetrios, Michael Michaely, and Armeane M. Choksi (1986). "The Phasing of a Trade Liberalization Policy: Preliminary Evidence." Paper presented at the annual meeting of the American Economic Association, 28–30 December, New Orleans.

Papanek, Gustav F. (1973a). "Aid, Foreign Private Investment, Savings and Growth in Less Developed Countries." *Journal of Political Economy* 81 (January–February): 120–30.

——— (1973b). "The Effect of Aid and Other Resource Transfers on Savings and Growth in Less-Developed Countries." *Economic Journal* 82 (September): 934–80.

Park, Jin Hwan (1981). "The Work of Agricultural Economists at Community, Village and Local Government Levels—Accomplishments and Challenges." In *Rural Change: The Challenge for Agricultural Economists*, ed. Glenn Johnson and Allen Maunder, pp. 147–85. Proceedings of the Seventeenth International Conference of Agricultural Economists, 3–12 September, 1979, Banff, Canada. Montclair, N.J.: Allanheld, Osmun and Co.

——— (1982). *Saemaul Movement in Korea*. Seoul: Agricultural Cooperative College.

Pastor, Robert A. (1980). *Congress and the Politics of United States Foreign Economic Policy*. Berkeley: University of California Press.

Patel, I. G. (1968). *Foreign Aid*. New Delhi: Allied Publishers.

—— (1986). *Essays in Economic Policy and Economic Growth*. New York: St. Martin's Press.

Pearson, Scott R., Gerald Nelson, and J. Dirck Stryker (1979). "Incentives and Comparative Advantage in Ghanaian Industry and Agriculture." Photocopy.

Pearson Commission. *See* Commission on International Development.

Peterson, Willis L. (1989). "Rates of Return Capital: An International Comparison." *Kyklos* 42 (Fasc. 2): 203–17.

Peterson Commission. *See* Task Force on International Development.

Pincus, John A. (1963). "The Cost of Foreign Aid." *Review of Economics and Statistics* 45 (November): 360–67.

Piñeiro, Martin and Eduardo Trigo (1983). *Technical Change and Social Conflict in Agriculture: Latin American Perspectives*. Boulder, Colo.: Westview Press.

Pitt, Mark M. (1981). "Smuggling and Price Disparity." *Journal of International Economics* 11 (November): 447–58.

Population Information Program (1985). "Fertility and Family Planning Surveys: An Update." *Population Reports*, series M, no. 8 (September–October).

Prebisch, Raul (1959). "Commercial Policy in the Underdeveloped Countries." *American Economic Review* 40 (May): 251–73.

President's Science Advisory Committee (1967). *World Food Problem*. Washington, D.C.: GAO.

Price, E. Frank (1970). *AID Educational Assistance to Turkey 1957–70*. Ankara: US/AID, July.

Psacharopoulos, George (1984). "The Contribution of Education to Economic Growth: International Comparisons." In *International Productivity Comparisons*, ed. John Kendrick, pp. 335–55. Cambridge, Mass.: Ballinger for the American Enterprise Institute.

—— (1985). "Returns to Education: A Further International Update and Implications." *Journal of Human Resources* 20 (Fall): 583–604.

Psacharopoulos, George and Maureen Woodhall (1985). *Education for Development: An Analysis of Investment Choices*. New York: Oxford University Press.

Rahman, M. Anisur (1968). "Foreign Capital and Domestic Savings: A Text of Haavelmo's Hypothesis with Cross Country Data." *Review of Economics and Statistics* 50 (February): 137–38.

Randhawa, M. S. (1979). *A History of the ICAR*. New Delhi: Indian Council of Agricultural Research.

Ranis, Gustav and J. C. H. Fei (1961). "A Theory of Economic Development." *American Economic Review* 51 (September): 533–61.

Ranis, Gustav and T. Paul Schultz, eds. (1988). *The State of Development Economics*. Oxford and New York: Basil Blackwell.

Raper, Arthur F. (1970). *Rural Development in Action: The Comprehensive Experiment at Comilla, East Pakistan*. Ithaca: Cornell University Press.

Raup, Philip M. (1967). "Land Reform and Agricultural Development." In *Agricultural Development and Economic Growth*, pp. 267–314. *See* Krishna (1967).

Redcliff, Michael (1983). "Production Programs for Small Farmers: Plan Puebla as Myth and Reality." *Economic Development and Cultural Change* 31 (April): 551–70.

Reid, Joseph D., Jr. (1976). "Sharecropping and Agricultural Uncertainty." *Economic Development and Cultural Change* 24 (April): 549–76.

Reiter, Stanley (1977). "Information and Performance in the (New) Welfare Economics." *American Economic Review* 67 (February): 226–34.

Repetto, Robert (1986). *Skimming the Water: Rent Seeking and the Performance of Public Irrigation Systems*. Research Report No. 9. Washington, D.C.: World Resources Institute.

Repetto, Robert, Tai Hwan Kwan, Son-ung Kim, Dae Young Kim, John E. Sloboda, and Peter J. Donaldson (1981). *Economic Development, Population Policy and Demographic Transition in the Republic of Korea*. Cambridge: Harvard University Press.

Ribeiro, Jose Paulo and Clifton R. Wharton, Jr. (1969). "The ACAR Program in Minas Gerais, Brazil." In *Subsistence Agriculture and Economic Development*, ed. Clifton R. Wharton, Jr., pp. 424–38. Chicago: Aldine.

Rice, Edward B. (1974). *Extension in the Andes: An Evaluation of Official United States Assistance to Agricultural Extension Services in Central and South America*. Cambridge: MIT Press.

Riddell, Roger C. (1987). *Foreign Aid Reconsidered*. Baltimore: Johns Hopkins University Press.

Rielly, John E. (1983). *American Public Opinion and United States Foreign Policy: 1983*. Chicago: Chicago Council on Foreign Relations.

Robertson, A. F. (1987). *The Dynamics of Productive Relationships: African Share Contracts in Comparative Perspective*. Cambridge: Cambridge University Press.

Robinson, Richard D. (1952). "Tractors in the Village—A Study in Turkey." *Journal of Farm Economics* 34 (November): 451–62.

——— (1958). "Turkey's Agrarian Revolution and the Problem of Urbanization." *Public Opinion Quarterly* 22 (Fall): 397–405.

Rogers, Keith D., Uma K. Srivastava, and Earl O. Heady (1972). "Modified Price, Production and Income Impacts of Food Aid Under Market Differentiated Distribution." *American Journal of Agricultural Economics* 54 (May): 201–8.

Rondinelli, Dennis (1982). "The Dilemma of Development Administration: Complexity and Uncertainty in Control-Oriented Bureaucracies." *World Politics* 35 (October): 43–72.

——— (1985). "Development Administration and Foreign Assistance Policy: An Assessment of Theory and Practice in Aid." *Canadian Journal of Development Studies* 6(2): 212–40.

Rosen, George (1985). *Western Economists and Eastern Societies: Agents of Change in South Asia, 1950–1979*. Baltimore: Johns Hopkins University Press.

Rosenstein-Rodan, Paul (1943). "Problems of Industrialization in Eastern and Southeastern Europe." *Economic Journal* 53 (June–September): 201–11.

——— (1961). "International Aid for Underdeveloped Countries." *Review of Economics and Statistics* 43 (May): 107–38.

Rosenzweig, Mark R. (1978). "Rural Wages, Labor Supply, and Land Reform: A Theoretical and Empirical Analysis." *American Economic Review* 68 (December): 847–61.

——— (1981). "Redistribution, Population Policies and Household Behavior: Implications for Population Growth and Economic Development." In *International*

Population Conference: Solicited Papers. Liege: International Union for the Scientific Study of Population.

Rostow, W. W. (1985). *Eisenhower, Kennedy and Foreign Aid*. Austin: University of Texas Press.

Rottenberg, Simon (1957). *How United States Business Firms Promote Technological Progress*. Washington, D.C.: National Planning Association.

Ruttan, Vernon W. (1956). "The Contribution of Technological Progress to Farm Output: 1950–75." *Review of Economics and Statistics* 38 (February): 61–69.

———— (1969). "Equity and Productivity Issues in Modern Agrarian Reform Legislation." In *Economic Problems of Agriculture in Industrial Societies*, ed. Ugo Papi and Charles Nunn, pp. 581–600. New York: Macmillan and St. Martin's Press.

———— (1975). "Integrated Rural Development Programs: A Skeptical Perspective." *International Development Review* 17 (December): 9–16.

———— (1978). "Induced Institutional Change." In *Induced Innovation: Technology, Institutions and Development*, ed. Vernon W. Ruttan and Hans P. Binswanger, pp. 327–57. Minneapolis: University of Minnesota Press.

———— (1981). *The Asia Bureau Agricultural Research Review*. University of Minnesota Economic Development Center Bulletin No. 81-2. St. Paul, March.

———— (1982). *Agricultural Research Policy*. Minneapolis: University of Minnesota Press.

———— (1984). "Integrated Rural Development Programmes: A Historical Perspective." *World Development* 12 (April): 393–401.

———— (1986a). "Assistance to Expand Agricultural Production." *World Development* 14 (January): 39–63.

———— (1986b). "Toward a Global Agricultural Research System: A Personal View." *Research Policy* 15 (December): 307–27.

———— (1989). "Why Foreign Economic Assistance?" *Economic Development and Cultural Change* 37 (January).

Ruttan, Vernon W. and Yujiro Hayami (1984). "Toward a Theory of Induced Institutional Innovation." *Journal of Development Studies* 20 (July): 203–23.

Ruttan, Vernon W. and Anne O. Krueger (1986). "The Impact of External Economic Assistance to Korea." *Journal of Rural Development* 9 (December): 219–56.

Samper, Armando (1957). *Secondary Education in Chile*. Washington, D.C.: National Planning Association.

Samuelson, Paul A. (1948). *Foundations of Economic Analysis*. Cambridge: Harvard University Press.

Sanderson, Fred and Shyamal Roy (1979). *Food Trends and Prospects in India*. Washington, D.C.: The Brookings Institution.

Schmidt, Wilson (1964). "The Economics of Charity: Loans versus Grants." *Journal of Political Economy* 72 (August): 387–95.

Schmookler, Jacob (1952). "The Changing Efficiency of the American Economy." *Review of Economics and Statistics* 34 (August): 214–32.

Schultz, Theodore W. (1940). "Capital Rationing, Uncertainty and Farm-Tenancy Reform." *Journal of Political Economy* 48 (June): 309–24.

——— (1956a). *The Economic Test in Latin America*. Bulletin No. 35. Ithaca: New York State School of Industrial and Labor Relations, Cornell University, August.

——— (1956b). *Latin America Economic Policy Lessons*. Washington, D.C.: National Planning Association.

——— (1960). "Value of United States Farm Surpluses to Underdeveloped Countries." *Journal of Farm Economics* 42 (December): 1019–30.

——— (1961). "Investment in Human Capital." *American Economic Review* 51 (March): 1–17.

——— (1964). *Transforming Traditional Agriculture*. New Haven: Yale University Press.

——— (1968). "Institutions and the Rising Economic Value of Man." *American Journal of Agricultural Economics* 50 (December): 1113–22.

——— (1971). *Investment in Human Capital*. New York: Free Press–Macmillan.

——— (1980). "Nobel Lecture: The Economics of Being Poor." *Journal of Political Economy* 88 (August): 639–51.

——— (1981). *Investing in People: The Economics of Population Quality*. Berkeley: University of California Press.

Schumpeter, Joseph A. [1911](1934). *The Theory of Economic Development*, trans. Redvers Opie. Cambridge: Harvard University Press.

Secretary General of the United Nations (1951). *Measures for the Economic Development of Under-Developed Countries*. New York: U.N. Department of Economic Affairs, May.

Sheetz, Arnold (1982). "Some Notes on Agricultural and Rural Development in Turkey." St. Paul: University of Minnesota, August. Mimeo.

Shenoy, B. R. (1974). *PL 480 Aid and India's Food Problem*. New Delhi: East-West Press.

Simmons, Ruth and James S. Phillips (1987). "The Integration of Family Planning with Health and Development." In *Organizing for Effective Family Planning Programs*, ed. Robert J. Lapham and George B. Simmons, pp. 185–211. Washington, D.C.: National Academy Press.

Simpson, James R. (1976). "The Origin of United States' Academic Interest in Foreign Economic Development." *Economic Development and Cultural Change* 24 (April): 633–44.

Singer, Hans W. (1965). "External Aid: In Plans or Projects?" *Economic Journal* 75 (September): 539–45.

Singh, Sateesh K. (1975). "Determinants of Aggregate Savings." In *Development Economics: Some Findings*, pp. 121–60. Lexington, Mass.: D. C. Heath and Co.

Small, Leslie E. (1982). "Investment Decisions for the Development and Utilization of Irrigation Resources in Southeast Asia." Teaching and Research Forum Workshop Report No. 26. New York: Agricultural Development Council.

Small, Leslie E., Marietta S. Adriano, and Edward D. Martin (1986). *Regional Study on Irrigation Service Fees: Final Report*. Kandy, Sri Lanka: International Irrigation Management Institute, January.

Soedjatmoko (1978). "National Policy Implications of the Basic Needs Model." *Prisma (Indonesian Journal of Social and Economic Affairs)* 9 (March): 3–25.

Solow, Robert M. (1957). "Technical Change and the Aggregate Production Function." *Review of Economics and Statistics* 39 (August): 313–20.

Somel, Kutlu (1979). "Technological Changes in Dryland Wheat Production in Turkey." *Food Research Institute Studies* 17 (1): 51–65.

Srikantan, K. S. (1977). *The Family Planning Program in the Socio-Economic Context.* New York: Population Council.

Srinivasan, T. N. (1979). "Trends in Agriculture in India, 1949–50 to 1977–78." *Economic and Political Weekly*, annual number, August.

——— (1985). "Neoclassical Political Economy, the State and Economic Development." *Asian Development Review* 3 (2): 38–58.

Srivastava, Uma K., Earl O. Heady, Keith D. Rogers, and Leo V. Mayer (1975). *Food Aid and International Economic Growth.* Ames: Iowa State University Press.

Stavis, Benedict (1979). *Agricultural Extension for Small Farmers.* Rural Development Series Working Paper No. 3. East Lansing: Michigan State University, September.

Steinberg, David I. (1982). *The Economic Development of Korea: Sui Generis or Generic?* US/AID Evaluation Special Study No. 6. Washington, D.C.

——— (1985). *Foreign Aid and the Development of the Republic of Korea: The Effectiveness of Concessional Assistance.* US/AID Discussion Paper No. 42. Washington, D.C.

Steinberg, David I., Sung-Hwan Ban, W. Donald Bowles, and Maureen A. Lewis (1984). *Korean Agricultural Services.* US/AID Project Impact Evaluation Report No. 52. Washington, D.C.

Steinberg, David I., Robert I. Jackson, Kwan S. Kim, and Hae-kyun Song (1982). *Korean Agricultural Research: The Integration of Research and Extension.* US/AID Project Impact Evaluation Report No. 27. Washington, D.C.

Steinberg, David I., Robert B. Morrow, Ingrid Palmer, and Kim Dang-il (1980). *Korean Irrigation.* US/AID Project Impact Evaluation Report No. 12. Washington, D.C.

Stevens, Robert D. (1974). "Three Rural Development Models for Small-Farm Agricultural Areas in Low Income Nations." *Journal of Developing Areas* 8 (April): 409–20.

Stewart, Frances (1971). "Foreign Capital, Domestic Savings and Economic Development: Comment." *Bulletin of the Oxford University Institute of Economics and Statistics* 33 (May): 138–49.

Stiglitz, Joseph E. (1974). "Incentives and Risks in Share Cropping." *Review of Economic Studies* 41 (April): 219–55.

——— (1986). "The New Development Economics." *World Development* 14 (February): 257–65.

Streeten, Paul (1977). "The Distinctive Features of a Basic Needs Approach to Development." Basic Needs Paper No. 2. Washington, D.C.: IBRD.

——— (1979). "Basic Needs: Premises and Promises." *Journal of Policy Modeling* 1 (January): 136–46.

Streeten, Paul P. and Shahid J. Burki (1978). "Basic Needs: Some Issues." *World Development* 6 (March): 411–21.

Streeten, Paul and Roger Hill (1968). "Aid to India." In *The Crisis of Indian Planning*, ed. Paul Streeten and Michael Lipton, pp. 323–49. London: Oxford University Press.

Stryker, J. Dirck (1975). "Western Africa Regional Project—Ghana Agriculture."

Somerville, Mass.: Associate for International Resources and Development. Mimeo.

—— (1977). "Western Africa Regional Project—Ivory Coast." Chapter 2. Economic Incentives and Costs in Agriculture." Somerville, Mass.: Associates for International Resources and Development. Mimeo.

—— (1988). *A Comparative Study of the Political Economy of Agricultural Pricing Policies: Ghana—Final Draft Report*. Somerville, Mass.: Associates for International Resources and Development. Photocopy.

Stryker, J. Dirck, Garry Pursell and Terry Munson (1975). "Incitations et coûts réels en Côte d'Ivoire. Photocopy.

Suh, Sang-Mok (1986). *The Evolution of the Korean Economy: A Historical Perspective*. Working Paper No. 8603. Seoul: Korea Development Institute.

Sussman, Gerald (1982). *The Challenge of Integrated Rural Development in India: A Policy and Management Perspective*. Boulder, Colo.: Westview Press.

Swanberg, Kenneth G. (1982). "Institutional Evolution: From Pilot Project to National Development Program—Puebla and Caqueza." Discussion Paper No. 132. Cambridge: Harvard Institute for International Development, March.

Symmonds, Richard and Michael Carder (1973). *The United Nations and the Population Question 1945–1970*. New York: McGraw-Hill.

Tansky, L. (1967). *U.S. and U.S.R.R. Aid to Developing Countries*. New York: Praeger.

Tarrant, John R. (1980). *Food Policies*. New York: John Wiley and Sons.

Task Force on International Development (Peterson Commission) (1970). *United States Foreign Assistance in the 1970s: A New Approach. Report to the President*. Washington, D.C.: GPO.

Taylor, Carl E., Ram D. Singh, R. S. S. Sharma, William A. Reinke, Robert L. Parker, and Rashid Faruquee, eds. (1975). *The Narangwal Population Study: Integrated Health and Family Planning Services*. Punjab: Rural Health Research Center.

Teece, D.J. (1977). "Technology Transfer by Multinational Firms: The Resource Cost of Transferring Technological Know-How." *Economic Journal* 77 (February): 49–57.

Tendler, Judith (1975). *Inside Foreign Aid*. Baltimore: John Hopkins University Press.

—— (1979a). *New Directions Rural Roads*, US/AID Program Evaluation Discussion Paper No. 2. Washington, D.C., March.

—— (1979b). *Rural Electrification: Linkages and Justifications*. US/AID Program Evaluation Discussion Paper No. 3. Washington, D.C.

—— (1982). *Rural Projects through Urban Eyes: An Interpretation of the World Bank's New-Style Rural Development Projects*. Washington, D.C.: World Bank.

Thirlwall, A. P. (1976). "When Is Trade More Valuable Than Aid?." *Journal of Development Studies* 13 (October): 35–41.

Thirtle, Colin G. and Vernon W. Ruttan (1987). *The Role of Demand and Supply in the Generation and Diffusion of Technical Change*. London: Harwood Academic Publishers.

Thomas, John W. and Richard M. Hook (1977). *Creating Rural Employment: A Manual for Organizing Rural Works Programs*. Washington, D.C.: US/AID.

Thomas, Woods D., Harry R. Potter, William L. Miller and Adrian F. Aveni, eds.

(1972). *Institution Building: A Model for Applied Social Change.* Cambridge, Mass.: Schenkman.

Timmer, C. Peter (1975). "The Choice of Technique in Indonesia." In *The Choice of Technology in Developing Countries: Some Cautionary Tales*, by C. Peter Timmer, John W. Thomas, Louis T. Wells, and David Morawetz. Harvard Studies in International Affairs, vol. 32. Cambridge: Harvard University Center for International Affairs.

Tolley, George S. and Vinod Thomas, eds. (1987). The Economics of *Urbanization Processes and Policies in the Developing Countries.* Washington, D.C.: World Bank.

Tollison, Robert (1982). "Rent Seeking: A Survey." *Kyklos* 35, fasc. 4: 575–602.

Toye, John (1985). "Dirigisme and Development Economics." *Cambridge Journal of Economics* 9 (March): 1–14.

Traxler, Gregory and Vernon W. Ruttan (1986). "Assistance for Water Resource Development in Pakistan." *Pakistan Journal of Agricultural Social Sciences* 1 (July–December): 72–91.

———— (1989). "An Evaluation of Donor Assistance to Agricultural Development in Pakistan." *Pakistan Development Review* 58 (Spring).

Truman, Harry S. (1949). "Inaugural Address of the President." *Department of State Bulletin* 33 (January).

United Nations (1975). *Report of the World Food Conference, 5–16, November, 1974, Rome.* New York.

———— (1986). *Coordination of Technical Assistance.* UN Document No. DP/1987/W6/WP.4 New York.

United Nations Economic Commission for Asia and the Pacific (UN/ESCAP) (1976). *Population of Sri Lanka.* Bangkok.

United States Agency for International Development (US/AID) (1965). *Technical Assistance Project History and Analysis Report: Agricultural Research.* TOAIDA-820 Ankara: November.

———— (1967). *Technical Assistance Project History and Analysis Report: Agricultural Planning and Economic Research.* TOAIDA-1317. Ankara, 15 February.

———— (1969). *Water Resources Management and Development: Technical Assistance Project History and Analysis Report.* TOAIDA-571 Ankara, 16 December.

———— (1973a). *Field Budget Submission, FY 1975—Ghana.* Washington, D.C.

———— (1973b). *Spring Review of Small Farmer Credit*, 20 vols. Washington, D.C.

———— (1974). *Technical Assistance Project History and Analysis Report: Family Planning and Rural Health Services.* Ankara.

———— (1975). *Country Development Strategy Statement, FY 1981—Ghana.* Washington, D.C.

———— (1980a). *Rural Roads in Thailand.* US/AID Project Impact Evaluation Report No. 13 Washington, D.C., December.

———— (1980b). *Third Evaluation of the Thailand National Family Planning Program.* US/AID Program Evaluation Report No. 3. Washington, D.C.

———— (1982a). *Approaches to the Policy Dialogue.* US/AID Policy Paper. Washington, D.C.

———— (1982b). *Community Water Supply in Developing Countries: Lessons from*

Experience. US/AID Program Evaluation Report No. 7. Washington, D.C., September.

——— (1982c). *The On-Farm Water Management Project in Pakistan.* Washington, D.C.

——— (1982d). *Recurrent Costs.* US/AID Policy Paper. Washington, D.C., May.

——— (1982e). *Rural Roads Evaluation Summary Report.* US/AID Program Evaluation Report No. 5. Washington, D.C., March.

——— (1983). *AID Guidelines on Program Sector Assistance.* Washington, D.C.

———, *United States Overseas Loans and Grants* (1962–86). Washington, D.C.

U.S. Congress, House of Representatives, Committee on Foreign Affairs (1973). *Mutual Development and Cooperation Act of 1973: Hearings.* 93d Cong., 1st sess.

U.S. Department of State (1982). *Maximum Travel Per Diem Allowances for Foreign Areas, Section 925, A Supplement to the Standardized Regulations (Government Civilians, Foreign Areas).* Washington, D.C., October.

Uphoff, Norman T., John M. Cohen and Arthur A. Goldsmith (1979). *Feasibility and Application of Rural Development Participation: A State-of-the-Art Paper.* Monograph Series No. 3. Ithaca: Cornell University, Rural Development Committee, January.

Uzawa, Hirofumi (1965). "Optimal Technical Change in an Aggregate Model of Economic Growth." *International Economic Review* 6 (January): 18–31.

Van Wijnbergen, Sweder (1986). "Aid, Export Promotion and the Real Exchange Rate: An African Dilemma." World Bank Development Research Department Discussion Paper No. 199. Washington, D.C.

Veit, Lawrence A. (1976). *India's Second Revolution.* New York: McGraw-Hill.

Viaria, Parvin and Anrudh Jain (1976). *India.* New York: Population Council.

Virmani, Arvind (1986). "Credit Markets and Credit Policy in Developing Countries: Myths and Reality." Background paper prepared for the World Bank *World Development Report, 1986.* Washington, D.C.

Von Pischke, J. D. (1980). "The Political Economy of Specialised Farm Credit Institutions." In *Borrowers and Lenders,* pp. 81–103. *See* David and Meyer (1980).

Wade, Robert (1982). "The World Bank and India's Irrigation Reform." *Journal of Development Studies* 18 (January): 171–84.

Walinsky, Louis J., ed. (1977). *Agrarian Reform as Unfinished Business: The Selected Papers of Wolf Ladejinsky.* New York: Oxford University Press.

Wang, In-Keun (1984). "Trends and Tasks of Korean Rural Development with Special Reference to the Integrated Approach." *Journal of Rural Development* 7 (June): 45–75.

Warriner, Doreen (1969). *Land Reform in Principle and Practice.* London: Clarendon Press.

Waterston, Albert (1965). *Development Planning: Lessons of Experience.* Baltimore: Johns Hopkins Press.

Weisskopf, Thomas E. (1972a). "An Econometric Test of Alternative Constraints on the Growth of Underdeveloped Countries." *Review of Economics and Statistics* 54 (February): 67–78.

——— (1972b). "The Impact of Foreign Capital Inflow on Domestic Savings in Underdeveloped Countries." *Journal of International Economics* 2 (February): 25–38.

Westphal, Larry E., Yang W. Rhee, Linsu Kim, and Alice H. Amsden (1984). "Republic of Korea." *World Development* 12 (May–June): 505–33.

Wharton, Clifton R., Jr. (1960). "The Economic Impact of Technical Assistance: A Brazilian Case Study." *Journal of Farm Economics* 42 (May): 252–67.

White, John A. (1967). *Pledged to Development: A Study of International Consortia and the Strategy of Aid*. London: Overseas Development Institute.

——— (1974). *The Politics of Foreign Aid*. New York: St. Martin's Press.

Williamson, Harold F. and John A. Buttrick (1954). *Economic Development: Principles and Patterns*. New York: Prentice-Hall.

Williamson, Nancy (1982). "An Attempt to Reduce Infant and Child Mortality in Bohol, Philippines." *Studies in Family Planning* (April): 106–15.

Wilson, John R. (1971). *A.I.D. Assistance to Agriculture in Turkey*. Ankara: US/AID, August.

Winch, Fred Everett III (1976). "Costs and Returns of Alternative Rice Production System in Northern Ghana: Implications for Output, Employment and Income Distribution." Ph.D. diss., Department of Agricultural Economics, Michigan State University.

Wittkopf, Eugene R. (1972). *Western Bilateral Aid Allocations*. Beverly Hills: Sage.

Wolf, Charles, Jr. (1960). *Foreign Aid: Theory and Practice in Southern Asia*. Princeton: Princeton University Press.

Wolfson, Margaret (1983). *Population Assistance*. Paris: OECD Development Centre.

World Bank (1972). *Agriculture—Sector Working Paper*. Washington, D.C.

——— (1975). *Rural Electrification*. Washington, D.C.

——— (1976). *World Tables: 1976*. Johns Hopkins University Press.

——— (1978). *The Study of Labor and Capital Substitution in Civil Engineering Construction: Report on the Bank Sponsored Seminars in Washington, Cologne, Copenhagen, London and Tokyo*. Washington D.C.

——— (1980a). *Health Sector Policy Paper*. Washington, D.C., February.

——— (1980b). *World Tables: 1980*. Johns Hopkins University Press.

——— (1981). *Turkey: Public Sector Investment Review*. 3 vols. Washington, D.C., December.

——— (1982a). *IDA in Retrospect*. Washington, D.C.: Oxford University Press.

——— (1982b). *Turkey: Industrialization and Trade Strategy: Methodological and Statistical Annex*. 3 vols. Washington, D.C., 18 February.

——— (1983). *World Tables: 1983*. 2 vols. Baltimore: Johns Hopkins University Press.

——— (1984a). *Annual Report, 1984*. Washington, D.C..

——— (1984b). *World Development Report, 1984*. Oxford University Press.

——— (1986a). *Commodity Trade and Price Trends*. Baltimore: Johns Hopkins University Press.

——— (1986b). *World Development Report, 1986*. New York: Oxford University Press.

——— (1987). *World Development Report, 1987*, New York: Oxford University Press.

——— (1988a). *Adjustment Lending: An Evaluation of Ten Years of Experience*. Washington, D.C.

———— (1988b). *World Development Report, 1988.* New York: Oxford University Press.

World Bank and the UNDP (1989). *Africa's Adjustment and Growth in the 1980s.* Washington, D.C.

World Commission on Environment and Development (1987). *From One Earth to One World.* New York: Oxford University Press.

Woronoff, Jon (1972). *West Africa Wager: Houphouet versus Nkrumah.* Metuchen, N.J.: Scarecrow Press.

Wortman, Sterling and Ralph W. Cummings, Jr. (1978). *To Feed This World: The Challenge and the Strategy.* Baltimore: Johns Hopkins University Press.

Wunsch, James (1986). "Administering Rural Development: Have Goals Outreached Organizational Capacity?" *Public Administration and Development* 6 (July–September): 287–308.

Zingler, Ervin K. (1974). "Veblen vs. Commons: A Comparative Evaluation." *Kyklos* 17, fasc. 2: 322–44.

Contributors

KEITH E. JAY is senior economist in the Policy Analysis and Review Division at the World Bank. He previously served as chief of the International Economic Affairs Division and deputy director of the Office of Economic Affairs at the United States Agency for International Development (US/AID). He has written on issues of foreign assistance policy. He received his doctorate in economics from the University of Wisconsin.

ANNE O. KRUEGER is Arts and Sciences Professor of Economics at Duke University. Her research has been on international economic policy, international trade, and economic development. Among her influential writings are *Alternative Trade Strategies and Employment* (Chicago: University of Chicago Press, 1983) and *Exchange Rate Determination* (Cambridge: Cambridge University Press, 1983). She has served as vice president for economics and research at the World Bank. Prior to joining the World Bank, she was a professor of economics at the University of Minnesota. She has directed the National Bureau of Economic Research projects on alternatives to trade strategy and employment and U.S. trade relations. A fellow of the Econometric Society and the American Academy of Arts and Sciences, she received her doctorate in economics from the University of Wisconsin.

CONSTANTINE MICHALOPOULOS is economic adviser to the vice president for Europe, the Middle East, and North Africa at the World Bank. He previously served as director for economic policy analysis and coordination at the World Bank and as chief economist at US/AID. Prior to joining US/AID, he was an associate professor of economics at Clark University. He has conducted research and written extensively on international economics, international finance, and development economics. He received his doctorate in economics from Columbia University.

GAYL D. NESS is a professor in the Department of Sociology and in the Department of Population Planning and International Health at the University of Michigan. He has written extensively in the areas of modernization and population policy. He is the author (with Hirofumi Ando) of *The Land Is Shrinking: Population and Planning in Asia* (Baltimore: Johns Hopkins University Press, 1984). He has been a consultant on population issues with the United Nations Fund for Population Activities, the United Nations Economic and Social Commission for Asia and the Pacific, and US/AID. He received his doctorate in sociology from the University of California, Berkeley.

VERNON W. RUTTAN is Regents Professor in the Department of Agricultural and Applied Economics and in the Department of Economics and adjunct professor in the Hubert H. Humphrey Institute of Public Affairs at the University of Minnesota. His research has been on the economics of technical change and agricultural development. His book (with Yujiro Hayami) *Agricultural Development: An International Perspective* (Baltimore: Johns Hopkins University Press, 1971 and 1985) is a basic reference in the field of agricultural development. His nonacademic experience includes service on the staff of the President's Council of Economic Advisors and as president of the Agricultural Development Council. He is a fellow of the American Agricultural Economics Association, the American Association for the Advancement of Science, and the American Academy of Arts and Sciences. He received his doctorate in economics from the University of Chicago.

J. DIRCK STRYKER is an associate professor of international economic relations at the Fletcher School of Law and Diplomacy at Tufts University. He is also president of the consulting firm Associates for International Resources and Development. He codirected a comprehensive study of the economics of rice in West Africa sponsored by the West Africa Rice Development Association and the Food Research Institute of Stanford University. He has served as a consultant to the World Bank in a number of African countries. His research has been primarily in the area of trade policy and agricultural policy. He received his doctorate in economics from Columbia University.

VASANT A. SUKHATME is Edward J. Noble Associate Professor of Economics at Macalester College. From 1976 to 1978 he was an economist in the Economic Analysis and Projections Department at the World Bank. He has written extensively on issues of agricultural development, macroeconomic policy, and labor economics. He received his doctorate in economics from the University of Chicago.

HASAN TULUY is an economist with the Occidental and Central Africa Country Operations Division of the World Bank. He has written extensively on agricultural development in West Africa and the Magreb and previously served as a consultant to the World Bank and the US/AID on African and Magreb development projects. He received his doctorate in economics from the Fletcher School of Law and Economics.

Name Index

Subject Index

Books in the Series

Designed by Martha Farlow

Composed by G & S Typesetters, Inc., in
Times Roman

Printed by Thomson-Shore, Inc., on 50-lb
Glatfelter Offset and bound in Holliston
Roxite A